The Alaska Native Reader

THE WORLD READERS

A Series Edited by Robin Kirk and Orin Starn

Also in This Series:

THE INDONESIA READER

THE ALASKA NATIVE READER

HISTORY, CULTURE, POLITICS

Edited by Maria *Shaa Tláa* Williams

DUKE UNIVERSITY PRESS Durham and London 2009

Typeset in Monotype Dante by
Tseng Information Systems, Inc.
Library of Congress Cataloging-in-
Publication information appears on
the last printed page of this book.

Duke University Press gratefully
acknowledges the support of the
Alaska Native Arts Foundation,
which provided funds toward the
production of this book.

Dedicated to the elders
on whose knowledge we have,
as indigenous people, been able
to survive for thousands of years,
and to the youth, who will
bring us to a beautiful future.

Contents

List of Illustrations

Maps

Figures

LANGDON AND LEGGETT

BANERJEE

MCNEIL

EATON

CORAY

Plates (between pages 194 and 195)

Preface

It is a great honor and privilege to present this volume to the world. Here are the words, wisdom, and beautiful histories and stories of Alaska Native peoples, from a variety of writers, artists, poets, scientists, historians, politicians, and educators. It has been a remarkable experience to work with such truly gifted individuals and to provide a voice for their important perspectives. I use the term "perspective" purposefully. Perspective is how something is portrayed from a particular point of view; in this case, it is an indigenous point of view. This volume is not primarily an anthropological study, a political history, or an art book (though it has all of these elements); it comprises an interdisciplinary collection of essays and other offerings from both Native and non-Native contributors that reflect the neocolonial experience of Alaska's indigenous peoples. Current trends in colonial and postcolonial studies have not effectively addressed the complicated legacy of the colonial periods. The colonial period applies to the older pre-twentieth-century geopolitical climate of European and American government domination and expansion of their respective empires. Although we have passed through this period, American corporate forces continue to dominate the planet in terms of control of resources such as oil, as well as to support and suppress governments and movements that operate counter to their for-profit capitalist model—a model that does not acknowledge environment or culture as valued resources. In this context, Alaska finds itself in a neocolonial period in which corporate interests are protected at the expense of indigenous cultures, languages, and land.

The writings in this volume are often "counter" stories or histories and relay new ideas and concepts that have not been included in most history books on Alaska. I grew up reading about the brave pioneers who came to Alaska or the early Russians who "discovered" my ancestral land. Most non-Native people do not realize what an affront this is—to read about the "discovery" of the place that is our home/heart/spirit and where my ancestors have lived and hunted since the end of the Pleistocene age, as if we have been somehow invisible all these tens of thousands of years.

The history of Alaska is a complex one and cannot be encapsulated within a one-dimensional perspective. For example, the first essay in this volume is an Athabascan narrative by Katie and Fred John, who are Ahtna Athabascan. It was recorded by the linguist James Kari. The narrative is in Ahtna with an English translation and reveals how an indigenous community reacted in a particularly heated exchange with a group of Russians in the nineteenth century. It provides a unique glimpse of early indigenous reactions to outsiders. The second essay is an excerpt from a major tome by the Russian scholars Solovjova and Vovnyanko that addresses the Russian colonial era, showing the depth and complexity of this period. These first two essays illustrate the interactions between indigenous peoples and their early colonial experience and the impact those interactions had on the colonizers as well as the colonized.

The history of Alaska is often told from the perspective of outsiders and those who view the resources of Alaska as amazing treasures to exploit. There are stories of eighteenth-century Russian fur hunters, of the brave miners who came to Alaska in the late nineteenth century to discover gold, of the companies that developed salmon canneries, and, in the twentieth century, of the oil companies that worked together to build the Trans-Alaska Pipeline, one of the engineering marvels of the twentieth century. These stories are often highlighted and even exalted, yet one must ask what was the impact on the indigenous people. It is imperative to present as many viewpoints as possible, especially about the historical discourse of the indigenous and European encounters. Most textbooks only provide one viewpoint, often muting the Native voice.

Explorers, colonizers, and writers who have been captivated by the landscape, people, and extreme climate of Alaska have often romanticized its history. However, no one knows this land better than the indigenous people who have lived here. Globally, the indigenous voice has often been silenced by overarching colonial governments, and Alaska is no exception.

Alaska is home to distinct cultural and ethnic groups that speak over twenty different languages. These include 225 federally recognized tribes.[1] Pejorative terms such as "Eskimo," "Aleut," and even "Indian" tend to diminish the diversity of cultures and are simplistic and in most cases mistaken. Within the past twenty years the self-designative terms such as "Yup'ik," "Yupiaq," "Iñupiaq," "Unangan," and "Alutiiq/Sugpiaq" are becoming symbols of the change that has taken place as Native people correct the colonial naming process.

Alaska is a vast subcontinent of North America and has over 33,000 miles of coastline, 440 million acres of land with numerous rivers, lakes, mountain ranges, and glaciers, and the tallest peak in North America (Denali). The indigenous people adapted to their environment in an equally diverse manner. The Russians "discovered" Alaska in the middle of the eighteenth century and named it "Russian America." They set up colonies immediately and began to establish fur companies that often enslaved local indigenous people to hunt the valuable sea otter and other fur-bearing animals. In 1867, under the Treaty of Session, the United States purchased Alaska for six million dollars. It was clear that the region had substantial natural resources, including fur, gold, silver, and salmon, and the new territorial government began to capitalize on the resource exploitation. In 1958–59 Alaska became the forty-ninth state in the Union, coinciding with the discovery of vast oil fields in the far Arctic coastal regions. This led to a huge land grab contest between the federal and the newly formed state government as they poised to lease the Arctic shelf for oil exploration and development. In response, young Native leadership began to question their rights to the land. In 1969, at the height of the land claims issue, William Hensley, who would go on to become a state representative, wrote a seminal paper, which is included in this volume. Oil leases and land selections came to a screeching halt as Native people organized, for the first time on the statewide level, and demanded that the U.S. Congress deal with their aboriginal claim to the land. This led to the landmark Alaska Native Claims Settlement Act in 1971, which extinguished aboriginal claim to the land for a settlement of forty-four million acres and nearly one billion dollars ($962.5 million).

The complex stories and history of Alaska have often been seen only through one perspective, that of Europeans and Americans, lacking the depth of knowledge that indigenous people have about their homelands. For a long time, most writings about indigenous people or Alaska Native people have been primarily by nonindigenous or non-Native people, and although there are some impressive contributions in this arena, by definition they lack the ideas, voice, or perspective of the indigenous experience. This is beginning to change in academic discourse, primarily fueled by grassroots movements that began in the 1960s, including the Civil Rights movement, the American Indian Movement, and the influence of other "radical" organizations. This seminal period of awakening created new programs in universities and colleges; the introduction of American Indian studies, Alaska Native studies, Chicano studies, African American studies, and women's studies resulted in new canons of intellectual thought and ideas.

One of the very early Native scholars from this period, Vine Deloria Jr. (Lakota), is arguably the father of Native American Studies. His early works, *Custer Died for Your Sins: An Indian Manifesto* (1970) and *God Is Red* (1973), were refreshingly honest and almost brutally frank. Deloria effectively used his wit and humor to illustrate how Native people feel, and how their ideas, histories, and lives have been devalued throughout the colonial and neocolonial periods. The titles of some of Deloria's chapters (for example, "Anthropologists and Other Friends") provide humorous commentary on how the Lakota felt when anthropologists arrived on their reservation to "study" them in order to write a dissertation or a book. Although Deloria expresses considerable sarcastic wit in his works, he also effectively communicates how it feels to be the "other."

The relationship between academia and indigenous communities globally has been somewhat strained by a past that includes theft of cultural patrimony and of skeletal remains, as well as an attitude of superiority and elitism. Archaeologists, anthropologists, and sociologists in the late nineteenth and early twentieth centuries created new definitions for indigenous peoples, using terms such as "hunter-gatherer" to define many indigenous groups without taking into account their wealth of scientific knowledge, math systems, linguistic diversity, and aesthetic traditions. The vestiges of the colonial past still remain in some measure, but new scholarship and new paradigms are painting a much more in-depth and realistic picture of indigenous societies. Scholars such as Oscar Kawagley, Claudette Engblom-Bradley, Beth Leonard, Deanna Kingston (all contributors to this volume) are providing new perspectives on Native math systems, geographic knowledge, and astronomy.

Today, indigenous scholarship is becoming more global and sophisticated in its use of analytical tools; in some cases developing its own theoretical paradigms, and in other instances using theorists such as Freire, Bakhtin, Fanon, and others. For example, Anna Smith-Chiburis in her essay draws on Bakhtin and Freire as she examines Sherman Alexei's film *Smoke Signals*. Erica Lord, another contributor, uses Fanon's *Wretched of the Earth* as a foundation for her analysis of indigenous identity. Indigenous scholars such as Jennifer Denetdale (Diné), Oscar Kawagley (Yupiaq), and Andrea Smith (Cherokee) are augmenting the canon in the area of Native history, science, philosophy, and epistemologies.[2] These are vital as indigenous people begin to reclaim their voices and to make a path for themselves in western settings such as universities. Oscar *Angayqaq* Kawagley's work is also reflective of the new paradigm that reveals how indigenous science is expressed in the Yupiaq world. It is especially important for me to mention here that Dr. Kawagley was my sixth-grade teacher. His teaching obviously went much further than my one-year experience with him. It resonated for me, a Native person, to actually have a Native teacher; he provided me with a role model and validated my "nativeness" in the very western setting of my school. *Gunalsheesh* (thank you), Oscar.

As indigenous scholarship increases at the global level, exemplified by publications such as *Decolonizing Methodology* (1999) by Linda Tuhiwai Smith

(Maori of New Zealand) and *A Yupiaq Worldview* (1995, 2006) by Oscar *Angayuqaq* Kawagley, the paradigm is shifting from one of nonindigenous people writing about indigenous people to indigenous people writing about indigenous people. This has provided new insight into Native perspectives on science, the arts, colonization, identity, education, and philosophy.

New research methods are now emerging because of people like Stephen Langdon, Beth Leonard, Claudette Englom-Bradley, James Kari, George Charles, Nancy Furlow, and Jeane Breinig (all contributors to this volume), who have highlighted indigenous math systems, indigenous language and its link to history and culture and other new methodologies. Other contributors to this volume, such as Ted Mayac Sr., a traditional Iñupiaq hunter and renowned ivory carver; the Tlingit photographer Larry McNeil; and Perry Eaton, an Alutiiq/Sugpiaq artist and mask carver, provide unique perspectives on identity, resilience, and culture. Linguists such as Beth *Ginondidoy* Leonard (Athabascan) and Walkie *Kumaggaq* Charles (Yup'ik) offer insightful selections on the cultural perspective of languages, as they work on these issues with students who are learning their traditional languages and orthographies in a university setting. Other contributions include poetry by Richard Dauenhauer and Nora Dauenhauer, titans in the Alaska Native community.

This reader also contains political histories that shed light on the Russian period in Alaska (see Solovjova and Vovnyanko), the seminal paper written (and delivered as a talk) in 1969 by William Hensley that provided a legal argument for Native land claims in Alaska, as well as Harold Napoleon's heartbreaking analysis of the impact of diseases and their lasting effects, which he identifies as a form of post-traumatic stress disorder. These selections are republished here because they are groundbreaking works that represent a nonwestern-focused experience.

The selections in this volume shed light on who Alaska Native people are, what their history has been, and the impacts of colonialism, in part by including a new cadre of indigenous leadership that has emerged in the twenty-first century. The first part, "Portraits of Nations: Telling Our Own Story," includes oral narratives in several Alaska Native languages and provides an insider's perspective on who Alaska Native people are. The second part, "Empire: Processing Colonization," contains some of the darker essays on the colonial experience. Struggles for land claims, identity, and protection of traditional land bases provide a variety of responses to the colonial and neocolonial experience. The essays in the third part, "Worldviews: Alaska Native and Indigenous Epistemologies," provide new models for viewing knowledge and the indigenous perspective on math, science, astronomy, and the cosmos. Excerpts from

Kawagley's *A Yupiaq Worldview: A Pathway to Ecology and Spirit* is included in this part. The fourth part, "Native Arts: A Weaving of Melody and Color," includes selections on indigenous music, the rebirth of Kodiak mask making, and the use of digital media as artists address their work in the contemporary twenty-first century. The final part, "Ravenstales," includes poetry, articles on Alaska Native literature, and even a recipe for moose ribs!

Certainly one of the newer paradigms in indigenous publications today, and one which informs this volume, is a result of Linda Smith's *Decolonizing Methodologies* (1999). Smith effectively addresses what she terms the "collective memory of imperialism" and the great imbalance between indigenous people and those who have studied them.

> It galls us that Western researchers and intellectuals can assume to know all that it is possible to know of us, on the basis of their brief encounters with some of us. It appalls us that the West can desire, extract and claim ownership of our ways of knowing, our imagery, the things we create and produce and then simultaneously reject the people who created and developed those ideas and seek to deny them further opportunities to be creators of their own culture and own nations. (1)

As the number of indigenous scholars grows, the imbalance will hopefully come to some equanimity and knowledge will be the privilege of all—not just a few. With this volume, perhaps what we are striving for is to provide another perspective that will result in a larger shared knowledge.

A Note on Style and Sources

Some selections in this reader are abridged, and some have had documentation removed or modified. Readers interested in the full version of a selection should refer to the Acknowledgment of Copyrights section. Most of the sources cited in abbreviated form can be found in full in the Suggestions for Further Reading.

Gunalsheesh

Notes

1. Bureau of Indian Affairs, Department of Interior, U.S. Federal Register, July 12, 2002, vol. 67, no. 134, pp. 46327–333.

2. Denetdale's work on Navajo/Diné history in her *Reclaiming Diné History* (Phoenix: University of Arizona Press, 2007) shows the dichotomy that exists between ex-

amining indigenous history from a specific cultural understanding versus a western perspective that overlooks cultural and social perspectives. Andrea Smith's work on colonialism and sexual violence, *Conquest: Sexual Violence and American Indian Genocide* (Boston: South End Press, 2005), addresses the colonial violence in regard to American Indian genocide. Both works are reflective of the broader movement in academia to present indigenous history from newer non-western-based paradigms.

Acknowledgments

I would first like to thank Miriam Angress, my editor at Duke University Press, whose patience and intelligence I have come to value a great deal. All of the contributors to this volume also deserve to be recognized for their words, ideas, and willingness to share and educate. Working with such a talented and recognized group of authors has humbled me and I have often thought "Am I dreaming?" The color plates in the volume were made possible by a grant from the Alaska Native Arts Foundation. I gratefully acknowledge its support.

I also want to thank several of my graduate students at the University of New Mexico who helped significantly with the making of the maps and also with the challenging process of Athabascan orthography in several of the essays. Aprell Emerson (Navajo) and Patrick Willink (Navajo) were especially helpful and gave willingly of their time and expertise. I must also thank my family, my mother, Marilyn, and all my sisters, who gave me lots of support and encouragement through the long editing process.

Sadly, one of the contributors, Joan *Pirciralria* Hamilton, passed away in June 2008. She would have been so pleased to see this book. She was a special person who will be missed by all.

I take full responsibility for any errors that have somehow been overlooked and hope that readers will take pleasure in this volume.

Alaska and Its People: An Introduction

Maria Shaa Tláa *Williams*

Alaska is a vast subcontinent of North America and the largest state in the United States, encompassing over 590,000 square miles with over 33,000 miles of coastline. Alaska is one-fifth the size of the continental United States and over twice the size of Texas, the second largest state in the union. Alaska also has nearly 100,000 glaciers; the Malaspina glacier covers an area of more than 1,500 square miles, larger than that of some states.[1] In physical characteristics, Alaska has thirty-nine majestic mountain ranges. Two of the larger ranges, the Brooks Range and the Alaska Range, divide the state into three major geographic areas. Of the twenty highest peaks in North America, seventeen are in Alaska, including Mount McKinley, which is referred to as Denali, meaning "the great one" in one of the Athabascan languages. It is the highest peak in North America at 20,360 feet and deserves the name Denali.

The environmental landscape distinguishes Alaska from other parts of North America. Volcanoes and earthquakes are daily events in this expansive state.[2] The largest volcanic eruption in North America in the twentieth century occurred in the Alaska Peninsula, when Mt. Novarupta erupted in 1912.[3] This became a time marker for the Sugpiaq people of the region. Most of the volcanoes in Alaska are in this region and the Aleutian Island area and are often referred to as the "Ring of Fire" in the Pacific Ocean basin. The more than 1,200-mile-long archipelago of these volcanic islands is homeland to the Unangan or Aleut peoples. The word "Alaska" actually comes from the Unangan language. *Alaxsxaq* means "place the sea moves toward" (Ransom 1978, 199). *Alyeska*, another Unangan word, means "the Great Land" (*Alaska Blue Book* 1993–94, 247).

Alaska's wilderness is host to many animals, birds, and plants. Migratory birds come from five continents to nest in Alaska during the summer months (Ewing 1996, 211). Salmon, a migratory fish, forms a vital part of most indigenous Alaskan Native diets; seven types of salmon come through Alaska's many rivers and streams from May through September. There are over 3,000 rivers in Alaska, the longest being the Yukon, which is over 2,298 miles long, with 1,875 of those miles in Alaska; its headwaters originate near Atlin, British Columbia, and its course ends in the Bering Sea. Rivers are not only an important source of salmon but also a major means of transportation (boats in the summer and snow machines in the winter). The largest freshwater lake in Alaska is Iliamna, on the Alaska Peninsula, which is over 1,150 square miles; Alaska has over three million lakes.[4]

As one moves through other geographic regions of Alaska, the light and the physical environments change dramatically. Alaska's indigenous peoples adapted to its imposing landscape, living in concert with its geographic diversity and extreme climate changes. There are twenty different Native languages spoken in Alaska and roughly eight broad cultural groups. Of the 562 federally recognized tribes in the United States, 225 are in Alaska. For example, the Iñupiaq people, who live in the upper one-third of the state known as the Arctic, form part of the larger circumpolar Inuit indigenous nations. Changes in the light are extreme in this northern region, especially above the Arctic Circle. The summer days are long and filled with sunlight. In Barrow, the northernmost community in North America, the sun rises in mid-May and does not set until the first part of August, which is why Alaska is often called "land of the midnight sun." The reverse is true in the winter when the sun sets in mid-November and does not rise again until the end of January (see Subhankar Banerjee's images in this volume).

Southeastern Alaska is a rainforest and part of the larger Pacific Northwest coast region, which stretches from northern California to Alaska. Average rainfall can exceed 200 inches and the thickly forested region is full of streams, fjords, glaciers, and wildlife. In this region the temperatures seldom dip below freezing. This region is homeland to the Tlingit, Haida, and Tsimshian peoples.

The interior of Alaska, a vast region with major rivers (including the Yukon) and the tallest mountain in North America, is subject to great temperature changes. In fact, Fairbanks, in the heart of the interior, experiences the greatest degree of temperature change of any city in the world. The summers can reach over 90 degrees Fahrenheit, while the winters can go below minus 70 degrees Fahrenheit. There are many different Athabascan villages in this region, and eleven different Athabascan languages (see the articles in this volume by Langdon and Leggett, Leonard, Kari and John).

Population estimates of Alaska's indigenous people vary. Some precontact estimates suggest an average population of 80,000 (Langdon 2002, 4). It is clear that the Native population is growing; in 1960 it was 42,522 and in 2004 was

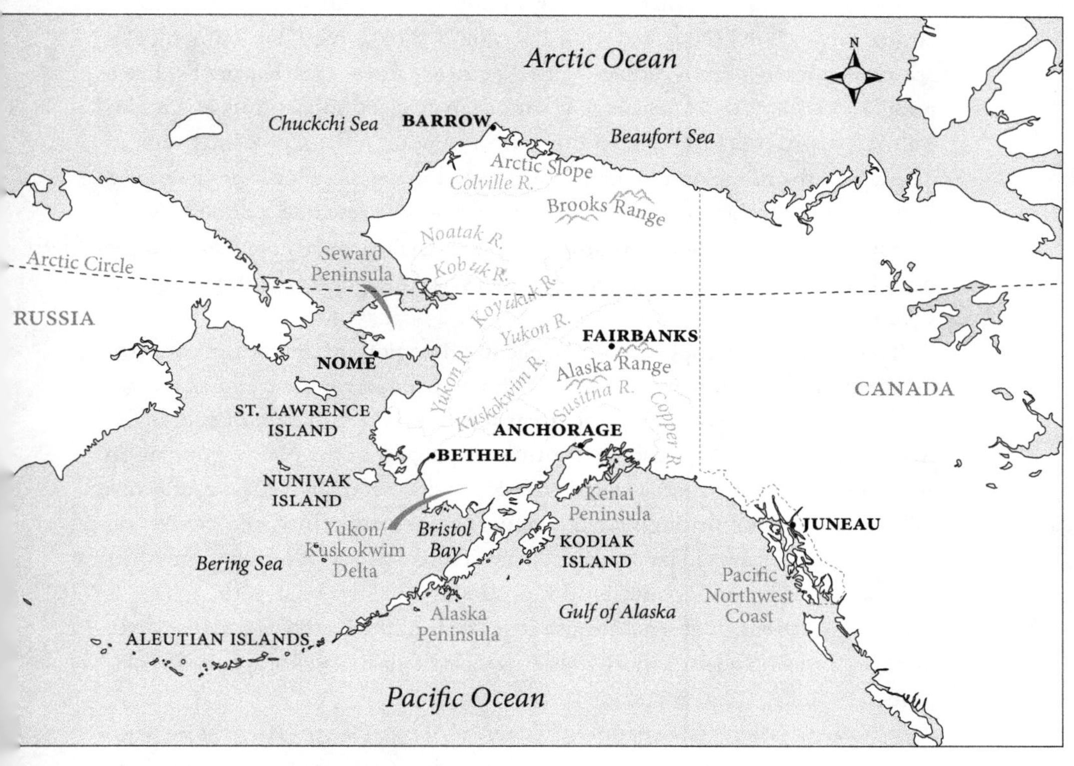

Map 1. Geographic map of Alaska

127,008 (Institute of Social and Economic Research 2004, 2–7). In comparison the non-Native population in 1960 was 183,645, while in 2004 it was 528,427 (ibid.). The population estimate for the entire state in 2006 was 670,253, with almost half of the population living in and around Anchorage, the state's largest city (Alaska Department of Labor and Workforce Development, Research Analysis, Demographic Unit). The next largest city, Fairbanks, has a population of 87,214.[5] Anchorage is a modern city, founded in 1915 as a major railroad town. It is located in south central Alaska in the Cook Inlet region. The area is the homeland to the Dena'ina Athabascan peoples, who have lived in the region for thousands of years. As Anchorage grew into a boomtown, it overshadowed the indigenous history of the Dena'ina, as happened to indigenous history in many other major U.S. cities (see Langdon and Leggett in this volume).

The indigenous peoples of Alaska occupy all regions of the state in over two hundred villages. However, there is a shifting demographic trend as indigenous people are moving to urban areas for jobs, education, and health care. According to the First Alaskans Institute, 58 percent of the Native population continues to live in what is called "rural" Alaska, referring to the numerous village settlements throughout the state. The over two hundred Native villages are not connected by roads and have a long history of occupation. Most transportation to rural communities occurs by air or by boat, if the village is along any of the large rivers. Almost 40 percent of the Native population lives in cities; these include the more modern settlements of Anchorage, Fairbanks, Juneau, Wasilla, Sitka, and Kodiak.[6]

Who are Alaska Native people? The term "Alaska Native" is a generic pejorative term, much like "American Indian." These are political designations that evolved in the colonial and neocolonial periods and established an overarching definition for indigenous people. Today, Alaska Native is the accepted definition for the indigenous peoples of Alaska; in actuality there are twenty different indigenous languages spoken in Alaska and seven or eight broad cultural groups, depending upon interpretation. The indigenous people adapted themselves perfectly to their environments, creating unique watercraft such as qayaqs/kayaks (now found all over the world), waterproof stitching, weaving traditions, specialized harpoons and other hunting gear, and ingenious dwelling places. The different cultural groups also had varied social practices that were as wide ranging as the landscape.

The twenty indigenous languages in Alaska can be categorized under four different language families: Eskimo-Aleut, Athabascan, Tsimshian, and Haida.[7] Eleven different Athabascan languages are spoken in Alaska.[8] The

Athabascan language family is a large one. There are over sixty Athabascan villages in interior Alaska. Groups in Canada, parts of Oregon, northern California, and the southwestern United States, such as the Navajo and Apache, are part of this large language family. Unangan or Aleut is spoken on the Aleutian Islands, where thirteen villages are spread out over 1,100 miles of volcanic islands. The Yup'ik/Cup'ik language, spoken in sixty villages on the mainland of southwestern Alaska; its very close linguistic relative Siberian Yupik, spoken on St. Lawrence Island; and Sugcestun, spoken on Kodiak Island and the Alaska Peninsula region, are mutually intelligible dialects. Sugpiaq or Sugcestun is spoken on Kodiak Island, parts of the Alaska Peninsula, and the Prince William Sound area and is closely related to Central Yup'ik, although the cultural and social practices of these groups are quite different.

Kodiak Island is the second largest island in the United States (the first is Hawaii). Sugcestun is spoken in seven villages on Kodiak Island, eight villages in the Chugach region, and twelve villages in the Alaska Peninsula. Eyak, found east of the Prince William Sound area and bordering Tlingit territory, is related to the Athabascan language families, but the cultural practices of the Eyak people are distinct. The Tlingit language is spoken in the northern part of southeastern Alaska and parts of British Columbia. Tlingit people traditionally lived in fourteen villages spread throughout the area. Haida is found in the southern portion of southeastern Alaska and is a linguistic isolate. The Tsimshian language is spoken in a small portion of southeastern Alaska (in the village of Metlakatla) and is part of the Penutian language family. The Iñupiaq language in Alaska is related to the larger circumpolar Inuit language family found in Russia, Canada, Greenland, and Scandinavia; it is spoken in several regions in Alaska and has several different dialects. Northern Alaskan Iñupiaq is found in the Arctic Slope area, home to seven villages; Seward Peninsula Iñupiaq includes the Qawiaraq dialect spoken in over twenty-seven villages including the island communities of King Island and Little Diomede Island; the Malimiut dialect is found in the Kobuk region, which has eleven associated villages.

The Alaska Native Language Center was established by the University of Alaska, Fairbanks in the early 1960s and has contributed greatly to the knowledge of Alaska's indigenous languages through publications, development of written orthographies, dictionaries, and translation of oral histories. Several of our contributors, among them James Kari, have long associations with the Alaska Native Language Center (see Kari/Johns article in this volume).

There has been a hyperfocus on the origins of Native Americans; Western scholars conjecture that there were three migrations out of Asia into North

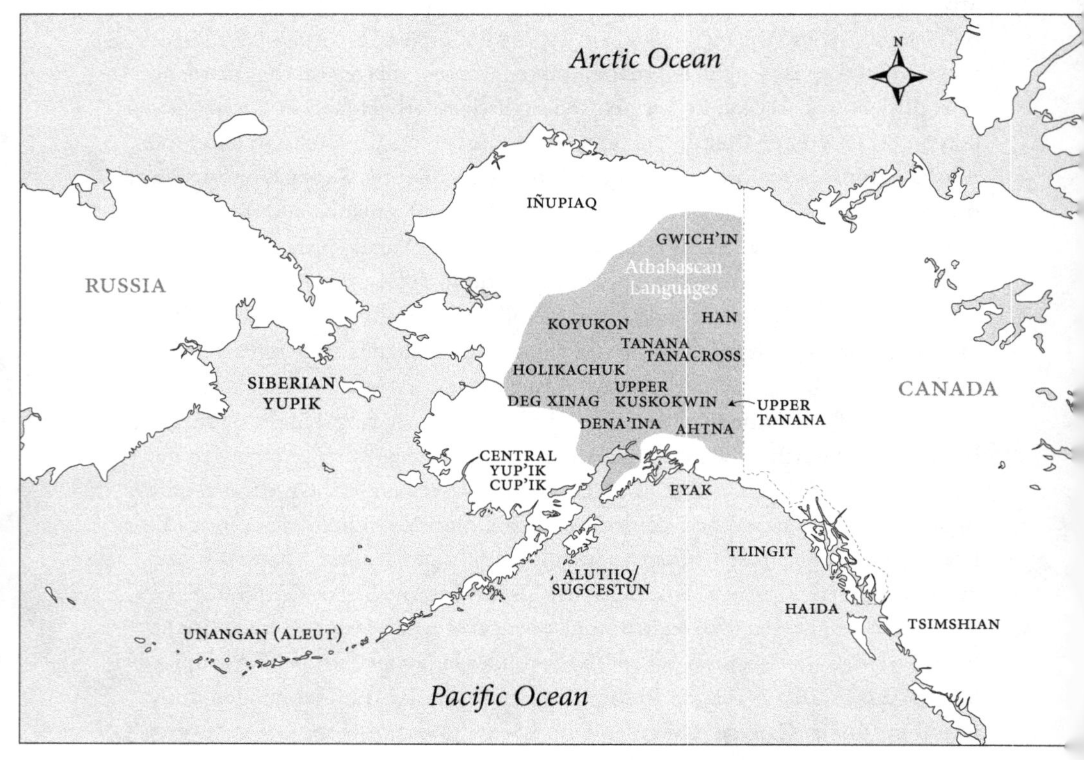

Map 2. Distribution of Alaska Native languages

America over the past ten to thirty thousand years or more. Indigenous origin stories are often more complex and much more interesting because they are related to both physical and metaphysical cosmologies. For example, each individual Tlingit clan has a separate origin story that describes a distant time when people and animals could speak to one another and even intermarry. Cajete (in this volume) addresses how astronomy and the stars can also relate the origin stories of indigenous peoples.

There are several different interpretations of how the indigenous people of Alaska can be viewed in terms of cultural groups. Today there is much discussion and debate on synonymy, or how people are called. The self-designative terms are quite numerous and village specific in Alaska. With over two hundred villages, this can get complicated. For example, the people on King Island or Ukivok, an Iñupiaq-speaking village, call themselves "Ukivokmiut"—or "the winter place people." The larger terms such as "Iñupiaq" or "Yup'ik" or "Tlingit" often translate into "people," or "real people" in the case of Yup'ik. Certainly the eleven different Athabascan-speaking peoples consider themselves related and share many cultural practices; politically they have formed alliances, even through modern times. This could be considered one culture group, even though they speak eleven different dialects and occupy the largest region of Alaska. Their current landholdings, after the 1971 Alaska Native Land Claims Settlement Act, are 12.5 million acres. They are the largest private landowners in Alaska. The Athabascan people continue to occupy and hunt in their historic land base. Athabascan people live, hunt, and seasonally occupy areas north to south from the Brooks Range to the Alaska Range. From east to west there are Athabascan settlements from the Canadian border to the interior of the Norton Sound area.[9]

The Unangan people of the Aleutian Islands historically were divided into nine subdivisions and spoke ten dialects (Bergland and Dirks 1990); however, beginning with the Russian period in the eighteenth century, they began to lose their political differences and could be considered as one culture group today. The islands stretch over 1,200 miles into the Pacific Ocean, and the Unangan developed the qayaq and unique hunting implements, elaborate body art and decoration, and a complex and stratified social system. They were also the first to face the brunt of Russian colonial practices.

The people on Kodiak Island, the Alaska Peninsula, and the Prince William Sound area speak Sugcestun, though they each have unique histories and cultural practices, resulting in complex relationships. Historically, Kodiak had over three dozen villages. After a major smallpox epidemic of 1835–40, and the harsh treatment they received from the Russian fur companies, only ten villages exist today. The Chugach people of the Prince William Sound area live in their long-inhabited traditional villages.[10] The Sugcestun-speaking people on the Alaska Peninsula occupy nearly a dozen settlements.

The Tlingit, Haida, and Tsimshian of southeastern Alaska speak three completely unrelated languages. They are not even in the same language family; however, their cultural practices are very similar in art, music, dance, and clan-based systems and patterns of reciprocity guided by moiety and status.

The Iñupiaq of Alaska, who occupy the Seward Peninsula, the Kobuk region, and the Arctic (North) Slope region, could be viewed as one group linked by language and subsistence patterns, though there are significant differences. The dialect of Inuit spoken in the North Slope region is not mutually intelligible with the languages spoken in the Kobuk or Seward Peninsula regions. Each of the over forty Iñupiaq villages has subtle, unique differences, perhaps because of their perfection in adapting to the environments they have lived in for so many thousands of years. Langdon (2002, 62–63) divides them into five major groups: the North Alaska Coast Iñupiaq, the Interior North Alaska Coast Iñupiaq, the Kotzebue Sound Iñupiaq, the Norton Sound/Seward Peninsula Iñupiat, and the Bering Straits Iñupiat.

The Yup'ik/Cup'ik people of southwestern Alaska certainly must be viewed as a separate cultural area. Historically, they were often called "Eskimo" along with the Iñupiaq. The term "Eskimo" is the outside or pejorative term and it is beginning to lose favor because it is simply too broad and inaccurate. The Yup'ik/Cup'ik or Yupiaq occupy the entire southwestern mainland portion of Alaska, including the Yukon/Kuskokwim Delta area and the Bristol Bay region.[11] These are rich ecosystems that continue to support over fifty-six villages in the Yukon/Kuskokwim Delta and eleven in the Bristol Bay region. The Yupiaq continue to live off the abundant salmon runs in the larger riverine areas, as well as the coastal marine mammals from the Bering Sea coast.

The Siberian Yupik of St. Lawrence Island, who number about 1,500, have historically been called Yup'ik or Eskimo; their language is mutually intelligible with Central Yup'ik (found on the mainland of Alaska) but their cultural and social practices are distinct and they are much more closely connected to their Siberian counterparts. Because their cultural practices are not directly similar to Yup'ik or Iñupiaq, they must be viewed as their own cultural area.[12]

Eyak, like the Siberian Yupik, provides another example of how difficult it can be to classify Native peoples of Alaska. Although the Eyak language is from the Athabascan language family, their cultural practices are different and they could also be considered a separate ethnic or cultural group. They have practices similar to their Sugcestun-speaking neighbors to the west, their Tlingit neighbors to the southeast, and their Athabascan counterparts to the north, but they developed individual art forms and subsistence and social practices that set them apart from their Athabascan relations.

Given all of this, one could say there are innumerable culture groups, but for the sake of clarity we identify eight broad cultural areas in Alaska. (1) Athabascan; (2) Northwest coast (Tlingit/Haida/Tsimshian); (3) Siberian Yup'ik (St. Lawrence Island); (4) Yup'ik/Cup'ik/Yupiaq; (5) Iñupiaq; (6) Alutiiq/Sugpiaq (Kodiak Island, Prince William Sound, Alaska Peninsula); (7) the Unangan of the Aleutian Islands; and (8) Eyak (Williams 2001).

The first European arrivals to Alaska were the Russians in the mid-eighteenth century, but other Europeans came to Alaska in the late eighteenth century as well, including the Spanish, French, British, and North Americans. By 1867 Alaska became part of the United States through the Treaty of Cession with Russia, and in 1958 Alaska became the forty-ninth state in the Union. The initial historic contacts are fascinating (see Kari/John and Solovjova/Vovnyanko in this volume).

The various contributions to *The Alaska Native Reader* will clarify and provide more detail on the colonial history and also the political history of Alaska and its indigenous peoples. The diverse geography of Alaska is matched by its Native people; one cannot separate them from "the last frontier." Alaska Native people have proven to be resilient and able to adapt to the larger geopolitical world. Many of the contributions in this reader detail some of the remarkable histories that set Alaska apart from any other place or people in the world.

Notes

Dr. Phyllis Fast, assistant professor of anthropology and liberal studies at the University of Alaska, Anchorage, helped draft an earlier version of this introduction. The introduction text has been substantially reworked since then, but I gratefully acknowledge her contribution.

1. http://www.dced.state.ak.us/oed/student_info.

2. Alaska has over forty active, monitored volcanoes (Wallace, McGimsey, Miller 2000). The largest recorded earthquake in North America took place in Alaska on March 27, 1964, on a magnitude of 9.2, which caused extensive damage and a tsunami.

3. http://www.volcano.si.edu.

4. http://www.dced.state.ak.us/oed/student_info.

5. Alaska Department of Labor and Workforce Development, www.dced.state .ak.us/dca.

6. http://www.firstalaskans.org.

7. http://www.uaf.edu/anlc.

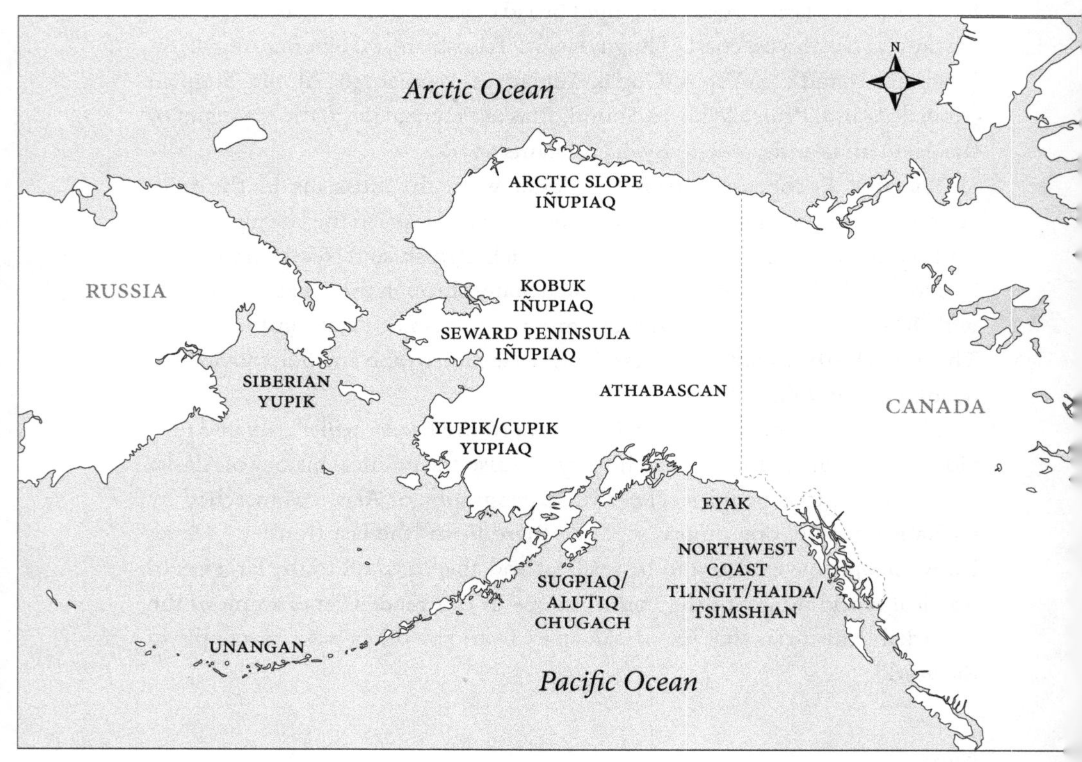

Map 3. Distribution of Alaska Native culture groups

8. The term "Athabascan" is from the Cree language and was adopted in the nineteenth century as the term for the related languages in this region and later became the name for the language family (http://www.uaf.edu/anlc/athabascan.htm).

9. http://www.doyon.com.

10. http://www.chugach-ak.com.

11. Yupiaq is the older term for people of this region.

12. Their dance and musical styles are distinctive, sharing some similarities with their Iñupiaq neighbors, but their subsistence practices, historic use of body art, and clothing decoration are very much their own.

I

Portraits of Nations: Telling Our Own Story

Part I of this volume provides new perspectives on indigenous languages and history by a variety of contributors. The first essay, "*Lazeni 'linn Nataełde Ghadghaande*: When Russians Were Killed at 'Roasted Salmon Place' (Batzulnetas)," is from an oral narrative by the Ahtna elders Katie and Fred John. I felt strongly that the first essay in this volume should be in one of the twenty Alaska Native languages so readers can get a sense of the worldview of Alaska Native people. The next essay, "The Fur Rush: A Chronicle of Colonial Life," is by Solovjova and Vovnyanko, two Russian scholars, and is an excerpt from a larger work. It reflects the exploration and subsequent colonization of parts of Alaska from a Russian perspective. History cannot be understood from one perspective, so these first two essays provide important divergent views.

That Alaska has over two hundred villages and twenty different languages is often overlooked and Alaska Native people are mistakenly viewed as monolithic. Part I will hopefully dispel that idea. Other essays address Alaska Native languages, correct misconceptions that indigenous people were not planners, describe the rich history of the city of Anchorage, and retell a story from the perspective of a young Native boy growing up in Alaska during the 1930s.

In too many instances Native stories and histories have been told by non-Native observers who do not speak the language or have an incomplete understanding of indigenous cultures and societies. Alaska has twenty languages; exciting work is being done on them at the university level by Alaska Native linguists. Jeane Breinig (Haida), Beth *Ginondidoy* Leonard (Deg Xinag), Walkie *Kumaggaq* Charles (Yup'ik), and George *Kanaqlak* Charles (Yup'ik) have written essays that directly address indigenous languages. Language is a window into a particular worldview and provides a means for understanding indigenous people. Beth Leonard uses Deg Xinag Athabascan narratives to illustrate the relationship between language and society and the subtle art of translating

Deg Xinag to English. She carefully describes the nuanced terms of Deg Xinag and thus makes the connection to that culture. Walkie Charles addresses the role of indigenous language teachers and linguists at the university level; he teaches Yup'ik at the University of Alaska, Fairbanks, where he focuses on the experiences of Yup'ik students learning their language in a western setting instead of a community setting. Jeane Breinig has been involved with Haida language revitalization and her essay provides an optimistic view of how endangered languages can be saved. George Charles's essay includes several narratives that illustrate Yup'ik culture and history. The Yup'ik language, like many indigenous languages, has no "he" or "she" and is gender neutral. Professor Charles also discusses the importance of names and the naming process within the Yup'ik or Yupiaq social protocols, thus providing a new way of understanding societies.

The part also contains an essay addressing the concept of planning from a western versus an indigenous perspective. Charlene Stern (Netsaii Gwich'in Athabascan) counters and corrects the ethnocentric idea that her people were not planners. In "Redefining Our Planning Traditions," she provides a detailed description of how the Gwich'in Athabascan planned and executed vital hunting expeditions so that they could survive in an Arctic environment.

In "*Dena'ina Elnena*: Denan'ina Country: The Dena'ina in Anchorage, Alaska," James Fall gives a wonderful account of how the Dena'ina lived in the area now known as Anchorage, the largest city in Alaska. The Dena'ina Athabascans occupied the site before the city was established in 1915 and remained there until World War II. Fall's essay should be read by all residents of Anchorage because it describes a rich heritage and contains remarkable photos of the first residents.

Maria Bolanz's "Memories of My Trapline" is based on a true story, retold from the perspective of a young boy who experienced life in the 1930s, a period in which remote areas of Alaska remained relatively untouched by western colonial expansion. The story is at once charming and sad, because the young boy's world was about to change dramatically.

Lazeni 'linn Nataełde Ghadghaande: When Russians Were Killed at "Roasted Salmon Place" (Batzulnetas)

James Kari, with Katie and Fred John *(Ahtna Athabascan)*

Oral history and narrative of Alaska's indigenous people are of paramount importance in terms of understanding their culture and worldview. Since indigenous languages in Alaska were not written, all knowledge was transmitted through oral narratives; these took the form of historical accounts, songs, and legendary history. This oral history, presented in the Ahtna language, one of the twenty indigenous languages spoken in Alaska, tells of one of the first encounters between the Ahtna and the Russians. It is an Upper Ahtna narrative, from a larger work of Upper Ahtna narratives, and has been transcribed in Ahtna and translated into English by James Kari.

In this account Katie and Fred John describe in great detail an altercation on the Upper Copper River between the Ahtna and a group of Russians, perhaps as early as 1794–95. This narrative relates how the Ahtna reacted to an intrusion by a group of Russian explorers, led by a Dena'ina Athabascan guide. The Dena'ina guide aided the Ahtna by purposefully mistranslating the Athabascan into Russian to give the Ahtnas the upper hand. The story illustrates the early colonial period and the indigenous reaction to encroachment by outsiders. The words of the Ahtna narrative about their attack on the Russians, "and the spears fell like frost crystals," are haunting.

Katie and Fred John are Upper Ahtna Athabascan from Mentasta. Fred was the traditional chief of Mentasta until his death in 2001. Katie John is well known for her leadership in protecting subsistence rights via her involvement with the landmark 1990 case, Katie John et al. v. the State of Alaska, *and for her subsequent work protecting traditional fishing and hunting lifestyles in rural communities. James Kari, a professor emeritus at the University of Alaska, Fairbanks, is a linguist who specializes in Athabascan languages and oral history. His landmark work with Katie and Fred John has resulted in publications of oral histories and narratives in Ahtna, one of the eleven Athabascan languages spoken in Alaska. Among Professor Kari's many publications are a collection of Belle Deacon's stories,* Deg Hit'an Athabascan, *and* The Ahtna Athabascan Dictionary.

Lazeni udetniinn 'iinn tseh xona 'udaadze 'Atna' daadze kadełe.
The ones called Russians first were coming from down the Copper River.
'Atna' daadze kadełde xona koht'aenn' iinn 'uka kadełde.
As they came up the Copper River they came (looking) for Ahtna people.
Łuk'ece'e Na' keniide yet c'a xona,
At the place they call "King Salmon Creek" (site where creek joins Copper River south of Drop Creek),
ts'utsaede tseh kughile'de, koht'aenn 'iinn hdaghalts'e.'
some Ahtnas were staying where about two hundred years ago there had been a site.
Kaek'ae kehwghił'aen'de.
They had a home there.
Yet xu nihnidaedl 'e ł kaskae, ukaskae' yilaenn 'uka c'ekudełketde.
They (the Russians) arrived there and they asked for their (Ahtna) chief.
Yen xugha tihniłtaen.
They brought him out to them.
Xeyuzniic ts'en' xeyełtsez.
They (the Russians) grabbed him and they whipped him.
Kedettsagh.
He was sobbing.
'Uniit Nataełde hwts'en ciił utsucde inełyaexi 'ae ł zdlaa.
From upriver at *"Roasted Salmon Place" (Batzulnetas) a young man who was raised by his grandmother had traps set.*
Decen 'ae ł tanatedaasi idezts'aan.
As he went back among the deadfall traps he heard him (sobbing).
Yii cu ugheldze' idits'agga 'e ł koht'aenn dadilaen ts'en.'
He listened carefully and it sounded like a person.
Detsucde ts'en' natesdeyaa ts'en' detsucde nahwnicdini'aan.
He returned to his grandmother and he brought the news to her.
"K'alii cu nkohnesi dadilehe.
"It didn't sound like an animal.
Koht'aenn k'a daasts'ak.
I heard a person.
Koht'aenn kedetsaghade de'ests'ak," dae' detsucde 'e łnii.
I heard a person sobbing," he told his grandmother.
Utsucde xona ka'ooxo koht'aenn 'iinn kugha'aay hdelts'iinn 'iinn tah łooyaał ts'en.'
His grandmother went over to the people staying nearby there.

"Naniit scaay xu 'ae ł tanatedaas nadaa'
"My grandchild was checking traps downriver
koht'aenn 'iinn hdelts'ii ts'en' xu' konii, dae' nii 'nts'e tkonii 'uzolyuunn.'"
where people are staying and he says *'you should be on guard.'"*
Lazeni 'iinn gaa htadeł koniix t'aenn kesdiłts'ak.
Someone let him know that the Russians would be coming here.
Xuk'a tk'ent'ae koniide," dae' koht'aenn 'iinn 'ełnii.
And this is how the situation seems to be," and so she told the people.
Yukahts'en' sacagha 'eł xona lazeni xuts'en' ghadeł.
Sure enough, in the morning Russians were approaching them.
Yene 'iinn xuts'en' ghadełi 'eł xona xugha hnidaetl.
They approached them and then they reached them.
C'uket Ta' c'ekudełket, "Bede 'iinn nuhkaskae' nlaen?" dae' xu'ekenii.
C'uket Ta,' ["Father of Buys Something"], asked, "Who are your chiefs?" they (Russians) said to them.[1]
"Yen, yen c'a nekaskae' nlaen," dae' kiiłnii.
"He, he is our chief," they (Ahtnas) said to him.
"Yen kaskae xona negha tinołtaes," dae' kenii ts'en.'
"Bring the chief out to us," they said.
Xugha tikiiniłtaen.
They brought him out to them.
Ba'aat xona c'ecenn' hwnidighi'aay 'ekeyiłtl'uun.
They (Russians) lashed him to a stump that stood near there.
Keyełtsez.
They whipped him.
Yii c'a xugha kiidettsagh yen da.
He was sobbing to them, that man.
"Yałniił Ta' da t'oł'aenn."
"You are doing this to Yałniił Ta'*" ["Father of He is Carrying It"].*[2]
"C'udaghalne' ts'en' cu'eł 'ohtnes da doht'aenn?" dae' da xu'ełnii.
"Do you know you are doing this to someone who is vicious?" he said to them.
Yen 'iinn k'alii kiidists'agga ts'en.'
They (the Russians) couldn't understand him.
C'uket Ta' kudełket, "Nts'e nii ts'en'?"
They asked C'uket Ta', "What is he saying?"
C'a nii dae, "Kedetsagh. 'Ebii, 'ebii,' dae' nii ts'en.'"
And he said, "He is sobbing. 'Ouch, Ouch,' he is saying."
C'uket Ta' yidi idits'ak k'alii xu'eł inakolnigi.
C'uket Ta' did not tell them what he had (actually) heard.[3]
Yeghak'ae xona dahnidaetl ts'en.'

They entered his (the chief's) house.

"Xantaey' tinohdaeł."

"You (men) leave right away."

Ts'iłten' keyizdlaay 'eł 'uyuunn 'eł hwtsicdze' xuc'a' kuzniic ts'en.'

They took from them (the Ahtna men) all the bows and spears that they had.

Xuyuunn' 'eł kuzniic.

They took their spears.

Xutandliidulneni gha tixuhniniyuut, denaey 'iinn.

They drove them out so that they might freeze, those men.

Ts'akaey 'iinn yaen,' ts'akaey 'iinn yaen' kuzniic ts'en.'

Only the women, they took just the women.

Ts'ins'taey 'iinn du' 'ałnaa gha kughines.

They took the old women, too, as slaves.

Denaey 'iinn yaen' tixuhniniyuut.

They chased out only the men.

Yii c'a xona Nataeł Na' ts'en' ngge' htezdaetl ts'en.'

And then they (the Ahtna men) started upland from "Roasted Salmon Creek" (Tanada Creek).

Yu' 'aede n'eł xutandliidulneni gha xu tkiilaak.

They had been forced to go without (adequate) clothing so that they would *freeze.*

Ts'instaey 'iinn lazeni 'iinn xukuzniic xu 'alnaa gha.

The Russians took those old women as slaves.

Łic'ae xugha nakighaan ts'en' xunansekele' ts'en.'

They (the Russians) killed some dogs and skinned them.

Xudezes łic'ae dezes ta xule' 'ehdelaes.

They gave them the skins, those dog skins.

Tadghusaex xu' 'ekenii.

They told them to tan them.

Yedu' takiide'aał.

Then they (the women) chewed on them.

Takiide'aał ts'en' tac'ehdesaex yii gha łic'ae zes.

They chewed all them and tanned them, those dog skins.[4]

Sasluuggu' cuu koht'aenn hdelts'ii ts'en' 'eł ts'eketniigi.

They (the Russians) didn't know that there were more people staying at "Small Salmon" (Suslota).

Gha yet tixuhniniyuut ts'en' xuk'a 'utgge tah Sasluuggu' tah kakezdaetl ts'en.'

When they chased them out, they (the Ahtna men) went up above to "Small Salmon."

Yihts'en tah xona yu' 'eł c'aan keyuyaan'a 'eł xule' ghalyaa.

There clothing and food to eat were given to them.
Yii c'a 'utsiit Nataeł Na' tah xona kii'eł nin'idaetl ts'en' xutah kedek'aas ts'en.'
Those who had come from down at "Roasted Salmon Creek" (Tanada Creek) were training (for war) among them.
Kadyiin' ts'en' c'etiye' 'iinn kadyiin.'
They made medicine, and the old men made medicine.
Sen 'eł niłtah nakehwdelaes.
They combined their medicine (powers).
Sen 'eł koht'aenn 'iinn ketk'aas.
The people trained with medicine.
Deyeni 'iinn, "Na'aat ts'abaeli c'eyits'e dighiłcaax gha yii tatnułghotlde.
The medicine men said, "You try to break the biggest spruce out there.
Yihts'en del 'eł tsighaa 'eł ta uyihts'en kadidaek xona k'etuhdeniił,"
If blood and hair come out of it, then you will get your revenge,"
dae' deyeni 'iinn xu'ełnii.
so the shamans told them.
Xu' tkedyaak ts'en.'
So they did that.
Ba'aat ts'abael yii c'eyits'e dighiłcaax xu xii'ekułdeł takiitnełghodli 'eł
Out there they charged against the largest spruce and they broke it and
del tah tsighaa del dilaenn 'eł ta kadedaex.
blood, hair with blood, came out (of the spruce).
"Yet c'a xona c'a k'et'ohdeyaak."
"There you will get revenge."
"Xona xu' tułiił. Xu' tuhghaan," dae' xu'ekenii.
"You will do like this. You will kill them," they told them.
Deyeni xu'ekenii.
The shamans told them.
Xona katk'aats.
Then they were trained.

Fred John (FJ):
Lazeni 'iinn nadaa'a nadaa'a 'Atna daa' tah c' ezdlaen dae' konii.
It was said that they (the Russians) had appeared downriver, down the Copper River.[5]
C'ets'en' nikidaek ts'en.'
They were fierce.
Yedu' kaydii xutah 'udaadze xu htezdaetl lazeni 'iinn.
They were coming among them from downriver, those Russians.
Natsii Nataełde yet ta xona yet hnidaetl ts'en' nahwtezk'aats ts'en.'

They arrived down there at "Roasted Salmon Place" (Batzulnetas) and the weather was beginning to get cold (in the late fall).

C'uket Ta' yen du' dastnaey ghile' kenii

That man (the interpreter), C'uket Ta,' was a Dena'ina they say.

Yen du,' "'Ene'!"

He told them (earlier), "Don't do it (don't attack them now)!"

"C'etsen' 'ekutsaas da su xona kuts'ughaan,'" kenii.

"It would be 'difficult meat' for us to kill them," they said.

Cetsen' 'ekutsaas da su," dae' kenii.

"It would be difficult meat," they said.[6]

Xona du' xona 'udaa' kaskae 'udaa' tezyaa.

Then the chief (of Batzulnetas) went downriver.

'Ilcuut ts'en' c'etsezi kaen' ltsez.

He was taken and whipped with a whip.

Xoxoxoon.

Oh-ho-ho.

Na'udedzii xu' yen da t'ghoł 'aen' da?" dae' nii.

"Should you do this to one calling his own name?" he (Yałniił Ta') *said.*[7]

"Yii su c'a t'ae 'Ene' c'etsen' 'ekutsaas."

(C'uket Ta' said), "Don't do it. It would be difficult meat."

"'Ene'!" yen 'unsogho dastnaey yiłnii.

"Don't do it (don't fight them now)!" the Dena'ina from the west told him.

C'uket Ta' yiłnii.

C'uket Ta' told him.

Xona 'unae' dana'idyaa.

Then he (a Russian) came back in.

"Nts'e nii?" udetnii.

"What is he saying?" he asked him (C'uket Ta').

"'Egedaa su nii le," dae' udetnii.

"He is just saying ouch," he told him.

Yihts'en duye' gaa xona lazeni yen 'iinn,

After that then the Russians thought that he (Yałniił Ta')

'Egedaa" nii geła dae' keyutnii ts'en.'

had simply said "Ouch."

K'alii 'a xiigha hwdił'axa.

They (the Russians) did not harm him (further).

Xunikelget ts'en' tixuhniniyuut ts'en.'

They were afraid of them (the Ahtna men) and they chased them out.

Tixuhniniyuut ts'en.'

They chased them out.

Nt'i c'a 'unae' Nataeł Na' tah 'ungge ta k'ehghidaetl xuhtah.
Well, up "Roasted Salmon Creek" (Tanada Creek) they reached the upland country (at Suslota).
Kon'ts'en' tah hdelts'ii ts'en' ketk'aas xoxo!
Staying by the fire they trained (for war). Oh!
Gaa ketk'aas tah xona lazeni 'iinn ts'ughaan' kiiniziin' ts'en' ketk'aas.
Here they trained and they trained thinking that they would kill the Russians.
Yet xuhtah t'ae' t'ae' katk'aats.
Then they were well-trained.
'Udaat 'udaa' xugha ts'enkedeł.
They came back downriver to them (the Russians).
Xoxo.
Ho-ho.
Xona tets xona xona c'edan'a ts'en' nayiis gha katk'aats ts'en,'
At night then, after they had finished training for war,
C'uket Ta' 'uyuunn 'e ł xuc'a' 'uzniic ts'en.'
C'uket Ta' *took the spears away from them (from the Russians).*
Xona tedze 'eł ketsihwku'aan.
Then the fight started at night.
Xoxoon'!
Ho-ho-ho!
Xugha dahnidaetl cu.
They (the Ahtnas) came in to them.
C'uket Ta' du,'
Saying to C'uket Ta,'
"'Uyuunn 'uyuunn tighuggot de' nlaaghe ts'ułtsesi," dae' kiidine' ts'en.'
They (the Ahtnas) said, "Pass the spears outside and we will take them from you."
Yen, "Ghat yet 'uyuunn zdlaa da k'e de?"
"Are there spears there?"
Zdaa ts'en' xona kedahwdilts'edi.
He (C'uket Ta') *sat there and a noise was heard.*
Be'eni be'eni nitsiił nu' xeyiłces.
He shoved them (spears) out through a hole in the house.
Da'eni da'ents'en' tixeyełdeł ts'en.'
Out there they took them away.
Tixeyełdeł ts' en.'
They took them (spears) away.
Yehwna du' gaa du' lazeni 'iinn xona tl'akahwdiłnen.
Meanwhile they killed the Russians here.

Katie John (KJ):

Ts'akaey 'iinn lazeni yuzniigi 'iinn denae C'uket Ta' yen xugha xu'ekenii ts'en.'

They (the Ahtnas) had informed C'uket Ta' *and those women taken by the Russians about it (the plan of attack).*

K'a' xiidziidi decen xiidzendutsiyde xu' li'i taldese.

They (the women) put sticks in the (Russians') gun hammers so they wouldn't fire.

Hwnaghalt'aets'en' nakusdeniic.

Many of them (the guns) didn't work.

K' a' li'i tildese.

The guns didn't fire.

FJ:

Yik'ets'en su xona ts'iłghan su nac'ustniic.

Afterwards one man (a Russian) grabbed something (a gun).

" 'Ene' nac'ustniic," yiłnii.

"Don't! He took something," he (C'uket Ta') *said.*

'Utggat kon' łet ghani'aade yet ts'esezyel ts'en' yen c'a xona kiizełghaen.

He (the Russian) stuck his head up out of the smoke hole and they killed him too.

Teldic ts'en' kiigha da'ilggaac ts' en.'

They shot him with an arrow as they ran inside to him.

Yen kiizełghaen.

They killed him.

KJ:

Lazeni 'iinn hghighaan xu tetsde xuxghighaan.

When they killed the Russians they did it at night.

Xona sacagha xakal'aen'e 'e ł kahwtel'aen'e 'eł,

Then in the morning at daylight, as it was just getting light,

"Xona c'etsen' nahzełghehe xona c'etsen' nahzełghehe."

"Then they killed the meat, they killed the meat," (they said)[8]

Sacagha xuts'en' nahtesdaetl.

In the morning they went back to them.

Iyuunn 'eł ta ts'ełten' cu 'eł xii'eł c'eghaan t'iłaen'i yii, yii 'eł 'unse tes 'enhdidaetl.

With the spears, bows, and weapons of war, with those they climbed up a hill.

Yits'en' xuts'en' c'eghaan c'eliis kadahdi'aan.

Then they sang a war song to them.

Yii bendadezelnak, just half.

I have forgotten some of it, just half (I remember).

C'uket Ta' tseh xuts'en' hghiya' kadahdi'a.'
They sang of what C'uket Ta' *had told them earlier.*
"C'etsen' 'ekutsaasi. Tsae' doht'ae!" dae' C'uket Ta' xu'edine.
"It would be difficult meat. You should wait!" C'uket Ta' *had told them.*
Yii xuts'en' kandahdi'a';
They sang this again to them:

> *(song)*
> K'adii c'etsen' 'ekutsaas.
> *Now it would be difficult meat.*
> K'adii c'etsen' nazelghaede.
> *Now the meat has been killed.*
> Yaa'aaaaaaa.
> *Yaa'aaaaaa.*

Ghayet lazeni 'iinn ghadghaande c'a koht'aenn 'iinn all xu'e'a' natesdaetl.
The Ahtnas left from where they killed the Russians.
C'ezaege' yaen' ghayet 'ila' ts'en.'
Only the corpses were left there.
Koht'aenn 'iinn kon' kukełtsiin.
The Ahtnas cremated them.
Ts'abael 'eł kugha ketsaeł ts'en' yii niidze kon' kukełtsiin xu xutl'ac'ihdełk'aan.
They chopped spruce for them and they built a fire in the middle of the area and burned them.
Yii gha k'adii C'ecenn'gha kedi'aan.
That is why this place is now *called "By the Stumps" (site below Batzulnetas).*
C'ecenn' kulaen gha lazeni 'iinn 'ughelk'aande.
Stumps are there where the Russians were cremated.

FJ:
Yihts'en xona lazeni ts'en' ni'ilyaan 'iinn ts'iłghan yen c'a nałkaay łtsiin.
Then there was one Russian half-breed who was wounded.
Yii su xona C'uket Ta' nakeztl'uun.
They gave C'uket Ta' *a set of clothes.*
Xuc'a' naytesdeyaa.
He started back away from them.
'Uniidze Stl'aa Caegge xuyae' nansogho yae' nakusdaetl.
They passed "Rear River Mouth" (Slana) going downriver.
Xona nałkaay łtsiinn du,'
Then the guy who was wounded said,

"Xoxoxoon,' Tatl'ahwt'aenn 'iinn nuhgha nahwtxelnic."
"Oh-ho, I will tell on you Headwaters People."
"Nen' k'et ni'ulyaał xa,'" dae' nii
"You will not live in this country," he said.
Yihts'en' gaa duu k'eze ts'ekedaeł.
Then they (some Ahtnas) came up beside him.
'Uyuunn kaen' xu'uggaet ts'en.'
He tried to thrust a spear at them.
Yii su xona C'uket Ta,' "Dii nanae' nanae' xuts'en' na'uhdaał.
Then C'uket Ta' *said, "You go back upriver to them.*
Ghan sacts'en' dadedlii xa.'
I don't like what he is saying.
Xona nakiizułghaełi," dae' nii ts'en.'
They ought to *kill him," he said.*
Yii su xona 'unae' ts'iłghan nateltlet ts'en' Baa Łaets T'aax ts'en.'
Then one guy ran back upriver to *"Beneath Gray Sand" (point near Slana).*
Yitah xona 'unggat kon' idik'aan.
Up from there a fire started.
"Nt'i c'a dats'ii su dzaenn kulaen?"
"How come (there is a fire while) it is still daytime?"
"Yidi gha kon' dghołk'aan?"
"Why are you building a fire?" (the wounded man asked).
"Nt'i tats'atnak gaa ts'edults'e'e."
"Well, we are tired and should stay here."
Xoxoxoon.'
Ho-ho-ho.
Xełts'en' 'eł naniidze 'uyuunn sogh k'ent'ae xu naniidze.
In the evening from upriver (came) spears like frost crystals.
Yii su gaa nałkaay nlaenen, "Tatl'ahwt'aenn 'iinn nuhgha nahwtxelnic 'iinn."
That wounded guy had said, "I will tell on you Headwaters People."
Xona 'uyuunn kaen' tikiiniłt'ak nanset tayenk'et.
Then they walked him out to the river flat with a spear (pointed at him).
'Uyuunn uts'en' kutkaes.
He was stabbed with spears.
Del yaen' 'unse diłta' kukulaak.
Only blood was left there.
Yii su xona C'uket Ta,' "Xona ugheli xu' t'ghołaexi gha su," dae' nii ts'en.'
Then C'uket Ta' *said, "That is good that you did this."*
Xona yihts'en nahtesdaetl ts'en.'

Then they returned.
Yet xona lazeni 'iinn tsilahwdelnen.
And then they had killed off the Russians.

Commentary by James Kari

There are two stories from the upper Copper River area in which Russians (or non-Ahtnas) are killed. The earlier incident, portrayed here, took place at Nataełde (Batzulnetas). The later incident occurred at Stl'aa Caegge (Slana). There has been considerable controversy about these events as depicted in the oral history of the Ahtna and other historic sources. I present here, in brief, evidence which suggests that the Batzulnetas incident occurred very early in the Russian colonial period, possibly in the winter of 1794–95, and involved the Samoilov party, and that the second incident at Slana occurred in June of 1848, and involved the Serebrennikov party. Confusion about these dates stems from Strong's interpretation that the earlier Batzulnetas incident involved the Serebrennikov party (Strong 1972; John and John 1973).

The Batzulnetas story takes place in the fall-winter, and the Slana story takes place in the summer. According to information in Serebrennikov's journal, which was brought by Ahtnas to Nuchek, in Prince William Sound, his party was killed in late June of 1848 (Doroshin 1866, 27–31, Hanable 1982, 28).

We have record of another incident in which a large group of Russians and creoles was killed on the Copper River; this involved the thirteen-man Samoilov party of the Lebedev-Lastochkin company, who ascended the Copper River in 1794. Baranov, manager of the Russian-American Company, first learned in Kenai in June of 1795 that this party, led by Samoilov, had been killed somewhere on the Copper River (Tikhmenev 1978, 42). Ketz (1983, 10) believes that Davydov's account, based on his travel in Alaska in 1802–7, refers to the Samoilov party. Davydov, who does not mention Samoilov by name, nor a date, notes that Copper River Natives, prior to 1801, had killed everyone in a group of Russians except their commander (perhaps C'uket Ta' in the Johns' account here), that Ahtnas had tortured one of the Russians, and that the Russians had provoked the incident by abducting women and driving out the men in the winter without adequate clothing (Davydov 1977, 189). The incident at Batzulnetas as told by the Johns corresponds with Davydov's account, except that there is no mention of Russians being tortured.[9]

Other factors in determining the chronology of these incidents are as follows: Yałniił Ta,' chief in this story, is the earliest chief of Batzulnetas that Fred and Katie John know by name. They cannot date his death. Katie John states that the Kluane Lake incident occurred sometime after the Batzulnetas incident and perhaps ten years or less before the Slana incident. Fred John states that Takol'iix Ta,' the chief of Mentasta who was the prime instigator in the Slana incident, was the son of an Ahtna woman and one of the Russians killed at Batzulnetas (and was Fred John's grandfather). I would thus estimate his birth date as 1795–96.

The most interesting figure in the account presented here is C'uket Ta,' the guide and interpreter for the Russians. He was a Dastnaey, or Dena'ina, probably from Kenai, who deliberately mistranslated and concealed information from other members of the group while the Ahtna men prepared to retaliate.

I give particular weight to the accounts presented here by the Johns because 1) they are told in their Native language, 2) both of these incidents took place in the narrators' own country, 3) the Johns have repeatedly told these stories to Native and non-Native audiences, and 4) the transcripts have been reviewed and cross-checked with both narrators and compared with historical sources. It should be noted that Ahtnas from the lower Copper River also tell stories about these incidents, and there are details in those accounts that are not mentioned in the Johns' stories.

Notes

1. C'uket Ta's identification as "Aleut" by Strong in John and John (1973) was the result of a mistranslation. The Johns and other Ahtnas identify the Chugach people of Prince William Sound as Skesnaey or (in English) Aleut. In this story C'uket Ta' is identified as Dastnaey (Dena'ina), he has an Athabaskan name, and he speaks Ahtna well enough to dupe the Russians.

2. Yałniił Ta' is chief of this territory. Here he calls out his own personal name, an act that is considered a very bold challenge.

3. This bit of mistranslation is the first evidence of collaboration between C'uket Ta' and the Upper Ahtnas.

4. The Ahtnas had never worked with dog skin before. It was 'engii,' taboo.

5. Fred John told this portion of the story prior to the previous section told by Katie John. Portions here duplicate Katie's longer version.

6. Note that this phrase *c'etsen' 'ekkutsaas*, 'difficult meat,' appears in the war song that was made after the battle.

7. Yałniił Ta,' chief of Batzulnetas, says his name to himself as his ultimate challenge to those who are whipping him. In other words, "Who are you guys? Are your names of higher value than my own? I am the authority over this country." The use of Ahtna personal names is a matter of complex etiquette.

8. That is, they ended the war.

9. Katherine Arndt (personal communication) cautions that the historic record of Russian entry into Copper River is very fragmentary and that the *Nataełde* incident might have involved one of the other parties reported to have been killed on the Copper River. These include Bazhenov, who was killed ca. 1804–5, and Galaktionov and his interpreter, who also were killed ca. 1804–5. Further work with Lower Ahtna history may clarify the record.

The Fur Rush: A Chronicle of Colonial Life

Katerina G. Solovjova and Aleksandra A. Vovnyanko

The following is an excerpt from The Fur Rush: Essays and Documents on the History of Alaska at the End of the Eighteenth Century *by Katerina G. Solovjova and Aleksandra A. Vovnyanko (Phenix Press, 2002). The book is a major work that provides detailed information on the Russian presence in Alaska during the later part of the eighteenth century, including substantial new information. This excerpt is from chapter 3, which traces the events year by year from 1784 to 1800 with detailed information on historical figures, the exploration, exploitation, and importance of furs, and daily life for both Russian and Native peoples. Solovjova's and Vovnyanko's work is exceptional and their documentation is impeccable, bringing to light sources that have not been available before now. The book should be standard reading for anyone interested in Alaska history, especially Alaska Native history.*

In the history of Alaska, at the end of the eighteenth century, specific evidence makes it possible to speak of a "fur rush" as the characteristic occurrence that influenced the fate of the country and people. The desire of the merchants' companies to enrich themselves by importing American furs led to sending Russian trading ships on voyages to the east. According to the renowned Russian historian N. N. Bolkhovitinov, "Just as the 'sable's tail' guided the Russians through the boundless expanses of Siberia to the Pacific Ocean, the invaluable fur of the sea otter brought them to the shores of North America" (1997, vol. 1, 5).

Different merchants sent about 80 fur trading expeditions. The 40-year epic of seafarers and promyshlenniki[1] sailing across the ocean and exploring the Aleutian Islands ended with G. I. Shelikhov's seizure of Kodiak Island, an event customarily considered as the culmination of the Russians' securing of America. The character of colonization was sharply changed with the introduction of big merchant capital and the monopolization of Alaskan natural resources. The grandiose plans of the merchant Shelikhov, harsh colonial politics, support for his activities in government circles of the Russian Empire, and persistent methods of wringing out furs—all reflected in the struggles and tense daily life of the people on the shores of northwestern America, who were greatly affected by the fur rush.

The end of the nineteenth century gave Alaska a gold rush, but earlier, in the eighteenth century a fur rush had emerged in this land. The scope of these two rushes and many of their features differ. These features are primarily connected with the situation that the people—the Natives and the unwelcome newcomers—were in. The economic interests of the Russian merchants and expansionist politics of the government of the Russian Empire had a significant impact on the fur rush.

This chapter attempts to illuminate specific aspects of the colonial process in which various people participated. These people acted, struggled, made decisions and mistakes, risked their lives, and perished. The essay seeks to examine the conditions of these peoples' lives and works, and does not claim to cover the full scope of the historical events in Alaska at the end of the eighteenth century. Thus, the essay centers on the issues and events that characterized the situation in the Russian colonies as extraordinarily dangerous and strained. Some of these events have been insufficiently or erroneously elaborated, or have been ignored by the researchers.

For example, a document, one of the first to be created on Kodiak, should be mentioned. Most historians narrating the account of G. I. Shelikhov's stay on Kodiak rely on his "Note" of 1787 or his book republished in 1971.[2] However, Shelikhov's testimony, as is well known, is not entirely reliable. Researchers have completely lost sight of a very interesting document: the resolution, adopted by Shelikhov on December 11, 1785, at the conference with the mariners of his company.[3] The document outlines for the first time the main problems regarding interactions between the Russians and the Native populations, and thus it became the basis for the process of their interaction.

In this resolution, signed by the mariners, the most emphasis was given to relations between the Europeans and peoples unknown to them, whom it was necessary to "find for bargaining and subdue into citizenship of the Russian Empire." These relations were called "reconciliation." As is noted in the document, within the first year Shelikhov's men found many peoples and their hunting grounds, but because of their lack of strength (some of the new arrivals died and tradable goods had run out) they were not able to procure furs or explore new regions. Because of the small number of people it was dangerous for the Russians to live even with the already "reconciled" Kodiak people.[4] Shelikhov's people realized that without successful barter they would suffer great losses, and some would fall into irredeemable debt. Perhaps Shelikhov tried to introduce these ideas to his men. Participants of the conference recognized that "with difficulty and great battles they conquered" the Native.

1784

Two such battles are known. Shelikhov carried out the first against the [Kodiak] islanders 35 miles south of Trekhsviatitel'skaia Harbor in the first half of August.[5] Shelikhov's cruel massacre subjugated the Kodiak people, who did not succeed in uniting for a repulse and could not retaliate without effective weapons. On the first days of the Russians' presence in Manikaksik Harbor, which they named Trekhsviatitel'skaia [Three Saints] Harbor, Shelikhov sent his people in baidarki (kayaks) to become familiar with the coast of the large island and its hostile inhabitants. The news of the arrival of two large ships caused unrest in the Native villages on the south shore of the island, and they, as was their tradition, sought safety on a kekur (seastack), that is, on a large rock separated from the shore.[6] The Kodiak people defended themselves with arrows and stones. The besieged expected reinforcements, therefore Shelikhov decided to "take possession . . . of the rock, which they occupied as a fortress."

Shelikhov directed a ship to the kekur. This vessel had 71 Russian employees on board and was armed with firearms and five cannons, whose firing scared the Koniag: "terror was born and timidity seized them." The assailants stormed the seastack, destroyed the huts, and took captive those islanders who stayed alive. According to Shelikhov's report, Russians drove captive Koniag to their camp. Later, this seastack was named on Russian maps Razbitoi (Crushed). The Natives called the cliff Avauk (Frozen with Fear). This battle was a great tragedy for the islanders. Shelikhov did not report the number of people killed, but precisely noted that "of the Koniag they took more than a thousand people captive" (Andreev 1948, 231). Only five Russians were wounded. Shelikhov named the peninsula, the cape, and the nearby bay after his wife Nataliia. Even after this bloody massacre, at a conference with the mariners he hypocritically recommended "bringing new natives to friendship through tender treatment."

The primary reason for the clash was the Native inhabitants' unwillingness to become dependent on the new arrivals. And the Russians used their frightful weapons wherever they encountered resistance. Navigator G. G. Izmailov reported that when the Natives did not consent to give *amanaty* (hostages), Shelikhov's detachment killed approximately 150 to 200 islanders of both sexes. Many Natives threw themselves out of fear from the seastack into the water and onto the *baidary* and drowned. About 200 to 300 people were taken captives, primarily women, children, and the elderly. They were kept in the harbor for a month and a half. Shelikhov himself selected a chief or *toion*, who was showered with gifts and entertained.[7] When the husbands, fathers, and relatives began to arrive, Shelikhov returned the children to them.

"According to our desire, these inhabitants who were subjugated peacefully began to arrive with friendly disposition and sought a comfortable livelihood, leaving me not a small number of their children as *amanaty*; through this a method useful to the future of our fatherland was also discovered" (Andreev 1948, 211). In this exchange Shelikhov considered that he had found a way to bind the Natives to himself. He punished the rebellious Native inhabitants with a pistol and whipped them with baleen.[8] Thus, Shelikhov brought the Americans under the authority of the Russian Empire.

It was necessary to seek out skilled hunters in the villages where the Koniag and Kodiak Aleuts lived, as the Russians sometimes called them. The colonists established control over the male population, taking more than 400 *amanaty* (Andreev 1948, 178).[9] Relatives of the captives brought food to them and paid tribute to the victors. They were forced to make contact with the Russians, who had run out of goods with which to trade for furs. As a result of dwindling trade and food supplies, the Russians needed replenishment from Okhotsk.[10] Lack of goods was used as the primary reason for Shelikhov's departure on 22 May 1786,[11] when he took with him only 12 Russians and "up to 40 captive men, women, and children from different villages" (Andreev 1948, 188).[12]

Employees of Shelikhov's company sought out local people on his order not only for making trade arrangements, but also to take hostages across the ocean. Shelikhov's employees continued his predatory practices. For example, his sailor D. I. Shirokov, with the crew of the ship *Sv. Ioann Predtecha*, wintered on Unalaska in Samganuda Bay, forcibly took "50 men and 30 women islanders," and set out for the Pribilof Islands to hunt.[13] In 1784 Shelikhov took 10 Unalaskans and 2 interpreters with him to Kodiak. In his "Note" he reports that "70 Fox Islands Aleuts, voluntarily [served him] for pay" (Andreev 1948, 183, 228, 240). He recommended that his mariner D. I. Bocharov "take out of necessity up to 20 people of our Fox Islands Aleuts." When Evstratii Delarov, already an employee of the Northeastern Company (NEC), was sent to Kodiak, in Unalaska he "wintered and took along with him 30 Aleut men and 2 Aleut women."[14]

The well-known partovshchik (a participant in the hunting party or sometimes its head) Egor Purtov, who transferred from the crew of merchants Panovs's ship *Sv. Aleksei* to serve in the NEC, thought that Shelikhov had falsely reported the total number of 20,000 inhabitants on Kodiak Island[15] and the 500 who paid tribute. In fact there were "no more than 3,000 people in the surrounding islands and no more than 50 *yasak* (government tax paid in goods) payers."[16] It is possible these were the relatives of the amanaty.

K. T. Khlebnikov considered that "Shelikhov, for enlarging his glory, rashly over-stated the number of subjected people on Kodiak as 50,000 souls and this frightful number was striking to all. Therefore, they lashed at Baranov when by actual calculation it turned out to be 6,000 souls" (Khlebnikov 1835, 182).

Shelikhov planned to strengthen the depleted artels of the Russian hunters by adding "reconciled" Native inhabitants and at the same time establish control over all Koniag settlements. He considered the Natives as serfs without rights who could be ruled at his will. Shelikhov called them "American bondsmen" (Andreev 1948, 201). He wrote to his governors that it was necessary "to select in advance young and good boys and girls from the Kenai and Chugach clans for transporting them for education and to teach some of them here [in America] Russian grammar and speaking for translations. And it became quite necessary to especially try to take some [future students] from the Alaska mainland to California from 50° N [south]" (Andreev 1948, 195). The Irkutsk governor I. V. Yakobii considered this a reliable course toward the Russianization of the "backward" transoceanic peoples and developing their devotion to the Russian Empress Catherine II.[17]

In his book and accounts to the government, Shelikhov tried to show that he aspired to protect the Natives, to care for them and their *amanat* children, to reconcile them and to provide an introduction to the customs and life of Russian people. Shelikhov pretended that finally he won such love that the Natives "all call me their father" (Andreev 1948, 232–37).

1785

Company employees conducted the first study of Kodiak and surrounding islands from May to August in the galliot Tri Sviatitelia. Navigators G. Izmailov and D. Bocharov commanded the ship for this voyage and described the shoreline of the island and the mouth of Cook Inlet, the Native villages, and the locations of rich hunting grounds, and marked them on a map and various plans.

The maps indicate that at the mouth of Cook Inlet the Russians reached *Sel'devaia* (Seldovia) Bay and set up camp there.[18] "When the Russians arrived for the first time in Kenai Bay [Cook Inlet] the ship's captain detached several people to seize the Natives in order to acquaint themselves with them," reported G. I. Davydov. "They found seven or eight families and led them to the ship, but the Kenaitzy (Dena'ina), thinking that they were being taken into bondage, strangled all their wives and children, and then hanged themselves" (1812, 2: 33).[19] Davydov, an officer of the Russian fleet, believed that this occurred because of lack of agreement and mutual trust. He did not take into account the mentality of the Native Americans, whose view of the world had developed during their struggle for the source of provisions in internecine warfare. It is natural that they also viewed the Russians as enemies who forcefully seized them and forced them to leave their dwellings. One father said this about his boy: "Better to let him die now than be made to grow up a kaiur [slave]" (1812, 2: 34–35).[20]

The Native people did not attack this expedition and some even gave up to 20 people as *amanaty*. "By contrast, there was almost no significant trade there at this time, because the local inhabitants . . . were afraid to join in such relations, in spite of the fact that they had given *amanaty*," Shelikhov ascertained.

Returning from the expedition, the Russians arranged to winter at the populous village of Karluk [on Kodiak Island]. They sailed along the shore of the strait, took hostages from the village, and procured furs.[21] According to maps and reports about these events, Shelikhov participated in the voyage; however, company employees wrote that he "did not leave from this harbor [Three Saints Bay] the entire time of his stay until 1786."[22]

On the northwestern side of Kodiak, among the hills, flows the large Karluk River. An old Koniagmiut (Alutiiq) village, Karluk, was located on the shore of a convenient lagoon. The residents occupied themselves primarily with catching fish. Initially the colonists constructed a fortified barracks in the Karluk artel. Later they enclosed their fort with a small earthen rampart and built a sentry booth and support structures. The artel leader, the *baidarshchik*, was in charge of several villages of Natives and forced the men to work for the company—hunting sea otters and stocking up on food supplies—while the women caught and stashed fish and picked berries.[23]

Colonists settled in various artels because they needed food from the adjacent Koniagmiut (Alutiiq) villages. The concentration of the crews of two ships in Three Saints Bay could lead to shortage of provisions and thereby result in hunger. Shelikhov planned to "keep 163 people in each artel" at eight locations (Andreev 1948, 184, 186).

The first description of Karluk in the historical documents was as a Russian artel that maintained control of both shores of Shelikof Strait, that is, the villages of Karluk, Geopolik, Katmai, Kukan, and Naushak. Promyshlenniki arranged themselves near the huts of the Natives in Karluk and began to build the structures necessary for the stay, not forgetting to guard them. The builders of the fortification at Karluk were the *promyshlenniki* Aleksei Chernykh, Egor Bronnikov, Emel'ian Nekipelov, Piotr Popov, Vasilii Gorin,

Piotr Kalmyk, Demid Kulikalov, Fiodor Kochnev, Filipp Reviakin, Protasov, Aleksandr Molev, Egor Baranov, Ivan Repin, and Nikolai Mal'tsov. Vasilii Malakhov managed this artel.

The living conditions of Shelikhov's company employees were elaborated in a document of December 11, 1785. By winter, scurvy had begun to rage in the Russian camp. "All were sick and in despair," wrote Shelikhov. At this time, the only food available for the sick was worm-eaten bitter yukola (dried fish) covered with mold, "from which many got various illnesses: fever and scurvy and ended their lives in misery." But Shelikhov did not provide provisions for even the people in most desperate need. After many had died, and food could not even save those who were dying, he "began on the 25th of December to provide one and a half pounds [per person] per week of the company provisions," but the promyshlenniki were now unable to use it because they were too sick and extremely exhausted.[24] Those colonists who remained alive were not strong enough to move to new places. The people lacked the provisions and goods to trade for furs.

Ivan Belonogov was "brutally whipped with lashes" by the company owner for defending the promyshlenniki's rights against the deception and fraud of the master. The hunters Basov and Kochnov were also beaten on the deck.[25] Shelikhov treated his crew as if they did not have rights. He threatened to his subordinates that they all "would be left forever in these islands."[26] Striving to construct permanent settlements and declaring that the company was established for a term of no less than 10 years, Shelikhov had not prepared the legal base for the long stay of the employees on Kodiak. He had intended with the help of various contrivances and by force to keep them there in spite of the fact that their passports were only valid for seven years. Ten years later he collected from his employees without warrant their payments for their passports, as well as their relatives' debts and government duties [taxes].[27]

In order to attract people to his company, Shelikhov promised to pay for their work at the rate of half a share to a promyshlennik, as was a tradition in the other companies in the Aleutian Islands. He also promised to sell provisions at an increase of only 10 kopecks. In fact, in his "Book on the Merits of the Vessels's Crew" Shelikhov wrote down each cup of grits, candle, and glass of vodka, as well as the amount of tea issued, pricing the items eight times higher than what he'd originally promised. In Okhotsk the price for provisions was less than 3 rubles, while on Kodiak the people were forced to pay 24 rubles. Shelikhov arbitrarily charged such impossible prices, conveniently forgetting his Okhotsk agreement to increase fees minimally.[28]

The drama-filled documents brim with facts that reveal Shelikhov's unfair and cruel practices. The inexperienced common people were so trusting that they signed papers committing themselves to work three more years after the return of the ship. In Okhotsk Shelikhov had promised them that they would receive part of the shares that belonged to the deceased. They believed that Shelikhov would honestly divide up the procured sea otters when employees were not present. They wrote: "In Okhotsk you, yourself, collect our shares in the furs and the small individual scraps of furs divide as payment of debts [to the owners]" (Andreev 1948, 181).[29] At the same time they realized that with the small quantity of remaining wares they would suffer great financial loss and even go into irredeemable debt to Shelikhov. Upon joining the company and in hopes of becoming rich, the people believed the promises of being able to obtain their portion of the furs. The feverish haste of preparations, the equipping and dispatching of ships, the false promises of the owners, and the strain of the situation before leaving the port of Okhotsk—all of these misled them. Starting on a distant journey across the ocean they believed that they would receive deserved pay for their labor. But the real events in America led to bitter disappointment. During the two years Shelikhov was present on Kodiak as the organizer of permanent settlements and the "peacemaker" with the Native peoples, the aspects of colonial life, which over the years led to steady antagonistic relations between the owner and the common employees, acquired clear outlines. These aspects also shaped the relations between the Russians and Native inhabitants, thus influencing the social status of the latter.

1786

For procuring sea and land animals, the company primarily used the labor of the indigenous islanders who were natural hunters. The Natives were forced to supply the colonists with fish, game, berries, and other products. They also carried out the duties of unskilled workers in the settlements and acted as guides on trails and portages unfamiliar to the Russians, rowers in three-hatch baidarki, and interpreters during the visits of unknown Native peoples.[30] Within the colonial pyramid of social status, the indigenous inhabitants were considered the base of it. The company owners and the chief governor managed the company employees—prikazchiki (managers of private or government enterprise appointed by an owner), baidarshchiki (heads of a hunters' party moving in baidarki), and promyshlenniki—who in turn supervised the Natives. Because of the hostile surroundings, the Russian employees were forced to carry out the duties of building and protecting the settlements. Yet they served only as middlemen during the purchase of furs.[31] The owners watchfully made sure that not one skin, not one scrap of fur went astray.[32]

Therefore, the promyshlenniki were not allowed to exchange furs among themselves. The employees gathered all the fur parkas the islanders wore, and eventually the Natives began to wear clothing sewn from cheap Chinese fabrics. From the traditional clothing they kept only the waterproof kamleiki (an outer garment Aleuts wore to protect other clothing from water) made from animal gut.

The shortage of goods was alleviated by the Kodiak people's growing demand for iron-made items. Shelikhov permitted the remaining promyshlenniki to exchange iron tools for furs without the knowledge of the government. It is notable that at the same time he feared that all the Natives' furs would go to Unga Island, that is, to the company of merchants Panovs, where Delarov served as peredoushchik. The latter did not know about Shelikhov's apprehensions, so he helped with advice and promised to send his people (Andreev 1948, 191, 213).

One of the most important aspects typical of Russian colonization was the Russians' dependence on the Natives. Among the Russians quarrels emerged over the division of hunting places and the seizure of Natives for work. The *promyshlenniki* took them by force from the villages: from Unalaska more than 100 hunters with wives were taken to the Alaska Peninsula and the islands of Sannakh, Unga, Unimak, and Kodiak, and "from those who remained they took baidarki, arrows, parkas, and food supplies. [Only] a small number [of people] returned, [the rest] died there of starvation. Great hunger devastated the villages." The *baidarshchik* Pshenichnyi violated and beat women with clubs, flogging six to death.[33]

According to the Canadian researcher J. R. Gibson, the Russians depended on the Natives for basic necessities such as furs, provisions, labor, and sexual relations (Gibson (1980–1986[?], 1–36). These needs of the newcomers were directly connected to their usurpation of sources for subsistence, land, villages, and the Alaskan peoples themselves. The Russians' primary goal was the acquisition of furs, but *promyshlenniki* chronically lacked the goods for exchange. Therefore they became embittered and disregarded the vital interests and customs of the Native Americans.

The Russian colonists were not able to effectively match the skills of the local hunters, who were unsurpassed in their ability to land marine mammals. As a result, the use of Native forced labor became a source of enrichment for the fur-trading companies. The Russians' effort to settle near the Native villages, to obtain furs from the inhabitants at inequitable prices, and to use them as hunters, servants without rights, concubines, and even slaves—all this brought on protests and armed conflict. A. A. Baranov confirmed that for a long time "many people and whole villages were not brought to their knees" (Tikhmenev 1863, 2: appendix 42). The Natives of Alaska, armed with their arrows and spears, were not able to withstand the force of the western arrivals, who were equipped with firearms and ship's cannons with 2½ pound shot. "Such weapons were not known and especially frightening to the people in a land where there were rarely thunderstorms with thunder and lightning." Eventually the Koniag became forced laborers for the Russians (Chaussonnet 1996, 29).

Characteristic features of Shelikhov's politics in the colonies were his striving to procure furs from the Natives at any price, bloody punishment of the indocile, and satisfaction of his selfish goals through deception and exploitation of the Russian employees. From the time of his voyage these practices became the standard of relations between the peoples in the colonies. Many contemporaries of the events have noted the lawlessness, the backbreaking work, and the coercion that caused the spiritual depression of the people in the lower classes of the colonial pyramid.

But Shelikhov worried least of all about the fate of the people whom his methods of conducting colonial economics most painfully affected. He represented the top of the colonial pyramid, where the profits were concentrated, and simultaneously he was a distinct buffer between the government and the company interests in the colonies. He camouflaged the true position of affairs in the colonies and his selfish interests with false promises and patriotic rhetoric.

The second battle occurred in May on Shuyak Island, the day before Shelikhov's departure for Okhotsk. In spring, he had sent the *promyshlenniki* Sekerin and Labanov into Cook Inlet with an interpreter, having secured the support of the *toion* (a chief or a wealthy noble Native) of Shuyak Island. But the *toion* betrayed his Russian khaskhak (friend), killed the messengers, and plundered the goods. The irritated Shelikhov took vengeance on the islanders and sent two armed flotillas to the place where they lived, including three baidary of Natives and fifty Russians under the leadership of Konstantin A. Samoilov and Vasilii I. Malakhov, who found the instigators of the murder and killed them. The ensuing battle, similar to the one on the seastack *Razbitoi*, took place on the east coast of Shuyak Island. Analogous evil deeds, dictated by Shelikhov, significantly influenced the decrease in Native population in the Kodiak Archipelago. In memory of this devastating battle, two islands there were named *Bol'shoi Fort* [Big Fort] and *Malyi Fort* [Little Fort]. Three days before his departure, Shelikhov obtained a report that "the enemy is annihilated."[34]

In spring Shelikhov experienced a shortage of working people. By April of the previous year he had turned to other companies for help because of the loss of people from scurvy and armed conflicts with the Natives.[35] For this, the Russian navigator Bocharov was sent to the Shumagin Islands and farther to Unalaska Island. In March Evstratii I. Delarov, *peredovshchik* of the merchants Panovs Company, visited Kodiak. Shelikhov formed confidential relations with him (Andreev 1948, 182, 238).[36] It is possible that at this time they had already agreed upon Delarov's move to the NEC.

Shelikhov sent Bocharov, with several accompanying Koniag in three-hatch baidarki, to Delarov's possessions on Unga Island in the Shumagin Island group, in order to confer about the possible number of people for transfer from the ship *Sv. Aleksei*, which was leaving Alaska, to Shelikhov's company. Shelikhov was hoping that they would sign a contract immediately on the conditions of each obtaining a half share of total procurement. Apparently this deal came to pass on Unga with Delarov's agreement. Bocharov was ordered "to send [the working people from Unga] in two baidary, fairly well armed" to aid the peredovshchik Maksimov in the Semidi Islands, where one of the first artels of the NEC hunted. Shelikhov also hoped to attract "64 promyshlenniki at 60 rubles each per year" from other companies located not only on Unga, but on Unalaska, where, after Unga, Bocharov went with seven letters addressed to navigators and peredovshchiki of other companies (Andreev 1948, 182, 185).

Navigator Bocharov was ordered to hurry in order not to miss the ship *Sv. Mikhail* in Unalaska, to take command of the crew, and to prepare for a voyage. He had to be on the refitted ship in Unalaska until the 25th of May. Shelikhov, leaving Three Saints Bay on the 22nd of May, counted on finding Bocharov there. However, he also foresaw the possibility of other events; therefore, in paragraphs 5, 6, and 7 of his instructions to Bocharov, Shelikhov included significant additions about the expeditions.[37] At Shelikhov's insistence, the NEC ships constantly went on voyages in search of new islands with sea mammal haulouts.

In this connection Shelikhov's plans were well thought out to the smallest details and were filled with assignments for his employees. He directed Bocharov to not only attract people, but also to procure *lavtaki* (a skin of marine mammal that was especially dressed to make a baidarka) and trade tobacco for furs while en route at the companies in the Fox and Shumagin Islands. Shelikhov placed great significance on this voyage, even promising Bocharov the position of chief governor upon his return, as well as a large sum of money as a reward. However, in less than two months, even before Bocharov's return, the merchant K. A. Samoilov, who had become acquainted with Shelikhov as early as the voyage of 1777–1782 on his ship *Sv. Andrei Pervozvannyi*, was assigned this duty.[38]

In March, the experienced Bocharov set out on a difficult baidara voyage.

The primary task was to keep the ship *Sv. Mikhail* at Unalaska until Shelikhov's arrival, but it was not fulfilled. Possibly complex relations developed between the two skippers, V. Olesov and D. Bocharov. On May 22, 1786, the two ships, the *Sv. Mikhail* and the *Tri Sviatitelia*, met near the shores of Kodiak Island. It took Olesov 999 days to reach Kodiak. Furious Shelikhov met with the navigator, who had not been responsive to his instructions. This dramatic moment was certainly explosive (Andreev 1948, 239–41).[39] Shelikhov, ready to set off for Okhotsk, had to make new decisions and assignments in a hurry.

Preparing to sail to Okhotsk, Shelikhov composed directions to chief governor Samoilov. He "expected to obtain from the Greek Delarov and his company 24 men, and 26 more after the arrival of the ship *Sv. Mikhail* from Unalaska." He considered that the total would be "163 employees who would be maintained in the artels" (Andreev (1948, 186). In instructions to chief governors Samoilov and Delarov, Shelikhov gave concrete figures: on Kodiak 113 employees remained and 26 people were going to arrive on the third ship *Sv. Mikhail*. According to the gross contract they were 44 men short; apparently these people were deceased. Besides, Shelikhov promised to hire 20 to 30 workers, above the specified number, in Okhotsk for wages, but then did not do so (Andreev 1948, 181, 183, 186). In 1795 by the time his employees, brought to despair, realized the extent of his deceitful operation—the unlawful division of procured furs, cheating in measuring and counting—and demanded justice from Baranov,[40] Shelikhov was already far away from them.

Translated by Richard L. Bland and Katya S. Wessels

Notes

1. Editor's note: Russian words are italicized and the names of Russian vessels are italicized. *Promyshlenniki* means fur hunter.

2. Andreev (1948, 226–50); also Shelikhov (1971), edited and with the introduction by B. P. Polevoi.

3. Andreev (1948, 178–82). Both *promyshlenniki* and sailors of the ships *Tri Sviatitelia* and *Sv. Simeon* took part in this conference. The resolution adopted at this conference suggests that Shelikhov tried to leave carefully, that is, to not aggravate the remaining people by his departure.

4. Kodiak Island was inhabited by Koniagmiut (Alutiiq). In the eighteenth and nineteenth centuries they called themselves Sugpiaq. Russians called them Koniag or Kodiaktsy.

5. Shelikhov's two ships arrived at Kodiak on August 3, 1784.

6. "From the old times [they] used such refuges during enemy attacks." See Veniaminov (1840, vol. 1, 8); *Russkaia Amerika. Po lichnym vpechatleniiam missionerov,*

zemleprokhodtsev, moriakov, issledovatelei i drugikh ochevidtsev (Russian America: Personal impressions of missionaries, explorers, sailors, researchers, and other eyewitnesses) (1994, 64).

7. Russia's State Archive of Ancient Acts (RGADA), f. 1605, op. 1, d. 367, 1. 4–5.

8. RGADA, f. 1605, op. 1, d. 367, 1. 5–6.

9. Here Shelikhov's data varies from Izmailov's.

10. The most necessary goods were: "50 *pud* (1 *pud* = 36 pounds) of fine seine, 100 ox hides, 30 *pud* of large kettles, 1 *pud* of copper leaf, 10 *pud* of seed beads, 100,000 blue *korol'ki* (large blue or pink beads), 2 *pud* of white and red seed beads, 200 *pud* salt, 20 gun locks" (Andreev 1948, 181). Later, employees of the Northeastern Company were puzzled because the imported goods were so quickly exhausted. Shelikhov distributed these goods to them at prices higher than the ones in Okhotsk. The cost was written down as a debt, which had to be paid in sea otter skins. During the sea voyage the employees suffered "great famine." See *K istorii Rossiisko-amerikanskoi kompanii* (Related to the history of the Russian-American Company) (1957, 63–65).

11. The establishment of the company was closely connected with Shelikhov's dispatch to America. Possibly the term of his stay there was planned to be more than two years. The company itself was established for the term of no less than ten years. In any case, the idea of completing the construction of villages and forts in only two years was unrealistic. See Andreev (1948, 208). At the same time, the reasons why Shelikhov hastened to return to Russia and "attest his zeal to the fatherland" are completely understandable.

12. Shelikhov sent some of these people to work in the Kurile Islands. See Archive of Foreign Politics of Russian Empire (*Arkhiv vneshnei politiki Rossiiskoi imperii*, or AVPRI), f. RAC, op. 888, d. 53, 1. 1, 5. Of the Americans he left in Okhotsk, Shelikhov "ordered three juveniles and girls to be sent to him in Irkutsk," and seven people were returned to Kodiak with Delarov on the *Tri Sviatitelia*.

13. Russia's State Archive of the Navy (RGA VMF), f. 913, op. 1, d. 168, 1. 53ob. The Russian colonists resettled the Aleuts far from their home: to the Pribilof, Commander, and Kurile islands, to Kodiak, to Sitka, and even to California. The Aleuts were removed during and after the Second World War. But the Aleuts consider the resettlement of the Klavangin tribe to the Pribilof Islands as the most devastating action. See Chaussonnet (1996, 31).

14. RGADA, f. 1605, op. 1, d. 367, 1. 2.

15. In the "Note," given to the government, Shelikhov exaggerated this number even higher, up to 50,000 Koniags. See Andreev (1948), 238.

16. RGADA, f. 1605, op. 1, d. 367, 1. 4.

17. RGADA, f. Senata (Senate), d. 4383/812, 1. 707–09.

18. AVPRI, f. RAK, op. 888, d. 932/12, 935/15; RGVIA, f. VUA, d. 23441, 23443. Later the Russians called this place *zimov'e* (winter quarters). Possibly several *promyshlenniki* were temporarily left there. A. A. Baranov called it: "the place occupied by us a long time ago for winter quarters." See Tikhmenev (1863, vol. 2, appendix 41).

19. Davydov erroneously calls the inhabitants of this place Kenaitzy (Russian name

for Dena'ina Athabascan). However, the Chugachmiut occupied the southeastern bays of this inlet. See Krauss (1975).

20. Davydov (1812, vol. 2, 34–35).

21. On the Russian maps of the eighteenth and nineteenth centuries this strait was called Kenaiskii or Aliaskinskii; then it was named Shelikof after Grigorii Shelikhov.

22. *K istorii Rossiisko-amerikanskoi kompanii* (1957, 64).

23. *Russkaia Amerika* (1994, 56–62).

24. *K istorii Rossiisko-amerikanskoi kompanii* (1957, 64).

25. *K istorii Rossiisko-amerikanskoi kompanii* (1957, 63); RGADA, f. 1605, op. 1, d. 292, 1.

26. RGADA, f. 1605, op. 1, d. 367, 1. 4.

27. *K istorii Rossiisko-amerikanskoi kompanii* (1957, 68).

28. *K istorii Rossiisko-amerikanskoi kompanii* (1957, 64).

29. Shelikhov betrayed these assurances, and the ship *Tri Sviatitelia*, which he promised to return that same year with reinforcements and people, arrived only two years later in April 1788.

30. AVPRI, f. RAK, op. 888, d. 51, 1. 2 ob.

31. *K istorii Rossiisko-amerikansko kompanii* (1957, 64, 69); Andreev (1948, 189).

32. AVPRI, f. RAK, op. 888, d. 123, 1. 310.

33. RGADA, f. 1605, op. 1, d. 367, 1. 1.

34. RGADA, f. 1605, op. 1, d. 367, 1. 6. Shelikhov exaggerated the number of enemies to 1,000 men and for unknown reasons called the enemy the "Kenaitzy enterprise." See Andreev (1948, 240–241). Shelikhov wrote about these events briefly and inconsistently. Evidently his goal was revenge on the *toion* of Shuyak Island, for the Kenaitzy people were not involved in this murder, especially since they rarely left Sumachik (Cook Inlet).

35. RGADA, f. 1605, op. 1, d. 367, 1. 6.

36. Delarov went from Prince William Sound to Unga Island, where his base was located. Until he started working for Shelikhov, he was obliged to fulfill the contract signed with Panovs merchants; to deliver to Okhotsk on the ship *Sv. Aleksi* people and the furs obtained on the islands of Akun, Unalaska, and Unga and in Prince William Sound.

37. Andreev (1948, 183–85). These expeditions were not carried out.

38. I. L. Golikov and G. I. Shelikhov outfitted the ship. This was their first joint undertaking. Gavrila Pushkarev was a mariner on the ship, and Konstantin Samoilov was the *peredovshik*. Over the course of five years they hunted on the islands of Attu and Amchitka and acquired furs amounting to 133,150 rubles at Okhotsk value.

39. Earlier Olesov had sent thirty men from Unalaska to Kodiak in a *baidara*, but six of them perished from cold and lack of food. Detained on the way by stormy weather, the remaining men were saved by Russians from a nearby artel, but upon arrival in the harbor five more workers died.

40. *K istorii Rossiisko-amerikanskoi kompanii* (1957, 63).

Redefining Our Planning Traditions: Caribou Fences, Community, and the *Neetsaii* Experience

Charlene Khaih Zhuu *Stern* *(Neetsaii Gwich'in)*

This chapter focuses on the significance of indigenous planning traditions in Alaska. The traditional planning systems that have enabled indigenous communities to survive in the Arctic for thousands of years have largely become undervalued in the modern context. By moving toward a renewed understanding of their planning traditions, Alaska Natives have an opportunity to redefine them in ways that are highly meaningful and effective. Charlene Stern is of Neetsaii Gwich'in and Hungarian-Russian descent. An enrolled member of the Native Village of Venetie Tribal Government, her first home is Arctic Village, Alaska. A writer and traditional bead artist, Charlene earned a B.A. from Western Washington University in 2002 and an M.A. in Community and Regional Planning from the University of New Mexico in 2005. She exemplifies the younger Alaska Native generation whose members are actively engaged in community-based work.

Planning as a tradition was not a concept imposed on indigenous peoples by Euro-Americans. Indigenous communities existed in myriad highly coordinated and planned towns and villages.
—Theodore S. Jojola

Introduction

Long before the arrival of explorers, missionaries, fur traders, or gold miners to Alaska, the *first peoples* were busy planning. Planning for the coming season. Planning for subsistence harvests. Planning the movements of entire camps. For countless generations, Alaska Native people have practiced community planning very often in the face of subarctic temperatures, variable animal migrations, and other persistent threats. The continued survival of our people over thousands of years is reflective of not only our capacity to plan but also to do it well.

This chapter discusses the significance of planning traditions in the north, focusing specifically on the *Neetsaii* Gwich'in, an Athabascan community whose ancestral homeland lies in the northeastern interior of Alaska. The *Neetsaii* Gwich'in, much like indigenous peoples elsewhere, possess a wealth of planning knowledge and experience. In retracing their planning history and the role of caribou fences, we see the emergence of a powerful story that encourages us to redefine our own planning traditions.

The Neetsaii *Community and Caribou Fences*

The *Neetsaii* Gwich'in, like many other Alaska Native peoples, have a relatively short history as a settled community.[1] For much of their existence, the *Neetsaii* community based its lifestyle upon a series of planned movements.

Early accounts of the *Neetsaii* people by outsiders often portrayed them as nomadic hunters who struggled to survive from day to day. Certainly, while a great deal of attention must have been placed on surviving "today" and "tomorrow," it remains highly unlikely that the *Neetsaii* community would have endured as long as they have if their foresight was that narrow. From a *Neetsaii* perspective, survival required planning from day to day as well as season to season, year to year, and even generation to generation.

Equipped with an inherited knowledge of the local environment, *Neetsaii* families moved in strategic accordance with the available resources. Often camping apart during more abundant times, *Neetsaii* families would typically gather together in the spring and fall to collectively harvest caribou.

The migratory porcupine caribou herd has long been the most important resource to the *Neetsaii* people. Before the introduction of rifles to the area in the late 1800s, the *Neetsaii* community had their own effective means of hunting caribou using a *thalt*, or caribou fence. From a planning perspective, caribou fences—also referred to as corrals or pounds—offer some of the oldest physical evidence of the inherent planning capacity of the *Neetsaii* people.

Made primarily from timber and lashing material, caribou fences were elaborate hand-built structures constructed for the sole purpose of entrapping migrating caribou. The basic design of caribou fences included a drift fence, point of entry, surrounding fence, a series of fish hook style corrals and snares anchored within the fence (Warbelow, Roseneau, and Stern 1975, 1–129).

Caribou fences functioned by directing migrating caribou into an enclosed

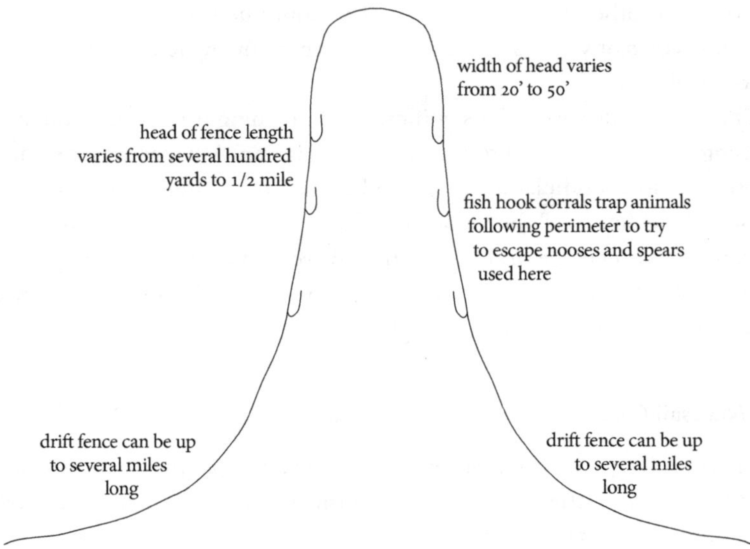

1. Diagram showing a common design for a caribou fence. Based on a drawing by Peter Stern.

area whereby they were more easily harvested using traditional weapons such as bow and arrows, snares, and spears.

Though caribou fences were generally considered to be the property of one individual or family, they often provided for much larger numbers of people who donated their labor in exchange for a portion of the harvest. In the words of the late *Neetsaii* elder Isaac Tritt Sr., "At this time [September] they would settle where people have caribou fence including those who doesn't have fences. This is the way people use to take care of one another they didn't hesitate to help one another" (*Nakai' t'in'in* 1991, 3).

McKennan (1965) and Hadleigh-West (1963) both discuss caribou fences but in limited detail. The most comprehensive study of caribou fences is a report by Cyndia Warbelow, David Roseneau, and Peter Stern titled "The Kutchin Caribou Fences of Northeastern Alaska and the Northern Yukon."[2] Theirs was the first account to present caribou fences as an involved planning process which occurred over several years and in four general phases—site selection, construction, operation, and maintenance—detailed below.

Selecting a site for a caribou fence was a critical planning decision that required knowledge of caribou behaviors as well as previous migrations. In their report, Warbelow, Roseneau, and Stern identify five criteria used in the site selection process: proximity to caribou migration paths, wind (assuming caribou move upwind in summer), water (assuming caribou are attracted to areas with water), topography (influenced structural orientation), and timber (availability of building materials) (14–15). Such considerations were important in judging the viability of a site well in advance of any actual construction.

Planning for the construction of a caribou fence required additional information concerning the practical design, orientation, materials, and labor needs. The orientation of the fence depended in large part on whether it was intended for the smaller spring harvest or the larger fall harvest. Open areas tended to be desirable locations for caribou fences, which made transporting the timber an issue. At least three of the eleven caribou fences identified in the region reached 8 to 10 miles in length (Warbelow, Roseneau, and Stern 1975, 61–106). These challenges ensured that the physical construction of a caribou fence necessitated a collective effort often involving men, women, and even children, as the following narrative describes.

> After a site was chosen, men cut trees for poles and set up two small upright poles at the site of each supportive tripod. The women and children, having prepared lashing material, followed behind the men, lashing the tripod sticks together to form an inverted V-shaped structure, usually adding supportive sticks to the two placed by the men. The women also helped the men set the rails and any additional supports. (Warbelow, Roseneau, and Stern 1975, 24)

If the site selection and construction of a caribou fence posed planning challenges, so did the actual operation. Larger caribou fences typically required the work of multiple families, with each person reportedly assuming a different role or responsibility, as an account by Isaac Tritt Sr. details:

> Back at the village, the Chief would plan out the hunting crew (in this story it's Chief Peter). They would go out early. They went up along the brush line and made a passage along the bushes where they set their caribou snares. There was signs of caribou tracks. Then the young men returns to the location of the caribou group. The snare was 20 miles from the caribou resting. The young men would surround it, direct it toward the snares. Then the women, children, all help surrounding also. The old women would babysit, and would get their share of meat. The elders hide on each side of the bush snareline while young men and women chase the herd toward the bush (snareline) once the caribou is in. The elders all come out. They surround the exit. Mass of snares have set for them (caribou). When a bunch of caribou get caught in the snares, it's quite a sight to observe. (*Nakai' t'in'in* 1991, 7)

The subsequent distribution of meat and skins after a successful caribou drive was critical to the survival of the *Neetsaii* community. When preserved, the meat could offer some assurance during an otherwise uncertain winter, while the skins provided much needed material for clothing and shelter. In order for a caribou fence to continue to provide for the *Neetsaii* community over time, it required maintenance after each use as well as annually. Replacing broken poles and tripods once again required a communal effort (Warbelow, Roseneau, and Stern 1975, 37).

The tremendous amount of work it took to select a site, construct, operate, and maintain a caribou fence was a large and highly effective community planning effort. The process proved so successful that it was also used for hunting moose and mountain sheep, though considerably less often (Hadleigh-West 1963, 139; personal communication with Peter Stern, July 15, 2006). Caribou fences remained in popular use until the early 1900s. According to McKennan, the last reported attempt to construct a caribou fence was in 1914 as part of what he describes as a "nativistic movement" conceived by the late *Neetsaii* leader Albert Tritt (86–87). Albert Tritt apparently persuaded the community to build a caribou fence, which his son Isaac Tritt Sr. later described as an attempt to provide a consistent food supply by domesticating caribou:

> I didn't understand what we're working for, but my family and I helped my father chop down spruce trees. As we continued to work on the fence, I began to understand what we're making. After we're done with it, we would chase the caribou into the fence and block the entrance so we can raise the caribou to increase the herd. People told him [Albert Tritt] that he would get in trouble with the game warden if he was caught. He discontinued the project. (*Nakai' t'in'in* 1991, 2)

Although the physical traces of caribou fences are still present today, the significance of their role in the planning history of the *Neetsaii* Gwich'in has been largely overlooked. Unfortunately this oversight has come at the expense of our general understanding of *Neetsaii* planning traditions and their value in the modern context.

Planning in a Modern Context

Over the past hundred years, the *Neetsaii* community has witnessed a phenomenal degree of change. The community is now centrally located in two villages, Venetie and Arctic Village. Tribal and village governments have assumed greater responsibility over most community planning efforts and the objective is no longer *physical* survival but *economic* survival. These changes and more have transformed the ways in which *Neetsaii* planning occurs.

The *Neetsaii* community, similar to many other Alaska Native communities, has struggled with the task of planning for their developing villages. Although subsistence remains a strong part of the modern lifestyle, villages have introduced new needs relating to housing, electricity, roads, running water, sewage, solid waste, and more. Unfortunately, most villages often lack the economic resources to financially respond to such growing needs and therefore must look to outside governments and other funding agencies. Increasingly such agencies are requiring some level of planning on the part of the community in order to secure funding. What is more, the process in which all this planning is expected to occur is typically not one which is indigenous to the community.

To further complicate the scenario, because of the way in which land claims were settled in Alaska, many Alaska Native communities have multiple governing entities which have a voice in community affairs. Tribal governments, village corporations, city governments, regional corporations, and nonprofit agencies share some role in local planning. The questions then arise: Who has planning authority? What are they planning for? On whose behalf are they planning? What processes are they using? All these questions pose important considerations for the community because it is the community that will be most directly affected by the outcomes of planning decisions. With the creation of the Denali Commission in 1998, additional resources have been made available to villages to develop community plans. Some communities have taken advantage of such resources while others have not.

Unfortunately the broader implication of our communities' modern planning struggles has been an internal questioning of our planning capacity. The planning skills that our ancestors traditionally relied upon seemingly have little or no place in the modern context, thus creating room for us to be self-critical of our local planning knowledge, tools, and capability. This perspective, however, could not be further from the truth.

Conclusion

As a young member of the *Neetsaii* community, I find significance in knowing that my people have a long legacy of planning, a legacy that demonstrates the important fact that planning is a natural part of our lives and that we have more experience doing it than we think. What is needed is for the *Neetsaii* community, and perhaps other Alaska Native communities, to become familiar with our planning traditions so that we are better positioned to redefine them in ways that will honor our past, serve our communities, and exceed any planning demands placed upon us. While this may seem a daunting challenge, it is like any other process in that it begins with a first step.

By learning as much as we can of our own planning traditions, we will find ourselves that much closer to realizing the full potential of our planning capacity.

Notes

1. McKennan dates the establishment of Venetie around 1895 and Arctic Village around 1910 (McKennan 1965, 19). Although this suggests a longer history of settlement, it was not until several decades later that either location could be considered a year-round residence.

2. "Kutchin" is one of the older variants for 'Gwich'in' Athabascan.

Memories of My Trap Line

Maria Bolanz

This selection, an excerpt from a novella by Maria Bolanz, is a composite of several Tlingit stories that her husband, Awêxh, related to her and is told from his perspective. The story focuses on a nine-year-old boy traveling by dogsled with his grandfather, checking the family's trap line, and is set in the 1930s, which for indigenous people living in remote areas of Alaska was a time of change and adaptation. Some call it the "time of twilight," the ending of one world and the beginning of the western or American period. Checking the trap line is an auspicious occasion for the boy, who is learning how to handle a dog team on his own in the isolation of a cold and dark subarctic winter. The excerpt here begins as the grandson and his grandfather have arrived at one of their small cabins along the trap line.

This story references western schools established by colonial governments, called boarding schools or residential schools, which had as their official policy "Kill the Indian, save the child." Established in the 1870s and active until the 1960s, these schools subjected many young indigenous students to trauma and abuse as they punished children for speaking their Native languages and shamed them for the color of their skin. Parents often were forced to send their children to these schools.

Maria Bolanz is the coauthor, with Gloria Williams, of Tlingit Art: Totem Poles and Art of the Alaskan Indians *(Hancock House, 2003). Both she and Gloria Williams are members of the Carcross/Tagish First Nation.*

My grandfather settled his dogs down, and began unloading his sled. I took the packs off my sled and unloaded the canvas bag my grandmother made for my sleeping bag, clothes and boots. I went back for the moose bladder bag; it had a yummy snack my mother made for me.

"I'll take my axe, and skinning knives back to the cabin along with my 30.06 rifle," he said as he unloaded a sack of dried fish. "You watch the dried fish while I get a fire going in the cabin. When I get back we'll feed each dog a fish. After that we can eat. Does that sound good to you?" He smiled, taking off his outer gloves that hung from a red string around his neck and patted a hand on my shoulder.

1. Frank Williams (Tlingit). Johns and Williams collection.

2. Bill *Aweix* Williams, ca. 1930. Johns and Williams collection.

"It sure does!" I cried out, barely able to contain the urge to jump up and down in the deep snow.

He kicked the sack of dried fish out of his way, and sat me on his empty sled. "Keep an eye on the dry fish, and give me five or ten minutes."

The dogs barked and leapt up and down because they knew they would eat soon. I knew how they felt because I was hungry too. Soon my grandfather called out, "The fire is going good."

I jumped off the sled and untied the sack of dried fish. The dogs leap, howl and whine like crazy.

"Throw each of them a fish," Grandfather said as he came to help me. "Be careful you don't get too close to them. They will jump up on you and knock you over."

The dogs leapt in the air as high as they could on their tethered lines. It was hard to throw them a fish without hitting them, but I finished all by my self without any problems. Soon they will calm down soon, and dig into the soft snow and go to sleep.

My grandfather is smiling at me. "Tomorrow you will hook up your own team. Now let's get to the cabin and warm up."

I follow him to the cabin on the path he made with his snowshoes. Smoke is coming out of the chimney, and as we enter, the fire in the metal barrel Yukon stove feels so good. The cabin is warm and cheerful in the lamplight, and like the dogs, I can barely wait to eat.

"You have done well, *Awêxh*." My grandfather says as he brushes the snow off my parka, and then sits me down on a wooden bench to untie my moose skin moccasins. "You must have run behind your sled most of the time," he added, placing my moccasins near the stove.

"Are your socks dry? You don't want to get wet feet." He cautions me. I nod my head yes and pull them off and hand them to him. He hangs them on a rope strung across the ceiling of the log cabin.

"Well let's get your parka off and hang it up too," he said, helping me pull my arms out of the sleeves.

"One time when your father and I were traveling near here, on our way back to *Â Tlèn* we killed a moose. We skinned and quartered it, and hung part of it in the cache behind the cabin. I'll show you this cache tomorrow. The wolves can't get it when it hangs in there. The rest of the meat we took back home."

"I miss my father," I whispered, watching him remove his parka.

"Just wait until I tell him what a good man you are in the woods, and what a great help you are to me," he said with a gleeful chuckle.

"When will he come home from Juneau?" I ask.

"When the work in the gold mine is over. He misses the life here, but he earns money setting the dynamite charges."

"Can we visit him?" I asked thinking of Juneau, the place where we go once a year when we take our two boatloads of furs down the *T'àkhú* river to Juneau to sell them.

"If he is there in the spring when we go to trade. You know *T'aww Chân*[1] told me your father fixed up a ski jump, and in his spare time he skis and jumps. *T'aww Chân* says he is a champion jumper and the miners take bets on him and other skiers, mostly white men come to challenge him."

"Will I learn to ski?" I ask.

"Of course, you will, but first you must learn to snowshoe well!"

"Are you cold?" he asked.

"No, grandfather. I am warm, even though I know it is cold and dark outside."

"You must be hungry and tired we had a long day?" He shook out his sleeping bag and laid it out on the bunk. Smoothing it down, little feathers flew out. "Hand me that small log from the wood box, and then shake out your sleeping bag."

He put the log in the stove and I shook out my bag and smoothed it out on my bunk. "Now we eat!" My grandfather exclaimed, getting tin plates and cups off the shelf and rummaging in his food pack.

Sitting on tree stumps, we ate our evening meal of dried moose meat, smoked salmon strips, tea and pilot bread. I opened up the moose bladder my mother had filled for us.

"What kind of trail treat did your mother give you?" he asked.

"I think dried bear meat mixed with cranberries and bone marrow."

"That is good and rich too, it will keep us warm all throughout our trip. I got a moose bladder bag too. Your grandmother filled with dry shredded moose meat, blue berries and moose fat. We will save some for the trail when we or the dogs need quick energy. You let it freeze on the trail it tastes just like the white man's ice cream." "Now, I have a surprise for you, close your eyes."

My eyes were already growing very heavy so it was easy for me to close them. "*K̲hàtgwèxh* made these snowshoes just for you." He laughed as I opened my eyes wide. "He bent the frames just to your size and finished lacing them with babiche last week."

My grandfather held out my new snowshoes, they were the most perfect snowshoes I had ever seen. "Tomorrow you will walk a long time in your new snowshoes. You will stamp down the snow to make camp. Just like I did today."

"*Â Tlèn* Shorty made my snow shoes!" I exclaimed. "He is the best snowshoe maker around, and he gets orders from the highest ranking clans in the northlands, even Athabascans traded dearly for a set of his snow shoes."

My grandfather laughed and said, "Yep, that's funny you use the nickname the white men call him."

I felt a bit ashamed at having said that and looked down at the floor.

"You are a good boy, my *Awêxh,*" my grandfather said as he reached over and brushed the top of my head. Don't ever forget how to behave well. Your *Dak̲ł̲awèdí* clan will be proud of you. Like you I am a Wolf, but a member of the *Yanyèidí* clan. We must always honor and respect our lineage and our ancestors."

The fire in the Yukon stove crackled and sputtered, and the lamplight flickered across my grandfather's face as he talked to me. We nibbled on the remnants of our dinner and drank our tea. My grandfather loosened his worn moose hide belt from his full stomach and let out a big sigh. Because I like to hear the story of this belt I asked, "Tell me again grandfather why you wear that old worn belt."

"Because once it saved my life. It is true the beads are gone and your grandmother has mended it many times, and if I am a lucky man she will mend it again.

"You value it that much?" I ask.

"I was hunting moose with *K̲hàtgwèxh* at the end of summer. I carried my 30.06 and *K̲hàtgwèxh* had his 30.30. I was wearing my new shell belt of thick moose skin that went around my waist and over my shoulder. Lanatk[2] had just made it for me. There were pockets for shells and over them rested beaded flaps made of moose calfskin, to protect the shells.

We walked along Inhini Creek and noticed Willow branches along the creek were chewed off high up. High enough that a bear had to stand up on his hind legs to reach it. There were tracks in the wet mud of a cow moose and calf and other tracks deep and round made by a bull moose. I knew then a bear was stalking them.

K̲hàtgwèxh nudged me and pointed to signs where a land otter had slid into the water. We were distracted by the honking sound of a small flock of wild geese flying overhead. I said to *K̲hàtgwèxh*, 'Not many geese remain. We will have an early winter.'

'Won't be back till spring,' *K̲hàtgwèxh* said to me." My grandfather paused a minute and then said, "That is how the *Takhú* River got its name, *Awêxh*. The Waters where the Wild Geese Nest."

"What happened, Grandfather?" I asked.

"Oh yes, *K̲hàtgwèxh* and I approached the clearing where the cache stood. In the tall grass we could see everything around the cache was smashed down and the ladder knocked to the ground.

Something was going on, grandson. And I raised my right hand. 'There's a bear around here!' I whispered. We waited for a bit, studying the area. Slowly we entered the meadow. We had our rifles loaded, hammer back, and ready to fire. We walked slowly, keeping each other in sight.

'We'll have to kill the bear. He'll be angry and will put up a fight,' *K̲hàtgwèxh* whispered to me.

Suddenly out of the high grass a big grizzly stood up. I kept moving slowly knowing that this would confuse the bear and let *K̲hàtgwèxh* get the first shot at the bear's shoulder. *Awêxh*, that shot spun the bear around and I fired a second one into his other shoulder.

That bear was in a frenzy but still able to charge and bite. His teeth were clicking together in pain and rage. That bear's shoulders were shattered, his fore legs were hanging like ropes at the sides of his bleeding body. I jumped on a dead tree lying on the ground. I wanted to get up higher to get a better shot and put it out of its misery. I thought I'd shoot at the bear's backbone to get the fatal shot, Grandson." My grandfather took a slow breath.

"I tell you, Grandson. That log was wet with melted frost and I slipped off. Fell right to the ground, on top my rifle. That bear was right on me. Those bears can roar real loud and this one did. He snarled and opened those mighty jaws and bit down on my stomach.

His teeth got stuck on this very belt I wear. *Awêxh*, this gave me time to put my thumbs inside his ears and hold his head away from my body. I had to use all my strength to keep him from turning sideways and biting my arms.

I called to *K̲hàtgwèxh*. 'Shoot, Shoot!'

I heard nothing, Grandson, nothing. Except the growling of the bear that had me locked in a terrible struggle.

'*K̲HÀTGWÈXH!*' I shouted again.

I finally heard him, 'My gun is jammed!' he shouted.

'Get it working,' I gasped.

He shouted right back, 'I'm trying!' He was working his knife under the rim of the shell so he could pull it out. It was slow and difficult. The bear kept growling and gnashing its teeth against my belt and trying to shake his head free of my hands. Those bears are strong, Grandson, very strong.

When *K̲hàtgwèxh* got that bullet out he yelled, 'I am coming in close and going to fire.' He pulled the lever down and got the shell in the chamber, crept close to the bear and fired through its neck. The blast struck the bear with such force that it blew him right off of me.

Somehow, I managed to jump to my feet, but my arms were too numb to grab my gun. That bear lay there paralyzed and dying and *K̲hàtgwèxh* had to put another bullet in it to finish it off, and *K̲hàtgwèxh* shot again at the bear's heart. Finally *K̲hàtgwèxh* was able to ask, 'Did the bear harm you?'

I said to him, 'Just a scratch on my belly where his teeth bit down. This shell belt saved my life! But it took all the strength from my arms, I can't move them yet.'

K̲hàtgwèxh went to the creek and came back with some water. After I had the use of my arms, we skinned the bear and took the hide, head, and claws back to *Â Tlèn*. 'You can't eat the meat, but the dogs can, so we will put it in the cache.' The women use the claws and the teeth to make decorations on our clothing and dancing outfits."

"You were very brave Grandfather."

"So was *Â Tlèn* Shorty, as you call him. He had to stand there and get his gun working."

"I guess so," I gasped.

I thought of asking if we should check the dogs again, but the cabin is so warm, the food so good, the cup of tea so hot that I fell asleep and dreamt about my new snow shoes.

Notes

1. His English name is Walter Soboleff and his ceremonial name is *K̲aajaak̲wtí*.
2. His wife.

Cultural Identity through Yupiaq Narrative

George P. Kanaqlak *Charles* *(Yup'ik)*

This selection derives from research that Professor George Charles conducted and is based on Yup'ik or Yupiaq identity from a Yupiaq perspective. Professor Charles's work reflects a detailed knowledge base of the Yup'ik language and culture. The first part, in which the author places himself within the larger context of his family and discusses how names reflect family relationships as well as physical locations, illustrates a non-western concept of identity. The essay also includes translations of song texts that capture important historical events in the Yupiaq world. The cultural expressions of indigenous societies, especially music, dance, and text, are reflections of their histories and worldviews. Oral narratives and histories are intrinsic to indigenous identities and reflect their unique placement within the physical world and the cosmos. Charles uses song texts to relay specific cultural values and knowledge systems.

Dr. Charles is currently director of the National Resource Center for American Indian, Alaska Native and Native Hawaiian Elders at the University of Alaska, Anchorage and is an assistant professor at the University of Alaska, Fairbanks. He is a Yupiaq originally from Nelson Island, Alaska, and is bilingual in Yupiaq (Yup'ik) and English.

AYAGNICUAQ (LITTLE BEGINNING, INTRODUCTION)

Yuuk eliskuni, qanruyutni-llu malgtaqukuniki
Nalluyagutevkenaki, tauna yuk
Umyuartuarkauguq.

If a person learns and follows what he
Is taught and does not forget it, that person
Will be wise

—*Kaligtuq* Marie Nichols, Lower Kuskokwim School District, 1981[1]

Yupiugua (I am *Yupiaq*).[2] I am the second son[3] of *Ayginar* (One Who Leisurely Travels), my father, from *Qaluyaaq* (Place of the Dipnet—Nelson Island) and *Nengqeralria* (One Pleasantly Extended), my mother, from *Nunacuar* (Place of the Little Land). My first given name is *Qugcuun* (One Who Gathers) given to me by my maternal grandfather *Makqalria* (One Who Remains Sitting Up) after one of his deceased relatives. My father gave my second name *Akagtaq* (One Who Was Rolled Over) to me after his brother in law, my first cousin *Ayaprun* (Johnny York)'s father. My third name is *Uksuqaq* (Suddenly Little Winter) given to me by my mother's great-aunt, *Passiqaq*, Lucy Jacob. My fourth name is *Kanaqlak* (Muskrat) given to me by my father after my paternal grandfather passed away.

This first person statement is the protocol followed by my family when introducing themselves to others and to elders. Even now, the speaker sometimes elaborates when needed by adding the grandparents' genealogies and places of birth. This introduction protocol and other notions such as a belief in the birth, death, and rebirth of both human and non-human sentient beings reflect basic notions inherent in *Yuuyaraq* (The Way of the Human Being) as understood and expressed in the *Yupiaq* language by my family. The remembrances,[4] stories, songs, and artist's impressions of my immediate and extended family will provide a synoptic view of the family's life experiences and give a glimpse of the meaning of *Yuuyaraq*, thereby giving us our identity and by extension our ethnicity. This essay focuses on the worldview of a contemporary *Yupiaq* family and is specific and illustrative rather than exhaustive and extensive. The *Ayaginar* family's worldview will not be compared to the worldview of other families and groups within the greater *Yupiaq/Cupiaq* society. This study is not an attempt to develop universals but to conduct micro-level inquiries concerning the transmission of cultural knowledge that exists in one family. It is an attempt to explicate indigenous ways of knowing from the Native point of view (Talamantes 1999).

I am an insider whose first language was *Yupiaq*. Later, I became a bilingual speaker with English as a second language. I am sometimes the source of this paper as well as the one analyzing[5] the verbal art of the sources. To put it in another way, this exercise is *Yupiaq* exegesis. There are both advantages and disadvantages to being an insider. One obvious advantage is the knowledge of the target language and the obvious language proficiency of the elders. As a bilingual speaker/writer of the target (*Yupiaq*) language[6] as well as being a speaker/writer of the contact (English) language,[7] the analysis would be more accurate. The family remembrances and songs were told or sung in the *Yupiaq* language that required interpretation and translation.[8] I have asked questions of my elders in situ. I first had a list of questions that I would ask my immediate and extended family members. While they answered the questions, I discovered later that the very questions I asked were limiting. A kind of unconscious gate keeping was taking place. My elders were answering my questions but the answers I received were precise but narrow in content. Part of the problem was that they realize I had a list of questions and I believe accommodating me so as to get the questions out of the way. It was several years later that I realized that I received far more detail when my elders were free to follow their mind's journey in whatever directions their remembrances went. When this happened their remembrances were filled with emotions whatever they were and became far more interesting and efforts were made to truly capture the original experiential moment. An obvious disadvantage of being an insider is being too close to the cultural material. However, my training and education in Western based colleges and universities and travel in the United States, Europe, and Southeast Asia have given me the insight to be conscious of potential difficulties.

It is also common among the *Yupiaq* to speak with authority on only those elements that one has personally experienced and verified with the phrase, "I can only speak of what I actually know." This idea is also expressed in the *Yupiaq* suffix, *-gguq*, which means "apparently" or "hearsay." The authority or truth is usually relegated to the *Yupiaq* elders in the various verbal arts; one such word is "*qanellriit*" (what they said). These notions point to using only pertinent, reliable, meaningful material. To rely on Western paradigms and theories would create universals out of data that come from different cultures resulting, in my opinion, in an erroneous conclusion.[9] Traditionally, Western scholars have done fieldwork in order to study "the other" and they have used bilingual interpreter/translators to analyze the material they have gathered. Then they have looked upon the persons as the object of their research and not as authorities of their own culture. To put it in yet another way, not all concepts translate across cultures accurately and precisely. This points to the use of analogies in the interpretation and translation of concepts from one culture context to another. I posit that the analogies chosen are best selected by a bilingual researcher/writer from the culture under analysis and one who demonstrates competence in both the Western and the particular First Nations or indigenous culture. In other words, an insider who speakers *Yupiaq* in this case would more accurately analyze the indigenous cultural ecology during the study (Woodbury 1984).[10] I am in the process of learning to write the *Yupiaq* language using the orthography developed by the Alaska Native Language Center at the University of Alaska, Fairbanks.

I have been mainly influenced by the encounter of two cultures, the *Yupiaq* and the Euro-American. By the middle of the nineteenth century, most of the non-Native external forces that would begin affecting the *Yupiaq* world of the *Ayaginar* family were well underway. Missionization, assimilation and acculturation policies of the United States government were just a few of these external forces. I was hit on the palm of my hands with a wooden ruler for speaking *Yupiaq* in the second grade. My younger sister, *Uyuruciaq* (Mary Stachelrodt), and I were sent to a Bureau of Indian Affairs boarding grade school in Wrangell, Alaska, a town in Tlingit territory of southeastern Alaska for one year. In Wrangell, I was taught table manners, to iron a white shirt, and to tie a double Windsor necktie without looking in the mirror. In a carving class, I was forced to carve Tlingit totem poles, although I wanted to carve something *Yupiaq*. We were lined up according to height and marched to our meals daily. The assimilation and acculturation policies of the United States government were efforts to westernize Alaska Native children and these policies further added to the cultural suppression practiced in the missionization process. There were relocation and termination policies carried out by the federal government that added to the cultural suppression of Native Alaskan as well as other Native Americans.[11] Even today, the residue of colonization persists in what is called the "certificate of degree of Indian blood." Native Americans who belong to federally recognized tribes within the United States carry a card that shows blood quantum in order to get various social services. My family members and I carry such a card.

Despite the cultural suppression and genocide that was practiced by the external forces, the *Yupiaq* culture is still alive through the *Yupiaq* language in the form of family remembrances, stories and songs, dances, rituals, and artistic expression in the *Ayaginar* family. As an insider who comes from the *Yupiaq* culture and with first hand experience in the *Ayaginar* family's ways of living, I think I can make an important contribution to the growing body of primary information on the *Yupiaq/Cupiaq* society.

Yupiaq ontology and epistemology as defined by the worldview of the *Ayaginar* family have their own theories and rhetorical categories and a self-evident philosophy of their own. These theories and rhetorical categories are best defined in their own linguistic and cultural contexts. To do otherwise would be to recreate the *Ayaginar* family in the image of the other.

I will now demonstrate a few examples of verbal arts that exist in the *Ayaginar* family. These examples define who we are and give meaning to our existence.

The songs demonstrate the ability of fluent and competent *Yupiaq* speakers who have been immersed in their culture to be able to compose the lyrics and the melody with seemingly little effort. My own father, to reiterate, was a prolific composer of new songs and dances in his later years. My father's uncle, *Angutikiayak* (Frank Amedeus), of Toksook Bay, was known for his abilities as a singer and composer. He, according to my mother, would break into song as he gazed upon the *nuna* (land) and compose a song in near perfect form. He would later add the dance motions to the lyrics and improve upon the melodic elements as well. He had apparently composed many songs but my mother was not able to recall any of them. Future research will be to musically notate my father's musical compositions with my wife, who has training in classical piano and composition.

Anguyagtem Yuarutii *(A Warrior's Song)*

This example is a war song my mother remembered from her youth. War, according to my family, had been not practiced *ak'anun* (for a long time). It was so long ago that it had become legend, part and parcel of *Yupiaq* mythology. It was according to them that *Apanuugpak*, a *Yupiaq* legendary mythical figure, convinced villages that war was a futile and wasteful activity.[12] I heard of the *Apanuugpak* story of the elimination of war in almost all of the villages I was able to visit in my youth. There are other *Apanuugpak* stories but I do not remember the details of them from my relatives from *Qaluyyaq* (Nelson Island). Ann Fienup-Riordan, an independent research cultural anthropologist, in her work has made references to this mythical figure.

War was an activity that was practiced not so much between villages as it was between areas, such as *Kuigpak* (Big River-Yukon River) and *Kusquqvak* (Kuskokwim River), according to my father. War was conducted according to my mother at specific times of the year and at specific intervals. My father also remembered wars between areas separated by the *Kuskuqvak* (Kuskokwim) River, the east versus the west bank areas. War was not a haphazard affair like guerilla warfare where no rules exist but to do as much damage, harassment and sabotage as possible against the opposing sides. True, some of these warriors, if they happened upon a hunter from the opposing area with a good catch of animals, would kill for the food for furs. But it appears to me that war was an organized affair following specific guidelines of time, areas and training time for young warriors by the elders. I have heard other stories of war but do not remember the exact. I am only detailing the stories I have heard in my family. Fienup-Riordan has written an excellent article on *Yupiaq* warfare and has identified warring areas in her article.

According to *Nengqeralria* young men would be trained to go to war at an early age by the elders. They were trained to build up their stamina, gain strength, endure physical pain, and to run great distances, sometimes pole vaulting, which apparently resulted in being able to move faster and further with the least expenditure of energy. Some of these warriors would pole vault over depressions in the landscape and over small streams. My mother had also heard that the young potential warriors during training drank very little water with the belief that this somehow increased their stamina in the event of actual war. They were trained to run in such a way as to dodge arrows. There are stories of warriors wearing bone armor. They were taught to extend what food they had by eating sparingly. My father, *Ayaginar*, pointed out that dried fish eggs were such a source of nourishment; a small amount of eggs would be placed under the upper lip and slowly sucked and the juices swallowed. There are references from my parents that sometimes these warriors would tattoo spots on their foreheads for the number of warriors they had killed. One warrior had killed so many that most of his forehead appeared to be black.

The most common war weapon was the bow and arrow, according to my grandfather. My mother also stated in the stories she remembers that the opposing warriors always seemed to like hiding in the cemeteries near the villages or in the isolation first menses huts, constructed for young women. Women would also bring their male first born into the *qasgi* (men's community house) and breast feed the baby bare breasted in the hopes that this son would become a warrior.

Nengqeralria remembers the following song that was sung in her village of *Nunacuar* and later in *Kassigluq*. This song had specific dance motions. She thought that the composer of this particular song was from the *Lilgayaq*[13] (Bristol Bay area). This demonstrates the distance some songs and dances are transmitted between villages and regions. Some songs, such as this example according to my mother, are readily shared between villages or regional groups contrary to the family motif women's dances.

According to my mother, a warrior was returning to his village and was being chased by his opponents. The warrior had been running for some time and was getting exhausted, fearing he would be captured. Imminent death was on his mind. He had to hide from one of the men who was wearing an old worn out caribou parka. He successfully avoided being caught or found by his enemies and especially the man wearing the old caribou parka. Later, as he was returning to his village, this man had to swim across a wide river known as *liussiq*. According to the song, this warrior cried as he swam, thinking he would not be able to cross over it successfully. Upon his return to his village, this man composed this song having survived a traumatic and harrowing life experience. My mother still likes to sing this song and my siblings and I have learned it by sheer repetition of her singing. My own grandson, Brandon, just two and a half at the time of the writing of this paper, had also learned the first part of this song. At a dance festival held in *Mamterilliq* (Bethel) my mother spoke to a man from the *Lilgayaq* (Bristol Bay) area about this song, asking whether if such a river existed and how big it was. The man replied that indeed that river existed and that its mouth, quite wide. My question is whether that man from the *Lilgayaq* (Bristol Bay) area also knows that song.

The next example is a war song my mother remembered from her youth.

ANGAYAGTEM YUARUTII (A WARRIOR'S SONG)[14]

Aa aa anga aa
Yi ii inga aa
Agi ii iya aa.
Yi ii inga aa[15]
Kia *un'a* *atu-u-u-liuu*
Who this one to sing for
"Atuqerluku"
"Singing it quickly"

Nannii-miiii *uiv-a-lag-cia.*
Where I was I do not know where to go.

Qali-lugpalgem[16] *pia-qa-tan-rani*[17]
One who has an old caribou parka just when he was about to pass him?

Kia *un'a* *atu-u-u-liuu*
Who this one to sing for

"Nemqerluku"[18]

"Wrapping it quickly"

Aa aa anga aa.
Yi ii inga aa.
Agi ii iya aa.

Nanii-miiii *qiar-lur-cia*
Where I was I crying

Iiussikun *kuim-qatan-um-ni*
By *Iiussikun* when I was swimming over

Kia *un'a* *atu-u-u-liuu*
Who this one to sing for

"Cali"
"More"

Aa aa anga aa
Yi ii inga aa
Agi iii iya aa
Yi ii inga aa

Kia	*un'a*	*atu-u-u-liuu*
Who	this one	to sing for

In the introduction there is reference to how a war was started in anger. A child accidentally blinded another during play with darts. The father of the blinded child in anger poked the eye out of the child who had blinded his son. This incident resulted in families taking sides in the *qasgi*. This started an irreversible village conflict. Soon the nearby villages also took sides, and later the entire area was at war. My maternal grandparents had also told this story, emphasizing the effect anger can have not only on one person but on many. I have also heard this same story in several other villages near *Kassigluq* (Kasigluk) and on the *Kusquqvak* (Kuskokwim) River. Fienup-Riordan makes reference to this same story in one of her articles.

In another story told by my father some *Kuigpak* (Yukon River) warriors came over the narrowest portage area between the *Kuigpak* and *Kusquqvak* (Kuskokwim) Rivers to attack one of their opponent's villages. Apparently some boys were upriver from the village hunting when they saw the *Kwigpak* (Yukon River) warriors moving in the direction of their village. They ran back as fast as they could, over quite a distance, to the village to warn them of the impending attack. The *Kusquqvak* (Kuskokwim) village warriors quickly headed upriver and set a trap. The strategy was to let the *Kuigak* (Yukon River) warriors pass in their qayaq (canoes) between two river points, and as the last qayaq (canoe) passed the upriver point the *Kusquqvak* (Kuskokwim), warriors made their attack from both sides of the river. The surprise attack was so complete that most of the *Kuigpak* (Yukon River) warriors were killed. So much blood was shed that part of the river looked red. To this day that part of the river retains a reddish hue.

In another story my mother relates how warriors captured one of their enemies. In this instance, the captured warrior was forced to drink copious amounts of rancid seal oil. While the captors were distracted, this warrior was able somehow to loosen the sealskin ropes and make good his escape. The captors upon seeing him running gave chase over the somewhat frozen tundra. The escaping warrior, upon running, began to throw up the rancid seal oil he had been forced to drink. The story tells of how this man threw up over both shoulders as he ran as well as his chest. According to my mother this story is commemorated by sewing areas of white caribou skins in the upper right and left arm sleeves of some fancy fur mink parkas as well as in the upper chest and upper back part of the parka. I asked a woman from *Akiaq* (Akiak) about the white areas of her parka and she told the same story. More research will need to be conducted to see how this particular story plays out in the greater *Yupiaq/Cupiaq* nation. *Arnaq* (Marie Meade), formerly Marie Nick of *Nunapicuaq* (Nunapitchuk), wrote a detailed article on the *Yupiaq* parka. She details the names of the various parts of the parka (Meade 1990). Marie Meade is also an excellent experienced translator and teacher of the *Yupiaq* culture.

The story about the reason the river has a red hue has some interesting implications regarding the validity of some stories. How much truth is there in this particular story? Was the story created to explain why the river appears to have a reddish hue? Again I have heard others ask this same question, but yet the story is told and retold in several villages near *Mamterilleq* (Bethel) in such places as *Kuiggluk* (Kwethluk), *Akiaq* (Akiak), *Akiacuaq* (Akiachuk), and *Tuulkessaaq* (Tuluksak). I have seen this river from the air while flying down from the Kilbuck Mountains not far out of *Mamterilleq* (Bethel).

Commemoration of war in the *Yupiaq* parkas is a statement in itself on how war is still in the psyche of elders such as my mother and other older, more culturally informed, fluent *Yupiaq* tradition bearers. While war is still remembered by the elders such as my mother, the details of their knowledge are being lost rapidly due to their passing.

Concluding Remarks

I am appreciative of the work of other researchers that have worked in this area and much more needs to be done to preserve what is left of that area of knowledge. The intimate knowledge of metaphor and double meanings inherent in the *Yupiaq* paradigm is paramount in getting the best interpretation of the discourse and narrative of the culturally rich verbal art of the *Yupiaq* elders. To be redundant, *Yupiaq* exegesis by the *Yupiaq* still is and will continue to be the mechanism to gain fuller understanding of *Yupiaq* discourse in its true cultural context. While we may judge that war is a wasteful and destructive human effort, this discourse nevertheless gives us a glimpse of what was in its proper place in the time when its cultural context had some meaning for whatever reason for the *Yupiaq*.

Is it that in our evolution we have to experience this waste of human life and energy before we find its true nature and realize that war is meaningless? In my own case, I am still pondering this dilemma. I am a Vietnam era veteran and am still perplexed with some trauma I carry from that experience. Part of me is still carrying guilt for having survived that conflict when so many had died. A cousin committed suicide having served several U.S. Army tours in Vietnam. A boyhood friend died of stomach cancer that I believe was caused by Agent Orange, the defoliant used by the military there. I had become unfeeling of human suffering as a defense mechanism, having seen so many wounded and suffering South Vietnamese. I remember being able to eat my lunch with other military personnel in the presence of suffering human beings without giving any thought to them. I was in a relatively safe area in a military compound stationed on the Mekong River. Many Veterans I knew were in heavy and more dangerous combat assignments.

I would hope to learn, as *Apanuugpak* had, that war, the killing of human beings, be eliminated from our psyche as a mechanism of honor. Perhaps we can still have a warrior code but with the emphasis to end war as *Apanuugpak* came to believe.

Notes

1. *Kaligtuq* is my maternal grandmother.

2. *Yupiaq Eskimo* is designated as a Central Alaskan Yup'ik Eskimo by the Alaska Native Language Center at the University of Alaska, Fairbanks (Himmelheber 1984).

3. There were two other children born before me. George the eldest brother, and a sister Margaret died as children.

4. I use the word *remembrance* here to indicate the personal first person life experience narratives of my immediate and extended family members. The word *story* or *stories* will refer to those macrocosmic verbal arts that come from the *Yupiaq* society that my elders and I have heard outside of the immediate and extended family.

5. The immediate or extended family member who told the story or sang the song sometimes provided the analysis or explanation.

6. The target language is the *Yupiaq* language of the material/data of the family remembrances and songs. The word *Yup'ik* is the designation used by the Alaska Native Language Center and refers to the Central Alaskan Yup'ik Language.

7. The contact language is the English language. I grew up bilingual, speaking more *Yupiaq* in my early years and later speaking more English as I grew older, going to grade school, high school, and college.

8. In my terminology, interpretation deals with orality and translation deals with written text.

9. This idea refers mainly to an earlier and antiquated type of research and attitude of the "other." During the last decades, one of the main tendencies has been to get away from "universals" and instead study local cultures based on their own preconditions. Earlier cultural anthropology research is referred to by some as Victorian Anthropology. Three sources that address this type of research are: Bernard McGrane (1989), Henri Baudet (1988) and Linda Tuhiwai Smith (1999).

10. Hanni Woodbury makes reference to the position of the bilingual cultural consultant and makes the case that this position needs further research (Woodbury 1984). The analogies used by the bilingual cultural consultant in research need to be clarified with appropriate disclaimers.

11. Relocation took the form of various training programs of non-managerial positions such as bookkeeping, automobile repair, and cooking, to name a few. The trainees were given one-way tickets to the job site and it was hoped by the Bureau of Indian Affairs that those people would assimilate in the dominant society. The termination policies were implemented by the U.S. Department of the Interior that determined that a particular "Indian" tribe was no longer a federally recognized tribe but "terminated" as a tribe and designated as part of the dominant society. These federal policies resulted in loss of culture and identity.

12. Robert Redford, the actor, attempted to make a movie about *Apanuugpak*, "The Winter Warrior." The movie was never completed.

13. This song, according to *Nengqeralria*, originated from the Dillingham area at least two hundred miles to the east of her village. This area is the westernmost part of the *Yupiaq* area. The *Akalmiut* had learned this song somehow. *Nengqeralria* asked a man from the Dillingham area about the river mentioned in this song. The river is a real place and quite wide at the mouth. *Akalmiut* refers to the area surrounding the villages of what used to be *Nunacuar, Kassigluq* (Kasigluk), *Nunapicuaq* (Nunapitchuk), and the present-day village of *Atmaulluaq* (Atmauthluk).

14. There are specific dance motions with this song. The dance motions will be described in a separate article for publication.

15. This phrase and the previous three are musical words structured with a specific musical beat and not based on general everyday *Yupiaq* language and grammar.

16. The root is *qaliluk*, an old worn caribou parka whose caribou fur has fallen out, used for summer. In this context, the one wearing this old parka was apparently a warrior looking for and or chasing the man who composed this song.

17. At this point the warrior had been hiding from his enemy, who was searching to kill him.

18. See note 5.

Dena'ina Ełnena: Dena'ina Country: The Dena'ina in Anchorage, Alaska

James A. Fall

James Fall's essay focuses on the upper Cook Inlet area of south central Alaska, which is home to over half the state's population, including Anchorage, Alaska's largest city. This is also the homeland of the Dena'ina Athabascans. Oral traditions, including personal and family histories, traditional stories, and place names document the upper inlet Dena'ina's rich history and culture, but until very recently, little note was taken of the area's indigenous people. Due to the work of Fall and others, Dena'ina Athabascan history and their cultural footprint, which have remained largely invisible to the newly arrived populations of south central Alaska, are beginning to be recognized by the larger population. This essay is based on a presentation at the Cook Inlet Historical Society in Anchorage in October 2004.

James Fall is a cultural anthropologist who works for the Division of Subsistence of the Alaska Department of Fish and Game. He lives and works in Anchorage. While a graduate student at the University of Wisconsin-Madison he worked with upper Cook Inlet Dena'ina elders to record their history and culture. He is the coauthor, with James Kari, of Shem Pete's Alaska: The Territory of the Upper Cook Inlet Dena'ina *(1987, 2003).*

The upper Cook Inlet area of south-central Alaska is now home to over half the state's population, and includes Anchorage, by far Alaska's largest city. The upper inlet area is also part of *Dena'ina Ełnena*—Dena'ina Country. The Dena'ina are the indigenous people of *Tikahtnu*, "ocean river." This is Cook Inlet on today's maps, one of many examples of the renaming of Dena'ina places that obscures the long and continuing Dena'ina presence (map 1). Indeed, into the early twenty-first century, there was very little public acknowledgment of Dena'ina history and culture in Anchorage. This essay will briefly highlight some aspects of this heritage by focusing on several significant places in and near Anchorage, including their Dena'ina names and their roles in the annual round of subsistence activities. We'll take our cue from the Dena'ina

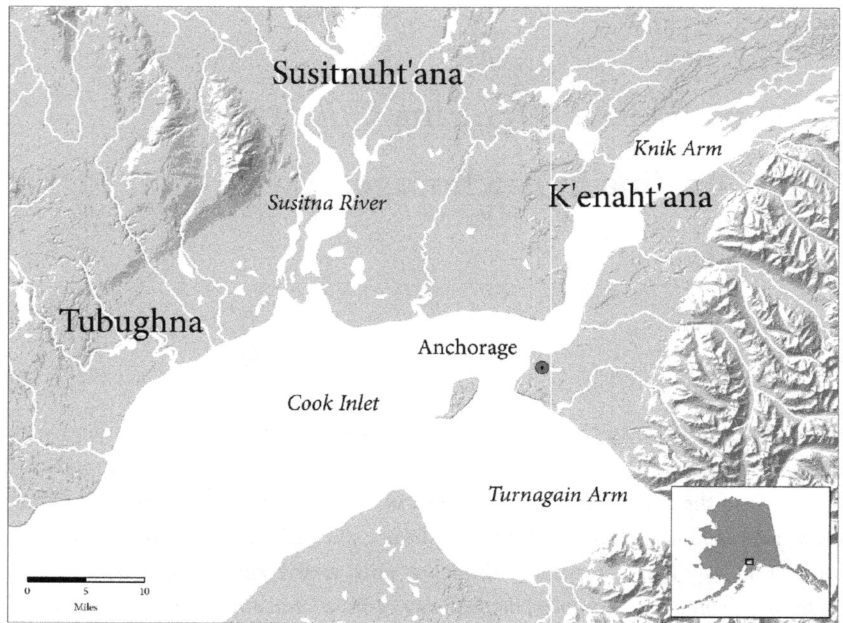

Map 1. Dena'ina regional bands, Upper Cook Inlet

historian Alberta Stephan, who wrote, "It is important to the Athabascan Indian people that their history of a well organized life style be known by everyone."[1]

First, let's travel back to 1914, at the very beginnings of Anchorage. A young Dena'ina man named *K'etech'ayutiłen* (the one who brings a gun among animals) from the village of *Tsat'ukegh* (later called Susitna Station) was one of the many Dena'ina eyewitnesses to the founding of a city in their homeland (figure 1). He remembered trapping in the spring and then rowing to the present site of Anchorage in its first year, and recalled:

> No Anchorage that time. No buildings. And that first street, it was right up top of the hill there. They're trying to make a street there. And lots of tents. They had a store in the tent. They carry the coat, dress, pants, and shirt. They put it over our neck. They hold our back. "That's big enough for you. Just right. Just right. Fifty cents. Sixty cents. Nice one seventy-five cents." We buy, and I got a job in the restaurant. I was fourteen years old. They give me four dollars a day. And they burn and cut the trees. It's full of smoke, fire, nighttime. So we stay there I don't know how many days, 'cause I work, get four dollars a day. And so we go back to Susitna in the dory. We tell the

1. K'etech'ayutiłen, about 1920. Shem Pete as a young man. From *Shem Pete's Alaska*, p. 335. Photo courtesy of Alexandra Allowan.

> story, "We see lots of white people. There's smoke all over Anchorage there now." At that time it was all full of trees and willows. Everything they cut down. Nights and days they work. (Kari and Fall 2003, 335)

Now, let's jump forward seventy years, to the mid-1980s. That young man had become the renowned Dena'ina elder and historian Shem Pete (figure 2). He and other Dena'ina elders have shared their knowledge of their people's traditions, culture, and history through stories, biographies, songs, and place names. A portion of that knowledge is featured in *Shem Pete's Alaska: The Territory of the Upper Cook Inlet Dena'ina* (2003). As that book shows, the Dena'ina names of places and their histories are an excellent portal through which to investigate and understand the past.

Shem Pete and other Dena'ina and Ahtna[2] people have recalled over 700 Athabascan place names in the upper inlet area. The present day Anchorage municipality stretches from its northern boundary at *Skitnu*—"Brush River"—the Knik River and *Ch'atanhtnu*—"trail comes out river," the Matanuska River, to its southern border along *Tutl'uh*—"back water" or, as renamed by the English Captain James Cook, "Turnagain Arm." As shown by the dots in map 2, about 130 Dena'ina place names have been recorded for the present Anchorage municipality. There are about 50 more for Turnagain Arm, 50 more for western Knik Arm, and about 120 Dena'ina and Ahtna names for the Matanuska River watershed.

Upper Inlet Regional Bands

Shem Pete, as a *Susitnuht'ana*, a person from Susitna River (*Suyitnu*, sand river) country, was really a visitor, a guest in the area that became Anchorage. This area was, and still is, within the territory of a second Dena'ina regional band, the *K'enaht'ana*, the people of Knik Arm, who today belong to the Eklutna and Knik tribes. Members of the third upper inlet regional band, the *Tubughna*, the beach people of Tyonek, also were, and are, frequent visitors to *K'enaht'ana Ełnena*. In the eighteenth century, before the Russians came, there were perhaps a thousand or more Dena'ina living in the villages of these three upper inlet regional bands.[3]

A Village People: Qayeh *and* Nichił

The *K'enaht'ana* lived along the water body they named *Nuti*, "salt water," called Knik Arm today. Before Anchorage, the Dena'ina were, in Shem Pete's words, "village people" (*qayeh quht'ana*). There were dozens of villages, called

2. Shem Pete at the University of Alaska, Fairbanks, 1983. Photo by James Kari.

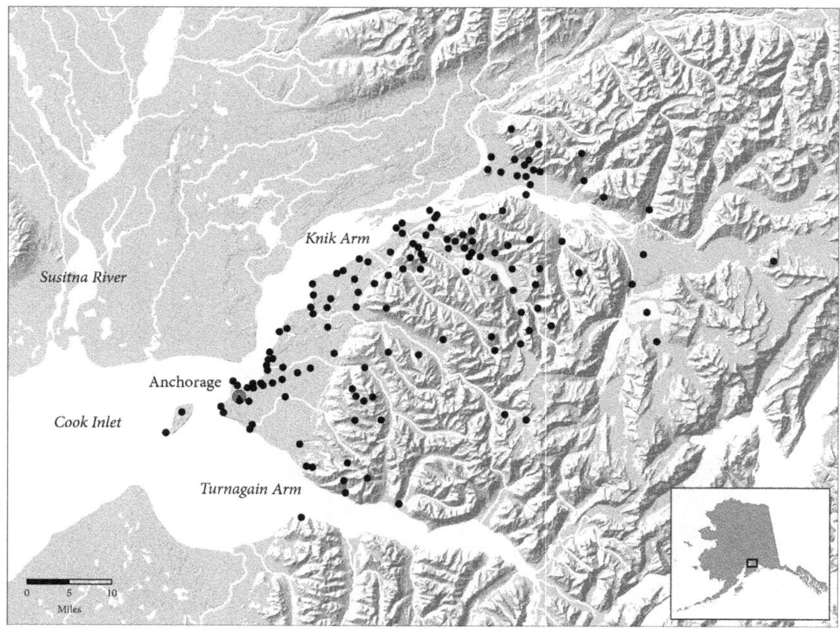

Map 2. Dena'ina place names within and bordering Anchorage

qayeh, throughout the upper inlet area. Around *Nuti* were villages, including these:

1. *K'enakatnu* (Knik)
2. *Biłni Ch'unaghelqeni* (bitter water), north of Knik
3. *Łajat* (silt place), Cottonwood Village
4. *Benteh* (among the lakes), present-day Wasilla
5. *Chuqilitnu* (fermented fish creek), village on Wasilla Creek
6. *Tuhnaghiłkitst* (where the bank extends)
7. *Niteh* (among the islands), Matanuska Village
8. *Nuk'dinitnu* (river that the bridge extends across), Chickaloon
9. *Hutnaynut'i* (that which is shining), Bodenberg Butte village
10. *Skintuk'ełaha* (fish run through brush), Swan Lake village
11. *Idlughet* (among the plural objects), Eklutna
12. *Ch'ak'dinłenghet* (by the current that flows out), site near Green Lake

Each village included one or more *nichił*, semipermanent multifamily houses made of logs and birch bark. Here people spent the winters, living from their caches of dried fish and meat but hunting, trapping, fishing, and visiting as well.

The Seasonal Round

From their central bases at their villages, the upper inlet Dena'ina fully utilized their homeland's seasonal abundance of natural resources, in preparation for possible times of scarcity in the late winter and early spring. They moved with the seasons to a set of traditional fishing and hunting camps. Before Anchorage, the beaches and streams of *Nuti* (Knik Arm) were the sites of Dena'ina fish camps with shelters, smokehouses, fish racks, and steam baths, occupied by extended families from spring to late summer. Within the present day Anchorage area were several particularly important Dena'ina subsistence salmon fishing locations.

Chanshtnu, "Grass Creek," now anglicized as "Chester Creek," was a major fish camp site. Figure 3 shows young Billy Pete, Shem Pete's son, with his mother Inga Jacko Pete and her brother, at their *Chanshtnu* fish camp, about 1922 (figure 3). Many Dena'ina families had fish camps in what is now downtown Anchorage. Dena'ina families used these camps until the non-Dena'ina newcomers changed the rules of land ownership and the Dena'ina were forced to leave.

Tak'at, near Cairn Point north of the Port of Anchorage, was another important Dena'ina fish camp. In the early twentieth century, several families with winter homes in Knik used *Tak'at*, including those of Rufe Stephan, his wife Annie, and their children (figure 4), and Annie's sisters and their families.

In an interview with Nancy Yaw Davis in 1998, one of Rufe and Annie Stephan's daughters, Alice Theodore, recalled:

3. Dena'ina fish camp at *Chanshtnu* (Chester Creek), in Anchorage. Photo courtesy Nora McCord.

4. Rufe and Annie Stephan and family. Photo courtesy of Alice Theodore.

> I remember every spring we go down there. They put us in a boat at Knik. And they row that—they didn't have no motor those days. They just row, my dad and my oldest brother. They took us down there to *Tak'at*. They put up a tent for us and then we stay there by ourselves. My mom used to cut wood like a man. She carry wood on her shoulder like a man. And we had a smokehouse there. All the time. Every year we come down. We had a steam bath and everything around there. They were all like that. My two aunties there. They had a smokehouse too.

At *Tak'at* and other sites, the Dena'ina used gill nets for salmon fishing from around 1900 or so, but before that a primary technology was the *tanik'edi*, the dipnet platform (figure 5). These pole platforms were built out over the mud flats. The name *Tak'at* commemorates the Dena'ina use of this technology. Isn't it somewhat ironic that the mud flats are an impediment to twenty-first-century commerce in the upper inlet but were an important asset to the traditional Dena'ina way of life?

Another example of the use of the tidal flats is the *yuyqul*, the beluga-spearing platform (figure 6). The Dena'ina uprooted spruce trees and embedded them upside down in the mud flats during low tide. A hunter armed with a harpoon stationed himself in the "nest" at the top of the pole and waited for a beluga to swim by with the flood tide. After he harpooned the whale, hunters waiting on shore chased the injured beluga with kayaks, stabbing and spearing it until it died. Shem Pete met the last Dena'ina person who hunted from the top of a *yuyqul*. His name was *Bidyaka'a*. The *yuyqul* was a unique Dena'ina invention for hunting beluga—a technology known nowhere else in the world but along the shores of *Tikahtnu* (Cook Inlet).

The Dena'ina name for Point MacKenzie, *Dilhi Tunch'del'usht Beydegh*, provides further clues about the Dena'ina seasonal round. The name means "Point Where We Transport Eulachon." It was here in spring that Susitna River Dena'ina brought large quantities of eulachon ("hooligan" or "candlefish") to trade with the *K'enaht'ana* for dried meat.

The Loss of Traditional Camps

Returning to the history of *Tak'at*, Billy Pete, Shem's son, visited this fish camp regularly in the 1930s. He remembered how the hundreds of years of Dena'ina use of that site ended. Billy said:

> The army guys burned that smokehouse down and they used that place for garbage dump.[4] *Tak'at* is right where that army dump used to be. And

5. *Tanik'edi* (dipnetting platform). From *Shem Pete's Alaska*, p. 65. Drawing by Diane L. Thedie, originally published in *Alaska Sportsman*, January 1965.

6. *Yuyqul* (beluga-spearing platform). From *Shem Pete's Alaska*, p. 75; drawing by Leonard Savage. Originally published in *Q'udi Heyi Niłch'diluyi Sukdu'a: This Year's Collected Stories (Tyonek and Iliamna Lake)*, ed. James Kari (Anchorage: National Bilingual Materials Development Center, 1980).

that *Tak'at*, 1941, that's the last time they use that place and after that there was nothing over there.

In the early 1940s, Alice Theodore stood at the dock in Anchorage during the Fourth of July celebration. From there, she looked northeast to where her family's fish camp had been. In 1998, she recalled:

> I look that way, where the tent, big smokehouse used to be lined up—my aunts' smokehouse, our dad's smokehouse too. All gone. They all gone. They tear it down, smokehouse and steam bath and everything. All them tent frame and everything they throw it down and then nothing around there. It didn't look like a fish camp anymore.

Another key Dena'ina fish camp was *Nuch'ishtunt*, "Place Protected from Wind," now renamed Point Woronzof. Before Anchorage, the Dena'ina used *tanik'edi*, dipnetting platforms, here also. More recently, into the 1940s and 1950s, it was the location of subsistence and commercial salmon fishing with set gill nets.

Figure 7 shows members of the Ezi family of Niteh and Eklutna at their Point Woronzof fish camp in about 1942. Figure 8 shows members of the Yakasoff family of Eklutna at their camp, also at *Nuch'ishtunt*, in the late 1930s. The Dena'ina fished at this site until federal authorities closed the area to commercial fishing. These families then moved to Fire Island and Point Possession.

7. Ezi family at their fish camp at *Nuch'ishtunt* (Point Woronzof). From *Shem Pete's Alaska*, p. 338. Photo courtesy of Alberta Stephan.

8. Yakasoff family fishing for salmon at *Nuch'ishtunt* (Point Woronzof). From *Shem Pete's Alaska*, p. 338. Photo courtesy of George and Susie Ondola and William Churchill.

Dena'ina elder Sava Stephan, Shem Pete's nephew, recalled spending summers in Anchorage with his grandmother and aunt in the 1920s. He described their subsistence activities at *Nuch'ishtunt*, providing a glimpse into the more distant past and an example of how the Dena'ina struggled to maintain their way of life in the midst of a growing population of outsiders.

> *Chidashla*, "little old lady," they called her. She was close related to my grandma. Our grandma used to go from Anchorage to Point Woronzof. They pack up. Both of them women was same age. They were pretty strong legs anyway. They go to Point Woronzof. You know how they do, old timers, they set net, they catch geese, ducks, everything like that, by set net on the beach at Point Woronzof. Grandma sometime she take me to Point Woronzof porcupine hunting. Sometime they come home with two, three geese. They got nothin' to do in town here. They just work every day trying to get some food.

In the Dena'ina seasonal round, after summer fishing came fall hunting. The *K'enaht'ana*, the Dena'ina of Knik Arm, hunted caribou, moose, bears, sheep, and goats in the Talkeetna and Chugach Mountains. Before Anchorage, and up to 1971, the valley of *Skitnu*, the Knik River, was an important hunting area, especially for moose and sheep. Figure 9 shows Peter Ezi Sr. at the Ezi family cache at *Skintuk'ełaha*, Swan Lake, in 1968. Alberta Stephan (2001) notes that hunting regulations imposed by territorial and federal game management authorities had by the mid-twentieth century curtailed much of the Dena'ina's traditional hunting within the rapidly growing upper inlet area.

Social Organization: The Roles of Men and Women

Before Anchorage, *qeshqa*, "rich men," organized Dena'ina economic, social, and political activities in upper inlet communities. They directed the hunting and fishing of their extended family members, managed the distribution of food, organized trade, and settled disputes. Among the important *qeshqa* who were active in the Anchorage area in the mid and late twentieth century were Mike Alex, who was chief at Eklutna until his death in 1977, and Simeon Ezi of *Niteh*, who fished at *Nuch'ishtunt* (Point Woronzof) into the 1930s.

Although the Dena'ina did not name places after people, non-Dena'ina who have arrived more recently have renamed several places in the upper inlet area in honor of Dena'ina leaders. Some examples are Alexander Creek, named after *Diqelas Tukda*; Kroto Creek, named after *K'ghedu*; Red Shirt Lake (*K'eł Nuts'ehen*); and Wasilla (*Bentehen*).

Figure 9. *Skintuk'ełaha* (near Swan Lake). From *Shem Pete's Alaska*, p. 316. Photo courtesy of Alberta Stephan.

As far as we know, all *qeshqa* were men. Their wives, traditionally up to eight, it is said, were *qiy'u*, rich women, and their children were called *jiggi*. Billy Pete translated *jiggi* as "prince and princess."

For hundreds of years in the Anchorage area, Dena'ina women fished and snared small game and harvested plants. They processed these foods for winter use. They raised young children, tanned hides, made clothing, and manufactured many key items of technology.

All Dena'ina belonged to the clan of their mothers — a matrilineal system — descent through the female line. Because much of Dena'ina life was organized around bonds of kinship, it can be said that women were the thread that tied Dena'ina life together.

Other Places, Other Stories

Space is too limited to discuss many more Dena'ina places and names in the Anchorage area in this essay. Here, briefly, are a few especially notable and interesting Dena'ina places in and near Anchorage (see map 1). For information about other places, see *Shem Pete's Alaska*.

Idlughet—"Place among the Plural Objects," or "Lump Station"—another Billy Pete translation. This is the Dena'ina name for village of Eklutna—the name refers to the small hills or "knobs" near the village.

Ch'ak'dinłenghet—Green Lake Outlet. This was the fish camp of the Alex family of Eklutna. It is now part of Elmendorf Air Force Base and not accessible to the Dena'ina.

Dgheyaytnu—Stickleback or Needlefish Creek. This stream is called "Ship Creek" on today's maps and is near downtown Anchorage. It was an important source of food in spring when other resources were scarce.

Nutuł'iy—"Object Standing in the Water"—Fire Island. Until recently, this was the site of more Dena'ina fish camps.

Ułchena Bada Huch'ilyut—"Where We Pulled up the Alutiiq's Boat"—Point Campbell at the westernmost point in Anchorage, was the site of the last battle between the upper inlet Dena'ina and the *Ułchena*, the Alutiiq people of Prince William Sound.

Esbaytnu—"Mountain Goat Creek," now called Bird Creek, is along Turnagain Arm.

Qeshqa Eł Tak'niqats't—"Where the Rich Man Sank"—This place in Turnagain Arm with a colorful Dena'ina name is now called "Gull Rock."

There are over a hundred more recorded Dena'ina names in and bordering on the Anchorage Bowl. Each has a story. Each has a history.

Opportunities for Acknowledging Anchorage's Dena'ina Heritage

In the late twentieth and early twenty-first centuries, it was difficult for residents of Anchorage or visitors to find any public acknowledgment of the city's location within *Dena'ina Ełnena* (Dena'ina Country). For example, the generally excellent "Historic Anchorage Walking Tour" in downtown Anchorage has but a single reference to the Dena'ina. On a kiosk at the corner of 3rd Avenue and F Street, and under an imposing portrait of Captain Cook, is an old photo of several anonymous Dena'ina. The text on the sign says two things: that the Dena'ina had not been in the inlet area much before Cook arrived, and that most Dena'ina died in a series of epidemic diseases. Ethnographic and linguistic evidence refute the first statement; the second is a tragic historical fact that the resilient Dena'ina population today continues to overcome. But in combination, the effect of these two statements in a public display is to dismiss the Dena'ina presence in Anchorage, both in the past and today, as largely irrelevant.

Through the efforts of the Dena'ina community and others, this situation is changing. With funds from the U.S. Department of Transportation and working with the Port of Anchorage, the Native Village of Eklutna in 2005 began designing a historical and cultural interpretive display near the mouth of *Dgheyaytnu* (Ship Creek) near downtown Anchorage. In 2007 and 2008, as part of its "Salmon in the City" program, the Municipality of Anchorage developed several interpretive signs that feature the Dena'ina's traditional uses of the city's waterways.

In June 2006, a citizen's panel appointed by Anchorage's mayor recommended that a new convention center in downtown Anchorage be named the "Dena'ina Civic and Convention Center." Further, the panel suggested that the major meeting rooms and exhibit halls bear Dena'ina names for places, such as *Tikahtnu* (Cook Inlet) and *Idlughet* (Eklutna) (Richtmyer 2006). On August 16, 2006, the Anchorage Assembly unanimously adopted the panel's recommendation. The Dena'ina Civic and Convention Center will open in fall 2008. Eklutna's interpretive site, the new interpretive signs, and the naming of the new convention center are positive steps toward broader recognition of Dena'ina heritage in Anchorage.

Closing: A Place for Remembering

Figure 10 shows a view quite familiar to residents of Anchorage—Mount Susitna. Here is another irony: Mount Susitna is perhaps the only geographic feature in the Anchorage viewscape that the public today readily links with Dena'ina traditions, the so-called Sleeping Lady. Tour guides often repeat a story they claim to be a Dena'ina legend about the mountain's origins. But according to Shem Pete and other Dena'ina elders, the name "Sleeping Lady" derives from no Dena'ina name and the Sleeping Lady Legend is part of no Dena'ina language oral tradition.

The Dena'ina name for Mount Susitna is *Dghelishla*, "little mountain." It is a sacred place. Here, Dena'ina elders said, the ancestors of the *Nulchina* clan descended from the sky on a frozen cloud. Here, the renowned Dena'ina *qeshqa, Diqelas Tukda*, obtained spiritual power. Here, centuries before, a young Dena'ina man from *Tuqen Kaq'* (Alexander Creek) discovered a deposit of copper and through its trade became rich.

10. *Dghelishla* and *Ch'chihi Ken* (Mount Susitna). From *Shem Pete's Alaska*, p. 13. Photo by Priscilla Russell.

The ridge sloping to the south of *Dghelishla* is *Ch'chihi Ken*, "Ridge Where We Cry." Shem Pete explained this name:[5]

> That big ridge going downriver from *Dghelishla* all the way to Beluga,
> They call *Ch'chihi Ken*.
> They would sit down there.
> Everything is in view.
> They can see their whole country.
> Everything is just right under them.
> They think about their brothers and their fathers and mothers.
> They remember that,
> And they just sit down there and cry.
> That's the place we cry all the time,
> 'Cause everything just show up plain.
> That's why they call it *Ch'chihi Ken*.

Let's end this essay with a wish: that when we who live in Anchorage and those of us who visit look to the west toward *Dghelishla* and *Ch'chihi Ken*, we, like Shem Pete, will remember the Dena'ina who were here before us and the Dena'ina who continue to live here today.

Notes

James Fall, Division of Subsistence, Alaska Department of Fish and Game; jim.fall@alaska.gov.

1. Alberta Stephan, "Report on the Dena'ina Team's Second Trip to Elmendorf Air Force Base Lands" (unpublished), August 19, 1998, files, Alaska Department of Fish and Game, Anchorage.

2. The Ahtna are the Dena'ina's Athabascan neighbors to the northeast.

3. For a discussion of Upper Inlet Dena'ina social organization and subsistence activities in the eighteenth and nineteenth centuries and the early twentieth, see Fall (1987).

4. Elmendorf Field, later Elmendorf Air Force Base, along Knik Arm in the northern portion of Anchorage, was established at the beginning of American involvement in World War II as part of the army's Fort Richardson.

5. This is Jim Kari's translation of Shem Pete's original Dena'ina (Kari and Fall 2003, 74).

Qaneryaramta Egmiucia: Continuing Our Language

Walkie Kumaggaq *Charles*

Walkie Kumaggaq *Charles's article focuses on indigenous language programs for indigenous peoples and the importance of language teaching at the university level. Currently traditional languages are in the decline worldwide and Alaska is no exception. Charles discusses efforts at language revitalization in the general central Yup'ik region through teacher training. Charles is Yup'ik and was born and raised in the village of Emmonak. He is currently a faculty member of the University of Alaska, Fairbanks, where he teaches the grammar of the Central Alaskan Yup'ik language. This article was previously published in* Anthropology and Education Quarterly *36 (2005).*

Orchestrating an Indigenous language program for Indigenous peoples within any academic environment is no easy task. In most cases, Indigenous languages are taught by a recognized community expert, in the community; teaching that same language in a university environment is much more challenging. This article responds to Mindy J. Morgan's description of a university-based Ojibwe language program by exploring and comparing it to the efforts of students and facilitators of the Yup'ik Eskimo language at the University of Alaska, Fairbanks, as they attempt to gain ownership of the language and grammar they are teaching or learning to use in their own communities. In the following article I address Indigenous languages, critical pedagogy, Yup'ik education, and the success of mentor apprentice programs.

The history of Indigenous language use and decline is similar throughout many communities in the United States. Since the time of European contact, what was once a common, everyday practice by language bearers has gradually weakened for religious, political, educational, and other reasons. In response to Mindy J. Morgan's examination of a university-based Ojibwe language program, I present a brief historical background on the use of Alaska Native languages, specifically Yup'ik Eskimo, and address the consequences of both the loss and the use of Yup'ik within the region where it is spoken. I then focus on what the Yup'ik language "looks like" in terms of its use today in academic institutions, as Indigenous professionals and paraprofessionals attempt to resuscitate it within their communities.

This is a challenging commentary to write, and it humbles me to consider what is most important to share about my culture and language within these few pages. My culture and language cannot be shared on paper—limited and limiting—alone. Hearing and learning from a single person also presents limits, and writing from the university level has its limitations. I cannot walk out of my office into an elder's home and collect information—gingerly formulating ways by which to acquire that information by stating, "I wonder if . . . ," or "I wonder why . . . ," or "I wonder when . . ."—as is the protocol in seeking answers from a Yup'ik elder. I hope that within these few pages I do justice to the people about whom I write. I offer this commentary as one story told by one person, at one time, at one place, and for one purpose.

As Indigenous Americans, we were faced with the sudden elimination of our languages at the time of European contact and the establishment of Bureau of Indian Affairs schools. Many Native Alaskan students were "shipped out" to distant boarding schools such as Wrangell Institute, or Mt. Edgecumbe High School in Alaska, or Chemawa and Chilocco Indian Schools in Oregon and Oklahoma, respectively (see, e.g., Lomawaima 1994). Those students who were left in their own communities also learned that their Indigenous language was secondary or non-existent in school. Soon, through verbal downgrading and physical punishments for using the language, most of us learned to silence our language from the heart (Philips 1983).

The efforts of parents of boarding school students, the development of rural attendance area schools within rural Alaska, and the promotion of the 1968 Bilingual Education Act brought Indigenous languages into the schools (Dauenhauer 1997; Krauss 1980; McCarty 1993). Initially, Indigenous paraprofessionals—most of whom were selected to teach because of their ability to speak both English and their heritage language—found positions as bilingual aides in many Alaskan communities. Although the intentions of the programs in which they worked were good, most language classes—often held for only 30 minutes each day—were conducted with limited success in helping children gain fluency in their Native language.

Initially, the curriculum consisted of translated material from other classroom sources. With minimal training for bilingual teacher aides, these programs hung on by a thread. One of the biggest challenges for teaching both Yup'ik as a second and a first language was the ability of teacher aides to teach the written form. As is the case for many Indigenous languages in the United

States, Yup'ik Eskimo was traditionally an oral language. Thus, for newly hired teacher aides, a primary task was to learn the writing system. Outside help in basic curriculum development occurred separately for each region and school district. Some of these efforts were more promising than others, and most of the schools and teacher aides made do with what little they were afforded to begin their teaching of Yup'ik. Still others carried remnants of a writing system introduced by early missionaries with limited knowledge of the culture. Most of the writing systems created by these missionaries had been developed for a single purpose; to indoctrinate Indigenous people in the teachings of the church.

For many bilingual aides, there was an underlying sense of procedural display even when facilitating their own heritage language in their own communities to their own children. Written curricula were faulty and limited, and because the language traditionally was used only in spoken form, written forms for classroom use just did not seem "right." The teachings became mirror images of what the Western teacher was teaching using Yup'ik vocabulary, and sometimes literal translations of Western phrases, songs, and "ditties."

In 1970, recognizing the need for a comprehensive and cohesive bond among Yup'ik speakers in Alaska, the Yup'ik Language Workshop was established at the University of Alaska, Fairbanks (UAF), under the leadership of Irene Reed. We owe much to Irene, affectionately known as "*Iitaruaq*" Irene, along with Osahito Miyaoka of Otaru University on Hokkaido, Steven Jacobson, and Michael Krauss—who, with the assistance of regional speakers such as Marie Nick Meade, Paschal Afcan, and Martha Teeluk, published the first teaching grammar of Central Yup'ik (Reed et al. 1977; see also Jacobson 1995). The work did not stop there. Since then, Steven Jacobson has published a comprehensive dictionary of the language that was first distributed in 1980 (Jacobson 1984; Krauss 1980). Many workshops and institutes followed, and bilingual aides of the Yup'ik region have generated ownership of the writing system that is consistent throughout the areas where it is spoken today. Of the 20,000 Yup'ik people in Alaska 50 percent speak the language fluently.

Following the development of a Yup'ik Eskimo grammar, a Yup'ik degree program was established at the UAF. Although few students have graduated with the degree, the program provides students from the Yup'ik region the option of taking Yup'ik Eskimo grammar as a humanities credit. The first-year class meets five days a week for two semesters, for five university credits. The second- and third-year classes meet three times a week for two semesters, for three credits each. When I asked what students liked about the first-year Yup'ik class, one student commented:

> [I]t's giving me an opportunity to learn and understand my own language and speak it when I get back home, I have always wanted to learn to speak and understand it because I get mad at myself when someone else speaks it and I can't understand them. I also like Yup'ik because it is a way to keep my native language alive.

Another student said:

> [that] is our culture. Yup'iks are Indigenous people; we have power. We are very strong with our cultural ways. And by taking a Yup'ik class, a grammatical course, I am learning how to write in our language.

The same student concluded:

> I wonder what I would be like if I were a true Yup'ik speaker. Would I take this class? How else would I communicate with others?

The students in this beginning Yup'ik class are aware of the weakness of the spoken language in their communities and within their peer groups. They want ownership, and they are learning that the challenge is to learn the grammar in order to be able to speak it fluently. This is not an overnight experience; it takes patience, commitment, and perseverance.

Today, some Yup'ik communities are struggling to hold on to their language. Most often, the only Yup'ik the children hear is what they passively witness among grandparents or other elders, and on rare occasions from their parents who either speak fluently or know enough of the language to "get by." Some communities still speak only Yup'ik, but that is becoming more rare with time. The other arena in which children hear Yup'ik is in school—but for a limited time each day (because bilingual aides typically teach six classes per day). After having been ridiculed or punished for using their languages (Manuelito 2005, 73–87) many elderly Yup'iks choose not to emphasize Yup'ik to the younger generation. They do not want their children to have access to the language and culture, yet most parents have lost the ability to speak.

Efforts to maintain Yup'ik in the communities with the help of schools have been a long, arduous process. There is still energy among those who speak or teach Yup'ik in the communities. The question for many is, how to strengthen the knowledge of the Yup'ik culture and language so that our children will be able to speak it in the future?

In response to this question—and, as a comparative example to the program described by Morgan at Michigan State—the UAF and its partner community college Kuskokwim Campus (KUC), have made strong efforts to maintain the language. Recently the UAF, KUC, the Alaska Native Language Center, and several school districts partnered in establishing the Yup'ik Language Institute (YLI) with funds from the U.S. Department of Education (2002).[1] The YLI career ladder program is designed to prepare Yup'ik Eskimo language teachers by

—offering special training, workshops, courses, and degree opportunities;
—empowering individuals eager to maintain the Yup'ik language in schools and communities; and
—developing high-quality, innovative language programs for schools and communities.

Courses are offered through YLI, a UAF/KUC summer session held in June each year, and distance delivery. Eligible participants work toward proficiency in Central Yup'ik through YLI's mentor-apprentice program.

Mentor-apprentice programs (also called master-apprentice programs) are perhaps best known in the California context (see, e.g., Hinton 1998; 2001). Such programs pair proficient Native speakers (often elders) with nonspeaking or limited-speaking apprentices. As Hinton describes them for California, master-apprentice teams work and often live together over extended periods of time, always communicating in the heritage language. Communication is natural, involving everyday activities; language teaching and learning use a great deal of contextual cues. UAF/KUC mentor-apprentice participants are selected by program partners. These participants receive financial support for costs related to the program. A limited number of graduate and undergraduate fellowships also are available for those who wish to enroll in a degree program on a full-time basis.

Talented high school juniors and seniors from participating school districts have enrolled in summer intensive-language and selected courses through YLI. All coursework carries full university credit and may be applied toward a four-year degree. Students earn credit toward a master of education degree in language and literacy by combining coursework for the endorsement of YLI with six graduate courses and completing a synthesizing research paper. The endorsement adds to an existing teaching license within the State of Alaska.

Once only a proposal, this program has become a reality for the Yup'ik region, giving self-determination a stronger meaning for these program participants from the Lower Yukon, Lower Kuskokwim, and Kuspuk school districts. They know that they have an academic and a professional future—a career pathway that will lead them to certification. Learning the Yup'ik language at the university level not only strengthens participants' language proficiency, their ability to write grammatically in Yup'ik, and their understanding of and skill in applying first- and second-language teaching methods; it also empowers them as educators and professionals. One participant from a partner school district had been teaching as a bilingual aide for over 20 years. This program gives him and many others in his situation greater confidence as a professional educator and language teacher. As Nieto (1999) so appropriately puts it, we see ". . . a light in their eyes."

This moment of academic ownership and facilitation of Indigenous language proficiency for the Yup'ik people is finally reaching its crest. Both students in the communities and their instructors realize that although there is still work to be done, it is good and important work that will return strength and vigor to the Yup'ik language and culture. Unlike the English-only legacy of the past, Yup'ik now belongs in the classroom where it can be spoken, developed, and used in all of its richness.

Note

1. United States Department of Education, Alaska Native Education Program (CDFA 84.356A), grant for Yup'ik Language Institute (2002).

Deg Xinag Oral Traditions: Reconnecting Indigenous Language and Education through Traditional Narratives

Beth Ginondidoy *Leonard* *(Deg Xinag Athabascan)*

Beth Leonard (Deg Xinag Athabascan) is originally from Shageluk, Alaska, a Deg Hit'an/Deg Xinag Athabascan community. Her father is James Dementi, who was raised in the traditional Athabascan subsistence lifestyle. Her mother is the late Reverend Jean Aubrey Dementi, originally from California. Beth Leonard is currently an assistant professor of Alaska Native Education in the School of Education, University of Alaska, Fairbanks, and a Ph.D. candidate in the UAF *Graduate School Interdisciplinary Studies Program. She earned her B.A. degree in linguistics in 1994 and an M.Ed. in language and literacy in 1996 from the University of Alaska, Fairbanks. Leonard's research on the Deg Xinag language includes work with elders in the community as well as the study of older recorded oral histories from the University of Alaska archives. As a community member, her cultural knowledge has given her insight into the language.*

"Deg Xinag," literally 'local language' (also known as "Ingalik"), is spoken in the villages of Anvik, Shageluk, and Grayling. Deg Xinag is the westernmost of the Athabascan languages within the Na-Dene language family. The language area is also referred to as "Deg Hit'an," literally, 'local people.' There are currently about twenty fluent speakers of this language remaining, some of whom reside in the referenced villages and others who reside in the large urban city of Anchorage. This article focuses on Deg Hit'an beliefs about the pike or "jackfish" through examination of *Niło'qay Nixidaxin* or "The Man and Wife," a complex cosmological narrative told in the Deg Xinag language by the late Deg Hit'an elder Belle Deacon.

As a woman of Deg Hit'an heritage who grew up in the villages of Shageluk and Anvik, I began my original research with the goal of finding ways to contribute to Deg Xinag language revitalization efforts. However, as I began my graduate research I came to understand the significance of indigenous language revitalization in relation to its potential contributions to indigenous and cross-cultural education. These contributions can include establishing and enhancing self-identity and self-esteem for indigenous students, as well as contributing in-depth knowledge about local environments, thereby enhancing place-based or funds of knowledge educational models. Underlying structures and meanings used in the contexts of Deg Xinag oral traditions are currently absent from most published materials for this language, making it difficult to both learn the language and develop culturally appropriate educational curriculum. This preliminary analysis draws on philosophical and pedagogical frameworks established by indigenous scholars including Gregory Cajete, Oscar Kawagley, and Greg Sarris.

I begin with an introduction to Deacon's volume *Engithidong Xugixudhoy: Their Stories of Long Ago*, including a brief overview of "Distant Time" narratives. I then review the recording context and introduce a morphological analysis of the narrative title. Following the narrative summary from the line-by-line translation, I discuss subsistence, including the pike's role in current subsistence practices of the Deg Hit'an. This section is followed by a discussion of the epistemologies and ontologies regarding the pike, including the literal meanings of Athabascan terms for pike, and beliefs about creation and transformation. The conclusion discusses my inter- and cross-cultural experiences as a Deg Hit'an researcher and language learner.

Introduction to Engithidong Xugixudhoy: Their Stories of Long Ago

All the narratives in this volume were audiotaped in 1973 by Karen McPherson, who was then working with the Alaska State Library's Alaska Native Oral Literature Project (Deacon 1987a, ix). The volume is organized with the Deg Xinag version of the story appearing first, with each facing page containing a line-by-line English translation. James Kari, currently professor emeritus with the Alaska Native Language Center, transcribed, translated, and edited the texts. Deg Xinag speakers who helped with translations included my father, James Dementi; Grace John and Bertha Dutchman of Shageluk; Hannah Maillelle and John Deacon of Grayling; Alta Jerue of Anvik; and the Koyukon linguist Dr. Eliza Jones of Koyukuk. According to the volume preface written by Kari, this volume represents less than half of all the narratives Deacon recorded for the Alaska Native Oral Literature Project.

Deacon introduces the volume with a short section titled *"Deg Hit'an Guxudhoy,"* literally, 'The People's Stories' (1987a, 2–3). In this section she talks about how children were told to listen carefully to the stories and instructed not to fidget or to fall asleep. They were told to "think about everything" to obtain the old wisdom. Deacon describes the process of storytelling, saying "[a story] is like a bright light ahead of us, just as though it were written as we speak" (3).

The other narratives transcribed and translated in this volume include "*Taxghoz*" or "Polar Bear" (41–60); "*Niq'odałin Notin Nixidaxin,*" "The Two Girls Who Lived There" or "Two Girls and Crow Man" (61–81); "*Niłeda Sugiluqye Yixo Dixodałdiyh,*" "Two Cousins Shooting Arrows" (83–89); "*Tr'an Sugiluq Tthux Ni'idhit,*" "The Old Woman Who Lived Alone" or "The Old Lady Who Lived Alone" (91–105); "*Nołdith Gixudhoy,*" "Hawk Owl Story" (107–9): "*Q'ivałdal Tixgidr Yił,*" "Spruce Grouse and Mink" (111–19); and "*Tr'an Sughiluq Chighiligguy Gho'in Xididhitl'ighanh,*" "The Old Woman Who Killed Herself Because of the Fox" (121–27). All but three of the narratives include an English version by Deacon.

Overview of "Long Ago" or "Far Distant Time" Narratives

> Koyukon belief stresses that in the distant past there was a time in the transition world when transformation of creatures was possible and all had transhuman aspects. Bear, wolf, wolverine, and lynx had two souls, like contemporary man, and could change from one form into another . . . After the great flood, man and other forms of nature underwent change. Man became denaa, or human, with other forms of nature taking on their distinctive features as we know them now, with transformation capacity lost at least to ordinary humans. (Wright 1995, 39)

In this passage, the Koyukon scholar Wright references two distinct Koyukon historical periods. According to Wright, the transition world existed before the great flood or "Raven's Raft," and major changes occurred afterward. This great flood is described in the narrative by the Koyukon elder Catherine Attla, "*Dotson' Sa Ninin' Atltseen*" or "Great Raven Who Shaped the World" (1983, 127–38).

Ruppert and Bernet (2001, 10–11) provide three categories or "eras" of Native oral genres along a continuum or "spectrum of narrative content." The first is the "origin era" or distant time when the world was in a state of flux. The second is the "transformation era" when beings move "toward social forms." After human-animal transformations become limited, there is an "historical era," that focuses mainly on "the actions of named and known people."

The Deg Xinag term *engithidong* refers to a far distant time, or "long ago"

Table 1

Deg Xinag	English	Related Koyukon terms
1. *adongdong*	long ago	
2. *yidong*		2. *yedone*
3. *dinanatthidong*		
4. *engithidong*		
5. *qi'dong*	Already, previously, in the past	5. *kk'edone "a long time ago in the legendary past (when animals were people)"*

(Kari 1978, 47). The suffix, *-dong*, is used in a number of other constructions or adverbs of time including a general term *q'idong*, referring to something that happened "previously," or "in the past." The root noun *xudhoy* in *xugixudhoy* is a commonly used term for story, historical narrative, or legend (Kari 1978, 94). The possessive prefix *xugi-* or *xigi-* functions as the third person plural reflexive pronoun, that is, "their own." Old stories can also be referred to as *q'iydong xunxinig* (Kari 1978, 95). Other adverbs of time using the stem *dong* from the *Deg Xinag Noun Dictionary* (Kari 1978, 47) are presented in table 1 with related Koyukon terms (Jette and Jones 2000, 147).

Overview of the Recording Context

The first voice heard on the audio recording is that of Karen McPherson, saying, "This is Belle Deacon from Grayling. She's going to tell the story 'The Man That Came Down from above the Second Layer of This World.' She's telling the story in Ingalik and she'll translate it into English. It is April 17, 1973." Deacon begins by recognizing the person who told her the narrative, and his advice about remembering and thinking about the traditional narratives. Most of Deacon's introduction is transcribed in the volume (Deacon 1973, 5); however, a few words were edited out, so I transcribed the following directly from the audiotape:

> The story came from Anvik when I was around maybe twelve years old I was. One, name of Old Jackson told this story to four of us girls. And he told us to listen to it good, because when you don't get the things that . . . if you don't even get the stories, even you never even think about it that's when you don't get the story, he tell us. And he told us to really think about it. It comes from way generation, from the story beginning, it's just. They pass it on to one another. It's what he told us.[1]

Deacon takes about thirty-eight minutes to tell the Deg Xinag version and approximately thirty-three minutes to tell the English version. The narrative is relatively long in comparison to the others in the volume. I mean "relatively long" in a contemporary context, as traditionally these kinds of narratives could have been substantially longer and told in sections over several evenings. For example, in order to tell the Koyukon narrative "*K'etetaalkkaanee*: The One Who Paddled among the People and Animals in Its Entirety," Thompson (1990) writes that the narrator would need "at least a week" (4).

All the narratives in Deacon's book were recorded in her home in Grayling, Alaska, thus the audio also captures sounds including knocking as visitors come by, Deacon's little dog barking, her husband John talking, and the kitchen clock ticking. My parents and I visited the home of John and Belle Deacon on many occasions, so listening to these recordings is like a trip back in time to those visits in the late 1960s and early 1970s. These background noises do not distract from the story but instead add to the context and overall appeal of the audio, effectively bringing the past into the present for those of us who knew John and Belle Deacon.

Nił'oqay Nixidaxin*: "The Man and Wife"*

As I studied the Deg Xinag language and became more familiar with the morphology and basic terms and expressions, I began to question the translation of the title *Nił'oqay Nixidaxin*. Further investigation using noun and stem dictionaries, and questions posed to the Koyukon scholar Dr. Eliza Jones, revealed the way the prefix *nił-* is used to mark vital, reciprocal social relationships. A morphological examination of the term *nił'oqay* reveals a reflexive prefix *nił-*, meaning "with each other." The "*'o*" is a contracted form of the stem for "wife," that is, *ot* (unpossessed form), and the final segment *qay* can mean "multiple persons" or "village." The reflexive term *nił'oqay* was not included in the referenced noun dictionary, hence my initial confusion. However, other reflexive forms, used in a number of creative ways, were recorded as noted in table 2 (Kari 1978, 26–28).

Thompson notes that many Koyukon stories "begin with the phrase '*Neełkkun kkaa łedo*' 'A man and wife were living together' . . . In such forms, the older or most important member of the pair is the only one explicitly stated . . . If a story begins with this phrase, one can assume that the couple will be broken up by either abduction or infidelity" (1990, 100–101).

After uncovering the deeper meanings of the term *nił'oqay*, the meaning of *nixidaxin* was still unclear. In examining the morphology of the word, the prefix "*ni-*" may refer to something specific in the environment. The areal prefix

Table 2

Deg Xinag	English translation	Comments
niłngonhye	mother and child	*ngonh* "your mother"
niłto'ye	father and son	*-to* unpossessed stem for "father"
niłq'uye	aunt and niece	*-q'u* unpossessed stem for "aunt" (mother's sister)
niłqing'qay	husband and wife	*-qing'* unpossessed stem for "husband"

xi- indicates something within the wider environment. The stem *-dax* is often used to indicate movement or travel within the natural world, for instance the term *tinh edax* is used to describe the movement of ice in the river in the fall or spring. The final portion of the word *-in* can be translated as "those who" are in a position or constant state.

A morphological analysis of the narrative title is presented in table 3.

Narrative Summary: Nił'oqay Ni'idaxin, *"The Man and Wife"*

Deacon (1987b) begins the narrative by identifying a couple living at the mouth of a side stream. When fall comes, the man spends a lot of time trapping, while the wife stays at home chopping wood, sewing, and cooking for her husband. The wife would always make ice cream for her husband and after he had eaten he would specifically ask for this. As the man continues to go out hunting and trapping for days at a time his wife begins to feel lonesome. This cycle of the same activities goes on for a number of years, with the wife making fat ice cream, or occasionally snow ice cream, for her husband. One day during the fall season she does not feel well, and does not make the ice cream for him. The man urges his wife to make the ice cream as he does not get full without it, and sleeps well after eating ice cream. His wife then goes outside for snow to make ice cream and does not return. The man searches for her and finds the bowl and spoon she had taken with her, but finds no tracks beyond the water hole. He mourns for her during the subsequent fall and winter becomes thin and weak, thinking that he will die.

At midwinter an old man (whom the husband later learns is Raven)[2] visits him and tells the husband that his wife was stolen by a giant and taken to "a land deep down in the water" (Deacon 1987b, 15). Raven tells the man that he will not be able to get his wife back without his (Raven's) help. After the man has eaten and rested, they begin work cutting down a large spruce tree with a stone axe. They then limb the tree, and cut the top off, making it about

Table 3

Deg Xinag	English translation	Morphological analysis
Nił'oqay	The man and wife	*Nił*
		'o contracted form of 'wife' (*si'ot=my wife*)
		qay plural person
Nixidaxin		*ni* continuative prefix
		dax can indicate movement or travel; or living in a place (for a length of time)
		in "those who" (aspect – in a position or constant state)

"twelve arm spans long" (19). The spruce is then peeled, and over the course of at least a month, carved into the shape of a pike, with the insides and mouth hollowed out. After the pike is complete, they tie a rope to it and drag it to the waterhole. The carved pike is then painted with white spots. At this point in the story, Deacon comments, "It was such a beautiful fish" (21).

On instruction from Raven, the man then goes to the cache and brings "things [beads] that were like eyes. Raven uses a medicine song on the beads and then puts them in place, whereupon they begin to wiggle and move. Raven instructs the man to go fetch an ice chisel. They then measure the fish (again) found to be twelve arm spans long. The man is instructed to chop a hole in the waterhole big enough to accommodate the fish and to fetch other items for his journey. These items include birch punk, a clay lamp to provide light for the man while inside the fish, and weasel skins to provide a disguise once he reaches the underwater village. Raven then "blew with his hands and made medicine with a song" (24). He hit the fish on the back and it sank to the bottom of the river, producing a humming noise that shook the man. In this part of the story Deacon uses the English word "electricity" to describing the sound made by the pike.

Upon reaching the underwater village the man leaves the fish and finds himself in the underwater village with a "big kashim and many winter houses" where there were people "hollering and playing ball" (25). Preparations were also underway for a mask dance. The man, hiding behind grass piled in the forks of trees, sees his wife being escorted by two women to the kashim. As the wife converses with the two women, she refers to herself at this point as their [the two women's] "sister-in-law." His wife tells her escorts she must relieve herself and then encounters her husband, who hands her a weasel skin. They both swallow the skins and turn into little weasels. At this point the punk the man left in the grass begins to talk to the two women in the wife's voice. The two women begin to look for the wife and discover the talking punk. Meanwhile, the man and wife return and enter the pike, whose head is resting on the shore. The giant and villagers prepare to shoot arrows at the pike when it swamps the canoe and swims around. The pike then swamps the village with waves, then straightens itself out and begins the humming sound again as it travels back to the home of the man and wife.

Upon their return, Raven is waiting for them and tells them to get a rag from the cache and urinate on it. Raven then washes the head and teeth with the rag, returning "the teeth-like bones to its mouth" (31). Raven then instructs the fish to "stay in a place where there are lakes, where no one will go," and "for people who step there on the ice of the lake, you will shake your little tail" (31), indicating "someone's impending death." The fish then "goes to the bottom"; however, they (man and wife) "don't know where." This is not the end of the narrative; but I will end the summary here as there are no more direct or indirect references to the pike.

Subsistence Beliefs and Practices

> If you look deeply enough, you'll see that animals can help us to understand life as it is . . . animals understand you, but only if you know how to talk with them. (Krupa 1996, 25)

Since subsistence beliefs and practices are central themes within the Deacon narrative, an exploration of indigenous knowledge systems and subsistence is essential. The words of the late Athabascan traditional chief Peter John, quoted above, initiate this brief discussion of indigenous knowledge systems and subsistence. Shallowly defined, the term "subsistence" seems to indicate a general knowledge of how to live off the land or subsist on what the land has to offer in terms of hunting, fishing, and trapping. For indigenous peoples, these limited definitions disconnect subsistence practices from spiritual beliefs. Chief John's words clearly articulate one of the disparities between Western and indigenous knowledge systems in terms of human-animal relationships and the status of these interactions.

In one of Deacon's English versions of Nił'oqay Nixidaxin, she provides more information about the pike's abilities to foretell death or danger. Here is Raven's final statement to the pike before Raven sends him to the bottom of the lake:

> But I'm going to send you down where there's nobody wouldn't see you anymore. In some big lake that's where you'll stay on the bottom. That, you'll, only sometimes when it's going to be big flu or something your tail will be this way [Deacon motions with her hand] and the ice will crack and they'll know that's a sign that sickness is going to come. Way back, this old man told this fish.[3]

These words directly correspond with Chief John's statement regarding the intellectual capacities of animals and their roles in assisting humans. In many Native American belief systems, animals were influential in the creation of the world, and all animals still have the ability to influence and guide humans (Cajete 2000; Deloria 1994, 2006; Kawagley 1995; Wright 1995).

Underlying differences between Western and indigenous knowledge systems or worldviews are difficult to summarize in a few words. The indigenous scholars referenced above observe the following major distinctions including: oral versus written transmission of knowledge; contextualized pedagogies; epistemologies, or worldviews that provide different hierarchies or classification systems for all parts of the environment; and perhaps most importantly, practices of complex reciprocal social and spiritual exchanges. Within this system, humans have specific responsibilities in maintaining balanced physical, psychological, and spiritual systems in all parts of the environment.

The Pike's Role in Subsistence Practices

> "They [pike] have a lot to do with the medicine man, shaman, you know. Some lakes, you know, they get pretty big, twenty feet long." (Grayling/Holikachuk interviewee, Brown et al. 2005, 46)

For the Deg Hit'an people, pike or jackfish were an important part of the traditional subsistence cycle as they can be harvested year-round from lakes, side streams, and rivers. Traditionally, pike were harvested in basket traps set as part of a fish weir during the fall and winter months or could be harvested individually, in clear water, using a double-pronged fish spear. Data from 1990–91 indicate that the pike harvest of the four Deg Hit'an villages ranged from 19.5 to 35 percent, confirming the continued importance of this fish in the current subsistence cycle (Wheeler 1997, 160–62).

Pike are aggressive, predatory fish and can grow up to six feet and fifty pounds. Their jaws and gills are laced with thin sharp teeth. Pike are currently harvested using gill nets and the meat is boiled, roasted, or fried. Pike is also used to make *vanhgiq*, or "ice cream," a subsistence food discussed in more detail in the following section.

VANHGIQ: "ICE CREAM"

Osgood (1958, 1959) observed that *vanhgiq* played an important role in Deg Hit'an society, served during most of the major feasts as well as on other social occasions. Deacon refers to several types of ice cream in both her Deg Xinag and English versions, including those made with fish, caribou or moose fat, or snow. Currently, pike is one of the fish used to make ice cream, as the meat flakes well and is readily available at most times of the year. Other white fish may be used as well. Deacon uses the Deg Xinag term *vanhgiq* to refer to several types of ice cream including fish, fat, and snow ice cream. She also uses the terms *ginot yił nintth'ix* as this refers to the mixing of the fish meat; *yith vanhgiq* for "snow ice cream" (8); and *giq'ux vanhgiq*, translated as "grease ice cream" (31). Kari (1978, 84) lists a different term for snow ice cream, *dhiyh vanhgiq*, and another term that refers to (caribou) rennet ice cream, *gichatlton vanhgiq*.

Traditionally, ice cream could also be made with the seed pods of the cottonwood tree as described by Osgood (1940, 193–94). This type of ice cream was usually made in the winter; however, Osgood (1959, 44) notes that the pods were collected in June or July or "may be gathered just as the cottony coma begins to appear, in which case the pods are stored in the smoke house until they open about a week later." The cotton seeds were discarded, then the cotton was saturated with fish oil. The saturated cotton was then mixed with warm fish oil and snow until fluffy. According to Osgood, lamprey oil was preferred, although any kind of fish oil could be used. Osgood also notes that favorite berries for ice cream included *niłanht'asr* or winter berries (crowberries), *nenhtl'it* or bunchberries (lowbush cranberries), and *xisrghed* (rose hips).

Fish ice cream is made by combining fat (fish oil, or more recently, hydrogenated vegetable oil) with the boiled meat of the fish, an extremely time-intensive process. After the fish is boiled, the skin is removed and the meat deboned. The liquid is then squeezed out of the fish by hand until the meat becomes dry and powdery. The fish meat and fat are combined and whipped using one hand until light and fluffy. During this process, people who are in the house must remain quiet as the ice cream is being made. Sugar, berries, and sometimes milk or a sweetened cream mixture are added to finish the dish. Blueberrries, lowbush cranberries, crowberries, or salmonberries seem to be the most popular fruit to add to the ice cream currently. Today the Deg Hit'an people continue to serve *vanhgiq* in large quantities at potlatches, mask dances, and funeral feasts.

Epistemology and Ontology: Aspects of the Pike

Moore (1998) defines epistemology as "the study of the cannons and protocols by which human beings acquire, organize, and verify their knowledge about the world" (271). In his introduction to *Native Science*, Leroy Little Bear talks about science as a "search for reality" and "knowledge," thereby encompassing both epistemology and ontology within a single term (Cajete 2000, x). Cajete emphasizes that Native science is a participatory process with the natural world (2) and that the understanding of Native science requires developing the ability to "decode layers of meaning embedded in symbols," symbols that "are used artistically and linguistically to depict structures and relationships to places" (36). Stories, or mythology, according to Cajete, "are alternative ways of understanding relationships, creation, and the creative process itself . . . how humans obtain knowledge, how they learn responsibility for such knowledge, and then how knowledge is applied in the proper context" (44). These mythologies contain "expressions of a worldview in coded form" (62).

Reflecting the epistemology and ontology of the Deg Hit'an, the name for pike in the Deg Xinag language is *giliqoy*, literally, "a lance" according to Osgood (1959, 24). There are several terms for pike in the *Koyukon Athabascan Dictionary* (Jette and Jones 2000); these include the related term *k'oolkkoye*, literally, "that which is speared at something" (345), *k'ootaah dletone* or large pike, literally, "that which stays on the bottom" (527), *dolel*, literally, "that which floats" (416), and *taah denaaltone* (502). The term *taah* refers to (something) being underwater, and *denaaltone* means a "slender stick-like object" (520). The term *k'ooleghos* (259) is also referenced with an indication that the stem is "probably from an obsolete verb theme . . . plural fish swim," but the stem *ghos* can also refer to "plural objects making noise" (258). The *Ahtna Dictionary* (Kari 1990) has a single reference, *'olgaadẓi*, or *c'ulgaadẓi*, which is said to originate from an "obsolete verb theme meaning 'fish swims rapidly'" (179); the Ahtna terms are similar to the Dena'ina term *ghelguts'i*, literally, "swift swimmer" (Kari 1994, 13). It is likely that the Deg Hit'an had additional terms referring to the pike. Tables 4 and 5 list terms for other Alaska Athabascan languages.

The spruce tree, or *didlang*, that was used to carve the pike was traditionally one of the most useful plants to the Deg Hit'an people, providing, for example, medicine in the form of new shoots in the spring, which could be collected and made into tea to treat colds; pitch, which was used for bandaging cuts and waterproofing canoes; and wood for burning, or the construction

Table 4

Language	Related terms for pike	Literal meaning
Deg Xinag	*giliqoy*	something that is speared at something (lance)
Holikachuk	*k'oolqoy*	
Koyukon	*k'oolkkoye*	

Table 5

Language	Other terms for pike	Literal meaning
Ahtna	*'olgaadẓi* (Central & Western dialects)	fish swims rapidly
	c'ulgaadẓi (Mentasta dialect)	
Dena'ina	*ghelguts'* (Inland dialect)	swift swimmer
Koyukon	*k'ootaah dletone*	that which stays on the bottom
	dolel	that which floats
	taah denaaltone	slender stick-like object underwater
	k'ooleghos	plural fish swim

of items such as sled runners or household items. According to Osgood (1959), the wood burns at a higher temperature than other woods and "is softer than birch," making it easier to work with (45).

The creation of the giant pike takes place through transformation of the spruce tree via medicine song and breath of Raven. Witherspoon (1977) indicates that the Navajo have established cultural categories or hierarchies that classify the world based on "potential for motion" (140) and acknowledge "air as the source of all knowledge and animation" (53). Posey (2001) also references the energy stored in inanimate objects that can be transformed into an animate being (7). In a similar vein, Cajete (2000) acknowledges that "in many Native myths, plants are acknowledged as the first life, or the grandparents of humans and animals and sources of life and wisdom" (108). In the Deg Xinag language, the word *yeg* means "breath" and "spirit." Deg Hit'an medicine men or shaman were often able to cure using their breath in ritual song, or blowing in a person's ear, for example, to cure an earache. When we examine these ontologies that acknowledge the power of air, the role of plants in the environment, and potential for motion, we can see that the transformation of the spruce tree into a giant pike becomes a natural process.

Conclusion

My research with Deg Xinag oral traditions has required a broad examination of my multiple "insider/outsider" roles (Smith 1999). This examination takes into account my general knowledge of the Deg Hit'an culture and my growing familiarity with the Deg Xinag language as a second-language learner; also, initially, my unfamiliarity with Deg Hit'an narratives, specifically, with Belle Deacon's narratives. In his book *Keeping Slug Woman Alive* (1993) the Pomo/Miwok scholar Greg Sarris discusses Bateson's notions of "culture contact," that is, that cultures will come into contact not only cross-culturally but interculturally as well. Intercultural and border themes are also prevalent in the publications of the Latina/o scholars Gloria Anzaldúa (1987) and Renato Rosaldo (1993). My research is, in many respects, a cross-cultural as well as decontextualized endeavor considering my background, a background that resulted in my initial experience with oral traditions in written formats, then secondarily through listening to audio recordings.

As a second-language learner of Deg Xinag, I have often struggled with identifying adequate processes and contexts that can facilitate this learning. Although some of us, as students, work directly with linguists, differences between English and Deg Xinag are perhaps not fully understood, and therefore not articulated. I believe this is due in part to the lack of knowledge of the deeper Athabascan cultural contexts and constructs and the "failure to document language beyond the lexical and grammatical levels."[4] Athabascan languages are classified by linguists as "prefix-agglutinative," that is, the stem or root of the word is preceded by a series of complex prefixes that signify "who is doing the action and when the action takes place" (Hargus and Taff 1994). This structure presents challenges for nonlinguists, as many dictionaries tend to be organized by word stems. The nonspeaker of the language, or speaker who does not know how to identify the word stem, needs to begin by looking at the English index to identify the stem for a particular word he or she is trying to research. For any one word, there can be multiple translations, hence multiple stems and multiple locations to research within a stem dictionary to find information related to one particular word or topic (see, for example, in the section "Epistemology," the multiple page numbers for pike terms from the *Koyukon Athabaskan Dictionary*).

I began my initial research into the language using the *Deg Xinag Noun Dictionary* (Kari 1978), and questioning my father, James Dementi, about literal translations for terms not provided by the dictionary. For a beginning language learner, literal translations offer fascinating glimpses into the system

Table 6

English	Deg Xinag	Literal translation
Raven	*Yixgitsiy*	your (plural) grandfather
rusty blackbird	*yixgitsiy vozra*	raven's nephew
puffball mushroom	*yixgitsiy nołchildl*	raven's (sewing) bag

of worldviews and values, providing further impetus for ongoing investigation. The entries for "raven" and "rusty blackbird" are taken from the "Birds" section of the dictionary (13), and the single entry for "puffball mushroom" is taken from the "Plants" section (23); see table 6.

At first glance, the novice or nonspeaker of the language can see that these three entries are similar in that *yixgitsiy* is part of each. The stem *-tsiy* means "grandfather." *Yixgitsiy* in the first example, literally means 'you guys' grandfather' or 'your (plural) grandfather.' "Rusty blackbird" appears farther down on the same page of the dictionary, and "puffball mushroom" in an entirely different section. Without seeing these entries grouped together, however, a novice learner looking at the dictionary would not be to see the connections among these entries; nor would he or she necessarily be able to identify the significance of the kinship term used to identify Raven. In my experience, significant knowledge can be hidden by the organization of, and limited translations provided by current dictionary formats. For the Deg Hit'an people, the entity "Raven" (sometimes referred to as "Crow") is significant as cosmological narratives document how he brought light and helped create different aspects of their environment. In Deacon's "*Nil'oqay Nixidaxin*" narrative, Raven calls the man and his wife *sitthey*, or "my grandchildren," and plays a central role in helping retrieve the wife through the creation and animation of the pike.

In her introductory chapter of *Reading Voices: Oral and Written Interpretations of the Yukon's Past*, Cruikshank (1991) discusses the educational processes of indigenous peoples that traditionally took place through the practice of oral traditions. Cruikshank emphasizes that youth in the Yukon Territory have experienced life very differently from their elders, probably in ways similar to my own inter- and cross-cultural experiences. Therefore, the construction of knowledge and the passing on of this knowledge through oral and written traditions become intercultural endeavors between older and younger generations. Traditional narratives such as *Nil'oqay Nixidaxin* were not "traditionally" analyzed in a literary sense by either the storyteller or the audience. However, I have had very different background experiences from those of

Deg Hit'an elder storytellers or fluent speakers, and I am learning the Deg Xinag language as an adult. As such, it is difficult to get an accurate sense of the depth of the narrative through the current English translation, so some exploration and analysis is necessary. These narratives, in turn, help me to further my knowledge of the language and to begin, in Chief John's words, "to understand life as it is."

Notes

1. Belle Deacon, interviewed by Karen McPherson on April 17, 1973, in *Grayling, Alaska* (audiotape), Alaska Native Oral Literature Project (Anchorage: Alaska State Library Media Services, 1973).

2. Raven, a "trickster" figure for Alaska Native cultures, is similar to the character of Coyote in the stories of indigenous peoples of the southwestern United States.

3. "The First Man and Woman," in *Athabascans: Strangers of the North*, Anchorage Historical and Fine Arts Museum Exhibit and Lecture Series (Anchorage: University of Alaska Media Services, Alaska Native Cultural Heritage and Information Bank, 1976).

4. Gary Holton, personal communication, Fairbanks, 2001.

The Alaskan Haida Language Today: Reasons for Hope

Jeane Breinig (Haida)

Indigenous languages are shrinking globally at exponential rates, a situation that has become the focus of many Alaska Native scholars. The following essay is one of several in this volume that address language revitalization and its placement within contemporary Native societies. Jeane Breinig is Haida originally from Kasaan village in southern Southeast Alaska. She is Raven, Brown Bear, Táas'Laannas Clan. She is associate professor of English at the University of Alaska, Anchorage. From 2003 to 2006 Breinig was the Haida language associate at Sealaska Heritage Institute (SHI), where she provided managerial oversight to SHI's Haida language revitalization projects. She is a contributing author and coeditor of Alaska Native Writers, Storytellers and Orators: The Expanded Edition *(1999), and coproducer of the video* Gá saá aan Xadaas Gusuu Kasaan Haida Elders Speak *(Kasaan Haida Heritage Foundation, 2002).*

In 1980 Michael E. Krauss, the noted Alaskan linguist and former director of the Alaska Native Language Center, predicted the imminent demise of the Haida language, stating that it, along with numerous other Native languages, would probably be "extinct by 2015" and several more "will be dead by 2030" (1980, 68). He identified approximately 100 Haida speakers, "the youngest of these in their forties" (33), and tied the remaining years for the language to the estimated life expectancy of these people. Krauss also posed and attempted to answer questions about whether schools might save the languages, and the role of bilingual education in language maintenance. He carefully distinguished between "transitional" programs, where the goal is to ultimately replace the Native language with English, and "maintenance" programs whereby "English would never entirely replace the Native language" (78), criticizing the fact that Alaska has followed the "transitional" model, which has done little to promote and hence regenerate Native languages. But Krauss also asserted that the "generation that is now able to speak Native and English, but is speaking

English only to its children is directly responsible for abandoning this heritage, irrecoverably" (67).

More recently, John Enrico, in the introduction to his *Haida Syntax* (2003), accuses the previous generation of Haida speakers of committing "linguistic suicide" (7) because they adopted the practice of speaking only English to their children. Given this situation, Enrico predicts that it is "extremely unlikely that even the most sophisticated and well-funded retention program could put off the imminent loss of the language" (7–8). Both linguists might be surprised to learn of the gains we are beginning to make here in Alaska. But before learning about our recent successes, it is important to understand something about our language situation.

Linguists have been studying the Haida language since John R. Swanton, anthropologist and linguist, traveled in the early 1900s to Haida *Gwaii* (Island), as it is affectionately called by the people themselves, in what is now known as the Queen Charlotte Islands, British Columbia, Canada. Swanton's foray into Haida country, which includes the southern portion of Southeast Alaska, where a group of Haida migrated northward sometime prior to contact with the non-Native population, was part of the Jesup North Pacific expedition, which aimed to describe and document apparently fast-disappearing aboriginal cultures. Swanton spent about a year in the area. In 1905 he published *Contributions to the Ethnology of the Haida*. It describes Haida beliefs, social organization, and customs as he found them after the devastating effects of contact had already taken their toll. By the time he arrived in Haida *Gwaii*, as many as twenty villages (280) had consolidated into two remaining villages, Masset and Skidegate in Canada, due primarily to the massive population decimation caused by infectious diseases such as smallpox, whooping cough, influenza, measles, and venereal disease, among others. In Alaska, the five or so original village sites had also moved and consolidated to two newly created villages, Hydaburg and (New) Kasaan. Some estimates put the overall Haida population at the time of contact somewhere between 10,000 and 15,000 with subsequent reduction of 80 to 90 percent (Boyd 1990).

In addition to writing the ethnography, Swanton spent a great deal of time transcribing Haida oral texts, and his publications include two large volumes of Haida stories collected mostly in the Queen Charlotte Islands: *Haida Texts and Myths: Skidegate Dialect*; *Haida Texts: Masset Dialect*; and *Haida Songs* collected in the southern and northern ends of the Queen Charlotte Islands, where two distinctly different dialects of the language are spoken. A small number of Alaskan Haida stories are found in the Massett collection. The Alaskan Haida language is most closely linked to the Massett dialect; differences between them are primarily ones of pronunciation. Swanton wrote down most of the stories he collected, acting as linguist transcriber, then translating the texts into English with assistance from bilingual Haida people. Until the 1970s, Swanton's texts were the primary source of Haida stories in print.

In 1972, Genevieve Soboloff, a fluent Alaskan Haida speaker, worked with the linguists Michael Krauss and Jack Osteen at the University of Alaska, Fairbanks, analyzing the Haida sound system. Shortly thereafter an Alaskan Haida writing system was designed and, in June of the same year, the first language workshop was held at Sheldon Jackson College, a former Presbyterian Mission boarding school for Natives, in Sitka, Alaska (Krauss, quoted in Lawrence 1977, 7).

Out of these workshops, the first Alaskan Haida texts written in both Haida and English were produced. These included several by Erma Lawrence and Robert and Nora Cogo developed specifically for language learning.[1] About the same time, in Ketchikan, the Alaska Society for the Preservation of Haida Language and Literature was formed to promote and perpetuate the language. In addition to producing texts, the society offered language workshops and classes, and many were inspired to learn or relearn their language.

My mother, Julie Jones Coburn (*Wahligidouk*), born in Kasaan in 1922, was one who took the opportunity to relearn her dormant Haida language when she had just turned fifty. She had grown up always understanding the language, because her parents spoke Haida regularly in the home to their children; however, my *chan* (grandfather) and *náan* (grandmother), like many other Haida people of the time, asked their children to answer in English because they recognized the importance of the immigrant's language to their children's future. They must have felt that they had to choose between two mutually exclusive options: saving their language or saving their children—and they chose to save their children. This is the generation accused of committing "linguistic suicide." Yet it was this generation who recognized and worked actively toward language revitalization with some success, as evidenced by people like my mother who chose to relearn the language.

Yet long-term language growth has been difficult to sustain due to many factors, including the fact that when Krauss published his assessment of the language in 1980, the number of *fluent* first-language Alaskan Haida speakers was small—perhaps no more than twenty or so, and they were all sixty years and older.

This small group, while dedicated to revitalizing the language, had no formal training in language teaching methods and no access to any kind of written language-teaching materials. The written materials were not so important to people like my mother, who had grown up hearing the language, but written materials were and are increasingly important to the children raised speaking English who have been educated in Western schools where developing literacy is paramount.

To their credit, this core group of elder speakers—Robert and Nora Cogo, Erma Lawrence, Christine Edenso, Jesse Natkong, Phyllis Almquist, Gladys Morrison, Beatrice Starkweather, Vesta Johnson, Walter Young, and Clara Natkong, among others, worked diligently to create the necessary teaching materials. Their contributions form the bulk of texts produced between 1972 and the mid-1980s. These texts did offer some support for the language workshops and classes, and dedicated students who were fortunate to study intensely with fluent speakers—and therefore had the chance to hear the language regularly spoken—made the most gains. But the teaching materials they created, while valuable as supporting bilingual texts for someone who has already acquired minimal fluency, are only modestly useful for beginning learners because they assume the ability to read Haida, as well as close access to a fluent speaker. With the increasing age of the fluent elders, this possibility dwindled year after year—especially given the fact that young people have often moved away from the villages to larger urban areas, primarily for better job or educational opportunities. Overall, the Haida population living in the United States is approximately 3,000, with only about 300 or so living in the two villages, Hydaburg and Kasaan, combined. Many Haida have moved to other larger towns or cities, but primarily to Ketchikan, Anchorage, Seattle, and the Pacific Northwest. This has increased the need for language-teaching materials that address the continuing loss of fluent speakers and the migration of people away from villages.

So while the desire to "save" our language has always been strong, the necessary material resources and training have not been there. The number of once-fluent speakers has continued to dwindle until we found ourselves in 2002 with only ten or so, all seventy-five years and older, whose language skills had grown rusty. Unfortunately, the dire predictions about the imminent loss of our language have always been in danger of coming true. What possible reasons could there be for hope?

Hope sometimes arrives in unexpected ways. Fortunately, there have always been a few dedicated younger Haida language learners who stayed interested and motivated and continued to learn the language as best they could. These people became an important part of the project that arrived like a gift in late 2003. This gift came unexpectedly from Sealaska Heritage Institute (SHI), the nonprofit arm of the "for-profit" Southeast Alaska Native Regional corporation (Sealaska Incorporated) located in Juneau, established through the Alaska Native Claims Settlement Act (ANCSA) enacted in 1971. SHI, established in 1980 at the direction of the elders who recognized the need for such an organization, assumed responsibility for administering the education, language, and cultural programs for Southeast Alaska's Tlingit, Haida, and Tsimshian peoples.[2] In 1997, SHI's board of trustees, after viewing Hawaii's successful language revitalization programs, made language restoration its top priority. In 2002 SHI sought and ultimately was awarded a three-year, $467,722 grant from the United States Department of Education.[3]

The Haida portion of the grant was written by Jordan Lachler, a linguist hired by SHI in 2002.[4] Lachler was completing a dissertation on the Laguna Keres language through the University of New Mexico and came to Alaska to finish his own work while gaining experience in indigenous language restoration, one of his primary interests. Soon after he arrived, he noticed how few Haida language materials existed. He traveled to Ketchikan and Hydaburg, met with the some of the elders, and returned excited about the possibilities of helping restore the language if adequate funding could be secured. This became the genesis of the Department of Education grant to provide bilingual education to Haida children in a semi-immersion setting. The project directly addressed one of the most significant previously identified problems: the need for appropriate beginning level teaching materials. It also took aim at the second problem: the need for Haida language teacher training.

As submitted, the proposal identified the ten Alaska Haida elder speakers who live in Hydaburg, Ketchikan, and Kasaan. These people were the master teachers to six younger apprentice language learners. The teams work closely together daily—the goal has been to develop the apprentices' language skills to the level needed to be able to teach the language themselves. The teams, with guidance from the linguist, also developed beginning-level teaching resources which have been incorporated into the final curriculum products.[5]

Additionally, two younger language learners with minimal fluency developed through years of persistent, intermittent study—Cherilyn Holter, raised by her grandparents Willis and Hazel Bell, and Linda Schrack, granddaughter of Robert and Nora Cogo—were called upon to work as Haida language "teachers-in-training." In addition to working closely with elders, they have continued to teach the language in school classes in Ketchikan and Hydaburg—Schrack in the local Head Start program, and Holter in the Hydaburg elementary school. They also produced teaching resources for the final curriculum and have field tested the products in their classrooms.

Interestingly, and as often happens with multiyear grant-funded projects written with high ideals and no crystal ball to predict the future, there have been many unforeseen benefits and many unforeseen challenges. One significant challenge emerged with the project team's realization that the final curriculum needed to serve at least two different audiences and at least two different teaching situations. The ideal arena, and the one in mind when the proposal was written, would be to use the curriculum in service of a Haida language immersion school, located near Hydaburg and Kasaan. But this school does not yet exist, and making it a reality will require time and much funding. The dream has been for beginning K-2 students to spend a half day intensely learning Haida. In the second half of the day, students would learn their regular subjects in English, with Haida used progressively more and more as their language fluency increased. As these students advanced, the language program would expand to include higher grade levels.

The other potential audience for the curriculum is certified elementary school teachers in Southeastern Alaskan schools, including Ketchikan, Kasaan, and Hydaburg, who are themselves not Haida, as there are no Haidas living in southern Southeast Alaska who hold elementary teaching credentials. But the non-Haida teachers often have significant numbers of Haida children in their classrooms. The most useful products for these teachers was identified as a curriculum that meets required Alaska state educational standards in each subject area and provides a strong "cultural enrichment" component, rather than focusing solely on Haida language growth. Additionally, in order for the curriculum to be useful in the regular nonimmersion classroom, it would need to address the reality that the certified teachers using it would, at best, understand only a few Haida language words or phrases. Their interest in the curriculum would most likely be that it addresses Alaska state standards and also integrates a strong local, cultural component into the classroom. Significant Haida language growth would not necessarily be the teachers' primary goal in using the curriculum. So as the project began, the overall aim was to produce curriculum that both Haida language teachers *and* non-Haida-speaking classroom elementary teachers could use for different purposes.

These apparently competing goals sometimes made for a confusing clash of expected outcomes, depending on whose perspective was viewing the curriculum. In practical terms, many hands were needed to work on specific parts of the pieces, with each person having little knowledge of the other person's expertise. Since neither the linguist, the Haida language teachers-in-training, nor the master-apprentice teams had ever written elementary school curricula, this meant that non-Haida-speaking elementary school teachers were contracted to create the basic format of the units, writing them from the perspective of how they might be integrated into mainstream Southeast Alaska elementary classrooms, with Haida language embedded in the units.

For example, Unit One, *Gíist Uu Díi Iijang* (Who Am I?), allows students to explore their own heritage and family lineages through introducing them to Haida oral history and kinship systems and then having them create their own booklets based upon their own personal histories. Students are taught related Haida words such as *íihlangaa* (boy), *jáadaa* (girl), *kíii* (name), *kugíin* (book), and questions with responses such as "*San uu dáng kya'áang?*" (What is your name?), "*hinuu díi kya'áng*" (My name is). In practical terms, in order for the students to actually have the chance to hear the language, either a guest language teacher will come to the classroom, or in cases where no speaker is available, audio CDs are included with the curriculum units. The linguist and language project staff added the actual Haida-language text portions and also created supplementary language-learning materials. The process was sometimes cumbersome, but it also generated several unexpected benefits.

These benefits included an abundance of materials actually produced, some not directly usable in any of the curriculum units, but available to potential language learners nonetheless. These include online resources and college credit classes sponsored by SHI and offered through the University of Alaska, Southeast in Ketchikan, Hydaburg, and Juneau. These have helped create a pool of adult second-language learners who have significantly increased their language abilities. So what was previously a steadily decreasing number based on ten remaining fluent elder speakers has expanded to a cadre of approximately thirty new adult language learners with the potential for many more to follow suit.

As it turned out, our largest audience for Haida language learning has been the adults who have long wanted to learn their ancestral language but did not live close to fluent elder speakers and had no access to any kind of audio-related language-learning materials. This project addresses this need through online resources now available through Sealaska Heritage Institute's website. See www.haidalanguage.org for examples and links to other language resources including an online discussion forum with words and phrases sent weekly to participants.

The college credit classes have become part of a plan to develop a "Teaching Indigenous Languages" Certificate, sponsored by SHI and offered through the University of Alaska, Southeast, to address the need for training a younger generation of teachers beyond the students able to work as apprentices directly with the elders. This entailed the linguist Jordan Lachler developing Haida language fluency through working closely with elders, so that his abilities were strong enough to teach the classes to adult learners.

In the process of teaching the classes, Lachler created numerous products including textbooks with accompanying audio CDs. He also has written several handbooks that explain Haida language grammatical features, written so students can understand and practice typical Haida language patterns in order to better learn how to create conversational sentences rather than simply memorizing words, which until now has been the case for most adult Haida language learners.

As someone who has had the good fortune to benefit from the project's language classes and teaching materials, I can attest to language growth in myself and others with whom I've had the good fortune to work and study. How thrilling to realize the dire predictions about our language do not have to come true. Our success is due in no small part to individuals who have committed to learning the language and to passing on what they know within their own families and communities. But it is also important to recognize that language growth of this magnitude would not be possible without institutional leadership buying into the premise that we *can* save our own languages, and then also providing the financial resources necessary to do so.

Notes

Portions of this paper, significantly revised, have appeared in "Alaskan Haida Stories of Language Growth and Regeneration," in *American Indian Quarterly* 30, nos. 1 and 2 (spring 2006) and "Wahligidouk: Giver of Gifts," in *Atlantis: A Women's Studies Journal* 29, no. 2 (spring/summer 2005).

1. The following participants are noted at the first, second, and third Haida language workshops held in Sitka, Alaska: Florence Adams, Edna Alexander, Phyllis Almquist, Lydia Charles, Verley George, Selina Peratovich, Marian Hawkins, Gladys Morrison, Julia Pace, Beatrice Starkweather, Fred Wallace, Jones Yeltatzie, Walter B. Young (*Xaada Gyaahlaang K'wa'andaa . . .*, Lawrence); Charles Natkong Sr., Jessie Natkong, Viola Lockhart, Nelson Frank (*Xaadas Kil Asgyaan . . .*, Natkong et al.); Mr. and Mrs. Louis Kitkoon, Vesta Johnson, Nancy McRoy, Clara Natkong, and Ada Yovanovich (*Haida Language Workshop*, Lawrence et al.). See Suggestions for Further Reading for texts by Robert and Nora Cogo, Christine Edenso, Charles Natkong, and Erma Lawrence.

2. Sealaska Corporation provides direct financial support to Sealaska Heritage Institute. Their commitment to supporting SHI cultural and language programs has been evident in the fact they continue to provide funding to SHI, even during years when Sealaska Corporation suffered financial losses.

3. Sealaska Heritage Institute is sponsoring the project through a $467,722 grant from the U.S. Department of Education sought on behalf of the Haida language and culture. The project is 97 percent federally funded and 3 percent funded by nongovernment sources.

4. This proposal was modeled after an earlier successfully funded grant written by SHI staff. The earlier grant provided $278,129 from the U.S. Department of Educa-

tion on behalf of the Tlingit language and culture. The project is 95 percent federally funded and 5 percent funded by nongovernment sources.

5. Recognizing a need for the project staff to have a central location from which the linguist and curriculum developers could work, SHI opened a second office in Ketchikan. Sealaska Timber Corporation, a subsidiary of Sealaska Corporation, donated the space.

II

Empire: Processing Colonization

It is such a secret place, the land of tears.
—Antoine de Saint Exupéry

This part contains selections that evoke the colonial and neocolonial experience of the indigenous people of Alaska as they were exposed to or exploited by colonial Europeans and, later, Americans. The colonizing process almost always has two aspects: resource exploitation and the forced remaking of the human cultural landscape. The indigenous people of Alaska during the colonial period were often forced to become Christian, were subject to deadly epidemic diseases, and lost control of their land base. By the 1950s and 1960s, with the discovery of oil, new pressures emerged to change the indigenous worldview from one of living in concert with the environment to one of exploiting natural resources.

A number of selections in this part address disease, struggles for land, and political issues. Harold Napoleon's heartbreaking essay relates the disappearance of the older traditional worlds of Native people and the terrible hardships endured from epidemic disease. He argues that because of large-scale epidemics, Native people dealt with trauma that is still with us today.

The Russian era of the eighteenth century was the beginning of the colonial period for Alaska's indigenous people. The early American period began in 1867, when the U.S. Army occupied the former Russian stronghold in southeastern Alaska. The bombardment of Angoon, a Tlingit village, by the U.S. Navy occurred during the early American period. In her essay, Nancy Furlow addresses the tragic impact of this event. Selections in part 1 capture the undisturbed world that existed before boarding schools arrived to "kill the Indian and save the child," the name of the policy referring to the boarding and residential schools established by the government to remove Indian and Native children from their homes and force them to speak English and give up their traditional religions and worldviews. This policy created long-term and multigenerational damage and trauma as children were often physically and psychologically abused.

As indigenous people began to take active roles in the twentieth century, their actions led to court battles over issues of "Indian Country," the 1971 Alaska Native Claims Settlement Act (see Maria Williams's and William Hensley's essays in this part), which led to a Native solidarity movement (see Williams) and a proactive political scenario. Steve Langdon and Aaron Leggett address how the Dena'ina people have survived as the city of Anchorage literally grew up around them, engulfing their traditional hunting and fishing regions, and how they have struggled to educate the newly arriving population about their land.

As indigenous people adapted to the modern American world and economy they have had to struggle with how to maintain a subsistence-based economy within a capitalistic system. Evon Peter, a younger Native leader, has been at the forefront of efforts to protect the indigenous land base from further loss and devastation and addresses this in his essay. Ted Mayac highlights the violation of indigenous intellectual and cultural property rights, as he writes about how his home Iñupiat community of King Island has been exploited by a musical based on King Island history.

Subhankar Banerjee's essay poignantly addresses the painful issues surrounding resource exploitation on indigenous lands. He is most recognized for his photographic works on Alaska's Arctic National Wildlife Refuge. Banerjee's perspective is sympathetic to the indigenous people who continue to hunt and fish on their ancestral lands and who are most impacted by oil, mining, and other destructive forces that affect the environment and also create challenging political situations.

To contextualize the diversity of the essays in this section, a brief outline of the different colonial periods in Alaska is in order. Although the colonial era effected many negative outcomes, there are positives to acknowledge as well, among them heroes who protected Native sovereignty and human rights. These included the first Russian priests and monks who came to Alaska in the 1790s, and also kind and compassionate American missionaries who attempted to protect Native culture and languages. It is sometimes difficult to show the complexities of the colonizing process and we hope this section does address some of the overarching issues.

Alaska Colonial History

1741	"Discovery" of Alaska by the Russian imperial government
1754–1799	Russian *Promyshlenniki* or Fur Rush period
1799–1867	Russian America Company established, operating as a monopoly controlled by the Russian imperial government and private investors
1867	Treaty of Cession in which Russia sells its investments in Russian America for $6.2 million
1867–1958	American period begins with army detachments in southeastern Alaska
1880–1915	Gold Rush period
1854–1880s	American whalers hunt beluga and bowhead whales, as well as walrus, along the Arctic coastal areas
1959–1971	Native Solidarity movement and oil era begins with statehood
1971–present	Alaska Native Claims Settlement Act (ANCSA) signed into law, initiating new and different types of struggles for Alaskans

The above dates indicate the periods of Russian and American colonial presence in Alaska and the years of subsequent resource exploitation as well. The Russian and U.S. periods in Alaska constitute a parallel story of resource exploitation, the twin of colonization.[1]

RUSSIAN PERIOD

Alaska is a beautiful landscape that has an indigenous population with a remarkable history. Most of Alaska's history is in the oral narratives of the many indigenous villages and societies that have populated this vast subcontinent of North America. The colonial history, which is the most painful, begins in the mid-eighteenth century, when Russian explorers learned from the indigenous Siberian people that there was a "great land" that lay to the east. The Russian imperial government sent several voyages to explore and map the area. Impressive exploits of Russian navigators document their first encounters with the indigenous people. The word "Alaska," dervived from an Unangan word, dates from this period. The earliest explorers, including Vitus Bering, George Stellar, and Alexei Chirikov, made great sacrifices (Bering died), and some suffered shipwreck in Alaska, but members of Bering's crew returned to Russia with an impressive cargo of fur.[2] Among the most prized fur was that of the sea otter, the densest fur of any animal on the planet. In the eighteenth and nineteenth centuries the fur market was global market, equivalent to oil in today's geopolitical climate. A fur rush ensued, leading to the establishment of Russian outposts in the Aleutian Islands, Kodiak Island, south central and southeastern Alaska, and a few places in mainland southwestern Alaska (see Solojova this volume).

The Russian period can be broken down into three subperiods. The initial Promyshlenniki period (1754–99) was the most destructive, primarily to the Unangan people on the Aleutian Islands, the Alutiit people on Kodiak Island, the Alaska Peninsula and Prince William Sound area, the southern Dena'ina Athabascan, and to a certain extent the Tlingit. In 1799 the Russian American Company (RAC) was established as a monopoly and controlled by the Russian imperial government and private investors. Other fur companies and independent fur companies were either absorbed by the RAC or eliminated. The first director, Alexander Baranov, ran the company from 1799 to 1817 in a rather despotic fashion. From 1818 to 1867 the RAC was run by Russian naval officers and a less brutal approach to colonizing Russian America began. Exploration of the Arctic coastline and establishment of trade posts in mainland Alaska occurred during this time.

Because of the Unangan and Kodiak peoples' skill and use of kayaks, the men were forced to go on long hunting expeditions, sometimes as far as California, while their women and children were held as hostages. The Unangan population between 1750 and 1800 was reduced by 90 percent. The villages on Kodiak Island had numbered fifty-six, but by the mid-nineteenth century the Russians moved them all to seven settlements, a consolidation following population loss and also a means of preventing rebellion. As the sea otter was hunted to near extinction, the Russian fur companies moved farther and farther east, coming up against some resistance. But it was not until they reached the Tlingit settlements in the late 1790s and 1800–1810 that Russian expansion in the Pacific was stopped. The Russians were not able to colonize mainland Alaska, although they did conduct successful explorations of the interior and the Arctic coastline.

DATES OF RUSSIAN EXPANSION IN ALASKA

1743–54	Near Islands, Commander Islands
1755–80	Remaining Aleutian Islands, parts of Alaska Peninsula
1781–98	Kodiak, Pribilof Islands, Prince William Sound, southern Kenai Peninsula, Iliamna, upper Cook Inlet, Yakutat area
1799–1812	Sitka, Wrangell, and Fort Ross (in northern California)
1819	Nushagak trade post only

1820–21	Copper River, Kotzbue and Seward Peninsula, Bering Straits (exploration only)
1830	St. Lawrence Island (trade only)
1832	Mid-Kuskokwim river area (exploration and trade posts only)
1833	St. Michaels in Norton Sound (trade post)
1835	Ikogmiut (trade post)
1838	Nulato (trade post)

AMERICAN PERIOD, 1867–1958

After the Russian colonial period ended in 1867, a new and different kind of colonial presence emerged: the U.S. government. The Treaty of Cession was signed in 1867, the United States purchased the Russian American Company's assets in Alaska for $6.2 million, and Alaska became a territory of the United States. Initially the United States did not know what to do with Alaska, first making it a military district and then, after the discovery of gold in 1880, a mining district. Among other resources that proved profitable for U.S. companies and investors were the whale industry, canneries, and the fur seal industry on the Pribilof Islands.

1867–1890s	U.S. military and naval presence; U.S. military exploration
1854–1890s	Commercial whalers in western Arctic
1880s–1915	Gold rush
1878–1930s	Salmon canneries[3] and Alaska Commercial Company, Northern Commercial Company, the "Syndicate" and corporate involvement in Alaska
1867–1940s	Lack of civil rights, lack of voting rights, etc.

Between the first and second world wars, Native people were subject to western educational practices, Christian missionaries, a changing economy, loss of lands, and lack of civil rights. In 1959 Alaska became the forty-ninth state in the Union and Alaska Native people were faced with loss of land as the newly created State of Alaska divided the land between itself and the federal government in order to profit from the upcoming oil leases. The discovery of oil in the Arctic Slope region was one of the main reasons that Alaska was pushed into becoming a state rather than remaining a territory. This led to a major Native solidary movement and the Alaska Native Claims Settlement Act (see Hensley and Williams in this section).

As Native people in Alaska have survived into the twenty-first century, there have been changes, adaptations, and tragedies, yet languages, music and dance, artforms, and subsistence lifestyles have remained intact. The population has reached the numbers estimated at the time of first European contact and it appears that indigenous people have survived. Today Alaska's indigenous people face new challenges mostly related to the friction of adapting to a western model based on resource exploitation rather than the indigenous philosophy of living in balance with the land and sustainable coexistence with nature.

Notes

1. The colonial interests in Alaska are a mirror of the larger colonial period in which European companies such as the Dutch East India Company, the Hudson's Bay Company, and the Russian American Company all categorically pillaged indigenous communities to obtain land, gold, furs, and new foods (potatoes, corn, beans, squash, avocados, tomatoes, chocolate, tobacco, etc.).

2. The official "discovery" of Alaska was in 1741 and is credited to the voyages of Alexei Chirikov and Vitus Bering. Bering's ship was wrecked on an island, but members of the crew, including George Stellar, built a smaller ship from the wreckage and sailed back to Russia the following year. Chirikov did sail back to Alaska in 1741 with reports of the "great land."

3. By 1888 the canneries near Karluk (on Kodiak Island) processed more than two and a half million salmon; the following year it increased to more than three million (Hinckley 1972, 128). Alaska became the world's "salmon capital," producing more canned salmon than any other place on earth (Gruening 1968, 75). The canneries practiced reckless overfishing, seriously depleting the salmon runs throughout Alaska with disastrous consequences. In 1889 the U.S. Congress passed an act to regulate salmon fisheries and banned the use of barricades, but no fund was set up to enforce the act until 1892, and as it provided for only one inspector and one assistant for the entire territory of Alaska, it was ineffectual at best.

Yuuyaraq: The Way of the Human Being

Harold Napoleon *(Yup'ik)*

Harold Napoleon (Yup'ik) was born and raised in Hooper Bay, Alaska. He lives in Anchorage with his wife, Margaret, and his family and continues to work for Native communities. The following is an excerpt from Napoleon's powerful narrative Yuuyaraq: Way of the Human Being, *written while he was in prison, about the stark and painful reality of Native alcohol abuse. It was a landmark publication, one of the first analyses of the history and impact of the epidemic diseases that destroyed many indigenous communities in the late nineteenth and early twentieth centuries. Although he explores painful issues, Napoleon conveys overall a message of positive hope, that understanding our history and dealing with what Native communities suffered is a path toward knowing where we are going.*

Introduction

For the past four years I have repeatedly tried to write letters and papers addressing the problem of alcoholism and alcohol abuse among Alaska's Native people. Each time I have stopped or thrown the paper away because the picture was never complete. There was always something missing. My efforts were like an incomplete sentence.

Since the death of my son, due directly to my own abuse of and addiction to alcohol, understanding the causes of this disease has occupied much of my time here at the Fairbanks Correctional Center. This prison has been like a laboratory to me; there is no shortage of subjects to be studied, namely, Alaska Natives from all parts of the state whose own abuse of alcohol also brought them here.

From my own family and village history and the histories and backgrounds of the hundreds of young Native people I have met, I have a profile of the Native addict or abuser. While the subjects may be from different villages and tribes, in almost every case the background remains the same. So now it is possible to make fairly accurate statements as to the cause or causes of this disease which yearly takes so many lives through suicide, homicide, accidental death, disease, and heartbreak. It also helps us understand the hopelessness, the frustration, and the anger, the prejudice so many people have, which tragically erupt in violence under the influence of alcohol.

The theory that Native people are somehow biologically susceptible to alcohol abuse and alcoholism may have some credence, but I have discounted it as being almost insignificant. Through my own studies of the history of Alaska Native people and the history of the abusers and alcoholics I have met here and by listening to elders, I have come to the conclusion that the primary cause of alcoholism is not physical but *spiritual*. And to carry this one step further, since the disease is not physical or caused by physical or biological factors, then the cure must also be of the *spirit*.

As to my credentials, I do not hold a master's or a doctorate, but I am a Yup'ik and I was born into a world that no longer exists. My education began in my village of Hooper Bay. I did not begin to learn English until I went to school at six years of age. I then was sent at age twelve to Copper Valley School, supposedly because the school in my village could not teach me what I needed to know. I love to read. From the first day that I learned the alphabet and acquired a dictionary, I have read everything I could get my hands on. I ruined my eyes reading. The whole world opened up to me and I drank it in thirstily. I do not wish to boast, but I think I know the English language as well as if not better than most English speakers. I learned it from books. I am also fluent in and think in my Native tongue.

I graduated from St. Mary's High School in May 1968 and was valedictorian of my class. Thereafter I went to Great Falls, Montana, for my first year of university where I chose to study history. From there I transferred to the University of Alaska where I also studied history. In 1972 I became executive director of the Association of Village Council Presidents and in that capacity got to know more intimately my own Yup'ik people. All I had to offer them was ideas and I never tired of presenting these. The germ of freedom and self-government was introduced to them then and, happily, today they still seek independence and self-government. I was 22, I was tireless, and I fell in love with them. Soon their problems became mine. Naively, I thought I could solve them all, but needless to say, I did not. I helped house them, clothe them, feed them, educate them, and protect their rights. I lobbied on their behalf and fought tooth and nail for them. But I now see I failed to look to the most critical part of our existence—our *spiritual* well being.

When I first started to work for our villages I did not drink; I did not like to drink—I didn't even like the taste. But after five years of countless meetings in Anchorage, Juneau and Washington, being with others for whom drinking was a part of their lives, like so many other Native people, I soon became addicted. But I did not know this; it just became a part of my life. Perhaps I took my responsibility and myself too seriously, but it was what I perceived to be my failures and the subsequent frustration and anger that led to my becoming an alcoholic. I was too young, too inexperienced, and I took everything to heart. But something in my soul, in my background, my family and village's history, had preconditioned me to internalize and personalize every perceived defeat.

This is not to say I did no good. Certainly I must have, because in many ways, I left our people in better shape than when they gave me so much responsibility at age twenty-two. I gave them my best, and so did my family. We sacrificed a great deal for them. I was hardly home but my children had to stay home waiting for me. Yes, I gave my best and my children gave me, their father, to others.

My whole adult life has been spent working for our Yup'ik people; I have had no other employer but them. I have been their executive director, vice-president, president and vice-chairman. This is my history until June of 1984 when my world, as I knew it then, ended with the death of my son.

I am now 39 years of age at the writing of this paper. The first 21 years of my life I was in school, and the next 13 years I spent working for our Yup'ik people. The last five years I have spent in prison as a direct result of my alcoholism. These last five years I have spent grieving, not only for my son, but also for all the others who have died in this long night of our alcohol-induced suffering. I have also spent that time looking into my own soul and the souls of my fellow Native people who have become afflicted with this disease.

It is a disease because the people who suffer from it do not volunteer to become infected. No one volunteers to live a life of misery, sorrow, disappointment, and hopelessness. No one in his right mind chooses to lose a loved one, to break his family's heart, to go to prison. It is a disease because no one will beat his wife, molest his children, or give them little rest, because he wants to. No man dreams of this. Yet sadly, this is what is happening too often in our villages and in our homes, and we have to stop it. We have to arrest this disease, this unhappiness, this suffering, and the good news is that we can.

This paper tries to deal with the causes of alcoholism and alcohol abuse among this generation of Alaska Native people. It is not intended to be a history or a study of the cultures of the various tribes. But because of the nature of the subject, pertinent aspects of the old Yup'ik culture will be briefly discussed so as to give the reader some background and a better understanding of the subject. Things don't just happen; there are causes and reasons, and if we try to understand these causes and reasons, then conceivably we will know how to better deal with the problem.

Although I am an Alaska Native, I am first a Yup'ik, and it is from this perspective that I think and write. However, I have found so many similarities among the important cultural aspects of the various tribes that it would be safe to say that we are, in fact, one tribe of many families.

Yuuyaraq

Prior to the arrival of Western people, the Yup'ik were alone in their riverine and Bering Sea homeland—they and the spirit beings that made things the way they were. Within this homeland they were free and secure. They were ruled by the customs, traditions, and spiritual beliefs of their people, and shaped by these and their environment: the tundra, the river and the Bering Sea.

Their world was complete; it was a very old world. They called it *Yuuyaraq*, "the way of being a human being." Although unwritten, this way can be compared to Mosaic law because it governed all aspects of a human being's life. It defined the correct behavior between parents and children, grandparents and grandchildren, mothers-in-law and daughters and sons-in-law. It defined the correct behavior between cousins (there were many cousins living together in a village). It determined which members of the community could talk with each other and which members could tease each other. It defined acceptable behavior for all members of the community. It outlined the protocol for every and any situation that human beings might find themselves in.

Yuuyaraq defined the correct way of thinking and speaking about all living things, especially the great sea and land mammals on which the Yup'ik relied for food, clothing, shelter, tools, kayaks, and other essentials. These great creatures were sensitive; they were able to understand human conversations, and they demanded and received respect. *Yuuyaraq* prescribed the correct method of hunting and fishing and the correct way of handling all fish and game caught by the hunter in order to honor and appease their spirits and maintain a harmonious relationship with them.

Yuuyaraq encompassed the spirit world in which the Yup'ik lived. It outlined the way of living in harmony within this spirit world and with the spirit beings that inhabited this world. To the Yup'ik, the land, the rivers, the heavens, the seas, and all that dwelled within them were spirit, and therefore sacred. They were born not only to the physical world of the Bering Sea, the Yukon, and the Kuskokwim rivers, but into a spirit world as well. Their arts, tools, weapons, kayaks and umiaks, songs and dances, customs and traditions, thoughts and actions—all bore the imprint of the spirit world and the spirit beings.

When the Yup'ik walked out into the tundra or launched their kayaks into the river or the Bering Sea, they entered into the spiritual realm. They lived in deference to this spiritual universe, of which they were, perhaps, the weakest members. *Yuuyaraq* outlined for the Yup'ik the way of living in this spiritual universe. It was the law by which they lived.

The Spirit World

To the Western explorers, whalers, traders, and missionaries who first met them, the Yup'ik were considered backward savages steeped in superstition. Their villages were small and hard to find because they were a part of the earth. Grass grew on their houses, making it hard to see the village. Only when the warriors came out in their kayaks and umiaks did the newcomers see them and then they were surprised that humans would already be in this part of the world. The riverbanks were red with fish drying on racks, along with seal, walrus, and whale meat. Women and children were everywhere, curious and afraid. The old men were curious but unafraid, their interest piqued by these white men who came on winged wooden ships. They could not communicate by tongue so they tried to converse by signs. The white men gave the Eskimo scouts small gifts. The Yup'ik soon saw that these whites seemed friendly so they allowed them into their villages although the newcomers did not want to eat when offered food. The visitors saw the semi-subterranean sod houses with underground entrances and they smelled the stench from within. They saw the oily, unwashed faces and the tangled hair. They saw the worn skin clothes and smelled the seal oil. They saw the labrets, the nose bones, and the beauty marks on the women, and the fierce, proud faces of the men. Then they were invited to a night of dancing. There they saw the wooden masks worn by them during their dances. They felt the beating of the drums and were carried away by the singers, drummers, and dancers.

To the explorer or missionary witnessing the dancing in a dimly lit, crowded, stifling *qasgiq* (men's house), the men, stripped of their clothing, and the women, dancing naked to the waist, must have seemed like heathen savages. The *kass'aqs* (white men) thought they were witnessing a form of devil worship and might even have been frightened by it. The white men did not understand what they were seeing. They did not know that for a brief time they had entered the spirit world of the Yup'ik Eskimo.

To the Yupiit, the world visible to the eye and available to the senses showed only one aspect of being.[1] Unseen was the spirit world, a world just as important as the visible, if not more so. In fact, Yup'ik life was lived in deference to this world and the spirit beings that inhabited it. What the white men saw was not worship of the devil, but a people paying attention—being mindful of the spirit beings of their world with whom they had to live in harmony. They knew that the temporal and the spiritual were intertwined and they needed to maintain a balance between the two. The Westerners had witnessed the physical representation of that spirit world as presented by dance, song, and mask. But they did not understand what they were seeing; they were strangers in the spirit world of the Bering Sea Eskimo.

Iinruq

The Yup'ik word for spirit is *iinruq*. The Yup'ik believed that all things, animate and inanimate, had *iinruq*. *Iinruq* was the essence, the soul, of the object or being. Hence, a caribou was a caribou only because it possessed a caribou *iinruq*, a caribou spirit. *Iinruq* were indestructible, unlike the bodies in which they resided. And in the case of men, fish, and game, death was the spirit leaving the body. This is why the Yup'ik prescribed respectful ways of treating even dead animals. They believed the *iinruq* would, in time, take another body and come back, and if it had been treated with respect, it would be happy to give itself to the hunter again. For a people solely dependent on sea and land mammals, fish, and waterfowl for subsistence, it was imperative that all members of the community treat all animals with respect or face starvation as a result of an offended spirit. For this reason, annual feasts were held to celebrate and appease the spirits of the animals the village had caught during that year. Some white men witnessed such feasts.

The Russian naval officer L. A. Zagoskin and the American ethnographer Edward W. Nelson witnessed the Bladder Feast in the nineteenth century. They called it that because the center of attention seemed to be the bladders of sea mammals hanging in the center of the *qasgiq*. Hanging with the bladders were spears, throwing darts, bows and arrows—all the hunting implements of the hunters. Both observers were moved by the dancing, the oratory they did not understand, and the ritual. But what they did not understand was the unseen, the spirits represented by the bladders. Not only the animals possessed *iinruq*, humans also possessed them. But human spirits were not called *iinruq*. In the Hooper Bay dialect, they are called *anerneq—literally*, "breath" and as in animals, a human being could not live without its breath. Death came when the *anerneq* left the body due to injury, illness, or by the will of the person. The human spirit was a very powerful spirit and, like the spirits of other living creatures, was reborn when its name was given to a newborn. These spirits were appeased and celebrated through the Great Feast of the Dead, as Nelson called it.

Even so, animal and human spirits wandered the earth, as did monsters and creatures of the deep and the underground, good spirits and evil spirits *(alangrut)* that either helped or caused havoc, even death, for humans and animals alike. Every physical manifestation—plenty of food or famine, good weather or bad, good luck or bad, health or illness—had a spiritual cause. This is why the shamans, the *angalkuq*, were the most important men and women in the village. The *angalkuq* were the village historians, physicians, judges, arbitrators, and interpreters of *Yuuyaraq*. They also understood the spirit world and at times entered into it to commune with the spirit beings in fulfillment of their responsibility as intermediaries between humans and the spiritual realm. *Angalkuq* are said to have gone to the moon, to the bottom of the sea, and to the bowels of the earth in their search for understanding and solutions to problems that faced their people, such as famine, bad weather, and illness.

In the old Yup'ik world, the *angalkuq* were powerful and indispensable forces because they represented, protected, and upheld *Yuuyaraq*, even against the spiritual realm, of which they were members. They were the guardians of an ancient culture that had become brittle with age, a culture whose underpinnings the rest of the world would never understand, a culture that was about to crumble as a result of temporal forces from the one direction the *angalkuq* were not looking—the physical world.

Illness and Disease

Not knowing of microbes, bacteria, or viruses, the old Yup'ik attributed illness to the invasion of the body by evil spirits. They knew that certain plants and spoiled food caused death and they strictly forbade the eating of them. But illness not attributed to the ingestion of poisons through the mouth was attributed to evil spirits. Such illness was treated by the *angalkuq* in their role as medicine men and women. Certain herbs, plants, and even animal parts provided commonly known remedies for many ailments suffered by the Yup'ik. They also had home remedies for small burns and cuts, sore backs, sprains, and other minor ailments. The *angalkuq* were not called in unless the illness was deemed to be serious and of an unknown nature, probably caused by an evil spirit and thus requiring a spiritual remedy.

The *angalkuq* must have known that some of the ailments were, by nature, physical. Their knowledge of the human anatomy was probably as good as that of their Western counterparts at that time. Some *angalkuq* were even said to have performed surgeries, amputations, and autopsies. They had names for all major bones, muscles, arteries, veins, and organs, and knew roughly the function of each. But their remedies for unknown disease were different from their Western counterparts who used bromides and elixirs, while the *angalkuq* used songs, dances, and chants. The important thing to remember is that the old Yupiit believed that illnesses not attributed to the ingestion of poisons or injury was caused by the invasion of the body by evil spirits. With the arrival of Western man, the Yupiit (and *Yuuyaraq)* would be accosted by diseases from which they would never recover. The old Yup'ik culture, the spirit world and its guardian, the *angalkuq*, were about to receive a fatal wounding.

The World Goes Upside Down

When the first white men arrived in the Yup'ik villages, the people did not immediately abandon their old ways. It is historical fact that they resisted Russian efforts to colonize them. They did not abandon their spirit world or their beliefs upon first hearing the Christian message of the priests. That the missionaries met resistance is clear from the derogatory and antagonistic references they made about the *angalkuq* in their diaries. They called them rascals, tricksters, even agents of the devil.

The Yupiit saw missionaries as curiosities, as they saw all white men. The Yupiit said of them, *yuunritut,* "they are not human beings." Obviously they were not impressed by the white men, even though they quickly adopted some of their technology and goods. But resistance to Western rule would crumble, *Yuuyaraq* would be abandoned, and the spirit world would be displaced by Christianity. The change was brought about as a result of the introduction of diseases that had been born in the slums of Europe during the dark and Middle Ages, diseases carried by the traders, the whalers, and the missionaries. To these diseases the Yup'ik and other Native tribes had no immunity, and to these they would lose up to 60 percent of their people. As a result of epidemics, the Yup'ik world would go upside down; it would end. This period of Yup'ik history is vague. There is no oral or written record of their reaction to this experience, but we can and must attempt in our minds to recreate what happened because this cataclysm of mass death changed the persona, the life view, and the worldview, of the Yup'ik people.

The Great Death

As a child I heard references to *yuut tuqurpallratni*—"when a great many died," or the Great Death. I never understood when it happened, nor was I told in detail what it was. But I learned that it was a time-marker for our Yup'ik people and that it was caused by disease. I heard references to *yuut tuqurpallratni* from three men, my granduncles, all of whom are now dead. Their white man-given names were Joe Seton, Frank Smart, and Sam Hill, but of course we did not call them that. To me they were my *Apakcuaq*, my *Apaiyaq*, and my *Angakalaq*. In almost every reference to the experience, they used the word *naklurluq*, or "poor," referring both to the dead and to the survivors, but they never went into detail. It was almost as if they had an aversion to it. From looking at the various epidemics, which decimated the Native people, I at first thought of them collectively as the Great Death, but I am now convinced that the Great Death referred to the 1900 influenza epidemic, which originated in Nome. From there it spread like a wildfire to all comers of Alaska, killing up to 60 percent of the Eskimo and Athabascan people with the least exposure to the white man. (Details are reported by Robert Fortuine in his book, *Chills and Fever*). This epidemic killed whole families and wiped out whole villages. It gave birth to a generation of orphans—our current grandparents and great-grandparents. The suffering, the despair, the heartbreak, the desperation, and confusion these survivors lived through are unimaginable. People watched helplessly as their mothers, fathers, brothers, and sisters grew ill, the efforts of the *angalkuq* failing. First one family fell ill, then another, then another. The people grew desperate, the *angalkuq* along with them. Then the death started, with people wailing morning, noon, and night. Soon whole families were dead, some leaving only a boy or girl. Babies tried to suckle on the breasts of dead mothers, soon to die themselves. Even the medicine men grew ill and died in despair with their people, and with them died a great part of *Yuuyaraq*, the ancient spirit world of the Eskimo.

The Survivors

Whether the survivors knew or understood, they had witnessed the fatal wounding of *Yuuyaraq* and the old Yup'ik culture. Compared to the span of life of a culture, the Great Death was instantaneous. The Yup'ik world was turned upside down, literally overnight. Out of the suffering, confusion, desperation, heartbreak, and trauma was born a new generation of Yup'ik people. They were born into shock. They woke to a world in shambles, many of their people and their beliefs strewn around them, dead. In their minds they had been overcome by evil. Their medicines and their medicine men and women had proven useless. Everything they had believed in had failed. Their ancient world had collapsed. From their innocence and from their inability to understand and dispel the disease, guilt was born into them. They had witnessed mass death—evil—in unimaginable and unacceptable terms. These were the men and women orphaned by the sudden and traumatic death of the culture that had given them birth. They would become the first generation of modern-day Yup'ik.

The Survivors' World

The world the survivors woke to was without anchor. The *angalkuq*, their medicines, and their beliefs, had all passed away overnight. They woke up in shock, listless, confused, bewildered, heartbroken, and afraid. Like soldiers on an especially gruesome battlefield, they were shell-shocked. Too weak to bury all the dead, many survivors abandoned the old villages, some caving in their houses with the dead still in them. Their homeland—the tundra, the Bering Sea coast, the river banks—had become a dying field for the Yup'ik people: families, leaders, artists, medicine men and women—and *Yuuyaraq*. But it would not end there. Famine, starvation, and disease resulting from the epidemic continued to plague them through the 1950s, and many more perished. These were the people whom the missionaries would call wretched, lazy, even listless. Gone were the people whom Nelson so admired for their "arts, ingenuity, perseverance and virtuosity," the people whom Henry B. Collins claimed had reached the "peak" of modem Eskimo art. Disease had wiped them out. The long night of suffering had begun for the survivors of the Great Death and their descendants.

The End of the Old Culture

The Yup'ik people of today are not culturally the same as their forebears. They are, however, linked to the old through the experience of the Great Death. One was wiped out by it, the other was born out of it and was shaped by it. It is from this context that we have to see the modern Yup'ik Eskimo. It is only from this context that we can begin to understand them.

Like any victim or witness of evil, whether it be murder, suicide, rape, war or mass death, the Yup'ik survivors were in shock. But unlike today's trauma victims, they received no physical or psychological help. They experienced the Great Death alone in the isolation of their tundra and riverine homeland. There was no Red Cross, no relief effort. The survivors of the Great Death had to face it alone. They were quiet and kept things to themselves. They rarely showed their sorrows, fears, heartbreak, anger, or grief. Unable to relive in their conscious minds the horror they had experienced, they did not talk about it with anyone. The survivors seem to have agreed, without discussing it, that they would not talk about it. It was too painful and the implications were too great. Discussing it would have let loose emotions they may not have been able to control. It was better not to talk about it, to act as if it had never happened, to *nallunguaq*. To this day *nallunguaq* remains a way of dealing with problems or unpleasant occurrences in Yup'ik life. Young people are advised by elders to *nallunguarluku*, "to pretend it didn't happen." They had a lot to pretend not to know. After all, it was not only that their loved ones had died, they also had seen their world collapse. Everything they had lived and believed had been found wanting. They were afraid to admit that the things they had believed in might not have been true. Traumatized, leaderless, confused, and afraid, the survivors readily followed the white missionaries and schoolteachers, who quickly attained a status once held only by the *angalkuq*. The survivors embraced Christianity, abandoned *Yuuyaraq*, discarded their spirit world and their ceremonies, and buried their old culture in the silence of denial.

Having silently abandoned their own beliefs, the survivors were reinforced in their decision not to talk about them by the missionaries who told them their old beliefs were evil and from the *tuunraq*, "the devil." They learned to sternly tell their grandchildren not to ask them questions about the *angalkuq*, the old symbol of Yup'ik spiritualism, as if they were ashamed of them and of their old beliefs. They would become good Christians—humble, compliant, obedient, deferential, repentant, and quiet. The survivors were fatalists. They were not sure about the future or even the next day. They told their children to always be prepared to die because they might not even wake up in the morning. They cautioned against making long-range plans. From their own experience they knew how fleeting life was, and from the missionaries they knew how terrible the wrath of the Christian God could be. As new Christians, they learned about hell, the place where the missionaries told them most of their ancestors probably went. They feared hell. They understood fear and they understood hell.

The survivors also turned over the education and instruction of their children to the missionaries and the schoolteachers. They taught them very little about *Yuuyaraq*. They allowed the missionaries and the schoolteachers to inflict physical punishment on their children; for example, washing their children's mouths with soap if they spoke Yup'ik in school or church. Their children were forbidden, on pain of "serving in hell," from dancing or following the old ways. The parents—the survivors—allowed this. They did not protest. The children were, therefore, led to believe that the ways of their fathers and forefathers were of no value and were evil. The survivors allowed this.

The survivors taught almost nothing about the old culture to their children. It was as if they were ashamed of it, and this shame they passed on to their children by their silence and by allowing cultural atrocities to be committed against their children. The survivors also gave up all governing power of the villages to the missionaries and schoolteachers, whoever were most aggressive. There was no one to contest them. In some villages the priest had displaced the *angalkuq*. In some villages there was theocracy under the benevolent dictatorship of a missionary. The old guardians of *Yuuyaraq* on the other hand, the *angalkuq*, if they were still alive, had fallen into disgrace. They had become a source of shame to the village, not only because their medicine and *Yuuyaraq* had failed, but also because the missionaries now openly accused them of being agents of the devil himself and of having led their people into disaster.

In their heart of hearts the survivors wept, but they did not talk to anyone, not even their fellow survivors. It hurt too much. They felt angry, bewildered, ashamed, and guilty, but all this they kept within themselves. These survivors became the forebears of the Yup'ik people and other Alaska Native tribes of today. Their experiences before, during, and after the Great Death explain in great part the persona of their children, grandchildren, and great-grandchildren who are alive today.

Post-Traumatic Stress Disorder: An Illness of the Soul

In light of recent cases of Vietnam veterans who witnessed or participated in war-related events repugnant to them, and who have subsequently been diagnosed to suffer from a psychological illness called post-traumatic stress disorder (PTSD), it is apparent to me that some of the survivors of the Great Death suffered from the same disorder.

The syndrome is born of the attempted suppression in the mind of events perceived as repugnant or evil to the individual who has witnessed or participated in these events. These events were often traumatic to the individual because they involved violence, death, and mayhem by which he was repelled and for which he felt guilt and shame. Not all veterans became infected by this illness. It was mainly the veterans who tried to suppress and ignore their experiences and the resultant feelings of guilt and shame who became ill. Post-traumatic stress disorder can cripple a person. The act of suppressing the traumatic event, instead of expunging it from the mind through confession, serves to drive it further into the psyche or soul, where it festers and begins to color all aspects of the person's life. The person who suppresses that which is unbearable to the conscious mind is trying to ignore it, trying to pretend it isn't there. In time, and without treatment, it will destroy the person, just as any illness left untreated will in time cripple and kill the body. Because of his guilt, the person suffering from PTSD does not like himself. He is ashamed of himself, ashamed of what he saw, or participated in, and is haunted by the memory, even in sleep. He becomes withdrawn, hypervigilant, hypersensitive, and is constantly living in stress. Soon he is unable to speak truthfully with other people about himself or his feelings and becomes unable to carry on close interpersonal relationships. Living under a great deal of stress in his soul, he becomes less and less able to deal with even the minor difficulties of everyday life.

To such a person, escape from self becomes a necessity because even in sleep he finds no peace. He becomes a runner, running from his memory and from himself. He gets tired and begins to despair. In this day and age, alcohol and drugs become a readily available escape from the illness. For a time, these numb the mind and soul. Without treatment, many veterans and others who suffer from PTSD become alcohol and drug abusers. Many become addicted, and as a result lose friends, wives, families, and become isolated, exacerbating an already bad situation. Being unable to hold jobs, some become dependent on others for support. Some become criminals, further isolating themselves and further depressing an already depressed soul.

Tragically, under the influence of alcohol and drugs, the pent-up anger, guilt, shame, sorrow, frustration, and hopelessness often are vented through outbursts of violence to self and others. Such acts, which are difficult for others and even for the sufferer to understand, drive him further into the deadly vortex of guilt and shame. Family and friends who knew him before he became ill swear that he is not the same person and that they do not know him anymore.

Post-traumatic stress disorder is not a physical illness, but an infection of the soul, of the spirit. I use the word infection because the person suffering from PTSD does not volunteer to become ill and does not choose the life of unhappiness, which results from it. I refer to PTSD as an infection of the soul because the disease attacks the core of the person, the spirit. The disease is born out of evil or of events perceived as evil by the person. And the nature of evil is such that it infects even the innocent, dirtying their minds and souls. Because it is infectious, it requires cleansing of the soul through confession. If PTSD sufferers do not get help, they will in time destroy themselves, leaving in their wake even more trauma and heartbreak.

Post-Traumatic Stress Disorder in the Survivors of the Great Death

Not all the survivors of the Great Death suffered from post-traumatic stress disorder, but a great many did. This may explain the great thirst for liquor that whalers and other Westerners found in the Eskimos along the Bering Sea and the Arctic. It was reported by whalers and the officers of the early revenue cutters that the Eskimos craved the liquor, trading all they had for it and almost starving themselves as long as they had molasses with which to make rum. Like the Vietnam veteran or victims and witnesses of other violent and traumatic events, these Eskimos found in liquor a narcotic which numbed their troubled minds. The reports of the whalers, the revenue cutters, and other observers confirm that the Eskimos quickly became addicted to alcohol.

The only explanation for this type of behavior is that for some reason these Eskimos were psychologically predisposed to seek relief through the narcotic effects of alcohol. And although in the case of the St. Lawrence Islanders this behavior was reported in the mid-nineteenth century, it must be remembered that they had already begun to see their world crumbling as a result of interaction with Western sailors and diseases much earlier than the Yup'ik, Iñupiaq, and Athabascan people who were located farther away from established sea lanes. The St. Lawrence story was only a precursor for the tragedy that would unfold on the mainland at the turn of the century. Judging from the abrupt changes the Yup'ik and other Native people accepted at the turn of the century, literally without a fight, one can assume that they were not themselves. No people anywhere will voluntarily discard their culture, beliefs, customs, and traditions unless they are under a great deal of stress, physically, psychologically, or spiritually. Yet for some reason, the Yup'ik people did exactly that, overnight in the span of their cultural history. There may have been pockets of resistance, but they were insignificant.

With the Yup'ik people and most Alaska Native tribes, the case can be made that resistance collapsed because of mass death, resulting from famine, illness, and the trauma that accompanied these. The case can also be made that many of the survivors of the Great Death suffered from post-traumatic stress disorder, and that it was in this condition that they surrendered and allowed their old cultures to pass away.

The survivors had been beaten by an unseen great evil (mass death) that had been unleashed in their villages, killing over half the men, women, and little children. They had witnessed the violent collapse of their world, of *Yuuyaraq*. Having barely escaped the grip of death, the survivors were shaken to the core. They staggered, dazed, confused, brutalized, and scarred, into the new world, refugees in their own land, a remnant of an ancient and proud people. The world looked the same, yet everything had changed. But the memories would remain, memories of the spirit world, the way life used to be, and memories of the horrors they had witnessed and lived through.

We who are alive today cannot begin to imagine the fear, the horror, the confusion and the desperation that gripped the villages of our forebears following the Great Death. But we have learned, through the experience of Vietnam veterans infected by PTSD, that the cries of horror and despair do not end unless they are expunged from the soul. Yes, the Yup'ik survivors cried, they wailed, and they fought with all they had, but they were not heard. They had been alone in a collapsed and dying world and many of them carried the memory, the heartbreak, the guilt, and the shame, silently with them into the grave.

But we hear them today. They cry in the hearts of their children, their grandchildren, and great-grandchildren. They cry in the hearts of the children who have inherited the symptoms of their disease of silent despairing loneliness, heartbreak, confusion, and guilt. And tragically, because the children do not understand why they feel this way, they blame themselves for this legacy from their grandparents, the survivors of the Great Death who suffered from what we now call post-traumatic stress disorder.

The Children and Grandchildren of the Survivors

At the time of the Great Death, there were white people in some of the villages, mostly missionaries and traders, but they were few in number. They witnessed the Great Death, and in many cases they did the best they could to help the Native people. Yet it would be these same people who would take advantage of the demoralized condition of the survivors to change them, to civilize them, to attempt to remake them. They, and the men and women who would follow them, had no understanding of or respect for the old cultures. They considered them satanic, and made it their mission from God to wipe them out. They considered the survivors savages and used derogatory adjectives in describing them in their letters and diaries. And because of what they had just lived through, and because of their disoriented and weakened condition, the survivors allowed these newcomers to take over their lives. What followed was an attempt at cultural genocide. The priests and missionaries impressed on the survivors that their spirit world was of the devil and was evil. They heaped scorn on the medicine men and women and told the people they were servants of the devil. They told the survivors that their feasts, songs, dances, and masks were evil and had to be abandoned on pain of condemnation and hellfire. Many villages followed these edicts. The masks and feasts disappeared.

The priests and missionaries forbade parents from teaching their children about *Yuuyaraq* and about the spirit world. They forbade the parents and children from practicing old customs and rituals based on *Yuuyaraq*, calling them taboo. Again, the survivors obeyed and their children grew up ignorant about themselves and about their history. When the children asked about the old culture, they were told by their parents not to ask such questions, as if they were ashamed or hiding something. From listening to the priest and observing the behavior of their parents, the children would come to believe that there was something wrong with their people, some dark secret to be ashamed of.

In the schoolhouse, the children were forbidden to speak in Yup'ik. The survivors did not protest even when it was learned that the schoolteachers were washing the mouths of their children with soap for speaking their mother tongue. In the schoolhouse, the children came to believe that to be Yup'ik was shameful and that to become like white people was not only desirable but essential. The children began to look down at their own people and began to see the observances of their people as quaint, shameful, and funny. That the survivors allowed all this is testimony to the degree of their individual and collective depression, especially in regard to the treatment of their children. Had Nelson made similar decrees during the time he was visiting these same villages (1870–1875), he would have been killed. Yet after the Great Death, some villages were ruled autocratically by a single priest. The survivors were stoic and seemed able to live under the most miserable and unbearable of conditions. They were quiet, even deferential. They did not discuss personal problems with others. If they were hurt, they kept it to themselves. If they were angry, they kept it to themselves. They were lauded as being so respectful that they avoided eye-to-eye contact with others. They were passive.

Very few exhibited their emotions or discussed them. The survivors did as they were told. They were not fighters or protesters. They almost lost everything: their cultures, their languages, their spiritual beliefs, their songs, their dances, their feasts, their lands, their independence, their pride—all their inheritances. This was their way of coping with life after the cataclysm of the Great Death. The survivors had gone into themselves and receded with their tattered lives and unbearable emotions into a deep silence. It was in this condition that they raised their children, who then learned to be like their parents passive, silent, not expressing emotions, keeping things to themselves, and not asking too many questions.

The survivors told their children about kindness, forgiveness, and sharing, yet they were unwilling to face and discuss the problems and unpleasantness in the family or the village. They did not teach their children about *Yuuyaraq*, the spirit world, or about the old culture because it was too painful to do so. Besides, the priest said it was wrong. Those who told stories told only the *harmless* ones. This would become part of the persona of the survivors and their descendents. Without meaning to, the survivors *drove* the experience of the Great Death and the resultant trauma and emotions deep into the souls of their children, who became psychologically and emotionally handicapped and who passed these symptoms on to their children and grandchildren.

The survivors' children are the grandparents of the present day Eskimo,

Indian, and Aleut. It is these traits, these symptoms of post-traumatic stress disorder, which are handicapping the present generation of Alaska Native people. Several generations of suppressed emotions, confusion, and feelings of inferiority and powerlessness now permeate even the very young.

An Anomaly

Since the early 1960s, Native people have seen their material lives improve. They are no longer hungry, they are well clothed, and they now live in comparatively warm, comfortable homes. This has largely been achieved by the anti-poverty programs, which were instituted in the years before and after the Great Society, of the Kennedy-Johnson administrations. Being by and large unemployed in the cash economy, Native people benefited greatly from the civil rights and anti-poverty programs of the 1960s and 1970s.

Yet, as their physical lives have improved, the quality of their lives has deteriorated. Since the 1960s there has been a dramatic rise in alcohol abuse, alcoholism, and associated violent behaviors, which have upset family and village life and resulted in physical and psychological injury, death, and imprisonment. Something self-destructive, violent, frustrated, and angry has been set loose from within the Alaska Native people. And it is the young that are dying, going to prison, and maiming themselves. Their families, their friends, their villages say they cannot understand why. Every suicide leaves a stunned family and village. Every violent crime and every alcohol-related death elicits the same reaction. The alcohol-related nightmare has now become an epidemic. No one seems to know why.

One thing we do know—the primary cause of the epidemic is not physical deprivation. Native people have never had it so good in terms of food, clothing, and shelter. We can also state that it isn't because the federal and state governments have ignored the problem. Hundreds of millions of dollars have been spent on Alaska Natives to improve their lives, their health, and their education. Hundreds of millions have been spent just trying to combat alcoholism and alcohol abuse among them. Local option laws have been passed that prohibit the importation, the sale, and even the possession of alcohol.[2] Yet the carnage goes on.

> From 1977 to 1988, the last year for which complete data are available, 1,789 Native Americans died violently in Alaska. These figures include 394 deaths by suicides, 257 by homicides, and 1,138 by accident out of a total population of only 64,000 (1980 Census), representing a claim of about 3 percent of the native population over a twelve-year period. (Berman 1991)

The numbers of incidents of domestic violence, imprisonments, alcohol affected children, and deaths from disease attributable to alcohol are equally shocking. Yet the numbers are misleading because they do not measure the true extent of the damage being done to the Native people. The numbers cannot quantify the heartbreak, discouragement, confusion, hopelessness, and grief. The numbers cannot measure the trauma. It is like repeating the Great Death all over again, and like then, the Alaska Natives blame themselves and do not know or understand why. And like the first Great Death, a whole generation of Alaska Natives is being born into trauma, just like their grandparents and parents. It is history repeating itself in a tragic, heartbreaking way. It is a deadly cycle that began in the changing of the times for the Yupiit and the other tribes of Alaska Natives.

Why?

We now know that our ancestors were besieged by diseases like smallpox, measles, chicken pox, and influenza that culminated in the Great Death at the turn of the century. Not knowing of microbes, they attributed these diseases to evil spirits and to their own weaknesses. They blamed themselves and their way of life, and abandoned themselves and their way of life as a result. But that did not end the suffering. Famine, poverty, confusion, polio, tuberculosis, and spiritual depression followed, ending in the death of the old cultures around the 1950s.

The present epidemic is a little harder to explain, but certainly it was born out of the Great Death itself, and the disease is one of the soul and the psyche of this present generation of Alaska Native people. It is an inherited disease, passed from parent to child. But it has been passed down unintentionally, unknowingly, and innocently. Nevertheless, it is deadly and unless treated, it will give birth to another generation of infected souls.

The cry of the survivors of the Great Death was why. That same cry is now heard from the confused, shocked, and heartbroken hearts of today's Alaska Native people.

A Generation Turns on Itself

Many of today's generation of Alaska Natives have turned on themselves. They blame themselves for being unemployed, for being second-class citizens, for not being successful as success is portrayed to them by the world they live in. They measure themselves by the standards of the television America and the textbook America, and they have failed. For this they blame themselves. There is no one to tell them that they are not to blame, that there is nothing wrong with them, that they are loved. Sometimes they don't even know who they are, or what they are. This, of course, does not describe all young Alaska Native people. But it describes the suicides, the alcohol abusers, the ones in prison, the ones with nothing to do in the villages. These are the numbers we hear in reports. They are living human beings—Eskimos, Aleuts, and Indians—the ones we pay no attention to until they become numbers. Chances are that their parents also were alcohol abusers, if not alcoholics. Chances are that they were disappointed, emotionally hurt, heartbroken children. Chances are they saw physical, verbal, and psychological violence in the home. Chances are that they were not given enough attention and thought themselves unloved and unwanted. Chances are they were hungry, were dirty, were tired, and were unsuccessful in school. Chances are they yearned for happiness and a normal home but were denied it. And now, chances are they no longer communicate with others—not their parents, not their relatives, not their friends, or anyone else.

By the time such children are grown, they are deeply depressed in their souls. They have become demoralized, discouraged, and do not think very much of themselves. Deep in their hearts they are hurt, angry, frustrated and confused. They never talk. They have turned inward. These are the ones who, when they drink alcohol, quickly become addicted to it, psychologically first, and then physically. When under the influence, they begin to vent their anger, hurt, frustration, and confusion, seemingly out of the clear blue sky. And sadly, their outbursts are directed at themselves and those closest to them: their parents, their brothers and sisters, their friends, and members of their villages. The most tragic events are those involving a blacked-out male Eskimo, Aleut, or Indian, who, while completely out of control, vents his deadly emotions in violence and mad acts resulting in dismemberment and death, thereby leaving even more traumatized victims and witnesses.

So what causes this? Is it the young man's or young woman's fault? Or is it the fault of parents who may have been abusers and alcoholics? Or is it the fault of grandparents who did not raise their children right because they themselves were traumatized by the Great Death and felt guilty about the subsequent loss of culture, language, and independence? *Whose fault is it?*

Certainly the dead will be buried, the suicides buried, the assaulter and abuser jailed and charged with the appropriate crime and put away in prison for a few years or a lifetime. But there are only so many prison cells. Can we seriously be thinking of putting everyone into prison? And do we keep burying the other victims of the Great Death until not a one is left? Is this to be our way of life until the end, burying the victims of the victims? When will all this end? How will it end? How can we end it? When can we end it? Or do we even want to end it? Have we become so callous, so hard-hearted, our spiritual senses so dulled, that we are no longer moved by all this? Is it to be as Darwin put it, the survival of the fittest? My answer at least is this: We who are also the survivors of the Great Death must end it. We must activate all our energies and resources to end it. And we must do it soon because as time goes by it will become harder and harder.

Every human life is sacred. Every Yup'ik, Iñupiaq, Athabascan, Aleut, Eyak, Chugiak, Tlingit, Haida, Sugcestun, and Tsimshian life is sacred. We are not so many that we can endlessly absorb the trauma each tragic death inflicts on our physical and psychic body. We are too few. The question is how to stop the epidemic.

Beginnings

If we were to look at the experience of the various tribes as the experience of individuals, and if they were exhibiting the symptoms we have described and which are now so well documented, we would have to spend some time just talking to them. We would have them truthfully tell their life stories, leaving nothing out, to see what was causing these disturbances in their lives. So it is in this way that we must begin to treat this particular syndrome of the various Alaska Native villages, beginning at the personal and familial levels. The living elders must tell all they know, tell their experiences, because theirs are the experiences of the whole village, whether the whole village is aware of them or not. The very oldest are the most important because they will be able to tell their remembrances to the whole village. They must relate the old beliefs of their people, no matter the subject. They must also relate the experiences of the epidemics, no matter how painful, because these haunt not only them, but their children and grandchildren as well. They must tell why they gave everything up, why they discarded the old ways, the old beliefs, why they allowed the culture to die. They must explain how and why they gave up governing themselves, why they allowed schoolteachers to wash their children's mouths with soap, why they gave up so much land. The elders must speak of all that hurts them and haunts them. They owe this to their children and to their children's children because without knowing why, the descendents feel the same as their elders do.

The one fear I have is that the first survivors of the Great Death, the ones who lived in the old world, were nurtured by it, and who loved it are now almost all gone. They are the ones to whom was born the disease that afflicts Alaska Natives today. They are the ones who felt the full brunt of the fatal wounding of their world. They are the ones who saw it, were horrified by it, and whose hearts were broken. Hearing them, we will recognize the emotions in our hearts, emotions we have long attributed to a weakness within ourselves. We would at least mourn with them, mourn together the passing of our old world. Then they and we would not be alone anymore.

The children of these survivors must also speak. They are now grandparents, even great-grandparents. They must speak of their childhoods, their world, what they saw, what they perceived, what they thought, how they felt. They too must share with us their life stories, leaving nothing out, the good and the bad, because their experiences are ours, and we are their seed. We also love them. Then the parents of this new generation must speak together, as a group, to the rest of the villages. They too must relate their life stories, their experiences, and their sorrows. They must turn their hearts to their children who so love them, who so long to know them. Their experiences are ours. We are shaped by them. Then we, their children, must speak to our parents, to our grandparents if we still have them, and to our own children. We, too, must tell our story to our people, because our experience is theirs too. We must tell our feelings, our anger, our frustrations, and ask questions of our parents. We must do this because we don't know each other anymore; we have become like strangers to each other. The old do not know or understand the young, and the young do not know or understand the old. Parents do not know their children, and the children do not know their parents. As a result of this silence, a gulf has grown between those who love and care for each other the most. It is so very sad. I have been in homes where members of the same household do not even speak to each other. I wondered how they could even stand to be in the same house together like this. And out of this will grow more hurt, misunderstanding, and unfulfilled love. Even in the family, while surrounded by those one loves the most, a person can become isolated, a stranger even to those who love him and are closest to him. Needless to say, there will be tension, stress, and frayed nerves. Only communication, honest communication from the heart, will break this down, because inability to share one's heart and feelings is the most deadly legacy of the Great Death. It was born out of the survivors' inability to face and speak about what they had seen and lived through. The memory was too painful, the reality too hard, the results too hard to hear.

Without knowing it, the survivors began to deal with the difficulties of life by trying to ignore them, by denying them, by not talking about them. This is the way they raised their children and their children raised us the same way. Holding things in has become a trait among our families and our people. The results have been tragic.

Over the many years of suppressed emotions, of not communicating from the heart, Native people and Native families grew apart. Somewhere along the line, something had to give. The body of the Alaska Native family, village, and tribe, being unable to withstand the stresses built up from within, began breaking down. The only way it will end is if the built-up stresses, misunderstandings, and questions are released and satisfied by truthful dialogue from the heart. It is only through this heart-to-heart dialogue, no matter how painful or embarrassing the subject, that the deadly stresses born of trauma on top of trauma can be released. Then slowly, we can all go home again, be alone and lonesome no more, be a family and a village again.

It is time we bury the old culture, mourn those who died with it, mourn with those who survived it. It is time we buried our many dead who have died in this long night of our suffering, then go forward, lost no more. We have been wandering in a daze for the last 100 years, rocked by a succession of traumatic changes and inundations. Now we have to stop, look at ourselves, and as the new Alaska Natives we are, press on together—not alone—free of the past that haunted and disabled us, free of the ghosts that haunted our hearts, free to become what we were intended to be by God.

Closing

I do not know if anyone will understand or agree with what I have written. Nor do I know that if it is understood, the recommendations will be followed. But I am convinced that what I have written is the truth and will be supported by facts. What I have written is the summary of five years' work, sometimes frustrating and anguishing work, but work nonetheless. It did not come to me in one flash; rather it came in bits and pieces. But finally the pieces fit, so I wrote them down for others to read.

Certainly there are others more qualified and more respected than I who could probably compose a more perfect letter. But this letter is from the heart and is born out of my own suffering and imprisonment. In suffering and imprisonment, I have found, life becomes starkly clearer, shed of the noise and the static of the world.

Yet I did not withdraw from the only world I have ever known, the world of my childhood and the world in which I struggled with seemingly insignificant results. No, while I might have been five years in prison, I have never left my village, nor my own Yup'ik people. In fact I return to them in spirit. While missing out on the seemingly good aspects of the life of my village and people, I certainly have not been spared their sorrows and their own suffering. These

I have shared with them fully, sorrowing with them, seeking all the harder in our collective soul for answers.

At times I have felt like giving up. Sometimes things look hopeless. But from the Apostle Paul I have been trying to learn to be content in whatever state I am in. I now see those things that brought me and still bring so many of my brothers and sisters to alcohol abuse and alcoholism. So now, when I see them, their suffering, their unhappiness, I see my old self and try all the harder to lead them to the truth, the truth that freed me even as I sat in this prison. The same truth that can free all Native people who have become prisoners of the unhappiness born of the evil of the Great Death and the subsequent trauma which it fathered.

This little that I have written is a part of that truth, the truth that was hidden from me by my previous life, by my own stubbornness, pride, unvented emotions, and my addiction to alcohol, which momentarily eased the suffering these bring.

This letter is not from a wise man, because were I wise I would not be where I am. This letter is from a man who learned only from suffering, the lessons literally beaten into his soul. But for this I am grateful, for now I have finally seen what was before my very eyes from the time I was a child. So I share what I have learned—been taught—in hope that the tragedy, which engulfed my life and that of my family and villages, may never happen again.

I will close by saying that I, once the most hopeless of men, no longer am without hope. I now live in hope. I also have faith that The One who started this good work in us by creating us will complete it.

Notes

1. Editor's note: "Yup'ik" can be a singular or plural form while "Yupiit" is exclusively a plural form.

2. Editor's note: Villages in Alaska can vote on whether alcohol can be sold in their villages or completely banned. Alaska villages are called "damp" if they prohibit sale of alcohol but do not deny importation for personal use. A village is "dry" if importation of alcohol is illegal.

Angoon Remembers: The Religious Significance of Balance and Reciprocity

Nancy Furlow (*Tlingit*)

In 1882 the U.S. Navy bombed and completely destroyed the Tlingit village of Angoon, an event bitterly remembered in Tlingit oral history. Nancy Furlow's research contextualizes the historical, cultural, and psychological effects of the destruction of Angoon. Furlow is Tlingit and of the Deisheetaan clan. She is presently the interim director of Alaska Native Studies at the University of Alaska, Anchorage and was formerly assistant professor in the Alaska Native Studies Department at the University of Alaska, Fairbanks. She received a B.A. cum laude in anthropology with a minor in music from Smith College, and did her graduate work in religious studies at the University of California, Santa Barbara. At Santa Barbara she studied under Ines Talamantez in the only doctoral program in the country that focuses on Native American religious traditions.

An important part of the American spirit involves mustering our strength to mourn, pick up the pieces, and then to move on together after tragedy. We take pride in our ability to rebuild and renew our "American values." We've seen this spirit in action countless times but most recently, after the horrendous events of 9–11. Since this spirit is such an integral part of our heritage as Americans, why can't the people in the village of Angoon, Alaska, pick up the pieces and move on past events that occurred over 120 years ago when the U.S. Navy bombarded the village? References to that day come up again and again when the people of Angoon speak to each other privately or publicly. Recollections about this event continue to bring strong feelings of grief, sadness, and even tears. What makes it impossible for Angoon to heal from that event—or at least put it in historical perspective? By heal I don't mean that the community should erase the event from memory; it was far too atrocious for that. By "heal" I mean to let the movement of time temper the memories, sand off the most painful edges, so that it finally feels settled and laid to rest on both individual and cultural levels.

I'd like to take a moment to discuss the importance of research into this event. Understanding Tlingit responses, both in the past and the present, to the bombing is important for many reasons, the most obvious being that we gain insight into a relatively unknown historical event in Alaska. This event has repercussions for Alaska Native history in the way that bringing to light the Aleut evacuation and the last Indian War in Nulato has (Wright 1995) and in the way the Japanese internment has for history at the national level. It also allows us to peer into Alaska Native/non-native relationships and glimpse the cross-cultural miscommunications between these groups at a crucial point in Alaska history—after the purchase of Alaska by the United States and prior to the establishment of a civil government. Tlingit oral traditions of the events leading up to the burning and bombing of Angoon also provide a counter-narrative to the official military records, which offer a much harsher portrait of the events. A letter found recently in a Boston dump, written by an officer and crew member of one of the Navy vessels involved, criticizes the official accounts and appears to support Tlingit historical versions. Part of my research, in this respect, is necessarily revisionist in nature. Linda Tuhiwai Smith, a Maori educator, researcher, and proponent of indigenous theory, has this to say about indigenous histories: "Indigenous peoples want to tell our own stories, write our own versions, in our own ways, for our own purposes. [We have] a very powerful need to give testimony to and restore a spirit, to bring back into existence a world fragmented and dying" (Smith 1999). A Tlingit telling of these events is just one way to breathe life back into the community of Angoon.

On a deeper level we become aware of some of the boundaries of Tlingit epistemology and ontology in a rapidly changing cultural environment. Where is the line drawn when it comes to partaking in American ideals, philosophies, and ways of life? What aspects of Tlingit culture are nonnegotiable and are important enough to continue to pass on from generation to generation as Tlingit cultural practices and ideals bend under pressures from Euro-American culture, and begin to conform to such Western ideals as individualization, English only, and a market economy, for example? This research also addresses issues central to the study of Native American religions. Lawrence Sullivan, a noted scholar of Native American religions, writes, "Religion stands at the heart of Native American life. Not the sort of 'religion' that is set apart from other domains of life. Rather, religion in Native American culture is robust, an entire lifeway that engages all that is vital and relates one to everything that matters" (2003, 1). The study of the bombing of Angoon and the aftereffects reaches into this heart.

Today these other important issues must remain in the background. I want to discuss the religious significance of two concepts central to Tlingit people, balance and reciprocity, to illustrate what keeps this event unresolved for the Tlingit people of Angoon. I will first provide a brief description of Tlingit social and cultural practices and then will set the bombardment of Angoon within a Tlingit context, highlighting the importance of balance and reciprocity in relation to this event to bring a greater depth of understanding to contemporary memories of the bombing. Of necessity, much will be omitted from this essay, including many important points and complex issues, not limited to but including issues related to the Americanization of Alaska, tensions between the Tlingit and white population, and the problems inherent in an area without any form of civil government.

This story must begin with Raven. Raven created the Tlingit world and the Raven stories tell us how Raven's cunning made our world what it is today. How he stole the sun, moon, and stars and brought light to the world or how water dripping from his beak became our rivers and lakes. The Raven stories highlight a time when the boundaries between the human and natural worlds and worlds of the spirits were fluid and communication and exchanges took place easily. Even though communication between these realms is no longer as direct, it remains very important. The world is a spiritual world, a sensing, feeling world. Strict rules guide behavior between the human, natural, and spiritual worlds that are passed down between generations even today. The rules of behavior promote respect, in other words, and show love. It is also a multidimensional world. Human actions, in other words, have effects in the human world, the natural world, the spiritual world, or on all levels.

All Tlingit are furthermore born into a world of duality, or what anthropologists call a moiety system. Additionally, this system is matrilineal, meaning identity comes through an individual's mother's line. For Tlingit people, this means that at birth each infant is born into one of two moieties, *Yeíl* (Raven) or *Ch'áak'* (Eagle), depending on the moiety of the mother. The children of an Eagle mother will all be Eagle, for example, because my mother is *Deisheetaan*, I am *Deisheetaan* and my brothers and sister are *Deisheetaan*. Although this may seem confusing to someone unfamiliar with this type of social structure, as humans we are all born into a system of duality—we're born either male or female and this makes sense to us. If we think about it this way the moiety system makes sense as well. The two moieties, *Yeíl* and *Ch'áak'* are further divided into clans and house groups. Marriage, ceremonial action, and actions like oratory and songs take place across moiety-clan boundaries. So exchanges take place back and forth. It takes both halves to make a whole.

Central to this Tlingit dual social structure are the concepts of ownership and balance. Ownership takes place at the clan level and includes such things as clan crests—the artistic and symbolic representation of the clan. Stories, songs, dances, artistic designs, names, geographical locations, subsistence areas, and clan histories are all owned. This sense of ownership was, and still is, strictly enforced, but in the pre-Russian and early American periods, this enforcement could be very harsh. If an individual(s) fished without permission on another clan's fishing stream, for example, they could be killed or the individual's entire clan could be required to pay compensation for trespassing. Although such harsh rules of enforcement no longer exist, ownership remains very important.

An important aspect of ownership involves *at.óow*. These are the most valued, religious objects for Tlingit clans. *At.*óow literally means a "purchased" or "owned" thing. Richard and Nora Dauenhauer, in their research on Tlingit culture and language, emphasize that both meanings are important. *At.óow* were purchased during events that occurred both in the time when boundaries between human, natural, and spiritual worlds were more fluid and in later times (Dauenhauer and Dauenhauer 1987; Dauenhauer and Dauenhauer 1990, 14–15). This concept includes physical objects such as mountains, glaciers, the sun, and clan crests and immaterial objects such as songs, stories, images (such as the beaver), and ancestors. These objects, though, in contrast to less valued objects, were often paid for or purchased by a human life and then brought out within a ceremonial context and publicly displayed and acknowledged by a clan of the opposite moiety. In other words, one cannot just decide that an object is going to be *at.óow*. Certain steps must be taken, but this does happen today. An important aspect of a*t.óow* within the Tlingit cultural context is that they are the symbolic representations by which the boundaries between human, natural, and spiritual worlds, the living and deceased, the past, present, and future become present and are maintained in balance with each other. The *at.óow* make this process possible.

This brings us to balance and reciprocity. Balance regulates all aspects of Tlingit life and it is essential that balance is maintained. Without it, Tlingit culture and peoples would cease to exist. For example, words spoken, especially when directed at the opposite moiety, cannot be allowed to "hang in space" but must be balanced by a verbal response from the opposite moiety. Words have power when directed at the opposite moiety, both to delineate or highlight the duality and to balance it at the same time. Love songs directed at the opposite moiety strengthen this sense of balance and reciprocity between the clans. Maintaining balance at the time of death is particularly important and strict rules of protocol must be followed in order to maintain cultural and spiritual balance at that time. Balance goes hand-in-hand with reciprocal acts and is necessary not only between opposite clans but with the spiritual world as well. It maintains respectful relations within the Tlingit cosmos and avoids insult. Duality, then, within Tlingit culture, is not viewed as oppositional but is understood within a context of balance and reciprocity. As we'll see, this misunderstood aspect of Tlingit culture had devastating effects for the village of Angoon.

I want briefly to point out where official Navy accounts disagree and then place the incident within the framework of Tlingit concepts of balance and reciprocity. Reports given by E. C. Merriman, commander of the United States Naval vessel the *Adams* and highest-ranking military official in Alaska at the time, and Lieutenant Commander Healy of the revenue steamer *Corwin* stated that two Northwest Trading Company boats and two white hostages were taken, that the hostages' lives were threatened unless a payment of 200 blankets to the Tlingit was made, and that other company valuables were taken. In a letter to Secretary of the Treasury Folger, Commander Healey stated that hostages and property were released upon arrival in Angoon. In other words there was no need to bomb Angoon other than, in Commander Merriman's words, to "do something they would remember." Most important, though, is what these reports leave out. Six children died that day of smoke inhalation.

Teel' Tlein was a Tlingit shaman or *ixt'*. He was working for the Northwest Trading Company and was killed in a work-related accident. According to Tlingit law his death required compensation from the Northwest Trading Company even though his death was an accident. Keep in mind that *Teel' Tlein* was an important and respected member of the community—he was the healer. Within the framework of Tlingit concepts of balance and reciprocity, 200 blankets were demanded as compensation for his death. The demand was not made in order to hold the Northwest Company or its employees hostage but because the shaman's death placed the community in a state of imbalance on social, cultural, and religious levels. There had always been accidents resulting in death, and Tlingit oral traditions are filled with stories about them from the long ago times and in the more recent past. This was a well-known fact of life, but the loss of life required compensation, a payment, to bring back balance, an act of reciprocity. In this case the payment of blankets was only one part of the process to bring back a sense of balance. Another part of the response would have been the ceremonial actions that started to take place between moieties immediately after *Teel' Tlein*'s death and the days leading up to placing his body in a grave house—the acts of reciprocal exchange between opposite moieties—and during the *k͟oo.éex'* that would take place in a year or two, but the bombing disrupted this process. The acts of reciprocity, which would have brought balance to the community, did not happen. This is the gravest insult of all in a Tlingit religious context. After the burning and bombing, people were struggling just to stay alive. In the words of a Tlingit eye witness to the event, "We were left homeless on the beach."

What I want to emphasize today is that when *Teel' Tlein* was killed, the community response—bringing the boats ashore, discontinuing work (which included not using sharp objects), painting faces black as a sign of mourning, and the gathering of the opposite clans to properly care for and place the body in the grave house were all natural responses practiced, as Tlingit say, "from time immemorial." They were not, as charged by the Navy, acts of aggression toward the "white" population. A death occurred. This required a payment as compensation for the loss and ritual action between two opposite clans to bring a sense of order and balance back to the cosmological world. Tlingit elder Jimmie George describes the powerful nature of reciprocal action between two opposite moieties in this way: "Men have constantly tried blending together oil and water—oil and water. No one succeeded in making it happen. But now on this *X'aalkweidí* land it has really happened to us at this moment. Just as one we have come together this evening. There is nothing that will blend them together. Yet this evening surely you can see the way our lives this evening are flowing together as one. There is nothing that can force this to happen. Love for each other, being one, perhaps that is what will blend our lives together, we who live in Southeast Alaska, we who live here" (Dauenhauer and Dauenhauer 1990, 167).

This idea of blending brings us to the root of the word "religion" and helps us to understand this concept in Tlingit lives. The word "religion" comes from the Latin *religare*—to tie fast or bind together. Duality, when viewed as only oppositional, distorts Tlingit perceptions of duality as that which binds our human, spiritual, and natural worlds with the past, the present, and the future—our ancestors—the time when Raven gave us this world—to the living, to our future generations—our children and children's children. This deepest meaning of duality forms the very basis of Tlingit religious meaning, and this meaning is expressed over and over in an eternal cycle of reincarnation—a cycle held within a container of reciprocity, balance, and love. Dualism governs "right relations," "correct relations," "proper relations" between the human social world, the surrounding natural world, and the spiritual world. In this view of the cosmos, balance and the maintenance of balance are not only central but absolutely necessary. In other words they are non-negotiable.

On October 26, 1882, as the people of Angoon were preparing to bind together the rift created by *Teel' Tlein*'s death, Commander E. C. Merriman proceeded to burn the village's storage houses filled with the winter food supply, to tie up and destroy the canoes, to bomb and then loot the village.

The sounds of the shells breaking apart the clan houses, the images of soldiers looting and taking the most valued objects, the *at.óow*, the bodies of the six children who died that day, remain in the present through the oral traditions and through the Navy uniform taken as a form of payment (and which is now *at.óow*) for that terrible day. Duality as the most powerful expression of Tlingit religious meaning, duality as expressed through acts of reciprocity leading to balance, a blending of oil and water—is nonnegotiable. The imbalance created by the death of a single individual was multiplied countless times in the bombing and has continued to multiply for 121 years.

I'd like to end by noting that the incident was severe enough, even with the inaccuracies of the official Navy accounts, to be used as a powerful example of the need for a civil government in Alaska.

Decades later, the Tlingit and Haida Central Council, on behalf of the village of Angoon, brought a lawsuit before the Indian Claims Commission. This case was settled out of court in 1973 for $90,000 compensation for property destroyed at the 1882 value. Governor Jay Hammond declared October 26, 1982, the date of the one hundredth commemoration, as Tlingit Remembrance Day and asked for flags to be flown at half mast on all state buildings "as a reminder that cultural misunderstandings diminish all of us spiritually." During that commemoration of the bombing, only silence filled the time set aside for an apology from the U.S. Navy. Without the apology, balance cannot be restored and the people of Angoon will remember.

But why not let it go now? There has been some compensation and acknowledgment of the horrific events. Because duality as expressed through reciprocity and balance is the central feature of Tlingit religious meaning. To forget—or give up—would mean the end, the death of Tlingit culture and peoples and would mean that the cycle of reincarnation would remain silent—forever—waiting for an apology—words that heal.

The Comity Agreement: Missionization of Alaska Native People

Maria Shaa Tláa *Williams* *(Tlingit)*

The following selection is an excerpt from an unpublished chapter on the effects of Christian missionaries and mission schools on Alaska Native people. The twin hallmarks of European colonization of indigenous people were resource exploitation and Christianity. Once indigenous people were subdued, the process to remake the spiritual landscape began. The purpose of the essay is not to criticize the Christian religion but to examine from a historical perspective how the indigenous people of Alaska came to be Christians.

Preface

Today most contemporary Alaska Native people consider themselves Christians although Christianity is a recent development in Alaska. Prior to the arrival of Christian missionaries, each indigenous group or nation in Alaska had their own religious and philosophical belief systems. It is clear from surviving religious practices, oral histories, and ethnographic, archaeological, and historical evidence that the indigenous people in Alaska had rich and varied ceremonial and religious lives. Their philosophical practices and elaborate ceremonies were expressed through prayer, dance, music, and other ritual practices; some of these have survived into the twenty-first century.

My journey into examining Alaska Native traditional religions and the effects of Christian missionaries developed over several stages. My parents are deeply spiritual people; my father prayed every day and wore a cross for most of my childhood. My mother is a devout Buddhist. I did not attend church regularly, although my older sister and I were baptized. I never questioned Christianity until after I became an adult. I am an ethnomusicologist by training, and my greatest passion in life is watching traditional indigenous music and dance performance. During the preparation for writing my dissertation, which focused on the renaissance in traditional Alaska Native music and dance, my research revealed a sharp decrease in religious and spiritual traditions among all Alaska Native peoples with the advent of colonialism. The masked dance practices and winter ceremonies that varied widely among the different cultures are well documented by early visitors, missionaries, and other westerners. Why did this change? What happened? Why are there only remnants of Alaska Native ceremonial practices? Why is the music and dance repertoire today primarily social songs and dances and not religious or ceremonial?

In 1993 I moved to New Mexico to teach at the Institute for American Indian Arts in Santa Fe. One of the epiphanies I had while being among the Pueblo, Navajo, and Apache peoples of New Mexico was that their traditional religions survived the colonial period. This revelation inspired me to examine the history of how Alaska became Christianized. One of my discoveries was the nineteenth-century Mission Plan or Comity Agreement that divided Alaska into a pie—assigning various Protestant denominations specific geographic regions to set up missions and schools—to remake the spiritual landscape. Catholics were of course not included because of the old schism that existed between the two systems of Protestantism and Catholicism.

In 1874 the American Home Missionary Society published an article about a meeting that took place, which resulted in a blueprint for a massive missionization plan for Alaska. This was called the "comity agreement." The purpose of the meeting was to openly discuss their evangelical plan for territories in the United States so that the missionaries would present a more effective front and not bicker over certain groups or regions. A paper read in October 2, 1874, before the National Council of Congregational Churches in New Haven, Connecticut, by Reverend David B. Coe, D.D., one of the secretaries of the American Home Missionary Society, refers to the meeting in New York. "We saw there a year ago, at the meeting of the Evangelical Alliance in the city of New York, where the representatives of all the Evangelical Christendom mingled together in council, sat down together at the table of their common Lord, and pledged themselves to cordial and loving co-operations with each other in extending his Kingdom among men" ("Comity between Denominations" 1874, 14). Another similar meeting followed, sometime in the early 1880s, reportedly organized by the Presbyterian minister Sheldon Jackson. He was appointed as agent for education in Alaska by the Department of Interior in 1885 but had been actively involved in establishing mission schools among other indigenous groups in the United States and in Alaska as well.[1]

The Comity Plan, or the Jackson Polity for Alaska, was a meeting that brought four or five main Protestant denominations to the table to divide Alaska into a pie of sorts. According to Dr. Henry Kendall, secretary of the Presbyterian Board of Home Missions at the time, Jackson "invited the Methodists and the Baptists and the Episcopalians. . . . to meet together and talk it over" (Stewart 1908, 364). The meeting took place in the mid-1880s, and although it appears to have been a small gathering, it had great impact on Alaska, still felt today.

> It was a small affair in outward appearance—only three secretaries and Sheldon Jackson—just enough to sit around a table; but this little company, meeting in an upper room, was sufficient to inaugurate a policy of peace, that, if adopted on a larger scale, would work for the benefit of all Christendom. And now I see these four heads bending over the little table, on which Sheldon Jackson has spread out a map of Alaska. . . . The allotment was made in perfect harmony. As the Presbyterians had been the first to enter Southeastern Alaska, they all agreed that they should retain it, untroubled by any intrusion. By the same rule, the Episcopalians were to keep the valley of the Yukon, where the Church of England [Anglican] following in the track of the Hudson Bay Company, had planted its missions forty years before. The island of Kodiak, with the adjoining region of Cook's Inlet, made a generous portion for the Baptists Brethren; while to the Methodists were assigned the Aleutian and Shumagin islands. The Moravians were to pitch their tents in the interior—in the valleys of the Kusko Kwim and the Nushagak; while the Congregationalists mounted higher to the Cape Prince of Wales, on the American side of Bering Strait; and, last of all, as nobody else could take it, the Presbyterians went to Point Barrow. (Dr. Henry M. Field, qtd. in Stewart 1908, 364–65)

The establishment of missions in Alaska was supported by the federal and territorial government and was publicly funded. Although this was, and is, in direct violation of the law that separates church and state, it was common practice, especially in regard to Native Americans. Once Native Americans were herded onto plots of reservation lands, the arrival of missionaries and mission schools was heralded as a means to "civilize" them, to make them learn English and to adopt the cultures and life ways of the Anglo-American society at the time. Nineteenth-century America was still an exclusive paternalistic society where women and African Americans could not vote and power was held in the hands of a few individuals. The federal and territorial governments facilitated the mission plans, providing not only funding but also land to build missions and mission schools.

The American missionaries of the late nineteenth century were not the first Christians to arrive in Alaska. Russian Orthodox missionaries arrived in 1794 with the early Russian expeditions. The priests and other clerics concentrated their conversion and baptism in areas where the Russian fur companies had the strongest presence—the Aleutian Islands, Kodiak Island, parts of the Alaska Peninsula, and parts of southeastern Alaska. The Russian monks and priests documented their work and exchanges with Alaska's indigenous peoples. These include Fathers Veniaminov, Netsvetov, German, and others. They learned Unangan, Sugcestun, Tlingit, and Dena'ina Athabascan and began to develop a system of writing these languages using a Cyrillic alphabet; they believed in a bilingual approach and translated passages from the Bible and other teachings. They often protested the treatment of the Native people; there are numerous examples of their attempts to protect them from the worst behavior of the Russian colonists and fur companies, who practiced slavery and rape. Russian Orthodoxy remains strong in most of these areas, due to the relationship the Orthodox priests had with the indigenous people. The priests did not wish to punish the indigenous people for speaking their languages, but they did want to make them give up their own particular religious beliefs, especially shamanism. Other early Christian missionaries included visiting Catholic priests who accompanied Spanish expeditions.[2]

With the arrival of the American missionaries in the 1880s and 1890s a whole new approach to evangelism was evident. The American missionaries, especially the Presbyterians, Quakers, Baptists, and most of the Catholics wanted to eradicate Native languages and incorporated very strict and punitive measures to do so. Further, the American Christians viewed music and dance practices and shamanism as dangerous and evil; it was common to see racist ethnocentric descriptions of Alaska's indigenous people, apparently made to justify the harsh means used by missionaries in the Christianization process:

> Hardy, but uncivilized and sadly debased Eskimos." (Stewart 1908, 374)
>
> That no trace or shadow of Christianity has found its way to their desolate regions [Yukon-Kuskokwim delta]; the dark night of Shamanism or sorcery still hangs over the human mind. (Stewart 1908, 366)

There are examples of American missionaries who did learn the Native language and practiced true Christian kindness and tolerance. These include Father Belarmine LaFortune, a Jesuit missionary who learned Iñupiaq; Archdeacon Robert McDonald, an Episcopalian missionary who learned the Gwich'in Athabascan language and with assistance from the local community translated the entire Bible into Athabascan; and the Moravian missionaries John and Edith Kilbuck, who learned the Yup'ik language fluently and developed written materials. These instances were rare; far more common was intolerance for indigenous language, family organization, and especially traditional religion. Due to the effectiveness of the mission plan for Alaska, virtually all traditional religions were eradicated.

The impact of each denomination and/or mission that was assigned to specific regions of Alaska still reverberates today. Each denomination and missionary had very specific methods for Christianizing the indigenous people—whether they tolerated indigenous language, dance, or even the indigenous design of the community. This helps to explain why some villages have higher levels of language retention than others, or some have new song composition and others do not. The following provides a thumbnail sketch of the impact of several of the missions and/or missionaries in Alaska in the nineteenth century.

Moravians

Presbyterian minister and educator Sheldon Jackson approached the Moravian church about establishing a mission in the Yukon-Kuskokwim delta area in 1883. In 1885 the first Moravian missionaries arrived. The Moravians believed in learning the Yup'ik language to better the process of evangelization and conversion. To this day, the Yup'ik language remains strong in those villages where Moravian missions were established. These include Atmauluak, Kwigillingok, Quinhagak, Togiak, Naptaskiak, Napakiak, Kwigillingok, Tuluksak, Akiak, Akiachak, Kwethluk (Kuskokwim orphanage and training school), Goodnews Bay, Kipnuk, Eek, Nunapitchuk, and Tuntutuliak. The Moravians did frown upon traditional dancing, which had to be practiced in secret or by the handful of village residents who did not wholly convert to Christianity. When traditional music and dance practices began to be openly celebrated in the late 1970s and 1980s, the Moravian villages had very strong dance groups accompanied by new song composition. This illustrates the close relationship between language retention and its fundamental importance to new song composition and music and dance practices. The Moravians were the first Christian missionaries and actively recruited converts or "helpers" who were Yup'ik, which proved to be an effective method of conversion. Other missionaries, including Catholics, also started staking out regions in southwestern Alaska. Russian Orthodoxy was present in just a handful of villages in the Yup'ik area and remained so. Russian Orthodoxy has remained strong in the Aleutian and Kodiak Island areas, even today.

Quakers or Society of Friends

The Friends or Quakers came to the Kobuk area in 1887. The nine villages in the Kobuk area had their own indigenous spiritual practices, including shamanism; prayer was expressed through ceremonial music and dance as well. The Friends believed in English-only as the best method of not only converting the Kobuk Iñupiaq into Christians but also changing their life-ways, social structure, clothing, and even house construction. They also frowned upon any type of dancing (western and especially indigenous). A standard of plainness, modesty, and simplicity are hallmarks of the Quaker belief system, and dancing was viewed as decadent. To this day, of the nine villages in the Kobuk area, only one village (Kotzebue) has a traditional dance group. The Kotzebue Northern Lights Dancers established their group in the 1980s, during the renaissance taking place throughout Alaska in the revival of traditional dance and music.

Father LaFortune, Jesuit Missionary on King Island

The Presbyterians, Catholics, and Baptists believed in very strict English-only policies. There are, however, rare incidences in which particular missionaries actually learned the language of their flock, and these are worth mentioning. King Island is a small remote island just off the coast of the Seward Peninsula. The King Island Iñupiaq people or *Okvokmiut* did not have a resident missionary until 1926, when Father Belarmine LaFortune arrived to the small island. Father LaFortune had learned Iñupiaq while in various Seward Peninsula villages.[3] He was deeply vested in the Iñupiaq community and when he came to King Island he learned their dialect of Iñupiaq. He built a church and a mission school. Father LaFortune did not practice harsh English-only policies but did teach the students English. He also is one of the very rare examples of a missionary who tolerated traditional music and dance practices. He even allowed the ceremonial Wolf Dance to continue, although he edited parts of it out (Kasgnoc, Mayac, and Ayek 2000). To this day, King Island has one of the most noted dance groups in Alaska. They have one of the largest repertoires of social songs and have also maintained their ceremonial Wolf Dance and Polar Bear Dances. The King Island people also had an unbroken masked-dance practice.

Father LaFortune allowed the mask dancing to continue as well. This is a highly unusual event, one that merits close attention. When the King Island people performed a Wolf Dance in Nome in 1980, it caught the attention of other Iñupiaq groups that had formerly practiced a similar version. The North

Slope Borough began to interview elders and resurrected the *Kivgiq* in 1990, which is their version of the Wolf Dance. Each village in the North Slope area has its own songs that were revived and relearned and brought back into community memory and practice. The *Kivgiq* occurs in January or February every other year, so that it will never be forgotten. During the 1980s when traditional social songs and dances were revived throughout Alaska, the villages that had maintained these traditions led the way and inspired many other villages to start dancing again, among them King Island, Tikigaq Point Hope, and Wainwright in the Iñupiaq-speaking areas. Today, all the North Slope villages have at least one dance group. Larger villages like Barrow have more than two or three.

Nunivak Island, a Yup'ik community, did not have a resident missionary until 1937. Their ceremonial midwinter event, called the Bladder Festival or *Ilgariq*, existed until the 1940s as a full five-day ritual. In many other Yup'ik villages it went underground or was given up due to the missionary presence. St. Lawrence Island is another example. The last person converted to Christianity in the 1960s. The level of language retention on St. Lawrence Island is close to 100 percent. There appears to be a direct correlation of language retention to the policies set by Christian missionaries, as well as the survival of any traditional ceremonial or religious practices.

DATES OF MISSIONS AND MISSION SCHOOLS IN ALASKA
(denomination, year, location)

Russian Orthodox	1794	Aleutian Islands (St. Paul's Harbor)
Russian Orthodox	1796	Kodiak Island (Three Saints Bay)
Russian Orthodox	1843	Sitka (with a school for 100 Native students)
Russian Orthodox	1845	Ikogmiut/Russian Mission (moved to St. Michaels in 1884)
Anglican Church	1847	Fort Yukon (with Hudson's Bay Company)
Canadian Catholic (Oblate)	1862–63	Fort Yukon
Canadian Episcopal	1862	Fort Yukon
Public School	1867	Sitka/for whites only
Canadian Catholic/Oblate	1872–74	Fort Yukon
Presbyterian	1877	Wrangell
Catholic	1877	Nulato

Presbyterian	1881	Sitka and Haines
Anglican	1883	Nukluklayet (Indian day school)
Baptists	1886	School in Kodiak
Baptists	1892	Orphanage and school established on Woody Island (run by the Women's American Baptist Home Missionary Society)
Moravian	1885	Bethel
Public School	1885	Juneau (for whites only)
Catholic (Jesuit)	1886	Juneau (Sisters of St. Ann)
Methodist	1886	Unga (mission and school)
Catholic	1886–87	Father Robaut in Anvik and Father Tosi in Nulato
Episcopal	1886	St. Michaels (Rev. Octavus Parker)—moved the following year to Anvik, because of the Russian Orthodox mission that was firmly established at St. Michaels
Episcopal	1887	Anvik[4]
Friends/Quakers	1887	Kotzebue and Douglas Island
Mission Covenant of Sweden	1887	Unalakleet and Yakutat
Mission Covenant of Sweden	1887	Yakutat
American Episcopal Church	1887	Anvik (Rev. John Chapman) (formerly Canadian Anglican Church)
Moravian	1886–87	Nushagak River area (abandoned in 1906)
Catholic (Jesuit)	1888	Holy Cross (Sisters of St. Ann, boarding school built in 1889)
Catholic	1888	Nelson Island and Nulato
Methodist Episcopal	1889	Unalaska (est. contract school)
Episcopalian	1890	Point Hope

Presbyterian	1890	Point Barrow
Congregational Church	1890	Wales (school and mission)
American Episcopal Church	1890	Point Hope
Methodists est. Jesse Lee Home	1890	Unalaska
Presbyterian	ca. 1895	Wainwright
Mission Covenant of Sweden	1893–94	Golovin
Presbyterian	1894	St. Lawrence Island
Lutheran	1894	Brevig
Moravians	1897	Ugovik and Quinhagak
Quakers/Friends	1897	Wales, Kotzebue, and Teller
Lutheran	1898	Teller
Catholic	1898	Nelson Island[5]
Methodist Church	1899	Sitka
Catholic	1899	Nulato; school opens
Salvation Army	1899	Skagway
Quakers/Friends	1901	Kotzebue (school established; also established a hospital and built the first high school in Kotzebue)
Catholic	1902	Nome
Quakers/Friends	1902	Shugnak, Kivalina, and Deering
Catholic	1902	Fairbanks
Catholic	1903	Nome and King Island
Catholic(?)	1906	Allakaket St. John's-in-the-Wilderness, first mission in Koyukok area
Catholic	1907	Sitka
Catholic	1926	King Island (resident missionary, Father LaFortune, and school)
Catholic	1927	Kashunak
Catholic	1928	Hooper Bay
Seventh Day Adventists	1940's	St. Lawrence Island

Negative Consequences

Why did Native people seemingly convert to Christianity so quickly? Native people in general, like all human beings, survived by adapting and changing to new ideas and teachings. The arrival of Russians and later Americans brought a host of epidemics with diseases that the indigenous people had no resistance to (smallpox, influenza, tuberculosis, STDs). The powers of their shamans and their traditional healers had no effect over these new diseases. When the Christian missionaries arrived, they knew how to prevent and treat these illnesses and provided sustenance and care for the survivors of some of the larger epidemics which occurred in 1835–40 (smallpox), 1900 (influenza followed by measles), and 1918 (influenza). The missionaries often built orphanages for the newly orphaned children and brought in canned foods to communities that were not able to build up their subsistence food storages for winters because of epidemic diseases, which crippled communities for months at a time. The shamans were powerless, the traditional healers were powerless, and the Christian missionaries took on new power. This combination, and the newly established boarding schools, ushered in a socialization process that attempted to eradicate traditional language and religion, along with music, dance, and related arts such as mask carving.

Revival

With the Native Solidarity movement of the 1960s and the landmark 1971 Alaska Native Land Claims Settlement, indigenous people in Alaska began to reclaim their identities. Dance festivals and new dance groups emerged as traditional dance began to be publicly embraced beginning in the 1970s and 1980s. By 1990 major dance festivals occurred annually in Bethel (Camai Festival), Anchorage (AFN Quyana Nights), Fairbanks (Athabascan Fiddling Festival, Festival of Alaska Native Arts), Barrow (Kivgiq), and Juneau (Celebration). There are literally hundreds of traditional dance groups in Alaska and young people are learning the regalia making, song composition, and the repertoires of their ancient cultural heritage. I will never forget the first time I attended a Camai Festival in Bethel in 1995 and saw all these young beautiful Yup'ik dancers. I had just completed extensive research on the devastating impact of disease among Alaska Natives. I had tears in my eyes as I watched the children wave their dance fans and drummers sing their songs. Tears of joy and pain. That moment stays with me when I see traditional dancing, which is why I love it so much; it is enduring and emblematic of survival.

In 2000 the Iñupiaq village of Wales hosted a *Nilgaq* for the first time in almost forty years. Wales, the westernmost village on the Seward Peninsula, is only a little over fifty miles from Siberia. The community was once known as the dance capital of the Seward Peninsula; given it size and strategic location for trade, it was a powerful and rich village. The village had at least five dance houses or *kagri*, where most villages usually had two or three. The number of dance houses was a sign of prestige in Iñupiaq villages.[6] The young people of Wales and other villages on the Seward Peninsula, including Brevig and Shishmaref, have traditional dance groups who participated in the *Nilgaq*. The youth seem to have an intuitive understanding of traditional dance, and it is an inspiration to see dance being reborn in communities where it has lain dormant. In 2004 the Native village of Wales received funding from the National Park Service to document their 2004 *Nilgaq*. The event had dance groups from Wales, Diomede Island, Shishmaref, Brevig, Nome, and Point Hope. The Point Hope dance group performed songs that their parents and grandparents had received in trade from the Wales people and were teaching them to the youth of the village, in essence repatriating them.

In 1991–93 the Catholic Church made an official apology to the indigenous people of the world. In 1999 Native Alaskans from five different Christian denominations met to discuss the issues related to Christianity. Sponsored by the United Methodist Church, a series of nationwide conferences examined spirituality and Native Americans. Healing and reconciliation were one of the main themes.[7]

Although Alaska Native people have revived their traditional dancing and drumming and even festivals, there are only a few surviving ceremonial rituals. The impact of Christian missionaries needs to be examined further, as indigenous people begin the decolonization process.

Notes

1. Vincent Colyer, secretary of the Board of Indian Commission, visited Alaska in 1869, two years after Alaska was purchased from Russia. During the winter of 1875–76 Sheldon Jackson wrote the Board of Home Missions of the Presbyterian Church to urge the establishment of missions in Alaska. In 1877 Sheldon Jackson and Amanda McFarland came to Wrangell, in southeastern Alaska, to start the first Presbyterian mission and school there. Since English was not commonly spoken at the time, they used two translators, a Tsimshian woman they called "Clah" and Mrs. Sarah Dickinson, who was probably part Tlingit. They opened their school in August 1877.

2. In 1779 a Spanish priest reportedly baptized several Indian children and took five "abandoned" Native children with him as converts (Balcom in Henkelman and Vitt 1985, 35).

3. Oral history of King Island indicates that a powerful medicine man told the King Island people, long before the arrival of missionaries, that one day a person would come and make the sign of the cross and they would have a new path, and the King Island people were to follow that path because this would be a good person (Catherine Kasnoc, Ted Mayac, Sylvester Ayek, personal interviews in Nome, Alaska, 2000; Paul Tiulana, personal interview, November 1993).

4. The local Anvik Athabascans were trading in St. Michael's and they mistook the Protestant missionary for a trader. They invited him to their village thinking that he would open up a trading post (Van Stone 1979, 136).

5. Father A. Parodi, S.J., came to Nelson Island in 1898. "This mission was a very difficult one at that time, as it was isolated and the food supply was scanty. Furthermore, many of the Eskimos [Yup'ik] were under the influence of the medicine men at that time, and did not exactly welcome the missionary, whom they considered an intruder. After several years at Nelson Island, the strain became too much for Father Parodi and he became mentally ill. Some of the friendly Eskimos took him to St. Mary's, where the priests and sisters took good care of him until he was able to be sent south for a complete recovery" (Balcom 1970, 88).

6. Kagri or dance houses were special structures in each community and membership was usually along kinship lines. Each dance house had its own repertoire of songs, and many of the houses were used for ceremonial events as well. Missionaries, of course, destroyed most of these.

7. Mike Dunham, "Ecumenical Meeting Explores Native Christianity," *Anchorage Daily News*, November 6, 1999, E-6.

Dena'ina Heritage and Representation in Anchorage: A Collaborative Project

Stephen J. Langdon and Aaron Leggett (Dena'ina Athabascan)

This essay emerged from a collaborative project undertaken by Stephen Langdon and Aaron Leggett at the University of Alaska, Anchorage with various Dena'ina Athabascan organizations in south central Alaska to develop accurate representation of Dena'ina heritage in the municipality of Anchorage and Matanuska-Susitna borough. The italicized texts are Aaron Leggett's personal experiences and reflections on issues of Dena'ina heritage and representation in Anchorage, which, with over 250,000 residents, is the largest city in Alaska. Founded in the early twentieth century, the city expanded over time and displaced the local indigenous Dena'ina Athabascan. Like most American cities, then, Anchorage has an indigenous past that has remained invisible. Stephen J. Langdon was raised in Anchorage and is a professor of anthropology at the University of Alaska, Anchorage. He has conducted numerous research projects throughout Alaska on a variety of public policy issues related to Alaska Natives but has specialized in southeast Alaska on topics related to precontact, historic, and contemporary fisheries of the Tlingit and Haida people. He is the author of The Native People of Alaska *(4th ed., 2002) and the editor of* Contemporary Alaska Native Economies *(1986). Aaron Leggett, a historian of the indigenous people of the Cook Inlet region, is a Dena'ina Athabascan and is a member of the Native Village of Eklutna, in the Cook Inlet region. He holds a B.A. in anthropology from the University of Alaska, Anchorage.*

The coast of south central Alaska is penetrated by a long watery arm that extends over 150 miles from the Pacific Ocean in the south to the mouth of the Knik River in the north. Dena'ina Athabascans occupy the shoreline of this inlet, which they call *Tikahtnu*, "Big water river" in the Dena'ina language. The uppermost reaches of the arm are the home to the *K'enaht'ana*[1] branch of the Dena'ina whose villages, fish camps, trails, battlegrounds, graves, and other sites dotted and crisscross the land and water of the area.

The *K'enaht'ana* region was never settled or colonized by Russians who established and maintained a trading post further south on *Tikahtnu* at present-day Kenai. Following purchase by the United States in 1867, the region remained isolated until late in the nineteenth century when several military exploratory expeditions and a few mineral prospectors briefly passed through the area (Kari and Fall 2003). A small port named Knik was established at a Dena'ina village site on the western shore of *Tikahtnu* in 1906 to provide mail and supplies to Euro-American settlers, but in 1914 things changed dramatically and rapidly. At a site at the mouth of *Dgheyaytnu*, today known as Ship Creek (see Orth 1971), a tent camp was built as a construction base for the Alaska Railroad and became Anchorage; today Anchorage is the largest city in Alaska and 50 percent of the entire population of Alaska lives in this area.[2] Little heed was paid to the *K'enaht'ana* fish camp at the mouth of Ship Creek as the bustling tent city of construction workers, 5,000 persons strong, completely engulfed them. By 1918, the *K'enaht'ana* moved their fish camp out to *Nutul'iy* (Fire Island) where they continued subsistence salmon harvesting and processing into the 1970s. The island location could only be reached and returned from by those with a detailed understanding of the working of the tidal flows of *Tikahtnu*. On the island, the Dena'ina families were able to reestablish camps and continue their customary and traditional salmon harvesting and processing activities in a spot away from the tumult of burgeoning Anchorage. At *Nutul'iy* they were protected by the turbulent tides to whose ways they were carefully attentive.

The explosive expansion of Anchorage prompted by Cold War militarization in Alaska after World War II ignored the fact that the region was the homeland to the *K'enaht'ana*. Dena'ina lands were appropriated without recognition or compensation by the businesses and residents of Anchorage as the *K'enaht'ana*, dramatically reduced by the 1918 flu epidemic, gradually abandoned their fish camps that were being swallowed up by Euro-American expansion. The *K'enaht'ana* were left to themselves, for the most part, in the village of *Idlughtet* (Eklutna) to the north of Anchorage, where a reserve was established around their traditional home. With the loss of their fish camps, trails, trap lines, and hunting grounds, they essentially became invisible in their homeland and absent from the consciousness of the newcomers to the "last frontier," as Alaska came to be known.

My grandmother was from the village of Eklutna and shared many of the stories that she experienced growing up. During this time of rapid growth, I believe most people were probably unaware that Natives lived and maintained a subsistence lifestyle within the Anchorage bowl until Statehood occurred in 1959. Speaking from my own experiences, the only way that I knew that there were Dena'ina people still within the area was through my grandmother, and I became frustrated whenever I would try to explain this to others in Anchorage. In fact, it was not until I was 19 years old that I read an article written by Eklutna elder Alberta Stephan and realized that my great-great-grandfather and our family had fished in Anchorage until about 1918. Just as with my situation, many Dena'ina did not learn our history as we were growing up. In my case, I feel my family had to be focused on adapting to and surviving within what has become Alaska's largest city. One of the reasons for this ignorance, I believe, is there is little in the way of public representation of our Dena'ina people's prior uses of significant places, streams and other aspects of the Anchorage area.

The Euro-American leaders of Anchorage have positioned the history of the city as a trajectory of European and American cultural history, primarily because the intellectual and cultural atmosphere of the mid-twentieth century viewed Native American rights and concerns as an unwanted relic to be eradicated from the political face of the United States. Federal policy initiatives in the 1950s such as termination and relocation sought to end the constitutional recognition of Native American governments and remove indigenous North Americans from their homelands through educational and employment programs (Skinner 1997; Arnold 1976). In Alaska, the tactic of promoting connection to European and American history, with no regard for its original indigenous inhabitants, was employed to raise awareness of Alaska and to create recognition of its strategic geopolitical position as a means to acquiring statehood, a status achieved in 1959.

Within Downtown Anchorage very little in the way of public recognition of Dena'ina is available. On the corner of 3rd and F, the heart of the tourist visiting area, there is one sign that presents two facts about the Tanaina (an older outdated spelling). The sign says that we have only been here for about 350 years, which is wrong, and that half our population died off in the flu epidemic. To me what this does is marginalize the Dena'ina existence by saying that we haven't lived here that long and that when Americans came in they just utilized the land they saw in front of them in one of the last acts of Manifest Destiny.[3]

This privileging of European and American history and culture is symbolically demonstrated by the prominent positioning of a statue of Captain James Cook, the first-known European explorer to view the area, in a park named after his flagship *Resolution*. The park is located on a high bluff overlooking *Tikahtnu* at the edge of the city's business district, where it fosters the impression of the commander gazing omnisciently from his ship, thereby assimilating the landscape he perceives, transforming it into what later became his

1. Signage in downtown Anchorage on the Dena'ina, the original inhabitants of the area. Photo by Stephen Langdon.

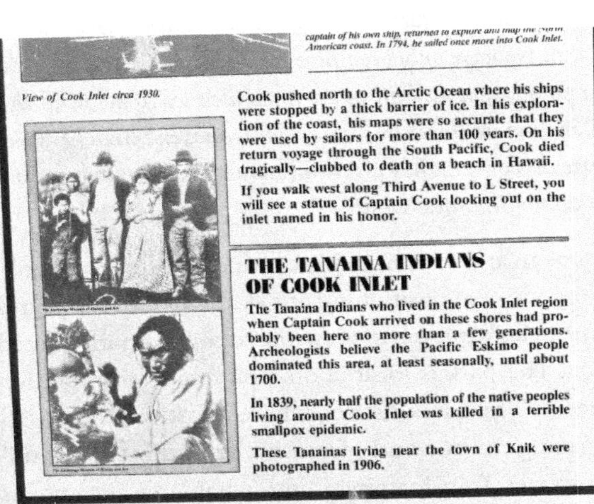

captain of his own ship, returned to explore and map the North American coast. In 1794, he sailed once more into Cook Inlet.

View of Cook Inlet circa 1930.

Cook pushed north to the Arctic Ocean where his ships were stopped by a thick barrier of ice. In his exploration of the coast, his maps were so accurate that they were used by sailors for more than 100 years. On his return voyage through the South Pacific, Cook died tragically—clubbed to death on a beach in Hawaii.

If you walk west along Third Avenue to L Street, you will see a statue of Captain Cook looking out on the inlet named in his honor.

THE TANAINA INDIANS OF COOK INLET

The Tanaina Indians who lived in the Cook Inlet region when Captain Cook arrived on these shores had probably been here no more than a few generations. Archeologists believe the Pacific Eskimo people dominated this area, at least seasonally, until about 1700.

In 1839, nearly half the population of the native peoples living around Cook Inlet was killed in a terrible smallpox epidemic.

These Tanainas living near the town of Knik were photographed in 1906.

2. Close-up of the signage in downtown Anchorage, with inaccurate information on the "Tanaina" (Dena'ina). Photo by Stephen Langdon.

namesake Cook Inlet. Nowhere in this symbolic hegemony is there mention that this place is the homeland of the *K'enaht'ana*. To the authors, this constant reminder of the lack of any respectful recognition of Dena'ina heritage in the self-conscious representations of Anchorage has been both painful and a powerful prompt to action.

> *Another item in Downtown Anchorage that has always bothered me is on 3rd and L Street at what is called Resolution Park where a statute of Captain Cook stands. A statue for a man who spent ten days here and never got off his boat and therefore because he "discovered" this area, we no longer use the far more descriptive name Tikahtnu or "Big water river" for the inlet.*[4]

Dr. James Fall, whose collaborative research with Susitnuht'ana elder Shem Pete began in the 1970s, was well aware of both the extensive knowledge of and use of the Anchorage area by the *K'enaht'ana* and the near total lack of recognition of their presence in contemporary public representation in Anchorage. In conjunction with a research project concerning Dena'ina heritage on the local military bases with Dr. Nancy Davis, Fall prepared a public lecture

3. Statue of Captain James Cook in downtown Anchorage, Alaska. Photo by Stephen Langdon.

for presentation at the Anchorage Museum of History and Art on October 14, 2004.[5] The title of the lecture was "Dena'ina Ełena, Dena'ina Lands" and Fall announced that he was prompted to prepare the lecture by the admonition from the Eklutna historian Alberta Stephan, herself a published author. She stated, "It is important to the Athabascan Indian People that their history of a well organized lifestyle be known to everyone" (Fall 2004).

Collaborative Course/Project

In the summer of 2005, in response to the University of Alaska, Anchorage, Community Engagement and Learning Program's proposal solicitation, an idea for a course/project to address issues of Dena'ina heritage and representation in Anchorage was developed and submitted. The course/project proposal was initially voiced and developed by Langdon with co-instructor James Fall and teaching assistant Aaron Leggett, a senior anthropology major at the time. Langdon and Leggett, both raised in Anchorage, were troubled by the absence of respectful Dena'ina heritage recognition in the Anchorage area, while Fall, whose research with Shem Pete on place names and Dena'ina cultural activities in the *Tikahtnu* area dated to the late 1970s, had endeavored to bring the lack of public recognition of Dena'ina to the attention of Anchorage residents and leaders on a number of occasions in the recent past. Our idea was to combine academic instruction on Dena'ina culture and history with investigation of Dena'ina heritage representation in Anchorage, culminating in the development of accurate, respectful, and meaningful heritage posters appropriate for public display in different areas of Anchorage. We hoped to integrate the heritage poster designs into an overall plan for markers to be appropriately placed throughout the Anchorage municipality.

After agreeing on the idea of the course/project at UAA, preliminary concepts for the course/project were shared with the tribal council of the Native Village of Eklutna. Subsequently a meeting was held in the Eklutna tribal chambers and received the support of the tribe. In late summer 2005, Langdon brought UAA Native Student Services director William Templeton (Iñupiaq) up to speed on the project; Templeton joined the collaboration by writing a letter of support for the Community Engagement and Learning grant proposal, identified potential Native students for the course, and invited the organizers to a Native Student Services potluck to announce the impending offering of the course in the spring 2006 semester. Templeton also facilitated the enrollment of Eklutna tribal members in the course and coordinated funding from the local Alaska Native Corporation's nonprofit arm, the CIRI Foundation.

At the same time, Langdon recruited UAA colleague Dr. Phyllis Fast (Koyukon Athabascan) to join the course/project team. As an Athabascan artist herself and a student of Alaska Native art, Fast had experience that would be beneficial in considering the aesthetic and communicative dimensions of heritage representation.

As the time for submission of the proposal grew nearer, letters of support were acquired from Cook Inlet Region Incorporated (CIRI), the for-profit corporation established by the Alaska Native Claims Settlement Act of 1971, the Alaska Native Heritage Center, and the CIRI Foundation. Our efforts were rewarded in fall 2005 when we received notification from the Community Engagement and Learning program that the course/project had been approved for the spring semester.

Course/Project Implementation

The course/project was designed to consist of four components: (1) Dena'ina culture and history; (2) student inventory of Dena'ina representation in the Anchorage area; (3) student design of accurate, respectful, and meaningful prototype heritage posters, and, (4) development of a spatial plan for the location of Dena'ina heritage posters in the Upper Cook Inlet area. Our outreach efforts drew fifteen students, six of whom were Dena'ina. The Dena'ina students were major contributors to the course and worked cooperatively with their fellow non-Dena'ina students in the inventory and design components of the project.

Dena'ina heritage content in culture and history was accomplished through readings, lectures by Dr. James Fall, guest presentations, films, and Dena'ina elder panels. Our objective was to convey substantive information about Dena'ina cultural heritage, especially in the area around Anchorage, focusing on themes, locations, place names, and activities. A substantial amount of Dena'ina oral literature was also incorporated into the course with volumes by Alberta Stephan (1996, 2001) and James Fall (Kari and Fall 2003) being used as primary texts. A number of guest presentations were made to the class. A panel of Eklutna Dena'ina elders provided a moving discussion of their experiences as Dena'ina growing up in the Anchorage area. They commented that this was the first occasion during their lives when the university had offered any courses that dealt with their cultural and contemporary history. The chief of the Native Village of Eklutna, Lee Stephan, provided an overview of the tribe's present programs and recent issues, such as the proposed blasting of the two rocky areas located near the village for gravel in the 1990s. Gravel is a needed resource for Anchorage roads and a way to bring income into

4. Dena'ina students in Dena'ina Heritage and Representation class point to their homeland. From left, counterclockwise: Maria Coleman, Marilyn Balluta, Deborah Call, Delia Call, Trescia Coleman, and Aaron Leggett. Photo by Stephen Langdon.

the small village. He also discussed the planning for a traditional Dena'ina house and associated cultural displays to be constructed on Ship Creek that was being designed by a Native Village of Eklutna team in association with the expansion of the Port of Anchorage. Jon Ross and Donita Peter (both Dena'ina Athabascan) of the Alaska Native Heritage Center presented information on their work with Dena'ina language preservation and curriculum development. Dr. William Workman (professor of archaeology, University of Alaska, Anchorage) and Dr. Douglas Reger (Alaska Office of History and Archaeology) gave an overview of archaeological research in the Cook Inlet portion of the Dena'ina region. Dr. Aron Crowell of the Smithsonian Institution Center in Anchorage delivered information on his approach to collaborative planning for the Anchorage museum expansion and preliminary thoughts on how the Dena'ina would be represented. The class also viewed the film *Tubughna* made by the Dena'ina people of Tyonek and Frank Brink about their culture and history (Brink and Brink 1988).

During the middle third of the course, students were assigned the task of taking inventory of various public representations of Dena'ina heritage in the Anchorage area. The students were provided with cameras and GPS instruments to document the locations and appearance of the images they identified. They covered much of the Anchorage bowl from Girdwood in the south to Chugiak in the north, while three students who lived in nearby Matanuska Valley communities to the north canvassed that area. The students then prepared PowerPoint presentations of their findings that were delivered to the class. The students discovered that there were very few public representations of Dena'ina heritage and that those that did exist were often inaccurate and demeaning. In addition, when any information appeared, it was typically presented in generic form, as either Dena'ina or Athabascan. Here and there streets and parks had been given Anglicized versions of Dena'ina names by some haphazard process but there was no additional information or context provided concerning the name. For example, the name Tikishla Park was based on the Dena'ina name for "black bear" but no information on the source of the name was provided on any of the signs on which the name appeared. This is an example of the random manner in which occasional nods to Dena'ina appeared within the general Anchorage municipal pattern in which the place names that are proposed and adopted reference specific persons and historic moments. Street and park names are primarily intended to provide reference points for management and use, and respectful recognition of Dena'ina or education about Dena'ina culture is not an objective of the practice.

The students discovered several other characteristics of Dena'ina representations. They observed that the information they encountered was presented in a depersonalized (named individuals were never presented) manner and paid no attention to Dena'ina knowledge of or use of an area. They also noted that Dena'ina representations were typically ahistoric with regard to the Dena'ina cultural experience prior to the coming of Euro-Americans. Dena'ina oral traditions and heritage concerning locations was nonexistent in the representations.[6] Another observation students made was that some organizations had erected totem poles as a form of generic recognition of Alaska Native culture. However, such poles were constructed by the Tlingit and Haida people of southeast Alaska and were not a part of the cultural heritage of the Dena'ina. Observers could misconstrue totem poles out of context and without explanatory information as either characteristic of Alaska Natives in general or of Dena'ina in the Anchorage area.

There is one exception to the above inventories. A respectful and contextualized Dena'ina representation was identified at Chugiak High School, located in proximity to the village of Eklutna, a mural depicting Dena'ina salmon fish trap construction and use; it was displayed with a detailed and relevant discussion of the design and operational principles upon which such fish traps operated. It is noteworthy that Dena'ina elder Alberta Stephan was consulted by the designers and played the central role in the development of the exhibit.

The final part of the course was devoted to student development of accurate, respectful, and meaningful heritage posters. The plan was these heritage posters would be prototypes of permanent signage. Groupings of students with Dena'ina and non-Dena'ina memberships were created with three to four students per group. A variety of possible forms and key issues were discussed in class as the topic of indigenous self-representation was explored. Key questions included: Who would be the decision-making authority to decide what was to be presented? What materials would be presented given possible differences of opinion and sensitivity over certain issues? How would postcontact relations be dealt with? What would be said about the manner in which Dena'ina in the Anchorage area had been treated?

Following discussions that explored these questions, we returned for guidance to the earlier remark from elder Alberta Stephan concerning the importance of demonstrating the "well-organized lifestyle" of the Dena'ina. Given the nonexistent or haphazard representations of Dena'ina heritage identified by the students, this statement was a powerful guiding principle.

In the class, a number of possible forms of cultural representation were discussed. Maria Coleman, a member of the Eklutna tribe involved in the design of the Ship Creek display, indicated that the fish camps in the Anchorage municipality were associated and owned by Dena'ina families. Family stories and photos were going to be the foundation of the displays prepared by the Native Village of Eklutna for the Ship Creek. We discussed various possible cultural themes such as salmon fishing, beluga hunting, trapping, berry gathering, processing and storage, clothing, song, dance, and historic events. Another possible form of representation was place names—but in our vision, place names were to be established in association with actual Dena'ina uses and contextualized with regard to why the name was given, what story went with the name, and what the name meant. Sites and associated activities constituted another possible form of representation. The actual physical locations of Dena'ina camps were of great significance to the Dena'ina elders who spoke to the class; therefore it was decided that this would be a primary emphasis in designing the heritage representations.

A final category of representation included that of vista; vistas provide the opportunity to present a large number of place names and associated heritage information displayed across photos of broad swathes of landscape and could be placed at strategic locations in the Anchorage area. Several such locations were identified, including the 3rd and L overlook (where Cook's statue is located); Chugach State Park, high in the mountains immediately to the east of Anchorage; Kincaid Park, which has a bluff view facing southward; and Eklutna Lake campground, from which the entire length of the lake can be viewed, backed by the spectacular looming Chugach Mountains. An important consideration in our thinking about the location of vista forms of heritage representation is that they should be positioned at places frequented by substantial numbers of visitors and residents in order to maximize the public education potential of the location.

Drawing on information and images presented earlier in the class, students returned to the field at various locations to fulfill their assignments. They took a variety of photos at their location to show how the sign could be positioned to best fit into the site. They selected various informational forms—text, art, photos, and drawings—and positioned them on PowerPoint posters. As the final component of the class, each student gave a presentation of his or her site, the information associated with the site, and the prototype design for heritage markers to be erected at the site.

Here are three examples of the Dena'ina heritage markers designed by students in the course. The first one concerns "Chanshtnu" (now known as Chester Creek) and the former Dena'ina fish camp located in the vicinity of modern Westchester Lagoon. The second is a design to memorialize a battle the Dena'ina fought against Alutiiqs (another Alaska Native group) at Point Campbell. The final example is a vista scene proposed for a parking lot at an entrance to Chugach State Park, high in the mountains overlooking Anchorage.

Our initial final objective for the course was to integrate the inventory and heritage marker prototypes into an overall presentation to deliver to the Anchorage Municipal Assembly as a call to action. Our efforts during the class to stimulate interest in the class/project in various municipal offices such as Parks and Recreation and Planning had met with little response. The mayor commended us in a letter for bringing forth important heritage information. Thus the class ended without completion of the objective of formally presenting the Dena'ina heritage representations to the municipal government. But the end of the course was not the end of the collaborative efforts or of the heritage posters prepared by the students.

Epilogue

In the summer of 2006, initial printings were done of a number of the prototype heritage markers prepared by the students. Some of the posters are of substantial size and are suitable for public presentation while others require additional editing and reprinting. Two of the posters ultimately did make an appearance before the municipal government in a somewhat unexpected way. In the summer of 2006, Leggett testified before and worked with a municipal committee responsible for recommending a name for the new civic and convention center being built in downtown Anchorage. After examining a variety of possible names, the committee decided to recommend "Dena'ina Civic and Convention Center" to the assembly. In August 2006, a public hearing was held prior to the Anchorage assembly voting on the recommended name of the new center. Leggett testified as the first pubic witness in support of the recommended name. Several of the posters were prominently displayed during the hearing, while Eklutna elders and spokespersons supported the proposed name and thanked the assembly members for the long overdue recognition. The assembly then voted 11–0 in support of the name "Dena'ina Civic and Convention Center" and following the announcement of the vote, assembly members, mayor, staff and the audience all rose to applaud the decision in a moving and memorable moment of public affirmation.

> *Today, however, things are finally changing. The Dena'ina have reached a place where we feel comfortable sharing our history of what we know about this landscape and how it has shaped who we are as a people. In other words, to borrow a phrase from a distinguished Dena'ina elder, we are no longer satisfied with being the "invisible people." We have a story to tell here about our land. But it is more than that; I think finally people are starting to realize the depth that we can bring to the table. In fact our new convention center in downtown Anchorage will recognize this by being named the Dena'ina Civic and Convention Center and that it will honor the people by using Dena'ina names for the various rooms throughout. This I think is a huge step forward and through the class we reinforced something that has been beneath the surface waiting to be exposed for far too long.*

Meanwhile, on the UAA campus, Langdon and Leggett have been working on having *Chanshtnu* signs placed at key locations along the route of the creek as it flows through the campus. These waters are the upper portion of the creek that previously was home to the Dena'ina fish camp depicted in the first of the heritage markers previously shown. Dr. Herbert Schroeder, coordinator of the Alaska Native Science and Engineering Program (ANSEP) and overseer of the new building under construction to house the program, has agreed to the name "Chanshtnu Commons" for a barbecue and picnic area that is located outside the new building in proximity to the stream. When she learned of this idea, Eklutna tribal member and class participant Maria Coleman wrote that it would be a good place to re-energize away from the glass and steel where sunlight, trees, and stream combine to lift your spirit.

The collaborative efforts on which the Dena'ina Heritage and Representation course/project were built have continued to grow and transform in various different contexts (Leggett 2006). While much work lies ahead, including another session of the course/project in the spring semester of 2007, the recognition of Dena'ina heritage in the municipality of Anchorage and the willingness to inclusively involve Dena'ina in Anchorage's future represent substantial strides. We hope that these positive developments will continue to grow in the future so that the residents of and visitors to Anchorage will come to know and appreciate the rich heritage of the Dena'ina Athabascans in this place.

Notes

1. The names "Knik" for the earliest Euroamerican town site in the area and "Knik Arm," the most northerly appendage of *Tikahtnu* (Cook Inlet), are derived from this term for the regional Dena'ina population.

2. The railroad had been routed through the area on its transit from a port to the south on the Gulf of Alaska from Seward to the gold rush town of Fairbanks on the Chena River in the middle of Alaska.

3. In the aftermath of the Anchorage Assembly's vote to name the Anchorage Convention Center the "Dena'ina Civic and Convention Center," Leggett was appointed to the board of the Anchorage Historic Properties Commission. That commission controls the signage of Anchorage's downtown streets. Incidentally, the matter of the offensive sign came up at a meeting in September 2008. Leggett indicated that the sign was offensive, whereupon the executive director invited Leggett to accompany him to the sign; he then unbolted and removed it. This act is a significant indicator of a change in attitude toward recognition and incorporation of the Dena'ina in the symbolic landscape of Anchorage.

4. In their poster presentations Dena'ina students invariably used the English phrase "upper inlet" rather than "upper Cook Inlet" to indicate their perspective.

5. Other contributors during Fall's lecture included Dr. Nancy Davis, the Dena'ina historian Alberta Stephan, and other Dena'ina elders.

6. A particularly egregious example of the lack of attention to Dena'ina oral tradition and cultural heritage is that of Mt. Susitna, a distinctive feature on Anchorage's western horizon across *Tikahtnu*. The term "Sleeping Lady" has been applied to the mountain and putatively linked to Dena'ina oral tradition in Euro-American writing. Dena'ina do not recognize the "Sleeping Lady" story and have entirely different oral traditions about the mountain (Kari and Fall 2003).

How It Feels to Have Your History Stolen

Ted Mayac Sr. *(King Island Iñupiaq)*

In the late 1990s a librettist named Deborah Baley Breevort and the composer David Friedman wrote an oratorio titled King Island Christmas, *which was produced in Juneau, Alaska, and later in New York. The libretto is based on an event that happened on King Island in the mid-twentieth century involving community members who are now deceased. The King Island Native community has vehemently protested the oratorio for its romanticized storyline, Disneyfication of the community's customs and lifeways, and crude representation of their language as cave man–like. The composer and librettist have rebutted the protest with the claim of creative license.*

Ted Mayac Sr. was born and raised on Okviok or King Island. He is a traditional ivory carver and singer, deeply involved in preserving his community's history, language, and life ways. He is a member of the King Island Native community's board and has also served on the board for the Alaska Native Heritage Center. The people on King Island have a distinct dialect of Iñupiaq and also a unique lifestyle resulting from their remote island location. In the late 1960s the U.S. government forced the King Island people to relocate to the mainland. The small community of several hundred has managed to remain a community by continuing their song and dance practice. The King Island music and dance repertoire is known all over Alaska as one of the most powerful groups.

Here are my reflections, recalling the meeting between the King Island people and the "King Island Record Company" in December of 1999. The librettist of an oratorio titled *King Island Christmas* notified the King Island people living in Anchorage, Alaska, about her desire to meet with them concerning the upcoming grand opening of this play in Juneau, Alaska, for the Christmas season of 1999. The King Island people agreed to meet with her. The debate and the eventual realization of her belated attempt to garner the blessing and the approval of the King Islanders became apparent. We agreed that she and her cohorts were really trying to forestall an angry outcry from the King Island people. She timed her meeting with the King Island people knowing full well that the oratorio was scheduled to open shortly after this meeting.

The meeting was strained from the beginning. As the meeting progressed, she became increasingly arrogant, confrontational, and overbearing. She dismissed the concerns and objections expressed by the King Islanders as meaningless and trivial, not worthy of consideration.

The King Islanders asked her if she had applied for the agreement and approval of the King Island IRA Council at Nome. She said she already had this permission, but in reality it was never given or formally granted to her company.

The King Island people objected to the story line of the oratorio, which blatantly misrepresented the King Island culture and the way of life. The objections included the arbitrary portrayal of the King Islanders, the inclusion of tribal customs outside the King Island practices, and the disrespectful dissemination of false information to bolster the successful outcome of the oratorio.

It is generally known and accepted that the differing groups in Alaska respect and honor the tribal ways and traditions, which are solely owned customs belonging only to those tribes which practice them. The librettist wrongfully attributed many customs to the King Island culture that did not in fact pertain to our culture. This is offensive to the King Islanders. The arbitrary insertion of these non–king Island customs within the King Island culture cast the islanders as usurpers of other tribes' practices and customs. The King Islanders are made to appear as if they do not honor or respect the other indigenous ethnic groups in Alaska.

The real damage caused by the inception and the performance of this oratorio is lasting and unforgettable. The young audiences are purposefully misled to believe that the King Island people live the idyllic life as portrayed. This play is adversely affecting the King Island people, who have been cast in a false light, misrepresented, and arbitrarily characterized without permission and agreement. This oratorio is an affront not only to King Island people but also to all the tribes residing in Alaska and elsewhere. It blatantly violates and dishonors the intellectual and the cultural property rights not only of the King Island people but also of those who live and practice a parallel way of life in Alaska, northern Canada, Greenland, and Siberia.

This example of the long-established protocol of "creative license" solely benefiting the theatrical industry has awakened the collective alienation of the King Island people and their indigenous neighbors. We must find ways to counteract this overbearing and paternalistic attitude, which logically and rightfully has no right to make up stories about our history, our culture, and our way of life.

They have stolen my history and misrepresented it.

Undermining Our Tribal Governments: The Stripping of Land, Resources, and Rights from Alaska Native Nations

Evon Peter *(Neetsaii Gwich'in Athabascan and Jewish)*

This essay focuses on the relationship between resource exploitation and its associated erosion of traditional indigenous values of caring for the land. The impacts of social, economic, political, and spiritual forces have riveted the foundation of indigenous ways of life. Evon Peter explores the history of colonization to find that the same epistemological roots that allowed for earlier violation of human rights on a global scale still have a stronghold in contemporary policy and attitude. The essay addresses the challenges indigenous communities face to decolonize thought and practice. Peter is Neetsaii Gwich'in Athabascan and Jewish and represents the emerging younger generation of Alaska Native leadership. He currently serves as chair of the Native Movement Collective and is former chief of the Neetsaii Gwich'in tribe of Arctic Village. He has also served on the board of directors for the Council of Athabascan Tribal Governments, Native Village of Venetie Tribal Government, Tanana Chiefs Conference, and Alaska Inter-Tribal Council. He is a well-recognized advocate of indigenous people's rights, youth, and a balanced world and is active as a speaker, strategist, writer, and organizer. His international experience includes work with indigenous people as well as within the United Nations and Arctic Council forum.

For the past couple hundred years the sovereign authority of Alaska Native nations has been undermined by both Russia and the United States as they have embarked on the process of western colonization. This has been a time of great transition and turmoil for Indigenous peoples in Alaska.[1] It is time for the truth to be told and a new dialogue opened regarding the decolonization of the Indigenous nations of Alaska. As this dialogue and process unfolds, Alaska Native nations should, at a bare minimum, be afforded the same rights and recognitions as Indian tribes within the continental United States.

At the time of first contact with European nations, Indigenous peoples were not considered "real" or "civilized" human beings, and, therefore, were afforded minimal recognition and rights. Our lands and resources were illegitimately claimed by Russia and later illegitimately sold to the United States through the Treaty of Cession in 1867. Indigenous nations were excluded from both negotiations of Russian land claims and the Treaty of Cession because of our lack of "human status" in the view of western thinking and legal systems. However, because tribes did exist (and still do exist) on the land, both Russia and the United States developed and implemented policies to address what is termed the "Indian problem."

Indigenous social and political systems as well as Indigenous land and resource management practices fell under attack by the U.S. government. The U.S. government utilized colonial mechanisms such as religious groups, military, local U.S. governing bodies, and schools to colonize Indigenous peoples. In this way they denounced Indigenous languages, spirituality, cultural practices, and belief systems. Fortunately, many of our tribes were remote and resistant, and therefore our ways of life were passed on.

Nonetheless, it has been a struggle for Indigenous peoples to first attain recognition as human beings and second to pursue justice within the political context of Alaska and the United States. The challenge our tribes face in reclaiming management over our lives, lands, and resources is a product of this history. Through self-determination and sovereignty, regaining ownership of traditional lands and resources, as well as implementing traditional practices of sustainability, our tribes can transition to a state of balance, both internally and with other nations.

Self-determination and sovereignty equate to the total freedom of an individual or group of peoples, such as tribes and nations, to make decisions on their own behalf without subjugation to another sovereign. This does not imply that one sovereign does not influence decisions within another sovereign, only that the final decision lies within each sovereign. Treaties are agreements made between two sovereigns. The United States has broken every single treaty made with tribes in the continental United States and they chose not to make treaties with Alaska Native tribes in an attempt to avoid the sovereign recognition of our nations.

Federal Indian Law

As a way of undermining the recognition of the full sovereignty of Indigenous tribes, the United States developed a body of law, known as Federal Indian law. This body of law outlines the relationship between the federal government and Indigenous tribes, from the U.S. government's perspective. Federal Indian law is based on a conglomeration of U.S. founding documents, federal legislation, administrative orders, as well as federal and state court cases. The result is that Indigenous tribes in the United States possess what is referred to as "limited sovereignty," through which tribes possess "limited self-determination." This is a form of sovereignty that is subject to the desires of those in power within Congress, the administrative branch, and the courts. Through this process the United States attempts to validate control and authority over Indigenous nations, our lands and our resources. Ultimately it is the U.S. military strength, willingness to use that strength, and the impacts of assimilation that maintain the compliance of Indigenous nations to U.S. subjugation. It has been through the struggles of many Indigenous people and their tribes that Federal Indian law has incorporated these limited policies of self-determination and recognition of sovereignty.

The Alaska Native Claims Settlement Act

In an attempt to legitimize U.S. ownership and governance over Indigenous peoples, their land, and their resources within Alaska, the U.S. Congress unilaterally passed the Alaska Native Claims Settlement Act (ANCSA) in 1971. The act created thirteen regional for-profit corporations and made Alaska Natives shareholders of the corporations based on regional areas. The act also provided for payment of nearly one billion dollars to the corporations for the taking of nearly all the lands and resources within Alaska. Although a few Native people participated in the debates surrounding the passage of ANCSA, it was not a legitimately negotiated treaty or settlement between the United States and Alaska Native tribes. ANCSA was void of direct negotiation with Alaska Native tribes and was not put to a vote of the Indigenous peoples.

Furthermore, ANCSA extinguished previously recognized Indian reservations in Alaska (with the exception of Metlakatla), extinguished Indigenous hunting and fishing rights, and paved the way for the oil industry and state government to access and transport oil from northern Alaska. This act was essentially a social and political experiment on Alaska Native peoples. ANCSA was a way of dealing with the "Indian problem" through assimilation, exploitation, corporatization, and extinguishment of Indigenous rights. It was a politically correct illusion that perpetuated colonization in contemporary times. Even so, many Alaska Natives viewed the act as "better than nothing," trying to make the best of the situation. These people realized that resistance might lead to massacre or incarceration, as was the practice with Indigenous tribes in the continental United States when they resisted the westward expansion and manifest destiny. When considering that just thirty years earlier Alaska

Natives were not even afforded basic civil rights, such as shopping in some stores and participating in certain business, it is not surprising that ANCSA was viewed positively among some people.

Over thirty years have passed since the enactment of ANCSA. In that time Alaska Natives have become better studied in the western professions, academia, and history. We understand that ANCSA, the Alaska Statehood Act, and the Treaty of Cession were all fundamentally illegitimate legislation that resulted in the unjust appropriation of our traditional lands and resources by the United States. In similar situations around the world, such as within Africa and India, the global community came together to support a process of decolonization based on moral integrity and justice. We need to reopen the doors of dialogue between Alaska Native tribes and the federal government to address the unjust colonization of our peoples, lands, and resources.

Indian Self-Determination and Education Assistance Act

In 1993, the federal government extended federal recognition to Alaska Native tribes. Prior to federal recognition, many federal Indian laws and programs were already applied to Alaska Natives, such as the Indian Health Service (IHS) benefits, Bureau of Indian Affairs (BIA) programs, and the Indian Self-Determination and Education Assistance Act (ISDEAA) of 1975. In particular, the ISDEAA paved the way for tribes, including Alaska Native tribes, to begin directly contracting with the federal government to manage programs that were intended for the benefit of American Indians and Alaska Natives. In a monumental speech to Congress supporting Indigenous Self-Determination in 1970, President Nixon stated:

> The first Americans—the Indians—are the most deprived . . . group in America . . . The condition of the Indian people ranks at the bottom. This condition is the heritage of centuries of injustice. From the time of their first contact with European settlers, the American Indians have been oppressed and brutalized, deprived of their ancestral lands and denied the opportunity to control their own destiny. Even the federal programs which are intended to meet their needs have frequently proved to be ineffective and demeaning.

Thirty-four years later this statement continues to hold true, particularly in Alaska, where the oil industry, state government, and congressional delegation openly pursue aggressive anti-tribal positions.

Self-determination under the ISDEAA is not complete but rather a form of "limited" self-determination that is strictly subject to federal oversight. Still, it was a step in the right direction and a benefit for both Indigenous tribes and the federal government. Since passage of the ISDEAA, federal Indian program operation and output has improved drastically. This is understandable and not surprising, considering it is in the best interest of Indigenous nations to manage programs in the best possible way for their people. For many Alaska Native tribes the ISDEAA gave birth to federally funded tribal government offices and programs managed at the local level.

The ISDEAA provided "limited" self-determination within a particular scope of federal programs meant for the benefit of American Indians and Alaska Natives. In Alaska the debate remains open with regard to inclusion of education programs (village schools) and other programs and projects, such as those funded through the Denali Commission and U.S. Fish and Wildlife Service. Progress toward tribal self-determination is being made in some areas, yet in other areas those who possess control over funding allocations are opposed to Alaska Native tribal sovereignty. This opposition is reflected in resource allocations, agency regulation, and legislative process.

Attacks on Tribal Sovereignty and Funding: "Regionalization"

Despite the acknowledgment and recognition of tribal self-determination, those opposed to tribal sovereignty continue to work to undermine tribal recognition and rights for Alaska Natives. In December 2003, Alaska senator Ted Stevens used a back door method to pass legislation (a rider known as "section 112" on a consolidated spending bill) that eliminates specific funds for small tribes and tribes located in select organized boroughs. This legislation also calls for the establishment of an "Alaska Rural Justice and Law Enforcement Commission." This commission would consist of members appointed by the Secretary General of the United States and is given direction to look into bringing tribal governance under state authority. There was no collaboration or agreement made with federally recognized Alaska Native tribes on this legislation. This process of eliminating tribal rights and funding has become known as the process of "regionalization." In reality, regionalization is a process of tribal termination that undermines tribal authority and cuts off tribal funding. It is the exact opposite of tribal self-determination and is in violation of the government-to-government relationship between federally recognized tribes and the federal government.

In an attempt to evade and subdue the issue of tribal sovereignty and self-determination, key leaders opposing tribal sovereignty use the term "rural" in place of "tribal." Furthermore, state leaders openly suggest that "tribal sovereignty is not the answer," as stated by Senator Stevens in an October 2003 speech to the Alaska Federation of Natives (AFN). While "rural" can be used as a descriptive word in relation to Alaska Native tribes, it should not be used to replace tribal recognition. The term "rural" and other similar language has been used to minimize recognition of the fact that the federal government has already recognized tribes in Alaska and that federal Indian law must be applied in relationships with tribal governments.

Asserting Tribal Sovereignty

Our tribes and individual Alaska Natives have struggled throughout recent history to establish recognition of our presence here and rights as Indigenous peoples. Leaders such as Elizabeth Peratrovich debated in the territorial legislature for the Alaska Native Civil Rights Act of 1945. Elder Katie John consciously violated state law in an act of civil disobedience to bring awareness to the injustice of extinguished Indigenous hunting and fishing rights. John Fredson led the Gwich'in people of the former Venetie reservation (extinguished pursuant to ANCSA) to struggle for tribal rights and resist unjust land appropriation. All three are visible examples of the struggle for Indigenous people's rights. Ultimately, the further we move toward full sovereignty and full self-determination the better positioned our tribes will be to provide effective management at the local level to meet the needs of our people.

Regaining ownership of our traditional lands and resources and becoming truly self-determined are two of the major challenges we face in healing our peoples and healing our relations with other nations.

This history poses challenges that we as Alaska Native nations must face as we begin to reclaim control over our land, resources, and institutions. Our struggle for justice and balance is reflected in the recent history of colonial rule by the United States government. Unless this history is appropriately acknowledged and addressed, we will continue to have greater struggles in the future for tribal sovereignty and self-determination. It is through a process of healing from colonization, reorganizing our institutions and political systems, and preparing ourselves for the future that we shall regain balance in our societies and with all our relations. The time has come for the truths of history to be acknowledged and a new discussion opened regarding the decolonization of the Indigenous nations of Alaska.

Note

1. Throughout this essay the words "Indigenous" and "Indigenous Peoples" will be used intermittently with "Native" and "Alaska Native."

Terra Incognita: Communities and Resource Wars

Subhankar Banerjee

Born in Kolkata, India, and currently based in Santa Fe, New Mexico, Subhankar Banerjee is an award-winning wilderness photographer and the famed author and photographer for Arctic National Wildlife Refuge: Seasons of Life and Land *(2003). He has traveled throughout the United States, Canada, and other countries to advocate for keeping the Refuge, a sacred area for the indigenous people of the region, protected from resource exploitation. The Lannan Foundation awarded its first Cultural Freedom Fellowship to Banerjee for his work to increase public awareness about issues that threaten the well-being of the planet. In the words of the foundation's president, J. Patrick Lannan Jr., "[Banerjee's] spectacular photographs achieved what others could not—exposing the lie that the Arctic Refuge is a frozen wasteland—put forth by those who place short-term profit above cultural diversity and the health of the planet."*

Because of his work, and long association with the land and environment, Banerjee has developed deep and longstanding relationships with the indigenous Gwich'in Athabascan and Iñupiaq people of Alaska. His work continues to capture the complex relationships between indigenous people, environmental organizations, the land, and the oil industry. One of his color images, Autumn on the Taiga, *is featured in plate 1.*

The eyes of the future are looking back at us and they are praying
for us to see beyond our own time. They are kneeling with clasped
hands that we might act with restraint, leaving room for the life that
is destined to come.
—Terry Tempest Williams from her poem *Wild Mercy*

I arrived in Point Lay on June 24, 2006, a small Iñupiat community of about 200 residents along the Kasegaluk Lagoon on the northern Chukchi Sea coast of Alaska. When I got off the plane the first time, a woman came up and gave

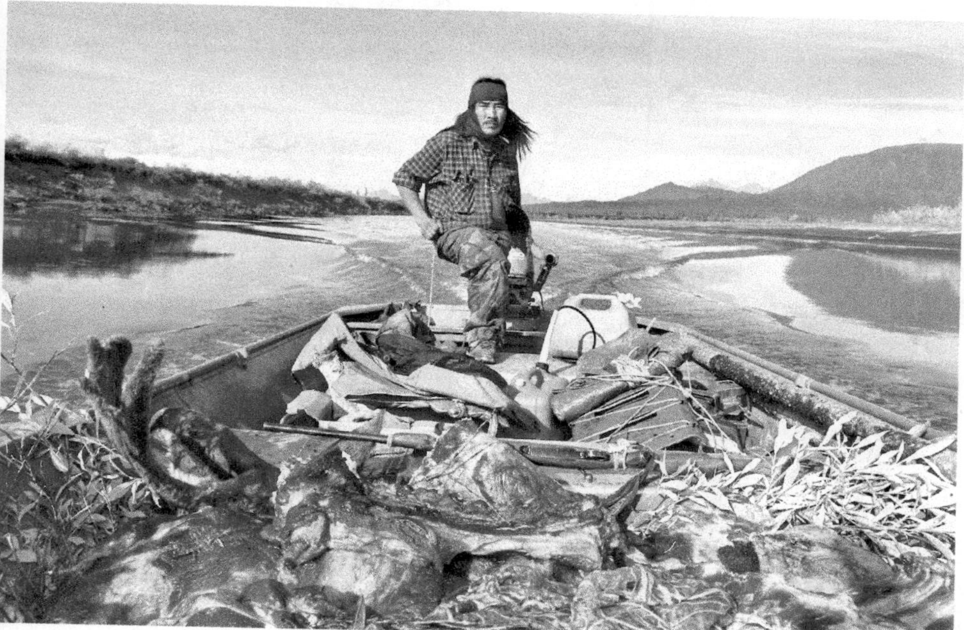

1. Iñupiat whale prayer. Photo by Subhankar Banerjee.

2. Gwich'in moose hunt, Jimi John. Photo by Subhankar Banerjee.

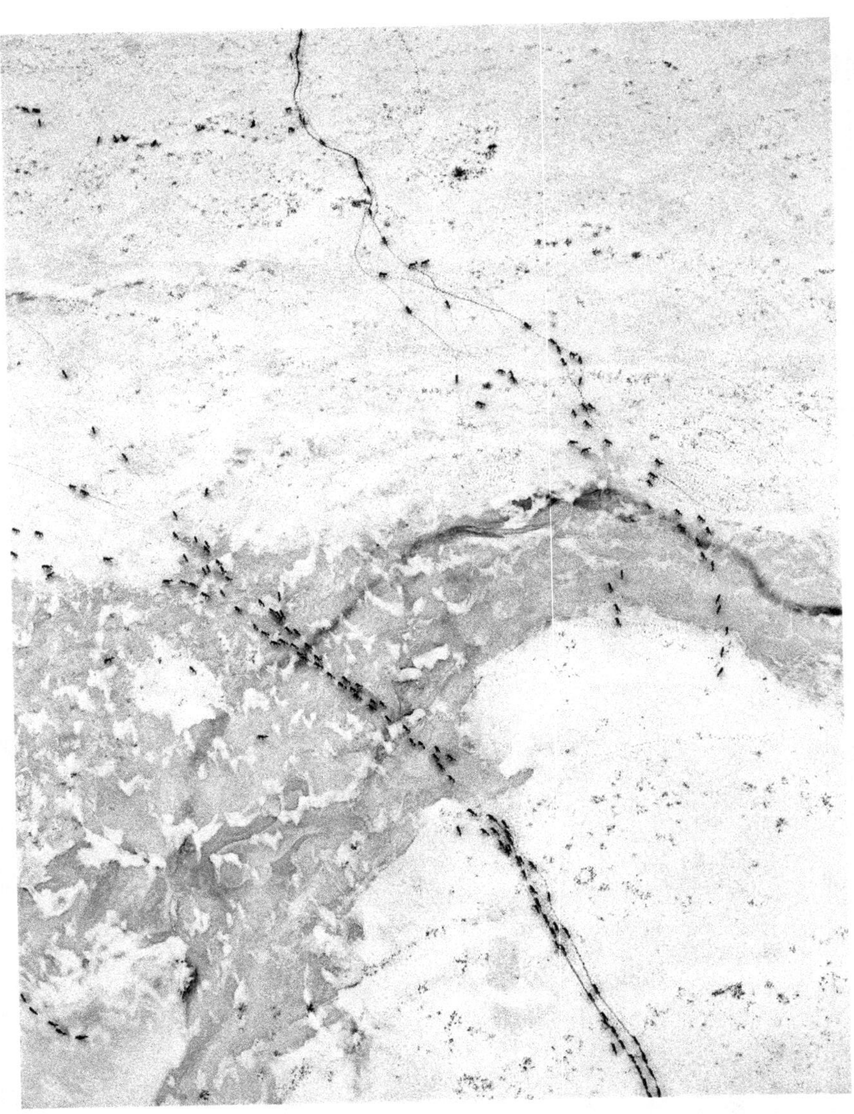

3. Caribou migration. Photo by Subhankar Banerjee.

me a hug. She is Marie Tracey, a council member of the Native Village of Point Lay. Over the next days I got to meet other members of the community, Julius Rexford Sr., Bill Tracey, Lily Annisket, Leo Ferreira Jr., among others. Every time I walk around the village on the main gravel road, *Qasigialik Street*, I hear my name being called, a welcoming sound, "Hey Subhankar." I look around, a group of children and youth of varying ages. I go up to them and we introduce each other. Everyone here is waiting for the Beluga whales to arrive any day now. A much anticipated annual harvest that brings the entire community together—children, youth, adults, and elders—four generations. Soon after the Belugas arrive on the Kasegaluk Lagoon, this year Shell Oil is scheduled to arrive to do extensive seismic testing on the Chukchi Sea followed by testing on the Beaufort Sea. Iñupiat communities across the North Slope are concerned about the offshore seismic testing and future oil exploration. They worry about the potential impact from offshore oil development on the marine life that they depend on for subsistence food—Bowhead and Beluga whales, seals, walrus, birds, and fish. For people of Point Lay it is the Beluga

4. Unnamed lake (Drunken Forest). Photo by Subhankar Banerjee.

whales that they don't want to be disturbed by development. Belugas are also known to calve along the Kasegaluk and the Oomalik lagoons.

Romans called the Arctic *Terra Incognita*—the unknown land. In broad public perception Arctic is still a mysterious place. However, today the Arctic is perhaps the most connected land on the planet. This global connection is both celebratory and tragic. Hundreds of millions of birds from around the world travel each spring thousands of miles to reach the Arctic to nest and rear their young—a planetary celebration that connects every citizen of the planet to these distant lands. On the other hand, global warming, migration of toxins, and resource extraction (oil, coal, and minerals) have connected these lands to the ways of lives of people thousands of miles away. In many cases, it has proven to be tragic for the people of the Arctic.

Before arriving at Point Lay, I was camping in the Utukok River uplands (about seventy-five miles from Point Lay), first with my friends the writer Peter Matthiessen, the philanthropist and conservationist Tom Campion, and the arctic guide Jim Campbell, and later with the bush pilot and retired wildlife biologist Pat Valkenburg and his wife and the wolverine biologist Audrey Magoun. Over a period of two weeks, I had perhaps seen 150,000 caribou and newborn calves. The herd is numbering around 500,000. Utukok Uplands, the core calving area of the Western Arctic caribou herd, happens to hold an estimated four trillion tons of coal, perhaps a future resource conflict of land, caribou, and coal. Pat Valkenburg, who had extensively studied the Western Arctic herd, told me that there are twenty-two Native communities that depend on the Western Arctic herd for subsistence food.

Petroleum and coal are the two key contributors to global warming. In addition, coal-burning power plants and oil refineries in the United States and around the world are contributing to toxins, known as Persistent Organic Pollutants (POP) at an alarming scale that are ending up in the arctic ecology. These toxic compounds bio-accumulate and bio-magnify in the animals—from polar bears, fish, seals, and whales, to women's breast milk, impacting women, children, and the unborn. The *Los Angeles Times* journalist Marla Cone, in her extensively researched book *Silent Snow: Slow Poisoning of the Arctic* (2005), details how the breast milk of high arctic women in Greenland and northern Canada has become contaminated to the point of being considered hazardous waste. Barbara Freese, an assistant attorney general of the state of Minnesota, in her book *Coal: A Human History* (2004), details the impact of coal on human societies. The United States government and Alaska Native corporations like Arctic Slope Regional Corporation and Doyon Ltd. are continuously looking into more and more extraction of oil and coal in the Alaskan Arctic. We have an opportunity to change the course of history by moving into a new energy future with solar, wind, biofuels, hydrogen, and other renewable sources that are cleaner for the environment and better for our health and for all other species we share this planet with; instead, for the profit of a few, we are looking back—to oil and coal to drive our energy future.

I had a remarkable opportunity to spend fourteen months over a period of two years in 2001 and 2002 in the Arctic National Wildlife Refuge to document a holistic story of the land, wildlife, and the peoples. Arctic Village, a Gwich'in village of about 150 residents on the southern edge of the Arctic Refuge, and Kaktovik, an Iñupiat village of about 280 residents on the Beaufort Sea coast, became my second homes during this sojourn. The Gwich'in, "people of the land," depend on the Porcupine River Caribou herd for food and cultural and spiritual identity. Their relationship with the caribou herd goes back many millennia. Every spring the Porcupine River Caribou herd migrates to the coastal plain of the Arctic Refuge for calving. Their calving ground has been the most debated public land in the United States. Whether to open up the coastal plain for oil drilling or to preserve it for future generations has been raging in the halls of the United States Congress for the past three decades. Gwich'in people from fifteen villages across Northeast Alaska and Northwest Canada are united in their opposition to oil drilling in the caribou calving ground, a land they consider *Iizhik Gwats'an Gwandaii Goodlit* (the sacred place where life begins). Sarah James, founding board member of the Gwich'in Steering Committee, said, "We are the caribou people. Caribou are not just what we eat; they are also who we are. They are in our stories and songs and the whole way we see the world. Caribou are our life. Without caribou we wouldn't exist."[1]

The coastal plain of the Arctic Refuge is also the most consistently used land-denning habitat for polar bears of the Beaufort Sea coast that spans across Alaska and Canada. Just when the caribou arrive on the coastal plain to calve, millions of birds, over 100 species, arrive from six continents to nest and rear their young on the coastal plain (Brown 2006). Many call the coastal plain *the biological heart* of the Arctic Refuge.

Proponents of oil drilling have described the coastal plain as a wasteland. In March 2002, then-senator Frank Murkowski (later governor of Alaska) held up a flat white poster board on the Senate floor and said of the Arctic National Wildlife Refuge, "This is a picture of ANWR as it exists for about nine months of the year. This is what it looks like. It's flat, it's unattractive; don't be misinformed." Secretary of the Interior Gail A. Norton, during a March 12, 2003, congressional testimony, famously described the Arctic Refuge coastal plain as an object of conceptual art, "a flat white nothingness." In an October 2, 2005, major front-page story in the *Chicago Tribune*, Senator Ted Stevens of

Alaska was quoted saying, "And they're [the American public] not susceptible anymore to misrepresentations that ANWR is some kind of pristine wilderness. It's empty. It's ugly." On November 5, 2005, Senator Stevens said on *PBS News Hour with Jim Lehrer*, "This is the area in wintertime. And I defy anyone to say that that is a beautiful place that has to be preserved for the future. It is a barren wasteland, frozen wasteland." My photographs convincingly countered these arguments and my photographic exhibition at the Smithsonian National Museum of Natural History in Washington resulted in a major controversy.[2]

What the Porcupine River caribou is to the Gwich'in, the Bowhead Whale is to the Iñupiat people of Kaktovik and other villages of the North Slope. Every September, the community of Kaktovik harvests up to three whales. After each whale is brought to shore, the entire community, elders, adults, and children, gather first to give thanks to the whale and the creator for providing food for their community, and then participate in the butchering and sharing of the *muktuk* (whale blubber and skin) and other parts of the whale. Come September, Shell Oil will be doing extensive seismic testing for offshore oil outside of Kaktovik. Robert Thompson and his wife Jane, who live in Kaktovik, are opposed to the idea, and so is the community. They fear offshore drilling will seriously impact the whales and other marine mammals and the entire ecology of the Arctic Ocean that they depend on and will undoubtedly bring not only environmental problems but also social and health problems to the community.

Nuiqsut is the only Iñupiat village on the North Slope of Alaska where oil drilling has been happening nearby—the latest oilfield, with the latest technology, the Alpine oilfield and its satellite stations. Rosemary Ahtuangaruak, former mayor of Nuiqsut, said in testimony, "When I started as a health aide, I had one patient as an asthmatic. This was almost 20 years ago, now I know of about 75. I have also seen increase in thyroid disease and breast cancer. These problems multiplied as oil development spread. During winter evenings, for instance, asthma attacks followed a pattern that pointed to causes other than the commonly recognized trigger of indoor smoking. I was often called to treat asthma patients during cold inversions, when a layer of ice fog hung over the North Slope. On those same evenings there was noticeable gas flaring in the oil fields."[3]

As I contemplate the resource wars on the land and seas of the Alaskan Arctic, people of Point Lay are getting ready for their annual Beluga hunt. Someone yesterday sighted Belugas at the Oomalik Lagoon. The wind is finally blowing from the northeast; that should push the ice out from the shore. Boats will go out soon. Last evening during a walk along the Kasegaluk Lagoon, the wildlife biologist Robert Suydam (local people call him the Beluga Man) showed me a couple of yellow wagtails, a songbird I so wanted to see in the Arctic Refuge but never did. I told Robert, "You know some of them migrate to the arctic from India."

Notes

1. Sarah James, Gwich'in Steering Committee website: http://www.gwichinsteeringcommittee.org.

2. See Finis Dunaway, "Reframing the Last Frontier: Subhankar Banerjee and the Visual Politics of the Arctic National Wildlife Refuge," *American Quarterly* 58, no. 1 (March 2006): 159–80.

3. Rosemary Ahtuangaruak, from the press release of REDOIL (Resisting Environmental Destruction on Indigenous Lands).

Why the Natives of Alaska Have a Land Claim

William Iggiagruk *Hensley* *(Iñupiaq)*

Willie Iggiagruk *Hensley was born and raised in Kotzebue, Alaska, on the Noatak River delta, forty miles above the Arctic Circle. His early years were spent in a traditional sod house. He was sent to boarding school and then attended George Washington University, returning to Alaska in the mid-1960s. In Fairbanks he took a class on constitutional law taught by Judge Rabinowitz and in 1966 he wrote a seminal legal analysis of the land rights of Alaska Native people.*[1] *Hensley was elected as state representative in the mid-1960s and served four years in that office, after which he was elected as a state senator. He helped to found many Alaska Native political organizations, including the Alaska Federation of Natives (where he served as president) and the* NANA *Regional Corporation (where he served as director and later president for twenty years). He also founded Maniilaq, the regional nonprofit representing the tribes in the Kotzebue region. Currently he lives in Washington, D.C., and is the manager of federal government relations for Alyeska Pipeline Service Company, the organization that operates and maintains the 800-mile Trans-Alaska Pipeline System.*

The following was a talk Hensley gave in 1969 at a conference in France, during the heat of the Alaska Native Land Claims battle. At that time, in Hensley's words, "We were desperate to seek any forum that would help us spread the word of the importance of our claims and the attendees were bureaucrats, anthropologists, doctors and other specialists on the North and included Inuit from Canada and Greenland."

Although I am an American citizen and a citizen of Alaska and I accept the responsibilities given to me as a legislator in the Alaska House of Representatives, I speak now as an Eskimo—as an Alaska Native—within the framework of our controversy with the State of Alaska and the United States of America. My purpose in this paper is to inform you of the present controversy in Alaska relating to the claims of the Eskimo, Indian, and Aleut people to land that we have occupied for centuries.

Although we recognize the fact that there is presently little that we can do to secure totally all of the land we occupied in the pre-Russian and American times, we do not believe that the simple planting of a flag on our soil secures that land for any country at no cost to it. We are now seeking to secure a settlement with the United States—through the Congress—of our land rights.

We recognize that when European nations secured colonies in parts of the world already inhabited by indigenous peoples that there never was gentle treatment of the aborigines. The European vanguards came to exploit the new land, and to civilize its peoples.

The Alaskan experience was no different. When Alaska was first sighted in 1741, the Native population numbered about 74,700. Thirteen years after Alaska was sold by the Russians, the population was decimated, leaving 33,000. The Eskimo population decreased from about 54,000 to about 18,000 in just 150 years.

Although this Congress is considering the future of Eskimo societies in relation to Arctic development, I will speak of the "Native" people of Alaska—Indians and Aleuts, as well as Eskimos—since we are all subject to the effects of the many changes brought to our ancient lands through industrialization and technological advances. Furthermore, if the Eskimo is to be successful in trying to influence public policy in Alaska and in the United States Congress, it is necessary that we Eskimos work with the Indians and Aleuts—which, in fact, we are doing, as will be described later.

Most of the world is now aware of the fact that vast deposits of oil have been found on the Arctic Slope of Alaska. It may be less well known that there is presently a great controversy as to whom that land and other lands actually belong. Since Alaska is the homeland of 55,000 Eskimo, Indian, and Aleut people; and since the land has never been specifically taken by act of the United States Congress, or in battle, or by abandonment; we declare—indeed, proclaim—that by reason of historic use and occupancy, this is our land.

In order to see our problem in accurate perspective, one must know the historical approach of the United States in dealing with the Indians of the main body of what is now the United States, what necessitated the encroachment on Indian territory, how the acquisitions took place, what the Indians received, and why it is that our present situation is so different in approach and in substance.

Background Concerning the American Indian: Theory of Indian Title

The American colonists came in search of a new life. They were not numerous and had to depend to some extent on the good will of the American Indian. Following the separation of the colonies from England, the new government had to deal with the Indian tribes as separate nations. They signed treaties with them and negotiated with them as equals. However, the number of Americans increased greatly and the pressures of settlement created greater demand for lands held by the Indians. Consequently, the Indians resisted American efforts at gaining more land since they did not care to be pushed further west, and the period of the Indian Wars took place. Being numerically inferior and having less firepower, the Indians were defeated and had to cede large areas of land to the United States. Usually a small area was left to each tribe for its use and held in trust for them by the federal government.

Today, the Indians of the mainland hold only 50 million acres of land and it is the poorest land in the nation. The Indians, however, have been allowed access to the courts to sue the federal government for compensation of land they lost, whether in battle or by act of Congress. In court the Indians have had to prove that they had "Indian Title" to the land—that is, that they used and occupied the entire area claimed. They have had to prove that this land was taken from them at a particular time. Once proved, compensation was paid to them for the taking, with compensation based upon the value of the land at the time of taking. The United States set up the Indian Claims Commission for the sole purpose of trying to pay money for depriving the Indian of his lands. To date, about $251 million has been paid to the Indian tribes.[2] The litigation usually takes many years and pits the Indian against the federal government. The compensation for millions of acres of land is usually a small sum when compared with the true value of the land.

It should be noted that the United States Constitution reserves to the federal government the responsibilities of dealing with the Indian tribes and the United States through executive order.

Tribe after tribe succumbed to the power of the United States. The Indian could not protect his land. How did the Eskimo fare? What about the Aleut and Indian in Alaska?

The Arrival of the Russians: Treatment of the Natives

The Russians first sighted the Alaskan landmass in 1741. At the time of their arrival, it is estimated that there were about 74,000 Alaskan Natives. Russia wanted the sea otter, the fur seal, and other resources of our lands. There was little penetration into the populous portions of the giant territory. Ports were established and trade ensued. The Aleuts were subjugated and made to gather food and work for the Russians. The Russians were under orders not to move into new territories among the Eskimo and Indian without consent. In practice, this was generally ignored. Nevertheless, the Russians exploited

PLATE 1. *Autumn on Taiga*. Photo by Subhankar Banerjee.

PLATE 2. *Kincolith*, 1998. Digital print. Copyright Larry McNeil, 2008. All rights reserved.

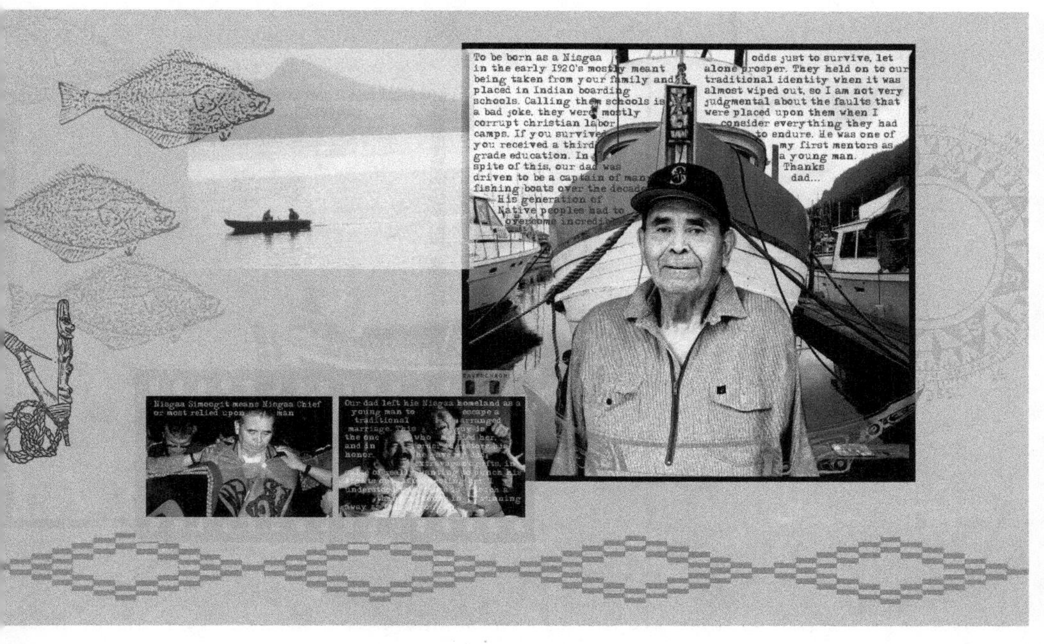

PLATE 3. *Dad*, 2002. Digital print.

In the true spirit of white man, I stole this car in my search for america. Just
call it manifested destiny. I asked the owner to take my picture in front of his
car before I took it and assured him that it was god's will that I take his car.
god meant for this fine machine to be flying down the freeway, I told him. Are
you a real indian he asked, I thought you were all vanished. As soon as you give
me the keys I'll be another vanishing indian I told him. Can you look more
noble? I told him sorry, this is as stoic as I can manage for now. He asked if I had
any regalia to put on, you know, to make it look authentic. This is as real as it
gets I told him. I saw in a book that you people were all vanished, he said again.
I asked him if he still has his native culture and who is the vanished one, you
or me... He told me that his grandfather was Edward Curtis and that he made some
of the best photographs ever of indians before they vanished. Like me? Kind of.
Thanks for the car I told him, but I've got some
serious vanishing
to catch up on...
RAVENCHROME
KODAK TXP 6049

PLATE 4. *In the True Spirit of the White Man*, 2002. Digital print.

PLATE 5. A mask carved by Perry Eaton, influenced by masks from the Pinart collection. Photo by Perry Eaton.

PLATE 6. Masks from the Pinart collection in France. Photo by Perry Eaton.

(OPPOSITE)
PLATE 7A. Woodpecker mask collected by Vosnesenskii in 1842 in the village of Lesnoi on Woody Island (Kodiak Archipelago), from the collection in the Kunstkamera Museum in St. Petersburg, Russia. Photo by Perry Eaton.

PLATE 7B. Masks from the Pinart collection on display at the Chateau-Musée de Boulogne-sur-Mer in France. Photo by Perry Eaton.

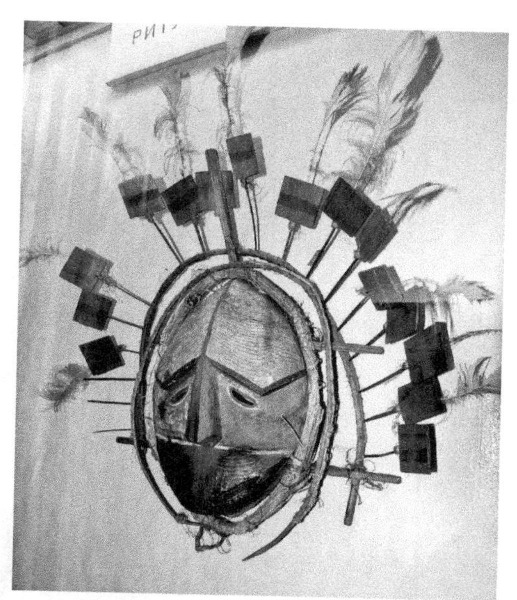

PLATE 8. Self-Portraits 007, 012, 022, 004, 008, 001 from the Un/Defined Self-Portrait series. Dates: 2004–6. Photos by Erica Lord.

Alaska from 1741 to 1867 and by the time of the transfer to the United States there were about 35,000 Native people in the territory.[3]

The Treaty of Cession—1867

Without consultation with the Eskimo, Indian, and Aleut people, the Russian government, for $7.2 million, sold Alaska to the United States. Russia was in a war in the Crimea and was in danger of losing Alaska to other countries. The Treaty of Cession did not provide for the citizenship of the Native people as it did for the white inhabitants. Section 3 of the Treaty stated that "the uncivilized Native tribes will be subject to such laws and regulations as the United States may, from time to time, adopt in regard to aboriginal tribes of that country."[4]

There was no confirmation of title to lands used and occupied by the Native people. Among some Natives there was discontent, but as the historian Bancroft put it:

> The discontent arose, not from any antagonism to the Americans, but from the fact that the territory had been sold without their consent, and that they had received none of the proceeds of the sale. The Russians, they agreed, had been allowed to occupy the territory mostly for mutual benefit, but their forefathers had dwelt in Alaska long before any white man had set foot in America. Why had not the 7½ million dollars been paid to them instead of the Russians?[5]

There was not then, nor has there ever been any agreement by the Eskimo, Indian, and Aleut people to the extinguishment of their ownership of lands in Alaska. At the time of the sale there were about 400 whites in Alaska; for all practical purposes, Alaska was still Native land but encumbered by the law between nations following "discovery" and the transfer of money.

The Organic Act of 1884

The Organic Act of 1884 was passed by the U.S. Congress in response to the clamor by whites who needed to receive title to lands they had discovered gold on and for the purpose of establishing civil government. Military detachments had governed the territory between 1867 and 1884. This act is the first specific policy pronouncement by the United States regarding the land of the Eskimos, Indians, and Aleuts. It provided strong terms for the protection of Native land rights:

> Indians or other persons in said district shall not be disturbed in the possession of any lands actually in their use or occupation or now claimed by them, but the terms under which such persons may acquire title to such lands is reserved for future legislation by the U.S. Congress.[6]

Although limited legislation has been enacted to allow for the acquisition of title by individual Natives or villages, there has not been specific congressional action to determine completely the extent of Native "use and occupation" and whether we should be granted title to those areas.

Statehood Act: The Built-in Conflict

By 1959, Alaska's total population had grown to about 200,000 persons, including about 43,000 Eskimos, Indians, and Aleuts. The Alaskan population sought and received Statehood. The Constitution of the newly admitted State of Alaska provided protection to the Native people by stating that:

> The State and its people further disclaim all right or title in or to any property, including fishing rights, the right or title to which may be held by or for any Indian, Eskimo, or Aleut, or community thereof, as that right is defined in the Act of Admission.[7]

There was hope that the Act of Admission to Statehood would dispose of the Native land issue, but it did not:

> As a compact with the United States, said State and its people do agree and declare that they forever disclaim all right title . . . to any lands or other property (including fishing rights), the right or title to which may be held by any Indians, Eskimos, or Aleuts . . . or is held by the United States in trust for said Natives; that all such lands or other property, belonging to the United States or which may belong to said Natives, shall be and remain under the absolute jurisdiction and control of the United States until disposed of under its authority.[8]

The new state allowed the Congress to retain jurisdiction over the disposition of the Native land rights issue. But a potential conflict was created when the Congress authorized the new state to select 103 million acres from the landmass of Alaska—land that was being used and occupied by Native people. How could the new state, on one hand, disclaim all right or title to our land and at the same time be allowed to select it under another provision of the Statehood Act?

This issue is being tested in the courts and it is the Native position that the

Native title has not been specifically extinguished and the State must await Congressional action to determine further the allocation of lands between the State and the Native people.

The Eskimo, Indian, and Aleut populations were adversely affected first by the Russians, who came in search of valuable furs; then by the whalers and fishermen from ports around the world; and, beginning in the 1890s for several decades, by fortune seekers during the great gold rush. Because of the influx of foreigners, the Native people suffered disease and, later, starvation due to the taking of much game and fish that the villagers utilized.

Furthermore, the Native people were not citizens. They could not hold land or stake mining claims. Consequently, the Native people were pushed off valuable lands that they used and lived on because they did not hold deeds or other written recognized evidence of ownership.

To this day, so little attention has been paid by government officials to the need for formal ownership of land by the Native people that only a tiny fraction of the privately held land in Alaska is owned by the first inhabitants—of the State's 375 million acres, Alaska Natives possess fee title to only 500 acres.[9]

As a result, in part, of the inability of the Native to hold title to land, or to acquire title, economic development has taken place but little benefit has accrued to the Eskimo and Indian people. This has been true of the gold rush period, the period of copper, tin, and other minerals—and it will be true of the oil era unless a change is brought about through federal legislation. It is just such action that the Alaska Federation of Natives is seeking to promote, and is the major reason for its creation.

The Alaska Federation of Natives and Its Position

As the State of Alaska began to make its first selections of land under the Statehood Act, it was plain that these selections were being made in areas used and occupied by us, the Native people. As a consequence, village councils began to protest the State selections and appealed to the Secretary of Interior (who is manager of America's public lands, and "guardian" of the Native people) to stop the granting of Native-claimed lands to the State.

Regional organizations of Native villages sprang up and, in a unified manner, claimed whole regions, which were used and occupied by the village people. This process continued and virtually the entire state was blanketed by Native claims. The Secretary of Interior was initially at a loss as to what should be done in view of the unclear legal directions provided in the Act of

Admission to statehood and his role as "guardian" of the Native people. At this point in time, the Alaska Federation of Natives was organized.

The Alaska Federation of Natives emerged as a moving force in 1966 because of the threat to Native lands. Initially, the Federation consisted of 19 regional and village groups. It presently is a vehicle through which the various regional groups are pushing for a settlement.

The creation of the Federation changed the political face of Alaska. Eskimos, Indians, and Aleuts comprise about 30 percent of the voting public in Alaska. The year 1966 marked a turning point for the Native people in that this was the first time in history we had a unified effort to promote an equitable land settlement, and organized to change public policy that was adverse to us.

The Federation was seen by the political leaders of the State as a vehicle with which they could work to become elected. In fact, 1966 was the year the present Secretary of Interior was elected Governor of Alaska, in part, by appealing to the Native vote.

The Federation now has programs in economic development planning, on-the-job training, health care, and village leadership training.

The Land Freeze

The Federation immediately began to work for a halt to disposition of land to the State until the U.S. Congress could make a determination regarding Native rights to the land. Of course, the State continued to seek to secure land for sale and development. Secretary Udall ordered the Bureau of Land Management, an agency in the Department of Interior, to cease processing of applications for patent in lands that were being claimed by Eskimo, Indian, and Aleut people. This came to be known as the "land freeze." This administrative order was later formalized by Secretary Udall by withdrawal of all Alaskan lands from disposal to the State or to any others until the U.S. Congress has an opportunity to act on the matter. But the "freeze" will be lifted at the end of 1970, if no action is taken.

The importance of the "land freeze" to the Native people is that it prevents anyone, including the State, from taking lands that may be granted to villages in a Congressional settlement. Furthermore, the pressure for a settlement continues on all parties so long as the status quo on land disposition remains. The Native people, the State, the Interior Department, and the Committees of Congress are all actively working toward a settlement.

Were it not for the "freeze," the State would go its merry way selecting

Native-claimed lands and would not lift a finger to help us obtain justice—unless some enlightened administration saw a value in doing so.

The Major Proposals before the U.S. Congress

Three legislative proposals are now pending before the United States Congress. Before this year ends, it is likely that in one house of the Congress—the Senate—the committee considering the land claims will have completed its work and a bill will have begun its way to becoming law.

The first proposal, and the one to which the Alaska Federation of Natives and the Department of the Interior have proposed amendments, is based upon elements of a legislative settlement suggested by the Federal Field Committee—a small federal research organization in Alaska. This bill includes conveyance of one township of land (23,040 acres) to each of 209 listed Native villages, payment of $100 million from funds appropriated by the Congress in a lump sum, and payment of a 10 percent share of the revenues derived from federal lands within Alaska—and outer continental shelf lands off the shore of Alaska—for a period of ten years. (It is important here to understand that the State of Alaska now shares in 90 percent of the revenues from onshore federal lands in Alaska.) All mineral rights under the village townships are to be given to and administered by a statewide Native corporation also charged with the management and disbursement of appropriated funds and shared revenues. During its first ten years the corporation—whose stockholders are to be all Alaska Natives—is to be rather closely controlled. At the end of that time it is to become an ordinary business corporation with its shares of stock freely bought and sold.

Very important to the content and form of any legislative proposal is the viewpoint of the executive branch of the national government. This viewpoint is expressed in an amendment submitted by the Secretary of the Interior, Walter J. Hickel. This provides for conveyance of one township of land to each of 13 named villages now located in a National Forest and two townships (46,080 acres) of land to each of an additional 192 villages. Locatable minerals—that is, gold, silver, lead, zinc, etc.—are also conveyed with the surface title to the land, but leaseable minerals—that is, oil, gas, and sulfur—are retained by the national government. As compensation for Native land use rights extinguished in the past and by this settlement a total sum of $500 million is to be appropriated by Congress in twenty equal annual sums. The closely controlled statewide, Native-owned Corporation to administer funds is adopted in this proposal, but the period of its control is extended to twenty years.

The proposal prepared b the Alaska Federation of Natives provides for either four townships (92,160 acres) or 500 acres of land per person, whichever is greater, for each 242 listed villages as well as four sections (640 acres each) in each township in the state to the appropriate regional Native corporation. These conveyances include all mineral rights. As compensation $500 million is to be granted by the Congress payable $100 million the first year and $50 million each of the eight years following. Because much of the land of Alaska is still occupied and used by Alaska Natives as their ancestors used the land, it is also proposed that 2 percent of the proceeds from the lease or sale of federal lands in Alaska be paid to Alaska Natives for the extinguishment of this present right of use and occupancy. It is this part of our proposal and its extension to the lands which the State of Alaska is entitled to choose under the terms of the Act admitting Alaska to the United States as a state which some say is alienating many non-Native Alaskans.

There are other obvious differences of degree in the three proposals—between 5 million acres and 40 million acres; between $500 million and $500 million plus a 2 percent royalty in perpetuity; between ten and twenty years of governmental supervision. But from one of these proposals—or from parts of all of them—it is anticipated there will emerge the terms of settlement of a century-old claim.

The Consequences of a Poor Settlement or No Settlement

The Native people of Alaska have had to be realists in dealing with the State and Federal officials concerning the land issue. Although we know that in terms of the legal theory relating to Indian Title, we know that we still retain the land—but only Congress can confirm—or extinguish—our ownership.

Our initial reaction in 1966 was to ask for confirmation to all lands we use and occupy today. But we knew this was impossible under the political circumstances.

Our position has been to go for what we feel is within reason—but not to buckle when pressure is brought to bear before we reach Capitol Hill.

Great pressure can be exerted to try to force us into going through the courts—which is a costly and lengthy route to go—and would result in no land grants and small money amounts. But, we feel that a Congressional settlement is within reach and are putting our efforts in that direction.

The Senate and House Interior and Insular Affairs Committees have both been to Alaska for hearings and we have traveled to Washington (as did the Indians a century ago) to present our case.

We are testing the American political system. We have found it responsive up to this time and have hope. We know the history of our country in dealing with the American Indian and want to see a final chapter not written in blood or in deception or in injustice. We are not numerous and recognize the pitfalls in securing this unprecedented kind of legislation.

We are seeking an alternative to wardship. We seek to offer alternatives to Eskimo and Indian people rather than a one-way ticket into the confused mainstream. We feel our people cannot convert to a cash economy overnight and will continue to fish and hunt for many years. On the other hand, we see that the young Natives seek education and new places. These should be available. We want to be able to live longer and more decently without having to stoop in indignity because of a degrading welfare system. We feel this is possible if we can secure the kind of land settlement we are proposing.

If there is no settlement or a poor one, we will have a generation of leaders who fought for years to protect their land and lost. This may start a chain of events in which it is seen by future generations of Natives as a disaster for us—an injustice that will mar the relationships between Natives and whites for many years. It may bring defeatism to the people and will prevent us from becoming an integral part of Alaska's social and economic development. Our present political influence will diminish and the efforts to develop our communities will falter. Such would be the consequences of a poor settlement or no settlement. Not only that, but America will have lost an opportunity to right old wrongs and, for once, allow the first Americans a fair deal.

Notes

1. "What Rights to Land Have the Alaska Natives? The Primary Question" can be viewed at http://www.alaskool.org.

2. *Annual Report of 1968*, Indian Claims Commission, 1968, 12.

3. *Alaska's Population and Economy Statistical Handbook*, vol. 2, 7 (1903).

4. Treaty of Cession, 1867, section 3.

5. *The Works of Hubert Howe Bancroft*, vol. 32, *1730–1887* (San Francisco: Bancroft Co., 1886), 609.

6. The Organic Act of 1884, May 17, 1884, 23 stat. 24.

7. Constitution of Alaska, article 12, section 12.

8. Alaska Statehood Act, 1959, section 4.

9. *Alaska Natives and the Land*, Federal Field Committee for Development Planning in Alaska, October 1, 1969.

A Brief History of Native Solidarity

Maria Shaa Tláa *Williams* *(Tlingit)*

This article was originally written for the Tundra Times *in a three-part series in October 1996 to mark the thirtieth anniversary of the Alaska Federation of Natives (AFN). It focuses on the statewide Native solidarity movement that began in the early 1960s and gave rise to most of the current Native organizations in Alaska, the Alaska Native Claims Settlement Act of 1971, as well as most political and government agencies that represent Alaska Native people.*

Although long-standing trade relations existed between the different ethnic groups or nations in Alaska, war and hostilities were also common and it was not until the twentieth century, as a direct result of colonial pressure, that unification between all Alaskan indigenous societies took place.

Up until the 1950s, Alaska Native people were subject to colonial and genocidal pressures. Disease, Christian missionaries, destruction of indigenous religions, forced Western-style boarding schools, restrictions on hunting, fishing and other subsistence practices, and the strict English-only policies all took a tremendous toll on Alaska Native societies and almost destroyed them. Alaska Native people were not considered or even consulted in decisions by the federal, territorial, or state government. During an era in which racism was commonplace, Native people were viewed as inferior.

A unique set of circumstances, along with a determined group of Alaska Native leaders, led to a statewide solidarity movement that ensured the survival of Alaska Natives into the twenty-first century. It is important to look at the overall picture, which begins with how Natives were viewed in the twentieth century, in order to understand the political and historical events that led to the Native solidarity movement of the 1960s.

Territory of Alaska: Status of Alaska Natives, 1900–1950

Native peoples were devastated and barely survived the crippling epidemics of the nineteenth and early twentieth centuries; the Christian missionaries, schools, and government organizations that supported complete assimilation of Native people did not tolerate their spiritual and philosophical beliefs. The mission, state and BIA schools oppressed traditional practices and languages. There was an expanding Anglo-American population that came north to seek land, wealth, and independence and escape, viewing Native people as primitive and therefore as obstacles to the development of Alaska's land and resources.

As with the rest of the United States, racism and segregation were practiced in most communities that had a mixed population until after World War II. It was not unusual to see signs in cities such as Juneau, Sitka, Fairbanks, Anchorage, and Nome that stated "No Dogs or Indians Allowed." Or areas that were reserved for "Whites Only" or "Eskimos Only." The newcomers to the Alaska territory were in search of opportunities, some on the run from their pasts; many were unfortunately racist and did not believe that indigenous societies had anything to offer. Schools were segregated until after World War II—a territorially run educational program for whites and a federally run program for Natives. It was thought best to keep white children from Native children since government officials felt, among other things, Native people "could not conform to white standards of health and sanitation." Newspapers such as the Fairbanks *Daily News Miner* and the Juneau *Empire* often had racist editorials. In 1926, the Fairbanks *Daily News Miner* stated: "Alaska—a White Man's Country." The article remarked, "Notwithstanding the fact that the Indians outnumber us, this is Whiteman's country, and it must remain such" (February 13, 1926). The editors of the paper reflected the Anglo populations' fears of any Indian or Native group having power or rights. The *Daily Empire*, a Juneau newspaper, called Tlingit attorney William Paul Sr. a "menace" in 1924 because he secured Native voting rights (October 7, 1924).

Alaska Natives had protested the encroachment of non-Natives onto their land for mining, trapping and settlement; however, most of their protests were ignored. In many cases the territorial or federal government supported the settlement of non-Natives onto traditional Native lands. In 1884 the U.S. Congress enacted laws that limited Native subsistence fishing but encouraged the larger white operated canneries. The canneries nearly wiped out entire salmon runs, leaving Native subsistence fishermen with nothing. The various gold discoveries in Nome, Fairbanks, and Juneau brought thousands and thousands of gold miners whose rights were protected, yet the Native people on whose land they were on had no rights or recourse whatsoever, and could not even stake their own claims.

In 1915 the Alaska Railroad had plans to build a railroad through burial grounds near Nenana. The Athabascan Tanana Chiefs protested the movement of non-Natives in their traditional hunting and fishing areas and stated that the land was theirs and they alone had authority over who could use the land and its resources. The Tanana Chiefs managed to get the Alaska railroad to reroute, but this type of action was an exception; usually Native protests fell on deaf ears.

The Alaska Native Brotherhood

The Alaska Native Brotherhood (ANB) formed in 1912 in Sitka and was the only Native political organization in the state until the 1960s. The organization had an active and radical political stance that enabled indigenous people to secure many rights. Little statewide political solidarity existed due to the large geographic region of Alaska and the scattered and diverse indigenous populations. The leadership of the Alaska Native Brotherhood represented a new generation of Tlingit, Haida, and Tsimshian; they had been educated by the mostly Presbyterian missions in Southeast Alaska, mastered the English language, and were familiar with Western laws and the U.S. government. The ANB recognized that Western acumen was necessary in order for their livelihood, culture, and land base to survive. They adopted Robert's Rules of Order and elected presidents, treasurers, and secretaries.

The ANB began exploring political and legal avenues to obtain equal treatment for Native people and made remarkable pathways for Native civil and human rights. William Paul Sr., a Tlingit attorney, secured Native voting rights in 1922, two years before the United States Congress established voting rights and U.S. citizenship for American Indians. In fact, William Paul was the first Native person elected to the territorial legislature in 1924. He and the ANB organized southeastern Indians into bloc voting. This became an effective means of getting Natives elected and other individuals that believed in equal rights. In order to counteract the new Native vote, the legislature enacted the racist Alaska Literacy Law in 1926, which mandated that an individual could vote only if they were able to read the constitution of the United States; at the time most Natives were not literate in English. William Paul managed to add a grandfather clause that kept the law from applying to people that had already voted, thus keeping intact over a thousand Tlingit, Haida, and Tsimshim votes.

Alaska Natives elected to the Territorial Legislature (House and Senate Seats) included the following:

1924 William Paul Sr. (Tlingit)
1944 Frank Peratrovich (Tlingit) to the House

1944 Andrew Hope (Tlingit) to the House
1946 Frank G. Johnson (Tlingit) to the House
1946 Frank Peratrovich (Tlingit) to the Senate
1948 Percy Ipalook (Iñupiat) from Wales
1948 William Beltz (Iñupiat) from Nome
1950 Frank Degnan (Iñupiat) of Unalakleet to the House
1950 James Wells (Iñupiat) of Noorvik to the House

The Alaska Native Brotherhood and Sisterhood (ANB/ANS) fought segregation and voting laws since their inception and pursued justice and equality for Native people. Because of their political activity they were viewed as progressive radicals by the existing press, but were effective and pro-active in securing many of their goals. William Paul Sr. sued and won a court case in 1929 that allowed Southeast Indian children to attend public schools. Previously only white students could attend these public schools. This was an initial step to end segregation in Alaska. It was not until World War II that segregation was outlawed in Alaska.

Several events occurred that led to the end of segregationist policies during the years preceding the end of World War II in Alaska. Territorial Governor Ernest Gruening sympathized and proposed an anti-discrimination law in 1943 to the territorial legislature. The law failed to pass. "I had found that the pure democracy and egalitarianism of Alaskans which had so impressed me was subject to one basic exception. It did not apply to the Native people—the Indians, Eskimos and Aleuts," said Gruening later. An incident occurred a few years later in Nome that brought unprecedented attention to segregation practices. Nome, a community that had a mixed population of Iñupiat and Anglo-Americans, practiced segregation. In 1944 Alberta Schenck, a young Iñupiat woman, protested the segregated seating in the Dream Theatre. Schenck worked as an usher at the theatre and was fired for complaining to the owner about the seating policy. She wrote a letter to the Nome *Nugget* on March 4, 1944 that called the segregation policy "Hitlerism." In a brave protest Ms. Schenck sat in the "white" section of the theatre. She was thrown in jail for violating the policy. The Native community was outraged and Iñupiats filled the theatre and sat in the "white" section. Schenck wrote a letter to Governor Gruening complaining about the segregation in Nome and explained how she was arrested for simply sitting in the "white" section of a movie theatre. Territorial Governor Gruening had taken an active stance in the discrimination conflict in Juneau, having racist signs removed. Later that year, an anti-discrimination law came before the territorial legislature. The Juneau *Daily Empire* and other newspapers had editorials that stated the law would increase the problem and supported what they viewed as a white businessman's right to refuse service to anyone of another race. An editorial appeared in the Nome *Nugget* on March 10, 1944, and stated the following:

> The theatre is a private institution and has the right to make its own house rules and until the Native people as a whole live up to public health standards, it would be hard for the management to change their present system. I therefore suggest to those of the Native group who are intelligent enough to complain and criticize, start working from within the Native population, raise their own standards and earn the right for which they are asking.
>
> Signed A Subscriber

Native people were viewed as unsanitary and savage. This supported the status quo of the values of the time, and unfortunately reinforced an illusion of superiority and justified any wrongful actions toward indigenous people. The 1945 Territorial Legislature came under fire for supporting the anti-discrimination bill. During the heated debate, Elizabeth Peratrovich (Tlingit) of the Alaska Native Sisterhood addressed the legislature. Her testimony was powerful and her dignity and answers to questions brought forward by Shattuck and others won accolades. Peratrovich's composure and wit received applause from the senate floor and the law passed. According to accounts, her presence and speech were unexpected and "stunned onlookers into silence" (Dauenhauer and Dauenhauer 1994, 538). Gruening later credited Peratrovich and her testimony for getting the act passed.

Because of the outspoken actions of people like Alberta Schenck, Elizabeth Peratrovich, along with other individuals, Native and non-Native, the Alaska Anti-Discrimination Bill passed and was one of the first equal rights bills in the United States. The U.S. Congress didn't deal with civil rights until the 1950s.

The Alaska Statehood Act—Status of Alaska Natives from 1950–1959

Ironically the Statehood Act of 1959 became a political turning point for Alaska Natives when Alaska became the forty-ninth state in the Union. By the 1950s Alaska Natives witnessed the demise of their traditional religions, educational practices, and self-determination. "In a period of sixty years, Alaska Natives had become a subject people, aliens in their own lands in spite of the work done by some of their leaders, especially the Tlingit people who had organized the Alaska Native Brotherhood to protect Native interests. By 1960 social, cultural and economic conditions for most Native tribes had deteriorated, just staying alive took most of their time with little left for addressing the dangers inherent in their decaying societies. . . ." (Napoleon 1995, 4). "In the 1950s, it was the hardest time for Natives. Many villagers were riddled with TB and Native people had no advocates and no rights," said Marilyn Williams, a physical therapist at the Indian Health Service Hospital in Anchorage from 1956–1981.

At the time of statehood, the average Native person had barely finished the sixth grade. The tuberculosis rate, which showed marked improvements since statehood, in 1966 was still ten times the national average. The infant mortality rate was among the highest in the world. When Alaska became a state the Alaska Native could look forward to a life expectancy of 34.7 years, while his fellow Alaskan who happened to be white could expect to live for 70 years (Gruening 1968, 544). Although Alaska Native people faced many challenges, little solidarity existed, except in Southeast Alaska. The ANB attempted to organize other Native people into ANB "camps" around the state, but geography, a scattered population, and cultural differences prevented the formation of other Alaska Native Brotherhoods from organizing. The ANB was viewed as a Tlingit, Haida, and Tsimshian political organization and non-southeast Natives did not feel comfortable with the aggressive political stance that the ANB represented.

The proverbial Phoenix rose from the ashes beginning in 1959 as a direct result of the Statehood Act. The Statehood Act recognized the Native right to aboriginal lands but did not include safeguards for protection or reference to the size of aboriginal lands. Though the rights were recognized, they still had to be fought for. The Act authorized the state government to obtain title to 103 million acres of land. This created problems for the Native people since the new state government began claiming lands that were used by Natives. The Statehood Act specifically stated that the only lands the state of Alaska could claim must be vacant, unappropriated, and unreserved. The state simply ignored Native rights to lands. Village land, including some burial sites, was selected without consultation with the local Native community. Even worse, plans were made for proposed nuclear testing and dam sites that would destroy the land on which local indigenous people were dependent for food and sustenance. The state also began enforcing laws through the U.S. Fish and Wildlife Service that restricted hunting. This created the greatest threat to Native cultures since the epidemics and Christian missionaries of the nineteenth and early twentieth centuries. Throughout the first half of the twentieth century Natives experienced traumatic hardships in terms of diseases, loss of self-determination, Christian missionaries, and encroachment on their traditional lands, and, because of the Statehood Act, were now looking at the end-of-the-line in terms of cultural survival.

Threats to the Native Land Base

Of the numerous threats to the Native population, the threat to the Native land base was one of the worst. The people behind the state and federal development schemes for Alaska's lands and resources viewed Native people as roadblocks to their plans. These included atomic testing and the building of massive dams. During the 1950s the Atomic Energy Commission (AEC) was experimenting with atomic explosions and underground testing in the Arctic. The AEC had begun doing nuclear testing and had plans to detonate atomic bombs that were over ten times larger than the bombs dropped on Hiroshima and Nagasaki in Cape Thompson, Alaska, just off the Chukchi Sea, under the ruse of creating a deep water harbor. Three Iñupiat villages, Point Hope, Noatak, and Kivalina, were within forty miles of the proposed blast site and the communities were not considered in the plans of the AEC.

The chairman of the AEC, Lewis Strauss, created a propaganda program called "Plowshares" with the stated intention of turning nuclear weapons into tools of constructive use, using the metaphor from the Bible of turning swords into plowshares. The Weapons Branch of the AEC, a military division, in fact administered Plowshares. The geographical engineering project for northern Alaska was called "Project Chariot" and Edward Teller, the "father of the hydrogen bomb," was the director. Teller came to Alaska several times, meeting with politicians and businessmen in order to advance Project Chariot. The AEC excluded the Iñupiat people from early discussions, even though they were touting the validity of Project Chariot to the Alaska Legislature, governor, and local business organizations. The AEC had no problem withdrawing over 1,600 square miles of land and water in the Cape Thompson area for their planned experiment in 1958, even though the Iñupiat people had made earlier attempts to claim the same land under the Alaska Native Allotment Act. The Iñupiat were initially fearful of having their environment contaminated. Unfortunately all of their fears became validated as they learned more about radioactivity. The villages depended on caribou and marine mammals. The short food chain would have poisoned the Native population with radioactivity. At the time, atomic testing was done above ground, causing the air to become contaminated. The Chariot blasts would have been below ground, but would have blasted significant amounts of radioactive debris into the air. Caribou feed mostly on lichen, a rootless form of vegetation that receives its nutrients from air. The lichen would have absorbed the radioactive fallout, and then been eaten by caribou, which are then eaten by people. Once the issue of the possible affects of radiation on the Iñupiat was raised, Teller counteracted the facts with lies. Teller stated that the Iñupiat people would actually benefit from the experiments. In November 1959, the Point Hope Village Council petitioned the AEC and condemned the project. The AEC finally visited Point Hope in 1960 to explain the project and to ally the fears of the community. At that time, the AEC stated that the fish in and around the area would not be radioactive and there was no danger of poison to anyone eating the fish and that the "effects of nuclear weapons testing never injured any people, anywhere, that once the severely exposed Japanese people recovered from radiation sickness . . . there were no side effects." The people of Point Hope were justifiably skeptical of the project and distrustful of the government and unanimously voted against the proposal. In 1961 the residents of Point Hope sent a letter of protest to President Kennedy stating that the blasts were "too close to our homes at Point Hope and to our hunting and fishing areas." Because of the impending threats, the Iñupiat villages began uniting in their struggles. Another incident that became part of the ongoing struggle of subsistence hunting was the Eider Duck Incident.

In 1916 the U.S. signed an international treaty with Canada and Mexico, which banned the hunting of waterfowl from March to September, called the Migratory Bird Treaty Act. Migratory waterfowl were only in Alaska from March through September. Indigenous hunters were prevented from hunting birds that continue to form a core of their diet. For many years the law didn't pose a problem because no one knew much, nor cared about Alaska Natives duck hunters. But when the Statehood Act of 1959 became a reality, more rigid control of federal laws followed—including enforcing the ban on hunting of waterfowl. Harry Pinkham, the white federal warden, arrested John Nusinginya, a resident of Barrow, for hunting an eider duck. Sadie Neakok, the first Alaska Native magistrate, and the Barrow villagers responded en masse.

> When one hunter was arrested for violating the absurd law, she [Sadie Neakok] quietly organized the rest of the village to protest—by breaking the same law, overwhelming the game warden's administrative capacities, drawing forth the spectre of mass jailings and community emergency, and, most important, pressuring the state to change the regulation. It was, perhaps, judicial activism at an awkward peak—but it brought necessary change for the people of Barrow.[1]

A delegation of leaders requested that Pinkham meet with the local residents. When Pinkham arrived, there were over one hundred hunters with eider ducks. The hunters had written statements that said they had taken the ducks out of season in direct violation of the law. They also had signed a petition to President Kennedy demanding that they be allowed to hunt migratory waterfowl since they had done it for thousands of years.

In 1961 the Association of American Indian Affairs (AAIA), under the direction of Laverne Madigan, sponsored a conference in Barrow because of the U.S. Fish and Wildlife Service's ban on hunting migratory waterfowl and concerns over Project Chariot. The AAIA was a progressive organization that supported indigenous rights. The 1961 conference in Barrow had the following opening statement:

> We the Iñupiat have come together for the first time ever in all the years of our history. We had to come together in meeting from our villages from the Lower Kuskokwim to Point Barrow. We had come from so far together for this reason. We always thought our Iñupiat Paitot [Aboriginal hunting right] was safe to be passed down to our future generations as our fathers passed down to us. Our Iñupiat Paitot is our land around the whole Arctic world where the Iñupiat live.

In the historic November 1961 meeting the Iñupiat people from several villages met in Barrow and formed the *Iñupiat Paitot* or People's Heritage, the first Iñupiat political organization. The newly formed organization focused on the proposed atomic blasts around Cape Thompson. Another outcome was the establishment of a Native statewide newspaper. In 1962, an Iñupiat artist from Point Hope, Howard Rock, founded the *Tundra Times*. Henry S. Forbes, the east coast multi-millionaire, provided about $35,000 in start-up funds for the paper. He was on the board of the AAIA and had been contacted by Laverne Madigan. who was trying to locate financial backing for the struggle. The first two issues of the paper included information on Project Chariot. Howard Rock was chosen as the editor and was assisted by Tom Snap, who had been writing for the Fairbanks *Daily News Miner*. This was the state's first statewide Native newspaper.

The *Tundra Times* gave a voice to Alaska Natives and communication on the statewide level was now possible—a real Native solidarity movement had begun. Growing opposition in the form of environmental and human concerns prevented Project Chariot from becoming a reality, but it was a major battle for the Iñupiat and one that motivated them into political action. The *Iñupiat Paitot* had a second annual meeting in 1962 in the village of Kotzebue. Twenty-eight delegates from all the northern Iñupiat villages met and stated the need for schools, housing, and employment and to counter the threats to their livelihood. The head of a newly formed Athabascan organization, Al Ketzler Sr., from Nenana, was a guest speaker. Ketzler proposed congressional action to establish land ownership for Native people, something the ANB had advocated for many years.

Dena Nena Henash—*Athabascan Political Action*

Ketzler was the head of the *Dena Nena Henash* (Our Land Speaks), an Athabascan organization formed in June 1962 to deal with land ownership and aboriginal rights. This later evolved into the Tanana Chiefs Conference (TCC). The first meeting took place in Tanana and over 30 Athabascan villages participated. Tanana was a traditional gathering place in the Tanana/Yukon River area (the Chiefs met there in 1915 at *Nochalawoya* [where the two rivers meet] to protest the Alaska Railroad's intention of routing a train track through a traditional cemetery). Momentum was in place for modern Athabascan political organization.

With the Statehood Act, Athabascan people were surprised to discover the state and federal governments were actively making land selections throughout the state, including the vast regions of the interior—homeland to eleven different Athabascan groups. The Minto Lakes Recreation Area was one such plan. The state planned to build a road to Minto from Fairbanks so access to a public recreation area would be possible for white hunters and sport fishers. The state selected the hunting, fishing, and trapping lands, and even the village of Minto itself. The state also selected the Minto land because of speculation that the area held oil and gas deposits. Minto had originally filed a land claim with the Bureau of Land Management (BLM) in 1951 for the area they occupied and depended on for subsistence, an area they had been intimately familiar with for thousands of years, but their claim was ignored by BLM. The village of Minto was not consulted and when they learned of the plans they protested to the U.S. Department of Interior. In 1963 a meeting was scheduled in Fairbanks to discuss the proposed recreation area. Richard Frank, the Chief of Minto, addressed the assembly of locals, sportsmen, biologists, and state officials, saying:

> Now I don't want to sound like I really hate you people, no. If we were convinced that everyone would benefit, that the people of Minto would benefit, we might go along. The attitude down there is that you people were going to put a road into Minto Lakes without even consulting the people who live there, who hunt and fish there, who use the area for a livelihood. . . . A village is at stake. Ask yourself this question, is a recreation area worth the future of a village? (in Arnold 1976, 101)

The pleas to prevent the Minto Recreation Area from being developed were ignored. The village of Minto hired Ted Stevens, a recent law school graduate, who took the case for free.[2]

Rampart Dam Project

The U.S. Army Corps of Engineers had plans of creating a dam along the Yukon River in the Athabascan area near Rampart which would flood several villages and destroy all the hunting, fishing, and trapping in the area. The Rampart Canyon Dam and Reservoir Project included plans to build a man-made reservoir larger than Lake Erie and bigger than the state of New Jersey. The federal Rampart Dam Project proposed that an electric power plant be created along with a recreation area. The five million kilowatts of power would hopefully attract industry and aluminum mining to the region. The village of Stevens fought the claim and filed a protest in June 1963. Over a thousand residents of the Yukon Flats area filed claims to over a million acres of land, which were adjacent to the Yukon River, their lifeline for survival. The dam was not built due to the protests of the U.S. Fish and Wildlife Service and not Native protests. Their studies indicated that the dam and reservoir would have detrimental affects on the fish and wildlife habitat in the area.

The Alaska Native subsistence and traditional way of life were increasingly threatened after the Statehood Act. The attitude at the time was anti-Native rights and the state and federal land selections presented a clear and immanent danger to Native people and their traditional way of life throughout the state. Another state land selection that drew fire from Athabascan people was the selection of the graveyard and village of Tanacross in 1963. The Tanacross people protested the sale and prevented it. The mood of the new state of Alaska was one of development and exploitation of the land and resources. Native people were viewed as roadblocks to development and economic gain. The development of programs like Project Chariot, Rampart Dam, and Minto Lakes Recreation Area had the support of most legislators, politicians, and businesses because it was viewed as an economic boom and the get-rich-quick mentality was prevalent.

The *Tundra Times* editor Howard Rock, and other Native leaders such as Al Ketzler Sr., began traveling and writing letters to different villages from 1962–64 in an effort to mobilize and instruct the villages on filing land claims with the Department of Interior to protect their homelands. They also sent a petition to Secretary of the Interior Stewart Udall in 1963, which had over one thousand signatures from twenty-four different villages. The petition requested a land freeze be imposed to stop federal and state land selections until aboriginal rights could be established. As a result of the petition, Udall created the Alaska Task Force. The Task Force Report stated that Native land rights needed to be addressed through Congress and this had to be done as quickly as possible.

As a result of the different activity, more and more regional Native organizations were forming.

1912	Alaska Native Brotherhood in Southeast Alaska
1935	Tlingit and Haida Central Council
1960	Fairbanks Native Association founded by Nick Grey (Yup'ik) and Ralph Perdue (Athabascan)
1961	*Iñupiat Paitot* formed in Barrow
1962	*Dena Nena Henash*, later renamed the Tanana Chief Conference
1962	Association of Village Council Presidents founded in Bethel to represent over 56 Yup'ik villages
1964	*Gwichya Gwich'in Ginkhye* (Yukon Flats People Speak)
1964	Cook Inlet Native Association founded in Anchorage by Nick Gray (Yup'ik) and Emil Notti (Athabascan)
1964–65	Kuskokwim Valley Native Association (Yup'ik) founded by Nick Gray for the Bethel area
1965	Arctic Slope Native Association formed for the North Slope Iñupiat villages
1965	Northwest Alaska Native Association (NANA) founded by Willie Hensley for the Iñupiat villages in the Kobuk area

In 1963 at a Tanana Chiefs Conference (formerly *Dena Nena Henash*) meeting, two representatives of the ANB, Steven Hotch and William Paul Sr., brought forward the idea of a statewide organization with ANB being the umbrella organization for the growing number of regional Native organizations. They were well received, but distrust of the mostly Tlingit dominated organization prevented this from happening. The following year, several Native leaders organized another meeting. Howard Rock of the *Tundra Times*, Al Ketzler of TCC/*Dena Nena Henash*, Ralph Perdue of the Fairbanks Native Association, and Marlow Solomon of the *Gwichya Gwich'in Ginkhye* met for two days with John Hope of the ANB as chair of the meeting. The agenda included the need for communication and activity between the different statewide Native organizations. This meeting and other events led to more communication between the different Native people and organizations. Another vital aspect to the growing statewide network of Native leaders was the Kennedy/Johnson Administration's anti-poverty campaign. The state of Alaska received funds to start an anti-poverty program and the Alaska State Community Action Program or ASCAP was organized. This was a grassroots operation led by Charles Edwardsen Jr. or Etuk of Barrow. Etuk had been influenced by the work of William Paul Sr. and the ANB. ASCAP later became RuralCAP. The process achieved more communication with different Natives throughout the state of Alaska and they began to work together.

The Petroleum Factor

For years the Iñupiat had cut out pieces of oil-soaked tundra for fuel use in an area southeast of Point Barrow at Cape Simpson and at another location southeast of Kaktovik in Angun Point. The petroleum find was originally recorded by Leffingwell, a geologist, as he and his Iñupiat guides and crew mapped the entire Arctic coast in a 1907–14 expedition, but due to isolation and limited technology, no test wells were drilled until the 1960s. In 1967, a test well hit pay dirt in Prudhoe Bay. The area represented the largest petroleum deposit in North America (to date it has yielded over twelve billion barrels of oil). The Arctic Slope Native Association flexed their political muscles in a shocking maneuver by claiming 58 million acres of land north of the Brooks Range—where the Prudhoe Bay oil fields lay. The land claim was based on aboriginal use and occupancy from time immemorial.

In 1966, Emil Notti, the President of Cook Inlet Native Association, called for a statewide meeting to address the issue of land claims. Notti was concerned over a BIA plan, the proposed "final solution" to the land problem in Alaska. He sent letters to different people around the state in an effort to discuss land claims. Howard Rock, beginning in July 1966, began headlining the meeting and urging people to attend. Over three hundred people, representing more than seventeen Native groups, attended the October 1966 meeting in Anchorage, Alaska. The meeting was financed by the Cook Inlet Village of Tyonek, which had recently won a major settlement from oil leases on their lands. Notti chaired the meeting and they elected a board of directors and called themselves the Alaska Federation of Native Associations. It was also at this meeting that Willie Hensley presented his legal study of Alaska's land, which indicated that Natives still owned Alaska's lands; the claims had never been extinguished. At their second meeting in 1967 the group renamed itself the Alaska Federation of Natives or AFN and elected Emil Notti as its first president. During the second meeting in 1967 the delegates from the different Native organizations cemented their constitution and solidified its political structure. The second meeting brought even more attention. Businessmen and government officials courted the Alaska Native delegates; especially since oil revenues were at stake. Native people now had a new source of power and everyone knew it. Native people were finally being considered in the land claims of Alaska.

The AFN became the first statewide Native organization and played a key role in the subsequent land claims settlement. One of the first problems they addressed was obtaining a land freeze to prevent the state of Alaska from gaining title to their aboriginal lands. The AFN's primary goal was a land settlement—they pushed for a land freeze and succeeded. Stewart Udall, the Secretary of Interior, imposed a land freeze on all federal land transfers to the state of Alaska until Congress could resolve the land claims issues.

By 1967 there were so many land claims in Alaska that they exceeded the actual size of the state by 20 percent. The process was exacerbated by the pending oil development plans for the Prudhoe Bay oil fields. The land freezes literally stopped any leasing of lands by oil companies. The state government and oil companies were upset over the land freeze. Alaska Governor Walter Hickel filed a lawsuit against Udall in an attempt to force the transfer of lands to the state. The Alaska District Court sided with the state, but the 9th Circuit Court of Appeals overturned the ruling. It was a very intense period of time. Sentiment in the late 1960s was still anti-Native. During a 1968 Senate Interior Committee hearing in Anchorage, the spokesman for the Alaska Miner's Association made a statement that reflected a common view at the time: "neither the United States, the State of Alaska, nor any of us here gathered as individuals owes the Natives one acre of ground or one cent of the taxpayer's money." Prominent Native testimony included William Paul Sr., Chief Andrew Isaac of Tanacross, Peter John of Minto, Walter Soboleff, John Klashnikoff of Cordova, and many others. The AFN land claims battle was very complicated because it involved the interests of state and federal governments and the oil companies. There were various bills that were introduced, and many were inadequate. AFN had to lobby hard for a fair and just bill that would include land entitlements and no involvement with the BIA and protection of subsistence hunting and fishing. There were many Native leaders, who fought hard, with little financial gain. Oil companies and a favorable climate for Native rights prevailed and, for better or worse, President Richard Nixon signed the Alaska Native Claims Settlement Act in 1971.

The rise in statewide Native political action did not begin until 1968, yet within eleven years Native people had managed to get the U.S. Congress to pass a law that established their land rights, and monetary compensation for lands that were lost. There were many factors involved in the decade preceding the ANCSA settlement, but the primary factor was Native solidarity. During the 1960s the growing number of Native organizations helped fuel a statewide solidarity movement and created the AFN and the *Tundra Times*. Initially these institutions were powerful organizations paving the way for a stronger Native identity.

The Native solidarity movement led to a stronger identity for Native people, coupled with a more local control of resources and for education of their children. Today, forty years after AFN's founding, new and younger Native generations are being born into a world with a fresher perspective of who they are and who they might become. The Native solidarity movement of the 1960s turned the tide of negative identity and racism around and created an environment of empowerment for Native people.[3]

Notes

1. See http://www.alaskool.org.

2. Ted Stevens was elected U.S. Senator and has served in Washington since 1970.

3. See the following periodicals for more information: Juneau *Empire*, October 7, 1924; Fairbanks *Daily News Miner*, February 13, 1926; Nome *Nugget*, March 4, 1944; Nome *Nugget*, March 10, 1944.

III

Worldviews: Alaska Native and Indigenous Epistemologies

Epistemology (from the Greek word *epistēmē* or "knowledge" and *ology* or "the study of") is a branch of philosophy that deals with knowledge and belief and worldview. Epistemology primarily addresses how knowledge is defined, acquired, and related to culture and worldview. Multiple, fascinating methods are being developed in this discipline by Native American and Alaska Native scholars.

The Native American philosopher Viola Cordova (Jicarilla Apache) states: "Each distinct cultural group, perhaps in an original isolation from other groups, provides three definitions around which they build all subsequent determinations about the world they live in. First, each has a definition or description of the world; second, there is a definition of what it is to be human in the world as it is so defined and described; and, third, there is an attempt to outline the role of a human in that world" (as quoted in Moore et al. 2007, 1).

Two of the contributors to this part, Oscar *Angayuqaq* Kawagley (Yupiaq) and Gregory A. Cajete (Santa Clara Pueblo), are leaders in the area of indigenous epistemology, along with Viola Cordova and Ines Talamantez (Mescalero Apache). Indigenous scholars are developing models that convey specific cultural worldviews and epistemology that establishes and defines the sophisticated ways of knowing that indigenous people developed over thousands and thousands of years. Western philosophers have overlooked the fact that Native Americans have philosophies, hence the importance of the work and research of Kawagley, Talamantez, and Cordova, who have painstakingly analyzed various indigenous belief systems and provided a window to understand them.

Talamantez's writings and research are focused in the areas of Native American spirituality and Native American female worldviews. She expresses her ideas in a forthright manner:

> The indigenous framework within which many of us work reveals the systems of relatedness, obligation, and respect that govern the lives of many native women. There is a driving purpose behind our work; we know what we are expected to do. There are political commitments to social justice, concerns for what constitutes activism in our present day, complex issues of identity and naming ourselves. The political survival issues of the day—land claims, freedom of religion, environmental racism, lack of appropriate health care, education, and employment, for example—engage us as to persons who labor under the twin oppressions of being woman and native. This narrative of inquiry requires deep reflection. It is an exploration in both humility and authority. Insight is gained through analysis, interpretation, and critique. (Talamantez 2005, 222)

There are a number of salient characteristics of Alaska Native epistemology, as pointed out in Kawagley's essay, such as the view that the natural and spiritual worlds are almost one and the idea that ties to the land and fellow creatures are profoundly linked to being a person. Kawagley writes, "Native people's reciprocity with the natural and spiritual realms implies a form of cross-species interaction." He offers examples by way of oral narrative, family ties, and social and religious practices.

The essays in part III offer perspectives on indigenous epistemology mostly through the lens of Native science, revealing how science and religion or spirit are indivisible in this worldview. Western philosophy compartmentalizes philosophy and science as opposed to the indigenous worldview, which is based on a more holistic model. It is exciting to witness the recognition of works by Kawagley, Talamantez, Cordova, and others. Kawagley's work, which focuses on traditional ecological knowledge, often referred to as TEK, has a science or environmental focus and brilliantly illustrates how indigenous epistemology and science are linked.

The first selection is an excerpt from Kawagley's book *A Yupiaq Worldview: A Pathway to Ecology and Spirit* (1995/2006), which accurately illustrates how Yupiaq science is still practiced, how important it was to the survival of the Yupiaq people, and how it can be made a relevant and powerful teaching tool.

Gregory A. Cajete's essay addresses astronomy from an indigenous framework of knowledge (or epistemology). Cajete believes that by studying astronomy one can learn much about the origin stories, religious beliefs, and cultural practices of people; he provides important examples of how the stars can tell stories.

Claudette Engblom-Bradley (Schaghticoke) contributes an essay on mathematics from an indigenous perspective, showing how math systems are culturally interpreted by and relevant for Native cultures. She discusses ethnomathematics, which is a way of studying the cultural context or epistemology of indigenous math systems. Whether teaching graphing through bead work (and vice versa) or showing students the mathematical relevance of indigenous navigational techniques, Engblom-Bradley exposes the connections between mathematics, a so-called artifact of Western knowledge, and her students' cultural heritage. Engblom-Bradley's other work focuses on traditional weaving techniques; she approaches the construction of material culture items and relates them to the specific culture they come from—in terms of counting, organizing, and other mathematical principles.

As indigenous people enter the sciences they are often taught to ignore their own intellectual and cultural traditions. In her essay, Lilian *Na'ia* Alessa questions how to come to terms with the two worldviews, indigenous and scientific. In many ways, her questions are relevant for disciplines outside of science as well. Can two worldviews or epistemologies coexist?

The concluding essay in this part is by Joan *Pirciralria* Hamilton (Cup'ik), who was the longtime director for the Yupiit Piciyararait Museum in Bethel, Alaska. The Cup'ik people are part of the larger Yup'ik culture group. Joan was raised in a traditional sod house speaking only Cup'ik until she went to the St. Mary's boarding School in St. Mary's, Alaska. Joan's life experiences and traditional knowledge contributed greatly to the development of the only Yup'ik Museum in Bethel, Alaska. Sadly Joan passed away in June 2008. Her contribution to this volume and to Native people will be forever cherished.

A Yupiaq Worldview: A Pathway to Ecology and Spirit

Oscar Angayuqaq *Kawagley* *(Yupiaq)*

This selection from Oscar Kawagley's groundbreaking book A Yupiaq Worldview *represents what contemporary indigenous scholars are doing in the twenty-first century on the theoretical as well as the applied level. In his book Kawagley proposes a pedagogical methodology that incorporates all ways of knowing—indigenous and Western alike. The excerpts here include the introduction to the book and a portion of the first chapter. Kawagley brilliantly uses oral narratives from various Alaska Native cultures and discusses how they convey indigenous ways of being, knowing, and understanding. Kawagley, a Yupiaq scholar, received his doctorate in social and education studies from the University of British Columbia. He has taught at the University of Alaska, Fairbanks in the School of Education for many years and has made major contributions to the curriculum and educational system.*

*Professor Kawagley was born near Bethel (Mamterilleq) and is a fluent Yupiaq/Yup'ik speaker. He has spent his life as a dedicated teacher and champion of indigenous peoples. He is a strong proponent of Traditional Ecological Knowledge (*TEK*), which is now a common approach used by many educational and research institutions. He has published articles and developed new programs that include indigenous perspectives in science and the importance of language in indigenous school programs; he belongs to a global indigenous network of scholars.*

The incursion of Western society has brought about many cultural and psychological disruptions to the flow of life in traditional societies. Indigenous peoples have become subservient in the Western system and are confronted with new social structures that they do not always find compatible with their needs. This assimilative process often alters childrearing practices and has brought about shifts from nomadic to sedentary lifestyles, changes in dietary orientation from natural to processed foods (often with less nutritional value), alterations in design and efficiency of housing, and dependence on numerous government institutions that control what people do. Traditional ways of knowing with the attendant life skills and self-regulating processes on which indigenous people have relied for many generations are usually left along the trail in the name of "progress" (Bodley 1982).

The Western educational system has attempted to instill a mechanistic and linear worldview in indigenous cultural contexts previously guided by a typically cyclic worldview. The "modern" view tends to be oriented toward the manipulation of the world's resources—including people—toward political, social, and economic "progress," with the presumed end result being an advanced quality of life (Berger 1976). This view is reinforced by an underlying notion of "manifest destiny," whereby the Western way of life is considered superior to those of traditional societies (Bodley 1982). Notions such as manifest destiny reflect the historical intent of Western society in its approach to indigenous peoples wherever they were encountered and the residue of such notions is still present today in the sociopolitical practices of governing institutions regulating the lives of indigenous people in such places as Alaska, Canada, New Zealand, Australia, and Norway.

Most indigenous peoples' worldviews seek harmony and integration with all life, including the spiritual, natural, and human domains (Burger 1990; Knudson and Suzuki 1992). These three realms permeate traditional worldviews and all aspects of indigenous peoples' lives. Their constructed technology was mediated by nature. Their traditional education processes were carefully constructed around mythology, history, the observation of natural processes and animals' and plants' styles of survival and obtaining food, and use of natural materials to make their tools and implements, all of which was made understandable through thoughtful stories and illustrative examples. This view of the world and approach to education has been brought into jeopardy with the onslaught of Western social systems and institutionalized forms of cultural transmission.

The indigenous peoples of the world have experienced varying degrees of disruption or loss with regard to their traditional lifestyles and worldviews. This disruption has contributed to the many psychosocial maladies that are extant in indigenous societies today. The Western worldview with its aggressive educational practices and technoscience orientation has placed indigenous cultures in "harm's way" (Bodley 1982). These cultures, having been characterized as primitive and backward, and therefore wanting, are subjected to an endless stream of assimilative processes to bring their practitioners into mainstream society. The indigenous peoples are forced to live in a constructed and psychic world not of their own making or choosing. Little is left in their lives to remind them of their indigenous culture, nor is there recognition of their indigenous consciousness and its application of intelligence, ingenuity, creativity, and inventiveness in the making of their world.

This is not to say that modernity has brought only negative consequences for indigenous peoples, for benefits have been derived as well. Infant mortality is down and childhood diseases greatly diminished. Disastrous fluctuations in food supplies have been reduced, and modes of transportation and means of communication have improved with telephones, radio, and so forth. However, in balance, the benefits to traditional societies are often offset by many new psychosocial and physical health ailments, problems of costly and inefficient housing, disruptions in parent-child relationships, domestic violence, suicides, alcohol and drug abuse, and other forms of dysfunctional social behavior; with the vast changes has come a general sense of powerlessness and loss of control over individual lives. Consequently, the issue of the long-term consequences of the collision of contrasting worldviews on the survival of indigenous peoples takes on an urgency that can no longer be ignored. Many studies and reports have addressed these concerns, but nearly all have been from a Western perspective. Rarely has the worldview and value structure underlying the way indigenous people look at such issues been examined and an attempt been made to approach the issues from an indigenous perspective.

Since this study is written from the perspective of a Yupiaq researcher, working in a traditional Yupiaq setting, the interpretations and generalizations pertaining to attributes of both the Yupiaq and Western worldviews will be presented as seen through Yupiaq eyes. This is not to deny that Yupiaq and Western societies include within them many variant perspectives and that ideas on values, lifestyles, and interrelationships among the human, natural, and spiritual worlds can differ markedly. Nor is it to ignore the fact that within Western society there are many ideas, practices, and artifacts derived from indigenous peoples throughout the world.

When representing the Western worldview from a Yupiaq perspective, it must be understood that the Yupiaq have experienced particular nuances in thinking, ways of doing things, and other idiosyncrasies of the Western world through the envoys of the various institutions established to administer to the needs of the Yupiaq people. From the Yupiaq person's perspective, the constellation of these new values, beliefs, and practices introduced through schooling, religion, government economics and numerous technological devices represents a worldview quite distinct from that of the Yupiaq. In Yupiaq eyes, Western society often appears as a monolithic entity; despite the fact that it is made up of many diverse institutions and divergent points of view.

This research will attempt to establish an indigenous platform from which to examine some of these issues, utilizing a case study of a Yupiaq Eskimo community in southwestern Alaska to identify ways in which the values extant in the competing Western and Yupiaq worldviews affect the lives and choices of the people in that community.

In this book the primary purposes of study are as follows:

1. To examine some of the historical consequences of the intersection of a Western and a Yupiaq worldview.
2. To understand how people in the contemporary Yupiaq community of Akiak, Alaska, have adapted their cultural values and principles to accommodate the intersection of Western and Yupiaq worldviews.
3. To document contemporary Yupiaq practices in the traditional activity and setting of a fish camp and explore implications for the development of social, political, economic, and educational institutions suited to the aspirations of Yupiaq communities and indigenous people generally.
4. To construct an epistemological framework and pedagogical orientation in which the Western and Yupiaq traditions of knowledge generation and utilization can be addressed, particularly as they pertain to the learning and use of scientific knowledge in a traditional Yupiaq environment.

I will then identify critical elements of the constellation of values and life principles currently operative in a Yupiaq community and explore the extent to which the existing configuration will allow the Yupiaq to reconstruct a world that will empower them with sufficient control over their own lives and give solidarity in their efforts. One dictionary, *The Random House Webster's Unabridged Dictionary*, defines *value* as "the quality of anything that renders it desirable or useful" and *principle* as "an accepted or professed rule of action or conduct." The Yupiaq terms that are roughly equivalent in meaning are *piciyarat* (qualities for life) and *yungnaqsarat* (rules of life). The first helps to make a life, while the second helps to make a living. These are the meanings that will be ascribed to the usage of the terms in this study.

A task of this magnitude requires the eventual narrowing of focus to a few of the most critical values and principles that define the intersection between the Western and indigenous worldviews, so that the implications can be examined in such social sectors as politics, economics, and education. The identification of certain core values and principles that are essential to the well-being of Yupiaq society is of central concern, and also the determination of how to make these values and principles an indelible part of a newly constructed school curriculum that can serve to revive and reorient the indigenous peoples to a more harmonious and sustainable life in a rapidly changing world. The exploration of contrasting values and principles in this way may open doors for further research and action to begin to implement initiatives that take the best from the two worlds and reconstruct a world to fit the times.

A Yupiaq Worldview: A Pathway to Ecology and Spirit analyzes available information on the lifeways, worldview, and ways of knowing of the Yupiaq people as they have evolved over time and then gives a detailed description of the ways in which the people in a particular community and region live their life today. Attention is also given to a Yupiaq perspective on the practice of science and technology, and how that perspective does or does not come into play in the context of education and schooling. Finally, some implications of the study for the application of science and technology and the practice of schooling in a Yupiaq setting are outlined.

Basic philosophical questions are raised in the course of observing and questioning people with respect to notions of inquiry, explanation, technology, science, and religion, as they relate to particular life ways. Accordingly, worldview as discussed here, will attempt to answer the questions deftly set out by Barry Lopez: "metaphysics epistemology, ethics, aesthetics and logic—which pose, in order the following questions. What is real? What can we understand? How should we behave? What is beautiful? What are the patterns we can rely upon?" (1986, 202). To his list will be added *ontology*: Why are we? Is there something greater than the human? Lopez goes on to point out, "The risk we take is of finding our final authority in the metaphors rather than in the land. To inquire into the intricacies of a distant landscape, then, provokes thoughts about one's own interior landscape, and the familiar landscapes of memory. The land urges us to come around to an understanding of ourselves" (ibid., 247).

The concept of worldview is very closely related to the definitions of culture and cognitive map (Berger, Berger and Kellner 1974, 148). A worldview consists of the principles we acquire to make sense of the world around us. Young people learn these principles, including values, traditions, and customs from myths, legends, stories, family, community, and examples set by community leaders (Deloria 1991a; Hardwick 1991). The worldview, or cognitive map, is a summation of coping devices that have worked in the past and may or may not be as effective in the present (Netting 1986). Once a worldview has been formed, the people are then able to identify themselves as a unique people. Thus, the worldview enables its possessors to make sense of the world around them, make artifacts to fit their world, generate behavior, and interpret their experiences. As with many other indigenous groups, the worldviews of the traditional Alaska Native peoples have worked well for their practitioners for thousands of years.

Alaska Native Worldview

Among Alaska Native peoples exist many languages and dialects, and as many worldviews or variations thereof. Thus, rather than attempt to describe them all, I will deal first with the more prominent shared characteristics of the Alaska Native worldviews and then focus more specifically on the Yupiaq.

Alaska Native peoples have traditionally tried to live in harmony with the world around them. This has required the construction of an intricate subsistence-based worldview, a complex way of life with specific cultural mandates regarding the ways in which the human being is to relate to other human relatives and the natural and spiritual worlds.

This worldview, as demonstrated historically by the Native peoples of Alaska, contained a highly developed social consciousness and sense of responsibility. As indicated by the writings of outside researchers and observers, Native peoples' myths, rituals, and ceremonies were consistent with their relationship to one another and to their environment (Fienup-Riordan 1990; Freeman, Milton and Carbyn 1988; Locust 1988). Ann Fienup-Riordan postulates that wisdom, insight, knowledge, and power were considered the prerogative of the elders, who were honored and respected in recognition of their achievements (1990, 55). Attitude was thought to be as important as action; therefore one was to be careful in thought and action so as not to injure another's mind or offend the spirits of the animals and surrounding environment. For one to have a powerful mind was to be "aware of or awake to the surroundings" (1990, 74).

To help practitioners along this reciprocal path, Native peoples developed many rituals and ceremonies with respect to motherhood, and child rearing, care of animals, hunting and trapping practices, and related ceremonies for maintaining balance between the human, natural, and spiritual realms. This intricate sense of harmony with all things has been identified by most observers as central to understanding Alaska Native worldviews (Freeman and Carbyn 1988; Locus 1988; Scollon and Scollon 1979). A hallmark of Alaska Native peoples was their success at adapting to ever changing environmental conditions "while strengthening their cultural integrity" (Bielawski 1990, 5). This was demonstrated in their ability to reconstruct and continuously modify their worldviews, so that "new" Native traditions have evolved even up to the present day (Fienup-Riordan 1990).

Fienup-Riordan has called the Alaska Native and other indigenous peoples the "original ecologists" (1990, 32). One reason for this is that their worldviews are dependent upon reciprocity—do unto others, as you would have them do unto you. All of life is considered recyclable and therefore requires certain ways of caring in order to maintain the cycle. Native people cannot put themselves above other living things because they were all created by the Raven, and all are considered an essential component of the universe. They were able to sustain their traditional subsistence economy because "they possessed appropriate ecological knowledge and suitable methods/technology to exploit resources, possessed a philosophy and environmental ethic to keep exploitative abilities in check, and established ground rules for relationships between humans and animals" (Freeman and Carbyn 1988, 7).

Out of this ecologically based emphasis on reciprocity, harmony, and balance have evolved some common values and principles that are embedded in the worldviews of most Alaska Native people. The following excerpt from Mary Muktoyuk's story, *Iñupiaq Rules for Living* (1988, 65–69), is an example:

> Back then, my parents would give us lessons on correct behavior, back when I was first becoming aware. My parents spoke with great wisdom of things that we did not know about.
>
> Also, when we were small, from time to time someone would kill a polar bear. The people were very happy when a hunter killed a polar bear, for polar bears were considered extremely dangerous then.
>
> Then after they had slept a certain number of nights, they would give thanks for it by dancing. They would give thanks for the polar bear.
>
> Then they would give some pieces of skin for sewing to those who were growing old, and they gave them food, too, because they were thankful for that polar bear and were celebrating it. They tried to make those who were growing old happy, too. These days, people are no longer like that, because we are no longer in our land, and because those wise people of long ago have died, all of them. They would give freely of food or skins for sewing. In those days they gave and gave freely. They lived a good life then. These days, they no longer live in a good way, for they are no longer as they used to be.
>
> The elders, in those days, we held in great respect. Whatever they told us, we would listen very carefully, trying not to make mistakes when we listened, because we respected them so highly because they knew much more than we did while we were still growing up. In those times, though, people seem to have stopped doing things in the old way. It is known that

> they no longer do things as they used to. And these days all of them have become that way. Even if they are close friends or relatives, they are no longer like members of a family.
>
> In the past we were aware that even people who were not closely related seemed like close relatives. Now what was is no more. You no longer see people like those who lived then. These people of one village all lived as close relatives; that's how they used to be. They probably can never be the same again. If somehow they could return to a village of their own, I wonder if they might go back to the way they lived long ago.[1]

This story incorporates three important ethical and moral teachings of Native people, namely, the importance of sharing, the role of cooperation in the extended family, and giving thanks to the creative force. It was the practice of the Native hunter to show his wealth and success as a provider by sharing what he obtained with his fellow villagers and invited guests. "In those days, they gave and gave freely," knowing that they would be repaid in-kind, respected and taken care of by others in their time of need. The food had been given freely by nature, so it was only right to share it. Particular attention was given to elders who did not have offspring for support, to widows with children, and to orphans. The gratitude of these less fortunates was considered powerful "medicine" that led to good fortune in future hunts. The more one gave, the happier one would be, and the more likely one would lead a long and satisfied life.

The extended family was important for survival and keeping a bloodline alive but did not necessarily consist only of the blood relatives. It included as family members those associated through marriage and "naming." When a family member died, whoever was named after the deceased became a member of the family and was accorded the kin term of the deceased. "Regardless of the familial relationship, "people of one village lived as close relatives" (Muktoyuk 1988).

The Native people continue to maintain a complex kin relationship, with a term for each person. The Yupiaq term for relatives is associated with the word for viscera, with connotations of deeply interconnected feelings. One must acknowledge and take pride in a relationship, and this feeling comes from within. Among the Athabascans, this sense of caring and respect derives from distant time (Nelson 1983) and is reinforced through many rituals and stories. These stories often include events in which humans become animals or vice versa, implying interrelationships with all living things, so care and respect must be shown all humans and nonhumans alike, to maintain harmony and balance.

Inherent in all aspects of Alaska Native worldviews is respect for the spiritual forces that govern the universe, so that following a successful hunt, "they would give thanks for it by dancing" (Muktoyuk 1988, 67). The creative force, as manifested in nature is more profound and powerful than anything the human being can do, because in it is the very essence of all things. Yet within this profound and powerful force are efficiency, economy, and purpose, the expression of which is dependent on the human being. As with other indigenous people, within the Native worldview is the notion that "a spiritual landscape exists within the physical landscape" (Lopez 1986, 273). This spiritual landscape provides a platform through which integration with other life forces is achieved. O. B. Bakar notes that "Careful observation was made of animal behavior and the inner qualities and the genius of a particular animal species with a view of deriving spiritual and moral lessons from that animal species. There is a metaphysical basis for the belief that animals have much to teach man concerning the divine wisdom and about his own inner nature" (Bakar 1991, 95).

Alaska Native worldviews are oriented toward the synthesis of information gathered from interaction with the natural and spiritual worlds so as to accommodate and live in harmony with the natural worlds and natural principles and exhibit the values of sharing, cooperation, and respect. Native people's reciprocity with the natural and spiritual realms implies a form of cross-species interaction that Caduto and Bruchac point out is perhaps only now being learned by Western scientists: "The science of ecology, the study of the interactions between living things and their environments, circles back to the ancient wisdom found in the rich and oral traditions of American Indian stories. Time and again the stories have said that all of the living and non-living parts of the Earth are one and that people are a part of that wholeness. Today, Western ecological science agrees" (1989, 5).

Note

1. Editor's note: The Iñupiaq people of King Island were forcibly relocated off their island in the 1960s.

The Cosmos: Indigenous Perspectives

Gregory A. Cajete (*Santa Clara Pueblo*)

This essay addresses the relationship between indigenous people and the stars, how they are linked to origin stories and their placement in the larger cosmos, similar to indigenous Alaska Native societies. The essay provides another framework for viewing indigenous perspectives on "star language" and astronomy. Cajete (Santa Clara Pueblo) is the director of Native American studies at the University of New Mexico. His work reflects Native American philosophical and epistemological perspectives; his numerous publications explore subjects from Native games to Native science. Professor Cajete has developed curricula for both the University of New Mexico and the Institute of American Indian Arts in Santa Fe, where he has served as dean.

Introduction

Contributions of Alaska Native Peoples to the stories and practical knowledge associated with indigenous astronomy are extensive. This is especially true when one considers the long history of circumpolar navigation in these regions based on their knowledge of the movements of sun, moon, stars and constellations, relative land formations, shifting ice masses, and the polar oceans.

As with other Native people, Alaska Natives believe that the places in which they live are sacred and the result of the activity of mythological beings. Guiding stories handed down through generations relate cosmological origins of people, plants, animals and places. Alaska Native stories relate the origins of life, particularly human life with activity of sacred beings, the sun, moon and stars. Thus, life as we know it was the result of biological, mythological and cosmological entities in dynamic and creative interplay.

The ancient origin of the cosmos, the earth and all living things provides the foundation for the consciousness and practical knowledge that are still acknowledged in Alaska Native societies today. Parts of these stories are held by different Alaskan groups with variations of stories found in different regions. They include such stories as those of Raven, the trickster-transformer, which are told by many Alaska Native groups. For example, among the Tlingit:

> Raven is responsible for the movement of the tides, for the existence of lakes and streams, for putting the stars and moon in the sky, and for liberating daylight. Many particular forms of the landscape are due to his activities. He brought ashore all the animals and birds now on the land, he determined the present form and habits of many species, or he created them from transformed men, according to various stories. He was responsible for obtaining fire from the sun. He taught men all the useful arts, and originated any customs. (de Laguna 1962, 792)

In these stories, every action of a mythological figure such as Raven is significant and reflects a web of relationship or "coming into being" which forms the foundation for the world as it exists today. Very much like the Australian Aboriginal stories of Dreamtime, Raven shapes the landscape as the Tlingit know it. These stories also imply the inherent and dynamically changing processes of a complex adaptive system of earth and cosmic processes. This is a system in which every action, including that of human beings, affects everything else. All things in this system are considered living and sacred. All things are seen to be in constant motion, interacting and interdependent at many levels of being. It is a system in which everything is paradoxically in chaos while at the same time moving toward some sort of dynamic balance.

The activity in the geophysical world "happens" as a result of the interaction of Raven, as transformer creator, with other players, old men or old women as well as spirit beings, who influence the changes we perceive in the natural world.

> The Tlingits say the world is supported by a pole, and an old women is always near, watching, and sometimes the Raven tries to pull away from her away from that pole foundation of the earth, and that is what shakes the earth and causes earthquakes. . . . [In another story version] . . . The "Old Woman Underneath" (hay'i ca' nak!) attends to the post, but it shakes when she is hungry, so people put food in the fire for her in order to stop the earthquake. (de Laguna 1962, 793)

The conflicts and antics instigated by Raven at times cause different events to occur among mythic beings. For example, the moving and ever changing ocean tides are important to the Tlingit by either allowing or preventing travel or providing rich harvests of beach foods.

> The tides were considered to be controlled by an old woman (or an old woman in some versions of the myth) called "Old Lady Who Watches the Tides" (qis 'axcuwu katsinnuq gu canuk). Once, according to the story, she seems to have kept the tide up all the time. Raven obtained a sea urchin

> by climbing a kelp stem down under the water, but she refused to believe him. So he became angry and rubbed her bare buttocks with prickly spines until she made the tides go down. "Raven only rubbed her bottom once, but its still sore. That's why she can't sit still, and keeps moving . . . That old woman don't sit still; and the tide moves up and down." (794)

The influence of the moon on the tides is also known among the Tlingit and represented in another version of the ebb and flow of tides.

> Once there was a great Flood, believed to have been caused by the same as described in the Bible. This was like an abnormally high tide that covered all the earth. It was caused by Raven's jealous uncle who became angry when his beautiful wife was molested by Raven. This personage is equated with Noah by some, and was called Tlingit Quiga (or Quige), and also 'He Who Orders the Tide' (qis' kuqek). In two versions of the myth this person is associated with the Moon. He became so angry at what happened to his wife that he went up into the sky, and his slaves accompanied him as the Stars. (794)

In the classic Tlingit story of creation of the Sun, Moon, and Stars, Raven plays the role of an instigator of the cosmological dynamic of chaos responsible for the creation of the Universe.

> The usual concept of the Sun, Moon, and Stars, is that they were objects kept in boxes by a chief who lived at the head of Nass River . . . At this time the world was dark. Raven transformed himself into a hemlock needle and was swallowed by the chief's daughter, to whom he was born as a baby. He cried for his grandfather's treasures, obtaining first the Stars and the Moon, which he threw out of the house so that they went up into the sky. When he got the box of Daylight, he resumed his Raven shape and flew away with it to Dry Bay. When he opened the box there the people were so frightened that they ran away, those wearing skins of land animals ran into the woods and mountains, while those wearing sealskin clothing ran into the water, and all were apparently transformed into various animals. The mountains also moved back and the rocks ran away. (796)

The Tlingit understood that there was fire in the Sun and metaphorically represented their perception in various stories. The phases of the moon as well as eclipses are also described. The Big Dipper, Pleiades, Jupiter, and Venus are all descriptively named according to how the people experience them in the night sky. The Yakutat Tlingit name for Venus as the Morning Star is translated to mean 'Morning Round Thing' (Keq ! acaguli') which is derived from the Yakutat verb 'to dawn.' All of these names imply or describe relationships to the entities which make up the cosmos.

Traditional stories of the cosmos are often the subject of oral, song or dance performance. And it is through the performance of these stories that the meaning and essence of Alaska Native sky lore comes alive in the hearts and mind of audiences. It is through performance that the Tlingit personify their ancestral connection to the Sun, Moon and Stars. Early ethnologists had difficulty understanding how indigenous performance could take the place of "scientific description." However, in relational thinking which engages the use of metaphor, creative imagination and active performance through story making and story presenting, the cosmos is made into an active participant in the lives and places in which the Tlingit live. And this perspective of the cosmos is very much in line with the indigenous notion of an interactive, interdependent universe.

Time, Space and Yup'ik Navigation

The work of Claudette Engblom-Bradley regarding Yup'ik navigation as practiced by Fred George of Akiachak, Alaska, exemplifies the practical use of astronomical knowledge by Alaska Natives. For while stories such as those of the Tlingit were imaginative and entertaining, coded in the metaphors and in the telling of the story was a wealth of practical understanding of how sun, moon, stars, and terrestrial forms could be used for practical orientation and navigation.

> Fred George travels by snow machine over snow covered frozen lakes and tundra in the Yukon-Kuskokwim Delta. In daylight, he uses the position of the sun and time of day to determine his direction. On clear nights, he uses the position of the Big Dipper and the time of night to determine his direction. In addition, he observes the frozen grass, isolated trees, and/or snow waves to reinforce his direction. The sun, Big Dipper, frozen grass, isolated trees, and snow waves function as a natural compass for Fred George. (Engblom-Bradley 2006, 90)

Fred George is one of a remaining few traditional Yup'ik hunters who continue to use traditional forms of Yup'ik knowledge of orientation and navigation based on "reading" the land, sky and waters. It is a form of traditional environmental knowledge that has served the Yup'ik in sustaining themselves in one of the harshest environments on earth for thousands of years. This way of reading and orienting in the Arctic tundra is founded on a deep observational understanding of the relationship between the movement of the sun in a directional circuit in time and the space of the Arctic tundra landscape and the night time movement of the Big Dipper during the year.

For example, when Fred knows the position of the Big Dipper and the time of night he can determine the four cardinal directions and the direction of his home base in a near featureless tundra landscape. This is an essential form of knowledge for finding one's way and surviving in the Artic tundra. Fred can find his way around from any place in this home territory because of his intimate understanding of the relative position and cyclic movement of the Big Dipper between the winter and summer solstices and his understanding of prevailing wind patterns and its affect on tundra plant growth.

This is only one type of knowledge of traditional orientation that was used historically by Alaska Native hunters and fishermen. It is a relational understanding which combines sky knowledge with knowledge of weather, land and ocean. This relational understanding is embedded in mythical as well as real stories handed down through the oral tradition. In this way stories of celestial cycles formed the basis for real integration of traditional environmental knowledge with mythical and historical traditions of Alaska Natives.

Traditional Environmental Knowledge and Alaska Native Astronomy in a Twenty-First-Century World

Traditional astronomical knowledge is held by only a few Alaska Native elders such as Fred George. However, the practical knowledge associated with Native Alaskan astronomy and traditional environmental knowledge is being revived in a number of ways through the work of Alaska Native people such as Oscar Kawagley. Kawagley has explored the ways in which Indigenous peoples' worldviews are about integration of spiritual, natural and human domains of existence and human interaction.[1] The characteristics of this reality include:

—a culturally constructed and responsive technology mediated by nature;
—a culturally based education process constructed around myth, history, observation of nature, animals, plants and their ways of survival;
—use of natural materials to make tools and art, and the development of appropriate technology for surviving in one's "place"; and
—use of thoughtful stories and illustrative examples as a foundation for learning to "live" in a particular environment.

Various overt and covert disruptions of these traditional educational systems have led to personal, psychosocial, and spiritual dysfunctions we now see in Indigenous societies. Benefits of "modernity" are offset by inefficient housing, disruptions in parent–child relationships, domestic violence, suicides, alcohol/drug abuse and other forms of dysfunctional behavior. With these has come a general sense of powerlessness and loss of control experienced by many indigenous people.

Kawagley (1995) argues that many indigenous people are forced to live in a psychically constructed world that is not of their making or choosing and essentially does not honor who they are either personally or culturally because there is little left to remind them of their indigenous culture. Furthermore there is little recognition of their indigenous consciousness and its application of intelligence, ingenuity, creativity, and inventiveness in making their world.

The work of Oscar Kawagley provides both a window and mirror into how culturally based indigenous science education curricula may be developed and applied. Working with traditional Yupiaq perspectives predicated on nuances in thinking, doing, and learning. Kawagley has embarked upon a comprehensive curriculum development process for a contemporary Yupiaq science education. It is this work that attracted considerable interest from the U.S. National Science Foundation, which funded a major ten-year initiative in Alaska focusing on documenting indigenous cultural knowledge and integrating it into school curricula, with a particular emphasis in the area of science. He also helped organize the Alaska Native Knowledge Network, aimed at furthering the involvement of Alaska Native people in research and education activities.[2]

Oscar's work recognized that the young Yupiaq child's worldview was challenged by the constellation of "new values, beliefs and practices" that had been introduced through the canons such as schooling, religion, government, economics and technology. He believed the best place to begin re-establishing the Yupiaq worldview was through a revitalizing and re-enforcing the traditional Yupiaq way of knowing and educating. Through his work Oscar Kawagley has attempted to:

—examine the sum of the historical consequences of the interaction and conflict between the Yupiaq and Western worldviews;

—understand how people in contemporary Yupiaq communities adapt their cultural values, principles, etc. to accommodate the intersection of Yupiaq and Western worldviews in constructive ways;

—document contemporary Yupiaq practices in the traditional activity and setting of the traditional fish camp (and) explore implications for the development of social, political, economic and educational institutions to the needs and aspirations of Yupiaq; and

—construct an epistemological framework and pedagogical orientation in Yupiaq traditions of knowledge as these pertain to the learning and use of scientific knowledge in a Yupiaq environment.[3]

As recognized in wider indigenous communities, Oscar's work identifies the values and life principles currently operative in the Yupiaq community and explores the extent to which existing configurations will allow the Yupiaq to reconstruct a world that will empower them with sufficient control over their own lives and give solidarity to their efforts. The need for expertise among Native people in the area of science has never been greater because of scientific and technical literacy and skill needed to effect self-determination in tribal resource management, health and economic development. Encouragement and support is crucial in the development of a foundation in science literacy. However, given the prior history of Western education of Native students, there is a need for a radically different approach. Such an approach necessarily requires the development of a new view of Native education in which new teaching and learning may unfold. Oscar Kawagley has provided such a new view of what Native education can be. May the good spirits which have guided Oscar's work also guide and keep us as we face the future envisioned by him.

Notes

1. The following list and subsequent paragraph are drawn from Kawagley's *A Yupiaq Worldview* (1995).

2. www.ankn.uaf.edu.

3. This list is adapted from Kawagley's *A Yupiaq Worldview* (1995).

Seeing Mathematics with Indian Eyes

Claudette Englom-Bradley (Schaghticoke)

Claudette Engblom-Bradley (Schaghticoke Tribal Nation) is an associate professor of secondary education at the College of Education of the University of Alaska, Anchorage. A member of the Schaghticoke Tribal Nation of Connecticut, Engblom-Bradley taught at the University of Alaska, Fairbanks for several years as an instructor for the former Cross Cultural Education Development (CCED) program, which was designed to facilitate education of Alaska Natives planning to teach in their village communities. She also served as chair of the Boston Indian Council. Her research at the University of Alaska, Fairbanks and the University of Alaska, Anchorage has centered on culturally sensitive mathematical teaching methods.

Ethno-mathematics is the study of mathematics that considers the cultural context in which the math system arises.[1] *Every culture has developed mathematical concepts through counting, measuring, creating designs, constructing artifacts, and navigating. As an ethnomathematician, Engblom-Bradley has researched Alaskan Native and American Indian cultural ways of doing mathematics. Her purpose is to develop mathematics programs and curricula for Alaskan Native and American Indian students, to develop an awareness of mathematics in the cultural ways of their elders, and to have Alaskan Native and American Indian students appreciate mathematics in the classroom, outside the classroom, and in their cultures.*

Schaghticoke Tribal Nation is an Indian tribe with a 400-acre reservation in the town of Kent, Connecticut.[2] The reservation is on the New York State border and on the Housatonic River, thirty miles south of Massachusetts. The word *Schaghticoke* means a place where two rivers run together, which gathers many fish to be caught for dinner.

My grandmother, Sarah Cogswell, was born on the Schaghticoke reservation to William and Gertrude Cogswell. She had seven sisters and one brother. Over the years while growing up in Connecticut I observed my grandmother's sister, Julie Parmelee, make loom-beadwork headbands and belts, which Julie would sell at Indian powwows. My grandparents and Julie would attend powwows every summer.

During those years I did not make a connection to mathematics and culture, but I did notice that my family seemed to be gifted in mathematics. In eighth grade I fell in love with mathematics and continued to enjoy math at the University of Connecticut where I earned my bachelor's and master's degrees in mathematics. While studying for my master's degree, I had a teaching assistantship and decided to become a mathematics educator.

From 1969 to 1972 I was a secondary teacher in San Francisco and would visit a Yaqui friend and his wife. They would make loom beadwork headbands and chokers to sell in the craft market. One day they invited me to try beading; it struck me: beading was like graphing! I was placing colorful beads in the loom to create a design; it was like plotting points on graph paper.

In 1974 I moved to Boston to teach mathematics in a community college and tutor young American Indian adults in math in preparation for their graduate equivalency diploma. The American Indian adults (mostly Micmac) were learning to add fractions for the third and fourth program in their lives. I started thinking about mathematics in American Indian artifacts and culture and felt my success in mathematics was a result of my Schaghticoke background.

At a community college faculty breakfast I discussed mathematics in American Indian culture with an MIT graduate student who happened to be sitting next to me at the breakfast table. He invited me to visit the MIT artificial intelligence lab and the LOGO lab (Papert 1993). During this visit he introduced me to Dr. Seymour Papert, who later invited me to conduct a seminar on mathematics in American Indian crafts. After the seminar Dr. Papert asked me to explore methods of learning mathematics from beading on a loom.

I purchased an assortment of beads, thread, needles, wood and nails to make looms, and beaded items. In the late afternoon I held beading classes for anyone at the Boston Indian Council. The fifteen participants were mostly males between the ages of eighteen and twenty-five. They readily sawed and hammered looms to fit their beaded item. Many wanted to make beadwork for a relative; some were planning to sell their beadwork at powwows or in trading posts located in Nova Scotia.

One afternoon I was half an hour late and certain that most of the beading students had given up and left. To my surprise all fifteen were patiently waiting for me. They were passing the time drawing or doodling with pencil and paper. The drawings grabbed my attention, for they were quite artistic, balanced in form and style. So I assembled my supplies; everyone gathered his/her loom and beads, and proceeded to bead as usual.

With the lessons learned from my beading class I completed a working paper titled "Loom Beadwork Can Teach Mathematics" for Professor Papert's LOGO lab. The paper eventually was archived at Harvard's Tozer Library.

In 1976 I reached a crossroad trying to decide if I should get a new job as a secondary mathematics teacher or develop a career for myself. I decided I would like to design mathematics programs based on culture and environment, so I became a doctoral student at Harvard Graduate School of Education (HGSE) to achieve my goals. Professors Fred Erickson and Karen Watson-Gegeo were the instructors for the ethnography courses in the Department of Teaching Curriculum and Learning Environments at HGSE. During my studies with Dr. Erickson, I explored navigation strategies of Micronesian people sailing 3,000 miles in the Pacific Ocean in outrigger canoes (Gladwin 1975). These sailors use the stars at night and ocean waves in the day to navigate from island to island.

Professor Eleanor Duckworth (1996) is an education psychologist at HGSE who had studied under Piaget and had considerable experience with LOGO, a computing language developed under the directorship of Seymour Papert. Dr. Duckworth became my thesis advisor. We decided I should research the mathematics knowledge gained by American Indian students using LOGO. I arranged for American Indian students from the Boston Indian Council to use the computer lab at the Boston School District Occupational Center. My treatment group worked with me creating designs and other projects using LOGO. My control group met with me in the same lab to use various education software in which the tasks were determined by the software. This project and the results of my assessments were written into my dissertation, "Responses of American Indian Students in a LOGO Environment" (1987). I graduated from Harvard Graduate School of Education in June 1987.

I was hired by the University of Alaska, Fairbanks (UAF) in March 1989 as an assistant professor of education, teaching mathematics for elementary teachers and computers for classroom use. My office was located in the "Red Building," later renamed the Harper Building in honor of the first Alaska Native to graduate from the University of Alaska (Flora Jane Harper in 1935). The Harper Building houses the Interior Aleutians Campus of the University of Alaska, Fairbanks.[3] My students were located in villages north or west of Anchorage. My math and education technology classes were to be delivered by audio conferencing, the U.S. Postal Service, and fax machines. During each semester I would fly to villages of some of my students to provide support for their course work in education classes.

In 1993 Herb Clemens, a mathematics professor at the University of Utah, invited me to visit Monument Valley High School in Monument Valley, Utah, near the border with Arizona. His purpose was to explore options for a program that would impact the mathematics skills of their student body, which was 99 percent Navajo. We discussed possibilities of combining mathematics and culture into a summer program. The principal, Pat Seltzer, liked the idea. I suggested that they hire elders to teach Navajo crafts of rug weaving, loom beading, and coil basket weaving and have the students learn LOGO in the computer lab. The students would spend equal time weaving with the elders and programming with LOGO in the computer lab. The first week the students would learn the weaving of the craft they selected and LOGO programming. During the second week the students would copy the designs they learned in craft class and bring them to the computer lab to program the design using LOGO. The third week the students would create a design on their computers to later use as a pattern to weave into a rug, beaded item, or basket (Engblom-Bradley and Reyes 2004; Engblom-Bradley 2005).

In 1994 the Monument Valley High School principal hired four elders as teachers in the summer program, which was a first for any school district program (MVHS, 1995–2000). Two college graduates were hired to manage the computer class and Vista volunteers were invited to be LOGO teachers. The program accepted forty Navajo students from Monument Valley High School to participate in the program. The elders were thrilled to teach, for they said the children were not learning the crafts at home, as had been the tradition. The principal was delighted and said the program had captured the interest of the entire community; and the elders enthusiastically participated in the program graduation event at the end of the three weeks. Prior school district efforts had not been able to attract as many community members into the school as this program had. Still teaching during the school year at University of Alaska, Fairbanks, I returned to Monument Valley High School for three consecutive summers to assist with the program, which continued for a decade. Each year new features and staff were added.

In July 2003 I collaborated with Tlingit elder Andy Hope of Juneau, Alaska; this was another opportunity to combine math, LOGO, and indigenous arts, but this time in southeast Alaska. Andy was the Alaska Rural Systemic Initiative (ARSI) coordinator in southeast Alaska. He wanted to have a place-based academy at the University of Alaska Southeast. Andy invited teachers from Juneau city schools and the Chatham school district to attend the five-day institute to earn graduate credit and to learn to develop a culture-based math curriculum. Teri Rofkar, her mother, and another traditional weaver helped the teachers and me learn the techniques of Tlingit basket weaving. Nora Dauenhauer, a Tlingit linguist, provided Tlingit stories of basket weavers. I provided the computer instruction for LOGO and the overall philosophical approach, and the instructor for the graduate level course provided for the teachers participating in the workshop (Engblom-Bradley 2005).

In August 2003 I left the University of Alaska, Fairbanks to join the faculty in the College of Education at the University of Alaska, Anchorage. I continued my work with mathematics and culture. During the fall semester the teachers of the July 2003 place-based academy institute developed lessons to teach LOGO and basket weaving to their students. They submitted a paper at the end of the semester for the graduate-level course. Their papers analyzed the lessons given to their students. Lori Hoover of Riverbend Elementary School in Juneau developed lessons for her third-grade class and a website to display their work and her teaching strategies. Lori was successful in teaching her students the weaving and LOGO programming. She termed the weaving experience as contagious among her students. Students did create basket designs on the computer with LOGO (Engblom-Bradley 2005). Lori was reminded how LOGO fits the constructivist theories of teaching and learning and has been inspired to use LOGO in other subject areas with her students.

In 1995 I started my collaboration with Jerry Lipka on developing Yup'ik culture-based mathematics education modules for K–6 grades (Lipka, Mohatt, Ciulista Group, 1995). Jerry Lipka received an education grant from National Science Foundation (NSF). Jerry and I met with elders and Yup'ik teachers to discuss mathematics in culture. They started with numeration, specifically, how to count in Yup'ik. After each talk or comment given by an elder, a Yup'ik teacher would translate what was said into English. So to establish the correct way in Yup'ik was a long process, for everything said had to be translated.

While studying at Harvard, I read *East Is a Big Bird* (Gladwin 1975), a book that tells stories of Micronesian navigators who traveled the Pacific Ocean in an outrigger canoe, using the stars and ocean waves to navigate 3,000 miles from island to island. They mapped islands to stars in the sky; sometimes they created an imaginary island as a marker to the navigator of their position in the ocean. When the stars were not visible, Micronesian navigators used knowledge of ocean waves, for example, that the large swells came from the north and the little waves traveled east.

I discussed navigation with Jerry, for the navigation strategies of the Yup'ik elders would have valuable application to understanding and using mathematics. The Yup'ik teachers in Jerry's project suggested we work with Fred George of Akiachak, Alaska, to learn about Yup'ik ways of navigating on the tundra.

During the many meetings with elders and Yup'ik teachers I would meet with Fred George and discuss navigation. At times Fred would share his way of navigating with the entire group of elders and Yup'ik teachers. Eventually we bonded and everyone shared in the understanding of navigation. In 1998

I began writing a teacher's manual for the Yup'ik way of navigation. I had identified some mathematical and science readiness skills for classroom teachers to explore with their students and have the student learn mathematics in the process. The teachers did not take Yup'ik students out on the tundra to practice navigation to develop navigation skills. But they could help students understand how the sun moves across the sky in the daytime and the stars move at night. They taught students to determine the four directions in the tundra by the sun's position in the sky or by the position of the Big Dipper as well as how the wind blows and the snow hardens into snow waves (Bradley 2002).

I made three trips with Fred George and his navigation crew on the Yukon-Kuskokwim Delta. They traveled in the daytime, but Fred prefers to travel at night. After the third trip, the fifth- and sixth-grade teachers invited Fred and me into their classroom to discuss their experience and to explain how Fred navigates. The sixth-grade teacher, Annie Kinegak, translated Fred's Yup'ik into English and my English into Yup'ik. I designed three board games for the students to learn how the sun moves in the sky in a given month at a given time. The students were interested in the games and enthusiastically played them in pairs. Three students made sky charts out of pipe cleaners, pony beads, and box carton (Bradley 2002; Engblom-Bradley 2006).

Dr. Ron Eglash of Rensselaer Polytechnic Institute (RPI) in Troy, New York, received FIPSE funding to have RPI students program culture-based software for the Internet, called Culturally Situated Design Tools (CDST). He invited me to submit my ideas for the three board games on the movement of the Big Dipper to be programmed and posted on the Internet among the CDST for the FIPSE grant. I supplied the rules and the design for the playing board, plus photos and cultural narrative to be posted with the games. Three games with cultural narrative are currently available on the Internet.

I returned to Akiachak to have fifth-grade and sixth-grade students preview the navigation CSDT software and cultural narrative. The students played the games in pairs and read the cultural narrative and acknowledgments on the software webpages. They especially enjoyed reading about their elders on a website. They are concerned about learning how to navigate on the tundra, for they know they will travel on the tundra as adults.

The students at RPI improved the website with my feedback. They added a second version of game 2, which is more difficult because many stars have been added to it which do not appear in the first game.

When I shared with Dr. Ron Eglash the geometric possibilities regarding the Tlingit basketry and LOGO, Eglash collaborated with me and the RPI students to create a basket-weave CSDT. We designed a graph with basket-weave-like cells. The x-axis and y-axis had a maximum of 20 and minimum of −20 cells. The user can select a basket pattern from the basket view window in the upper right corner of the screen. A color palette appears when the user clicks the down arrow beside the tiny color window. The student can select a point, line, rectangle, or triangle to create on the screen by selecting the x and y coordinates of the corners or endpoints (Eglash 2003).

I worked with teachers in Juneau during the 2005 place-based academy. These teachers used the CSDT software to create designs on the computer, as well as Geometer sketchpad. The CSDT software is good to use at the start of learning about designs. Geometer sketchpad is good for exploring transformations of the designs, like stretching in the horizontal direction or rotating shapes and discovering alternate tessellations of the designs. The Geometer sketchpad allows for angle measurements and lengths of line segments to appear on the screen and provides the opportunity to explore variations.

In the summers of 2004 and 2005 I was the primary instructor for the Math Institute in the Alaska Partnership Teacher Enhancement program at UAA College of Education. I collaborated with Rhonda Niemi of Kentucky and Ruth Mount of Anchorage School District to develop the class sessions for the two-week institute using the activities from the navigation manual, which I had started in Fairbanks while researching navigation in Akiachak. For two summers twenty teachers attended a two-week workshop; most of the teachers were from village schools but a few were from Anchorage. In 2004 Fred George attended with Annie Kinegak to participate and talk to the teachers about his way of navigating on the tundra.

The teachers learned to make a sundial and trace the sun shadow each hour. They discussed the decreasing and increasing shadow and location of true north. In July the teachers discovered that local noon is 2:04 p.m. in Anchorage, so that led to a discussion of time zones and local noon in Juneau, Anchorage, Akiachak, and Chevak. Fred George decided to learn about degrees, for Yup'ik elders have clearly stated they do not know about degrees (Engblom-Bradley 2006).

The teachers made board games for understanding the movement of the Big Dipper using my rules but adding new ways of scoring. The 2005 Math Institute teachers created more games to add to the collection of games to understand navigation on the tundra. The teachers, staff, and Fred George visited the Imaginarium to have a special session in the planetarium. Fred George was able to see the Dipper as he sees it on the tundra and explained how he finds the location of north on the horizon and the direction to Horseshoe Lake near Aniak. Dr. Travis Rector of the UAA physics department joined the teachers to present an overview of his work in astronomy and to answer questions about the stars. The teacher made star theaters out of cylinder boxes. They developed role-playing activities to understand how the sun, Venus, and the Earth move in relation to each other. At the end of the institute the teacher wrote lesson plans for their classes to learn and understand navigation with the stars, trees, frozen grass, and snow waves.

Teachers have worked with their students to understand the stars, the sun, four directions, and weather and its effect on the tundra, creating snow waves and frozen grass. They have used many of the activities in the institute and developed some to customize lessons for their students. I have enjoyed the enthusiasm and work of the teachers with their students. Currently I am writing a book chapter on navigation on the tundra and the impact on education in the south central Alaska for a book on ethnomathematics edited by Dr. Arthur Powell of Rutgers and Dr. Marilyn Frankenstein of the University of Massachusetts, Boston. I am collaborating with William Clark Bartley, a retired teacher of Harold Kaveolook School in Kaktovik, Alaska. In the 2006 National Council of Supervisors of Mathematics (NCSM), Dr. Bartley and I gave a session presentation on Clark Bartley's work with the Kaktovik students on developing the Iñupiat symbol set for Iñupiat numbers, which are base 20 with sub base 5. Those students explored addition, multiplication, subtraction, and division using the numerals. I have collected data on the students, which was my contribution to the 2006 NCSM presentations with Clark Bartley. They are planning to publish articles and give more presentations on the Kaktovik numerals.

Many Alaskan Native and American Indian students feel that mathematics is an artifact of the Western world. Those that want to continue studying in college or university realize that math is necessary to pass the college entrance exams. They probably will need to study more mathematics courses in college. Those planning not to attend college tend to feel mathematics is unnecessary for them. My work in ethnomathematics is helping Alaskan Native and American Indian students understand that mathematics is embedded in their cultural heritage and will continue to be a part of their life (Cajete 1988). For the non-Native students, learning that mathematics is embedded in Alaskan Native and American Indian cultures broadens their perspective of mathematics as an intellectual activity exercised by indigenous people as well as by modern society.

Notes

1. Editor's note: See definition of ethnomathematics at http://en.wikipedia.org/wiki/Ethnomathematics.

2. R. Velky, *Schaghticoke Tribal Nation* (Derby, Conn.: Schaghticoke Tribal Nation, 2006), http://www.schaghticoke.com (accessed July 8, 2006).

3. "Interior-Aleutians Campus: College of Rural and Community Development," University of Alaska, Fairbanks, 2006, http://www.uaf.edu/iac (accessed July 8, 2007).

What Is Truth? Where Western Science and Traditional Knowledge Converge

Lilian Na'ia *Alessa*

Lilian Na'ia *Alessa received her Ph.D. from the University of British Columbia in cell biology and now works in the area of adaptive resource management in Alaska. She approaches systems from an integrated, holistic perspective, utilizing tools from the two traditions of western and traditional ways of knowing. She is a global citizen of mixed heritage from the Salishan lands of British Columbia.*

I grew up in family where Bible study was mandatory. Yet, despite the firm Christian branches that shaded my home there were traditional roots that anchored daily life. My grandmother spoke no English and went about her tasks singing. She sang to things I couldn't see, to stones and water. She spoke to the breezes that came off the sea. This was not odd to me. No question of sanity or need of counseling entered my mind. It was simply the mechanics of living, of praise to God, to the Creator. She wove fibers into amazing patterns, placing them in water while singing. When she finished singing, the coarse strands would be soaked and pliable and she would sing again until the pattern was done. Her songs, I came to realize, were timers for different tasks. She had no watch, knew no math, indeed had been denied the opportunity to get the education that became the currency of her adulthood and old-age. Instead, she had acquired a sophisticated methodology to transform the resources that yielded to her hand and her hand only. There were no power tools, no mechanical devices to ease her work. There was only an elegance of skill that no machine could replicate. As a child, she was magic to me and at her deathbed the shock of her mortality severed my faith in these songs. I turned to the precision of western learning, so that such a fate would never befall me. So I would know the world and in that knowledge, somehow control it.

My desire to shun those things which had no firm margins grew as I came to learn the beauty and remarkable perfection of the universe through the eyes of those scholars which, like the elders of my youth, had discovered these things before. As I sat in uncomfortable chairs in lecture halls, a number in a sea of students, and despaired at the pain of examinations in those same chairs, a profound awe of the very molecules which composed my body and everything surrounding me settled. When I realized that the ability to pursue this learning fell squarely on my ability to navigate a system of hard edges I panicked. I had been raised in a home swirling with soft, fluidity of being.

And now, my learning rejected these things.

* * *

But numbers sing, too. Their words are clear and distinct and their combinations were refrains of certainty. The slow draining of the deep convictions of my upbringing and generations of women who had sustained children with their hands became a steady flow. Here lay the solution: I could understand all things by measuring them and, in knowing those words I felt I could re-write the song.

The profound awe I felt as a student failed me when I took a job as a faculty researcher at a university. I came to realize that western science hummed the words much of the time. I could see it coming, there were too many failures, too many times when it was apparent that politics, egos, and cliques were the white noise that drowned out the song. Like the death of my grandmother, it was a sound blow.

Western science as a way of knowing has precision and discipline and unlike most other ways of knowing, it can be faithfully replicated (most of the time) and understood by practitioners around the world, regardless of their language. But I was led to believe that it could explain more than it really could. Its limitations could be found not only in the over-simplification of the world but also in the murky stupidity of politics, greed and hubris. And so, in my thirties, I found my faith in western science fall away like a rock cast off a mountain for the second time in my life. In my rush to compose, rather than hear, the song, I was missing the synergy of the wisdoms of two worlds: one called "traditional" and the other called "western."

The phrases "traditional ecological knowledge," "traditional local knowledge" and "folk knowledge" are often associated with "fuzzy knowledge," the kind that comes from funneling information through a human instrument whereas "western science" suggests an absolute objectivity, "immune" from human bias. In order to discern between the two, one must understand how different cultures, including the "knowledge seekers" of both, come to exist, survive, and thrive in their worlds. The bottom line is that both address knowing the world using different yet ultimately similar approaches. Western science excels at unraveling the unseen, our medical technology a testimony to this precision, while traditional knowledge reveals the dynamics of larger systems, particularly animals, plants and habitats, and the wisdom of our place among them.

And so, as a cultural schizophrenic, I have a confession to make. It will likely earn me scorn from those who feel I am selling out the Chosen Residents of the Ivory Tower and those who feel that losing my faith in the first place should banish me from ever coming home. But it feels good to confess to this double life, this odd marriage of cultures, mainly because I have come to peace with it and with this enlightenment I have rediscovered the humility, and harmony, of my grandmother's eyes.

For those of you who don't know, there is an ongoing quiet tug of war between scientists of the western ilk and those who reside in the areas of interest for study. This subtle battle is one of recognition: whose way of knowing how the world works is the "right" way? Western Science and Traditional Knowledge (WS and TK from now on) vie for validity in the minds and ledgers of everyone from residents to practitioners, to the people who dole out the money, so that someone's favorite pursuit of knowing can continue. For me, growing up with my grandmother's habits, this tug of war didn't impress me all that much. It made no sense to subscribe to one or the other completely. It went against the basic logic that the more you knew from different angles, the more likely you were to understand the workings of the world around us.

In general, WS and TK are usually perceived as two separate, distinct, and somewhat incompatible entities. Why is this? In part, it is simply stubbornness and fear on both sides. In practice they are very similar and in outputs (results) they are highly complementary because one works well at small scales and the other at large scales but in their origins, they differ. Western science is relatively new and evolved from the philosophies of Aristotle and Bacon that sought to standardize information so that it could be used by groups of people who did not necessarily live in the same region. People who moved from one region to another relied on this information to aid the growth of their crops, the health of their livestock and the survival of their young, not to mention the development of weaponry, defenses, and trade. Aristotle stated that humans were separate from the rest of the "natural" world (this including animals, plants, and the places they lived). This was one of several interesting times (often repeated) in history: medicine was advancing, connections between a reasonable level of organization and cleanliness were being made that protected food resources from competing interests, such as rats, who also were vectors of life forms, such as viruses, of which humans were not fond. Government and economic structures were providing security for more and more people, most of whom had descended from tribes of peoples who survived by hunting and gathering and competing for these resources with neighboring tribes through conflict and, less often, fragile treaties of cooperation. With this shift from conflict to more and more centralized organization came more time to observe the components of the world not directly related to survival. While not new speculations, a class of "observer" started documenting the way humans behaved with each other and other curious habits of the species. This class of observer was more often than not comprised of members of religious sects, such as the clergy, and likely evolved from the strong shamanic heritage of their ancestral traditions. As these observations amassed and humans were ideologically "cleansed" of their increasingly socially offensive ties to the animal world, human nature sought to explain the observations. Tied into this desire was an increasing belief that the surrounding world was less and less a living, interacting system and more and more a source of resources, composed of "parts," each of which could be isolated, understood, and manipulated, usually for the benefit of humans. At this point, any oral histories which linked society to their environments were rapidly being relegated to the outlying villages and remnants of nomadic peoples. In other words, the "uneducated." So the "observers" or "scholars" had isolated themselves from their environments and were increasingly reliant on a hierarchy of workers to support their existence and lifestyles, distancing them from the lands and waters that sustained them. Could this be the point where WS and TK diverged as two distinct socially constructed approaches to "knowing"? That remains to be studied but perhaps one can link this early form of systematic observation and explanation to the relatively recent process called the "scientific method" which is often invoked to settle information-dependent conflicts.

The scientific method prescribes five steps regardless of what is being studied. These involve (1) posing a question about something for which you need an "answer" (e.g., do plants need sunshine to survive?) or for which you would like to predict an outcome, (2) proposing an answer or answers to that question (e.g., plants need sunshine to survive and grow), or in other words developing hypotheses that can be tested by (3) gathering information about the way things (like leaves and sunlight) appear to work in relation to each other, (4) testing the hypotheses by manipulating those things while observing the same ones without any manipulation at all (e.g., growing plants in sunlight, artificial light and no light) and (5) drawing conclusions from steps 1 to 4 so that you can refine your prediction of what the outcome will be and which is the cause and effect, or, in an ideal world . . . get an "answer." The purpose of these steps is to keep the user from being distracted by other events and phenomena that might be occurring simultaneously in the system being studied and, through repeating the process and getting similar results, to assert that it is something "normal" in our world, rather than an isolated phenomenon. While it's not perfect, and most of the time doesn't really yield an "answer," in some fields, like medicine, the scientific method has given rise to technologies which serve us in our daily lives and which allow us to develop strategies to utilize, cope with and enjoy our surroundings.

It is my opinion that an important distinction must be made between scales of knowledge with respect to the scientific method and TK. Technologies such as microscopes and antibodies have given us insights to the unseen worlds of micro scale processes that we would otherwise never have acquired. As you increase the level of space (for example a cell in the body) and time (which divides on a daily basis) you increase the level of complexity, or how many things interact with each other at any given time. By the time you arrive at ecosystems, the interactions of organisms and their habitats, you have accumulated an enormous amount of complexity. As you can imagine, it becomes increasingly difficult to resolve what is causing which effect. As a consequence the scientific method and the western approach to "understanding" is more tenuous and it is at this intersection of time and space that traditional knowledge is most apparent as another approach. By necessity, western science must simplify things to develop testable hypotheses about how they work, which is both precise and useful at smaller scales. In the process, however, and as you increase in scales of complexity, it eliminates details, many of which are considered "descriptive" and either not important to understanding or too confounding. A hallmark of TK is that details are exquisitely noted and communicated in such a way that the user can detect small changes and respond accordingly. Having said that, TK has developed around the processes which sustained indigenous peoples and historically all our ancestors: primarily interactions of plants and animals with their environments, whereas WS has enticed us to explore the range of existence, from the way the mind works to the quantum physics of northern lights, a reflection of some of the luxuries of time afforded certain societies as they secured reliable food and shelter.

Much evidence, never mind common sense, suggests that TK has existed as long as we have as a species (and having said that, who is to say that it is limited to humans, I'll get to the elephants later). The act of residing, surviving, and thriving in a place means that the resident must "know" her environment in such as way as to repeatedly have a high likelihood of acquiring the types of resources, whether they are physical or not, on a regular basis. The consequences are not the ridicule of one's peers, or the failure to get a research grant, they are sickness, suffering, and death. One could say that the stakes in TK are much higher and hence so is the precision. Traditional Knowledge requires something that, with few exceptions, WS has failed to accomplish:

long periods of observation in the same place and the transmission of these observations to others in that place so that they can use them practically and often, from a young age. Some western schools of thought romanticize TK, and perceive that somehow possessing it brings ultimate harmony of the user with his world. No mistakes will be made because there exists a magical link where all things are known. This is part of the de-validation of TK because it fails to acknowledge that it, like the scientific method, is a process where information is accepted or rejected based on receiving knowledge continuously, both directly from the system and from one's colleagues, friends, family, and mentors usually to benefit the community and future generations. The same can rarely be said for WS.

When I first learned the scientific method, I appreciated the discipline it brought to my tangential thinking: I was taught that everything is connected to everything else, which made thinking about cause and effect just slightly paralyzing. Particularly at smaller scales, such as those in beakers and tubes, it really did reveal the workings of the molecules within. The "controls" in the scientific method allow you to "prove" that your explanation of what might be going on is actually what is most likely going on. Note that I said "smaller scales." And this may be truly where the synergy of WS and TK is best revealed: where one scale leaves off, the other picks up.

It should not be surprising that somebody suggests that TK is not limited to humans. We have only recently become aware that elephants have very calculated ways of using and moving through their environments. They will find their food, raise their young, interact, and bury their dead in ways that are distinct to their clans, location, and preferences and they will transmit this information from one generation to the next using a complex subsonic language. It is only in our arrogance as western scientists that we would assume that we are the only animals who have the ability to use data to control our world. My grandmother told me similar stories about Ravens, that we were really not that different and that if we searched our memories really hard, we could actually see someone we knew in those brilliant, wise winter eyes.

The Yup'ik and Cup'ik People

Joan Pirciralria *Hamilton (Cup'ik)*

The Cup'ik and Yup'ik people inhabit the entire southwestern mainland of Alaska in fifty-six villages. Joan Pirciralria *Hamilton (Cup'ik) wrote the following essay to give visitors to Alaska a better understanding of the Yup'ik and Cup'ik people and the unique linguistic, cultural, and artistic practices that reflect their environment and relationship to the larger cosmos. Hamilton is working on trying to change some of the museum terminology used for Cup'ik/Yup'ik cultural patrimony. She states: "I don't like the impersonal word 'artifact.' It looks at empirical objects as 'things' rather than the sacred objects they are to us . . . like communion, handed down to us through the generations. We need to begin to change the words that are used by outsiders."*

Joan Hamilton was born and raised in Chevak, Alaska, a Cup'ik-speaking community near the Bering Sea coast. Cup'ik was her first language and English her second. She had a forty-year career directing substance abuse programs and served as the director of the Yupiit Piciryarait Museum, run by the Association of Village Council Presidents, in Bethel, Alaska, from 1997 to 2007. Joan passed away in June 2008 and is dearly missed by her family and the Native community. She was a kind and giving person who generously shared her life and knowledge.

For cultural groups to be successful and survive, the people must adapt to their environment, and more importantly, must create rules of conduct that govern their behavior for the benefit of the community's survival. Two closely related Alaskan tribes, Cup'ik and Yup'ik, continue to live in the area known as the Y-K (Yukon-Kuskokwim) Delta, as they have for at least ten thousand years. The Yukon River to the north, the Kuskokwim River to the south, and the Bering Sea to the west form the geographic boundaries of this Oregon-sized part of western Alaska. There are fifty-six villages in the region today, as well as the central hub of Bethel. More than 23,000 people live in the Y-K Delta, and many other Yup'ik and Cup'ik people live in Anchorage, Fairbanks, and all over the world.

The Y-K Delta appears to many as an endless, treeless tundra that is often labeled as a "barren wasteland." However, to its Natives, the land is exquisite and vibrantly alive, a stunningly abundant resource. We believe that all things in this world and universe have life, as humans have life. The land provides birds, animals, perennial berries, vegetables, moss for cleaning, sod for making houses and grass for weaving. Additionally, the land serves as a pharmacy, a source of many medicinal plants. The lakes, rivers, shallow creeks, and the sea provide a variety of fish, birds and marine mammals.

Life that follows the rhythm of the seasons is not without its stresses, but it also holds definite rewards and benefits. Those benefits come from learning and practicing a discipline of centuries-old knowledge that strikes a chord of harmony in the village and on the land. It is understandable how the people and culture have survived when the values required by this discipline are examined.

We are expected to improve ourselves by observing and listening in order to learn from Elders. Life's lessons are best learned by observation. As we watch, we are expected to continually analyze the activity. Elders then watch and guide our attempts to follow what we have learned. They evaluate us by stressing what was done right and what methods may improve our next steps. They emphasize that teaching is based on personal experience. We are also expected to help our families with daily chores and to contribute to the needs of the family, and we are rewarded for this. We are taught to welcome and to be generous with all people, to respect belongings and all the sources of our food. We strive to live well to reach venerated old age. We are taught that we learn best when we maintain a balance of leisure, learning, and work—with work being our first responsibility.

There have been major changes in our region over the last one hundred years. Many of the Elders were born in sod houses and lived their lives harvesting from the land and sea. By foot, *qayaq*, and large skin boats, people moved each year with the seasons to sites which are known to provide the optimum supply of resources to sustain the communities and to add to the quality of their lives. Today we continue our subsistence activities with the use of fuel-powered snow machines, motorized boats, and, occasionally, planes.

Today people live in established villages most of the year, leaving their home villages only for summer fish and berry picking camps. Children must attend school, and many people need to have 9-to-5 jobs to generate cash to augment subsistence living activities. Elders no longer gather in the communal men's house to speak to our young people, and many of our time-honored traditions are in danger of being forgotten.

But with all the changes we have experienced through the years, we continue to do the things that are most important to us. Families continue to hunt and gather from the land, the rivers, and the sea. We teach our children that if they respect the land and waters, they will provide for them. Family members still gather every day to share meals and laugh and tell stories. The Cup'ik/Yup'ik philosophies of how to be a human being remain intact and the family and village are central to these tenets, which dictate patience, kindness, and respect for all things in this world.

Despite the impact of outside contact in the last one hundred years that brought devastating loss of life due to epidemics, and more recently attempts by government policies, educators, and missionaries to "Westernize" our way of living, the people held, dearly and often secretly, to their languages, festivals, and ceremonies. This includes *yuraq* (Native dance), which may involve the use of *kegginaquq* (masks). Today, at the insistence of indigenous peoples, many of the schools and mass media continue in their efforts to incorporate the Native language use, in addition to education on regional and local histories as well as the ancient arts of skin sewing, manufacturing tools, and basket-making. Non-profit agencies further this effort with annual cultural camps to immerse the younger generation in the lives and times of the elder generations. Villages have and are recreating annual rituals and festivals that continue to be important benchmarks in the village seasonal cycles, such as recognizing each child's first catch, holding potlatches, and celebrating Bladder Festivals. Each of the fifty-six villages has at least one or more traditional dance groups, a testament to the importance of dance practices and music, especially the *cauyaq* (drum). The drum represents the combined heart-beat of the people; thus, as long as its sacred beat is allowed, the people will continue to live.

Bethel has hosted the Camai Festival, an annual gathering, for over fifteen years. The Camai festival brings Cup'ik/Yup'ik dancers and state, national, and international groups together for a four-day festival. The groups compose new songs each year that illustrate the subsistence life ways of today's Cup'ik/Yup'ik people. The traditional regalia, the *tegumiaq* (dance fans), the *nasqurrun* (women's headdresses), *cauyaq* (drums), traditional style outer garment or *kuspuq*, and the *piluguk* (footwear) are all made by the dancers and their families and everyone is allowed to participate.

Regional museums, which are more accessible to rural residents than urban-located museums, play a key role in preserving and providing a safe home for our cultural collections, which we see as venerated relics of yesterday. Museums serve as a modern resource of learning the past and present. This will hopefully assist the younger generation to walk boldly into the future with a solid footing in the past. We approach museums as places of reverence that sustain our time-honored traditions.

At our museum here in Bethel, today, it is not uncommon for an Elder, viewing the sacred collections on display, items he or she either used as a child or observed others use, to show striking emotion. Tears of awe and appreciative smiles reflect deep gratitude for this treasure trove of personal and generational memories.

During the late nineteenth and early twentieth centuries, many collectors traveled to Alaska and took many Cup'ik/Yup'ik baskets, dance masks, regalia, hunting implements, ceremonial items, and other objects. Sometimes the objects were stolen from burial grounds, taken to museums far removed from the Yukon/Kuskokwim Delta. The U.S. government and Alaska territorial policies also suppressed the beautiful cultural practices of the Cup'ik/Yup'ik people. Dance, music, and drum went underground and ceremonial mask-making was becoming increasingly rare.

In the 1970s and 1980s a renaissance occurred, and highly respected cultural leaders and elder artists such as Nick Charles (Yup'ik),[1] Uncle John (Cup'ik), Kay Hendrickson (Cup'ik), and Joe Friday (Cup'ik), with the financial assistance of Suzi Jones, formerly of the Alaska State Council on the Arts, began to teach mask carving to a new generation of artisans and traditional bearers. Dance groups reemerged from decades of repression, and language immersion programs have been created within the past five to eight years. The artists, dancers, community members, and youth will be further enriched with the return of cultural artifacts from the Smithsonian to Alaska. These sacred items have their cultural and spiritual home here in Alaska and as Elders have directed, "They want to come home and they need to be united with their people."

Note

1. Editor's note: Nick Charles is the father of one of the contributors for this volume. See George Charles's selection in part 1.

IV

Native Arts: A Weaving of Melody and Color

Native American arts form a fundamental aspect of cultural expression and are deeply tied to science, technology, creative expression, spirituality, ceremony, and identity. Indigenous arts are holistic, meaning they are related to all other aspects of society and even environment.

By tradition, Alaska Native arts, as they are now called, were so much a part of the web of life and living they were not separated by the idiomatic use of the word "art." The remarkable seal gut parkas made by indigenous groups all along the coastal regions of Alaska used a waterproof stitch—the garments were not only practical and made with great skill but the seamstresses used tufts of feathers in the seams and dyed thread made of sinew so that each garment was individually blessed and unique. The same can be said of countless other types of what is commonly referred to as "material culture"—those items used for everyday living. Hunting implements were almost always endowed with additional blessing or power by use of amulets and special feathers, in addition to being extremely accurate hunting tools.[1] The kayaks or skin boats which have their origins in Alaska, now popularly found throughout the world, were made of skins, using the inventive waterproof stitch, with frames of steamed bent wood, and almost always had additional protective amulets of ivory, bird feathers, and other ritually protective devices. The marriage of science, aesthetics, and ritual is so complete in the traditional arts of Alaska Native people that it is impossible to discuss one without the others.

Unfortunately there exist very few publications or ethnographies that use an indigenous approach in examining the arts; most are framed from the Western art history approach that only includes the one-dimensional "object analysis" approach. Recently Native authors have used the arts to prove the "science" behind them (see the selections by Kawagley and Engblom-Bradley this volume). Even music is tied to society (see Kingston selection in this part) with unique genres that reinforce family and community relationships.

The relationship between arts, society, identity, and environment can be seen in the myriad of design elements found in Alaska Native arts. Woven baskets, made of various materials, including grass, split willow roots, birch bark, baleen from whales, and other materials, always have design or motifs that reflect clan, family, and individual identity. The Iñupiat of the Arctic Slope, Seward Peninsula, and Kobuk areas have footwear made of various types of fur (polar bear, caribou calf, seal) and soles of a harder material made from walrus flippers. The top part of the boot or "mukluk,"[2] consists of elaborate geometric patterns that use black and white fur—geometric patterns that are owned and passed down from mother to daughter. Hence one can tell by the trim on the footwear which family a person is from and, by the style of the boot and crimping of the sole, which village. Art objects also reflect clan affiliation. All the material culture in Tlingit, Haida, and Tsimshian societies has design elements of clan crests; the clan houses were elaborately painted with the image of the clan crest, and within these societies even music is owned by the clan (Williams 1989).[3]

In the postcolonial world, especially from the mid-twentieth century to today, indigenous artists have incorporated new tools, new ways to express their ideas, identities, and personal aesthetics. As has been noted, music is reflective of society. Deanna *Paniataaq* Kingston writes about *Ugiuvangmiut*, or King Island teasing cousins songs, a genre that illustrates the intricate relationships between cross-cousins. Perry Eaton, an Alutiiq/Sugpiaq artist and rural community development specialist, writes about his personal journey as a mask carver and how he has traveled the world to locate Kodiak cultural patrimony, which had been removed in the nineteenth century. Larry McNeil's essay uses Raven, an important figure in Tlingit cosmology, to make commentary on modern-day life and offers humorous commentary on colonial institutions, by way of digital photography. Another contemporary digital photographer, Erica Lord, addresses identity using Frantz Fanon's concepts of the "other" in her essay and self-portraits. Anna Smith writes about "re-creation" stories and how the Native American author Sherman Alexie employs contemporary commentary based on the much older models of creation stories found in indigenous societies. James Ruppert, longtime professor of literature at the University of Alaska, Fairbanks, provides an overview of Alaska Native literature, including contemporary writers. Frank Francis-Chythlook, a contemporary videographer, offers his thoughts on digital media and identity.

Craig Coray, a composer and professor of music at the University of Alaska, completed a major project that involved repatriating early recordings of traditional Alaska Native music. In another essay on music and dance, Tim Murphrey, one of the organizers for the Festival of Native Arts, addresses the history of the oldest statewide music and dance festival in Alaska.

The voices in this section reveal the vitality of Native art and suggest how difficult it is to define it, as well as precolonial arts. Today in Alaska, a number of regional Native cultural centers and foundations recognize the vitality of the arts and their relationship to indigenous society.

Notes

1. The Alutiit of Kodiak had a water-skimming arrow specifically designed to be shot from their kayaks (Eaton).

2. *Mukluk* is more a commercial term or generalized term for footgear worn by Arctic peoples.

3. Music or song ownership is actually important in all Alaska Native societies, but particularly with the clan-sensitive Tlingit, Haida, and Tsimshian. In the precolonial period, performing another clan's song could be punished with a death sentence (Williams 1989).

Ugiuvangmiut Illugiit Atuut: Teasing Cousins Songs of the King Island Iñupiat

Deanna Paniataaq *Kingston* *(Iñupiaq)*

Deanna Paniataaq *Kingston's essay describes what she refers to as "teasing cousins" songs of the King Island Iñupiaq Eskimo Community. Kingston places these songs, which are rich with poetic metaphor, within the contexts of social relationships between teasing cousins in Iñupiaq society and the role of music and song in Iñupiat culture. Kingston, a descendent of the King Island Native community, is an associate professor of anthropology at Oregon State University and a member of her uncle Alex Muktoyuk's dance group (the Northwest Iñupiaq Dancers) in Oregon.*

My Uncle Alex Muktoyuk tells the story of how he fell asleep one day while out in a boat that was on its way to Nome from *Ugiuvak*, or King Island, Alaska. Two women saw that he had fallen asleep. They snuck up and kissed him over and over again in front of the other hunters. He woke up and became very embarrassed. There was little he could do about it, however, because the women were my uncle's cross-cousins and they were exercising their right to make fun of him in public. They were his "teasing cousins."

This chapter is an introduction to the fascinating Iñupiaq relationship referred to as "teasing cousins." In particular, I want to discuss the performative aspects of the relationship, because it usually manifests itself in the form of *illugiit atuut*, or teasing cousins (*illugiit*) songs (*atuut*), which are a variation on the common, circumpolar song tradition known as song duels among the Inuit.[1] In 1991, I learned several *illugiit atuut* as a member of my maternal uncle's dance group (the Northwest Iñupiaq[2] Dancers). Today, fifteen years later, this group still dances a few times a year.

Among the Iñupiat, like elsewhere in the Arctic, songs were composed for religious reasons, particularly to influence the weather or animal behavior, but they could also commemorate important community events, such as when a community member appeared on television (see below) and there were also songs sung to children (Koranda 1972, 1). In addition, songs also served to correct deviant behavior, to socialize youth to community norms, and to establish and maintain peace between villages (Kingston 1999).

Illugiit atuut were and are composed by individuals who are cross-cousins[3] to each other, people that Iñupiat refer to as "teasing" or "joking" cousins. Sometimes, two individuals in this teasing cousin relationship would compose songs about each other over the course of their lives. Usually, the songs reflect Iñupiat social norms, which places them within the broader context of the North American Arctic to what scholars refer to as Inuit song duels. The purpose of the song duel was for two participants to fight through songs rather than physical combat. The participants were men (and sometimes women) who composed songs about each other until one person was not able to reply and conceded the victory. Because the song duel was couched in humor, physical violence was avoided (Kingston 2005). This was necessary because survival in the Arctic necessitated sharing and cooperation. From the time they are born, Inuit generally, and Iñupiat more specifically, are encouraged to be friendly, happy, and to share. For example, among the Wainwright Iñupiat, a "child's outward expression of aggressive tendencies towards siblings or other children is discouraged. Mothers . . . can be frequently heard admonishing children not to fight" (Milan 1964, 57). In addition, Milan states that this lack of aggression "seems to be a highly pursued value among adults and is internalized at an early age" (57–58). This system of socializing children fosters cooperation and sharing and the avoidance of conflict.

Song duels varied from region to region in North America. In West Greenland, a person initiated a song duel when he or she became jealous or resentful of someone from another settlement. The first party would challenge the second to a song duel and a time and place for the event was scheduled. Both parties then prepared a series of songs about the other person, pointing out activities and behaviors that the other person committed that were considered inappropriate. Inappropriate behavior ranged from stealing from another's food cache to not providing for one's family. At the scheduled time, the two exchanged songs in front of both settlements until one person could not reply. Songs that produced the most laughter determined the winner of a duel. The ideal outcome was a peaceful relationship between the participants and their settlements so that the exchange of material goods, marriage partners, and news of weather and hunting could occur. Sometimes, songs were improvised and performed on the spot. Not only was peace maintained, but youth learned what others felt was inappropriate behavior by listening to the songs and observing how transgressors were treated.

In Canada, song duels occurred between participants, usually men from the same settlement, who were involved in a serious conflict. These men were generally not kin. As in Greenland, the two participants exchanged songs of insult and accusation until one could no longer respond. Although the whole event was meant to be humorous, an undercurrent of aggressiveness and animosity remained. Ideally, the audience's laughter diffused the negative feelings between the contestants and encouraged friendly behavior. Another genre of songs among the Canadian Inuit is "joking songs" in which song insults were exchanged. However, participants shared a very friendly relationship and the event was only in fun. Since people in the community knew the participants of a song contest, they did not confuse which genre was employed in a particular situation.

In Alaska, song duels are still performed today in some areas, primarily in Yup'ik and Iñupiaq communities where singing and dancing have continued into the twenty-first century. In contrast to Greenland and Canada, Alaskan song duels occur between teasing cousins (both men and women), who could live in the same or different communities. Teasing cousins enjoy a close relationship, taking every opportunity to tease each other by calling names or insulting each other in public without getting angry. Since the relationship is based on a fun, close relationship, teasing cousins could point out inappropriate actions by couching it in humor. Teasing could include the composition and exchange of songs. Because songs are performed in public, everyone is witness to the ridicule of the transgressor, usually causing a change in behavior. Thus, Alaskan song duels are closer to the Canadian "joking song" events in manner and intent than to the animosity exhibited in Canadian song duels.

The Illugiit *Relationship*

According to Burch, "cousins were expected to share, to work together, and to help each other" (1975, 55). In addition, he explains that "cousins" did not necessarily have to be "blood" cousins.[4] This sense of sharing is evident in the cousin relationships among the Bering Strait Iñupiat. They distinguish between their parallel ("partner") and cross cousins (Kaplan 1988, xx; Oswalt 1967, 202–3). According to Burch, expression between *arnaqatigiik* (parallel cousins) was similar to that between siblings (186, 188). The difference between the two types of cousins is that help would be expected from a parallel cousin as it would be from a sibling, but the formality of asking would have to be used for cross-cousins (Kaplan 1988, 97). Oftentimes, some sort of payment was expected from teasing cousins in return for the help.

In addition to helping each other, *illuq* (*illuriik*—plural),[5] or in English, teasing cousins, enjoyed what Burch (1975) calls a "radical departure from all other Eskimo kin relationships as far as expression was concerned" (188). This relationship is characterized by joking and teasing and "by extreme lack of restraint" (188). In most all other family relationships, expression of affection was restrained. Burch (188) elaborates: "*illuriik* could 'talk to each other any old way.' By this they meant that joking cousins could tease and insult each other as much as they wanted to without evoking *ill feelings*" (emphasis mine). In addition, *illuriik* were "mature adults who had gradually developed their association from a solid foundation, and who were *very* fond of one another" (188). Finally, Burch states of this relationship that a person "would often go to considerable lengths to contrive a situation that would provide him with an opportunity to make fun of his *illuq*" (188).

Ugiuvak

As Burch stated, *illuriik* would often go to great lengths to embarrass each other. This was true on King Island, or *Ugiuvak*, where my mother and uncle grew up. *Ugiuvak* is located in the Bering Sea. *Ugiuvak* is approximately 85 miles northwest of Nome and approximately 70 miles south of Little and Big Diomede Islands. Captain James Cook named the island "King Island" after his executive officer, Lieutenant James King. "*Ugiuvak*" means "winter home" because the approximately 150–200 *Ugiuvangmiut* on the island traditionally lived there during the winters, spending their summers trading along the mainland (Renner 1979, 67).

The *Ugiuvangmiut* lived in a small village that was built on the south side of the island, which sloped in a 40–45 degree angle to the ocean. The island is very rocky and is described as barren by some. However, the location of the island assured its people of abundant sea mammal life. The annual spring and fall walrus migrations pass right by *Ugiuvak*. Seals, whales, king crab, polar bears, shrimp, and cod were also plentiful. Murres, auklets, cormorants, and puffins nested on the cliffs of the island. Greens and berries grew on the island. The islanders were also fortunate in having a large ice cave that was used to preserve their food.

Today, the *Ugiuvangmiut* no longer live on the island. Many of them moved to Nome in the 1950s and 1960s "to be closer to the health care and other services Nome provides" (Kaplan 1988, 30). In addition, the Bureau of Indian Affairs closed the school on *Ugiuvak* in 1959, claiming that it was unsafe and too isolated for teachers to live there. According to my uncle, the *Ugiuvangmiut* were threatened with arrest if they did not send their children to the mainland to go to school. After that, some families without children attempted to stay on *Ugiuvak*, but said that it was too lonely and the last families moved to the mainland permanently in 1966. Today, the *Ugiuvangmiut* live in Nome, Fairbanks, Anchorage, and throughout the lower 48 states.

Performative Aspects of Ugiuvangmiut Illugiit *Tradition*

Traditionally, the *Ugiuvangmiut* performed their songs and dances mainly in the winter in the *qagrit* or clubhouses. They usually began dancing during the month of December, or *Sauya.tugvik*, the "Time of Drumming" (Kaplan 1988, 72–73). Teasing between cross-cousins occurred throughout *Ugiuvangmiut* social life. As mentioned above, teasing cousin relationships can take the form of name-calling, practical jokes, or teasing one another in song. For example, my Aunt Margaret's male teasing cousins called her "toothless" relentlessly during her growing up years because she was missing her two front teeth. I already mentioned Uncle Alex's female teasing cousins who caught him napping while traveling on a boat. In addition to verbal and physical taunts, songs were an effective way to tease each other because the entire community would witness the performance of the song.

Songs Composed by Illugiit *and the Stories behind Them*

Composing Iñupiaq songs is not easy and there were not many *Ugiuvangmiut* who were gifted in doing so. My uncle has mentioned only a few song composers: my stepgrandmother, Mary Muktoyuk; Charlie Mayac; John Kimenac (originally from Little Diomede Island); and Paul Tiulana. According to DeNevi, Inuit song texts "are often meagre, since the audience is expected to be familiar with the whole subject and fill in most of the meaning" (DeNevi 1969, 66). Although he was talking about the Inuit of Hudson Bay, Canada, I found this to be true of the *Ugiuvangmiut* songs. Most of the song texts below are approximately ten to twelve lines long. When our group learned these songs, my uncle would laugh to himself as he translated the song. The rest of us could not understand what he found so funny about the song until he explained the story behind it.

Among the *Ugiuvangmiut*, there were two gifted song composers who often composed songs about each other. Charlie Mayac was a teasing cousin to a man named John Kimenac, originally from Little Diomede Island, who moved to *Ugiuvak*. One song composed by Mayac was based upon lack of communication between Charlie Mayac and an airplane pilot. The airplane pilot was called to the island in order to transport a girl (one of my cousins) burned by boiling water. He was supposed to land on the north side of the island on the shore ice. However, he landed on the south side of the island where Mayac happened to be hunting. The pilot asked Mayac for directions, but Mayac did not understand English and the pilot did not understand Eskimo. Fortunately, Mayac knew why the pilot was there and finally said, "King Island udder [other] side!" The pilot then understood that he was then to go to the other side of the island to get the girl. Mayac was somewhat chagrined, given the seriousness of the situation, about the lack of communication between him and the pilot, so Mayac composed a song blaming Kimenac for potentially endangering the health of the girl by causing Mayac's confusion. The Iñupiaq[6] version, with English translation, follows:

Nugia sugnik atugia
I was filled with confusion
Ya eeyung ee yah[7]
Yaghi yah ah ah
Nalooagmiu, oorri yungi yah
When a white man, oorri yungi yah
Oorri yungi Aveksha manga
Oorri yungi asked me a question
Yaghi yah ah ah
Soona Ooa Kimenac
It turned out to be (because of) Kimenac
Ya eeyung ee yah
Yaghi yah ah ah
Oorri yungi yah eeyungi, ya ah

Another song was composed by Kimenac about Mayac. In this case, however, Kimenac was proud of his teasing cousin because Mayac went to California to appear on the old television show *This Is Your Life*, but he may have also been warning him not to get too proud of himself since boasting and pride were not desired traits. On this particular show, a man named Father Bernard Hubbard, the "Glacier Priest," was featured. Father Hubbard spent one winter on *Ugiuvak* (1937–38) and he considered Mayac a close friend. As a surprise, the producers flew Mayac down to California for the occasion. Kimenac's song about Mayac, in Iñupiaq and English, follows:

Ahtootookloo
I want to shake his hand
Kinnakiaklee
Who is that I saw?

Televishiuroova
On the television?
Amuni
Way over there
California mi yah Ay yah
In California?
Ah Ah Kayunga
Eeyunga Ah yah
Soona Uva Mayac
It turned out to be Mayac
Ozzingiloo yah ah yah anga
I thought so
Ahtootookloo
I want to shake his hand

These two men composed many songs about each other. When one man made up a song, shortly thereafter the other one would compose one in retaliation. (However, the above two songs do not fall into this pattern.) When performed, most of the village would witness their teasing.

Today, the composition of new songs is in decline. To my knowledge, the most recent *illugiit atuuq* was composed by my Uncle Alex about his teasing cousin, Paul Tiulana, in 1985 and Tiulana "retaliated" within the next year. In Alex's song about Tiulana, he teased Tiulana for having a piece of land "inside the wind," in other words, because he chose to camp where it is always windy. The story behind this song is: In 1983, Alex went to Alaska to visit. He hoped to go walrus hunting on *Ugiuvak*. The take-off point from the mainland to *Ugiuvak* is a place called Cape Woolley, where many *Ugiuvangmiut* maintain cabins. The wind must be fairly calm there before the boats can leave. On this trip, my uncle was constantly cursing the wind and the bad weather because he really wanted to see *Ugiuvak*. Tiulana and Yahmanni, Tiulana's wife, invited Alex to stay with them at their camp while they waited for the weather to change. Both Tiulana and Yahmanni are Alex's teasing cousins.[8] While they were waiting, Tiulana and Yahmanni teased my uncle about the weather. My uncle would tease them back, pointing out that they should not have built a cabin where it is always windy. At one point, Yahmanni complained about how the rocks and pebbles always got into her shoes. Alex teased her by telling her to put on some snow shoes, as if they would help keep the rocks and pebbles out of her shoes. (In other words, he pointed out that it was her own fault that she got rocks in her shoes because of her choice of shoes.) The weather never improved and my uncle had to go back to Oregon before he got a chance to hunt or to see *Ugiuvak*. After he got back from his trip, he spent two years composing the following song:

Anughim ilooanay
Inside the wind
Tiulana tonnee
Tiulana again
Noonakazimaroo
Has acquired a piece of land
Anughim ilooanay
Inside the wind.
Yah angi, ya angi, ya angi, yah
Ah ya eeyungee
Yahmanni loosaw
Poor little Yahmanni
Ya angi, ya angi, ya angi yah
Ah yah eeyungee
Pu'yooya annitoo
Wouldn't put her snowshoes on
Anughim ilooanay
Inside the wind

In 1985, Alex went back to Alaska. On his way to Nome, he had a layover in Anchorage, so he called up Tiulana and Yahmanni to say hi. Alex said "*So-yah-ghlay*" to Yahmanni, which means "Time to beat the drums!" He wanted to share his composition with them that night. For some reason, Yahmanni was not able to hear the song that day. However, while he was in Nome, he taught the song to the Nome *Ugiuvangmiut*. A couple of days later, Tiulana flew to Nome for a King Island Native Corporation meeting. He was present when Alex taught the song to other *Ugiuvangmiut*. Since then, this song has been part of the *Ugiuvak* song repertoire.

The next time my uncle went to Alaska, he discovered that Tiulana "retaliated." Alex has two Iñupiaq names—Allughuk and Kipkatasinak. He never liked Kipkatasinak because it sounded too close to the Iñupiaq word for earring, *kipkatak*. When he was an adolescent, the other children teased him by calling him "earring" all the time. Also, when he was a young child, the adults called him "Lookoostalk," which is more of a nickname than an actual name. He acquired this nickname because the adults would make him dance to an old song that was popular at the time on the radio called "Look Who's Talking." He would dance by bending the knees slightly, moving his knees back and forth (similar to the "Charleston"), and, with his elbows next to his ribs, wave his forearms back and forth in front of him. Because he would dance to "Look Who's Talking," the adults called him "Lookoostalk." Tiulana's retaliation song used both of these names in it:

Lookoostalk
Oolungnarakatonnee
Last spring
Kipkatasinak
This man Kipkatasinak
Soyayghlay
Said, "So-yay-ghlay"
Kuniksootioong
By the telephone
Soona ooa kaatonnee
It turned out that he wanted
Atughloonee
To sing a song
Eeyah, ah-ungah
Anugitowooni noonakaghlonee
Just because his land has no wind
Ah-eeyah, ya, ah eeyah,
Yungah, ayaa, eeyah, ah ungah
ah eeyah yung, ah eeyah
Yah-eeyah, yah!
Lookoostalk!

Tiulana retaliated by composing what is considered a clever song—he used two of Alex's names that Alex does not like and then referred to Alex's song about Tiulana in the line "Just because his land has no wind," which is like an admonishment for complaining about the weather, which people have no control over.

Conclusion

From an outsider's perspective, *Ugiuvangmiut illugiit atuut* do not appear to be humorous and an outsider would probably not understand their significance in terms of how these songs reflect something of the social structure of the *Ugiuvangmiut*, nor might they understand how the songs contribute to the transmission of cultural norms. By couching admonishments within humorous songs, *Ugiuvangmiut* could point out inappropriate behavior while still maintaining a peaceful and cooperative relationship. Most importantly, in terms of social relations, the teasing cousin songs demonstrate to the community the way the playful rivalry between cross-cousins traditionally works itself out in performance settings. The relationship between cross-cousins is different from those between siblings and between parallel cousins. It involves a certain amount of freedom to pursue friendly competitiveness—a competitiveness that often takes the form of friendly song duels. In a sense, then, the composition of teasing cousin songs models appropriate behavior: the songs suggest what is appropriate (and by its absence what is not) in cross-cousin relations. We also saw that the song composed by my uncle's cousin upbraids my uncle for complaining about things beyond his control, like the wind. Thus, the content of the songs themselves provides one way of transmitting societal norms about what should and should not be the subject of complaints. Remember that these songs were performed in public, so the entire community would learn from the songs, not just the two individuals involved. Today, unfortunately, although *Ugiuvangmiut* youth still learn to dance, sing, and drum, they usually do not understand the words to the songs they are singing, and so they are no longer learning some of these traditional norms. Perhaps if more of these songs were translated into English, we could reverse this trend.

Notes

I would like to give my appreciation to all of the teasing cousin song composers who created these songs, to my Uncle Alex for sharing them with me, and to the various King Island dance groups that still perform today. In addition, I would like to thank my master's degree committee, who helped me in the writing of my thesis, upon which this chapter is based. Finally, I would like to thank the current (2006) chair of my department, David McMurray, who gave me the "nudge" that helped me put this chapter together and who had helpful editorial comments. Thanks also to the editors, Maria Williams and Miriam Angress.

1. "Inuit" is the term used across the circumpolar North American Arctic for what was formerly known as "Eskimo" people.

2. The Iñupiat are those Eskimoan peoples that live in north and northwest Alaska. *Iñupiaq* is the singular form of the word and *Iñupiat* is the plural form.

3. Cross-cousins are the children of a brother and a sister.

4. See Burch's discussion on "The Scope of Eskimo Kinship in Northwest Alaska" (1975, 50–61). Not only were people considered "blood" relatives through descent from a single ancestor, but also through marriage (including step-relations), adoption, and sexual intercourse ("Any offspring of any person with whom one ever had sexual intercourse could be a child" [Burch 1975, 52]). These relationships were also considered permanent—"any kinship bond, once established, lasted for the lifetimes of the people involved" (1975, 52). In Burch's words, "it was almost more difficult for an Eskimo to

determine who was *not* a cousin than who was one . . . the number of one's cousins could run into the dozens even in one's own local group or village" (1975, 55). Thus, theoretically, one person could be related to most everyone else within the village, and they were not necessarily related by blood.

5. Burch spells the plural of *illuq* as *illuriik*. However, the "official" orthography of the Alaska Native Language Center would spell it *illugiit*. In my master's thesis, I used my uncle's spelling of *illuweet*. However, when discussing Burch, I will use his spelling of the word.

6. Here, I use my Uncle Alex's way of transcribing these songs. The words are not spelled according to the orthography used by the Alaska Native Language Center.

7. If there is no translation, it is because the words are just song syllables, like "la, la, la" in English.

8. Tiulana's mother and Alex's father were cousins, making Tiulana and Alex third or fourth cousins. Alex called Yahmanni's mother an "aunt," although Yahmanni's mother was not really Alex's father's sister. Yahmanni's mother and Alex's father were related in some way. Thus, they are teasing cousins because they are related through people who are of the opposite sex.

fly by night mythology

An Indigenous Guide to White Man, or How to Stay Sane When the World Makes No Sense

Larry McNeil *(Tlingit and Nisga'a)*

Larry McNeil was born and raised in Alaska. As a member of the Tlingit and Nisga'a Nations (from both the United States and Canada), he has a unique perspective of the world that is evident in his creative work. McNeil is an artist and educator, having taught at the Institute of American Indian Arts in Santa Fe and at Boise State University, where he is currently an associate professor of photography. His work has been exhibited around the world and has been published extensively; he is also a frequent lecturer and visiting artist. McNeil describes his most recent work as "exploring what it means to raise hell for the special benefit of Christians," a part of his fly by night mythology work. These visual images, using digital photography, are related to themes and stories that are often humorous yet also provide social commentary on Native history. In the following essay McNeil has Raven, the trickster, commenting on what he sees in the larger mainstream world. McNeil weaves personal history, narrative, and humor as he addresses the intersection that exists between the indigenous and western perspectives. His images provide a complexity of thought and ideas in a highly creative manner.

The title of this series of works is *fly by night mythology* because it is about Raven, or in Tlingit, *Yéil*, the trickster. It is fly by night because according to Tlingit mythology, Raven brought light to the world as part of the creation story. The series of art pieces is also about the intersection of cultures between the mainstream and Tlingit people. A lot of absurdities happen in that sometimes inane intersection, and if we can't laugh about it, we'll likely end up as one of the hapless characters we find along the way. I give full credit to our

1. *Yéil*, from the *Raven Asks Pontiac* series, 1998. Digital print. Copyright 2008, Larry McNeil. All rights reserved.

Elders for the spirit of the stories, because all of the work is inspired by them and their gentle, yet biting humor. Now they *knew* humor. They say that humor and tragedy go hand in hand, which is peculiar until you go through the fire of tragedy yourself and find yourself laughing for whatever reason. Humor heals. The Elders knew that crucial yet simple truth, but never actually came out and said it; instead, choosing to make you laugh, or at least chuckle a bit. In this sense, my work is very traditional and aspires to look at what is going on in our world and offers an interpretation that maybe makes a bit of sense in a sometimes-senseless place . . .

. . . after watching a
bird and shadow

dance on a very white
wall, I was going to
cross the street, but
came to a "don't walk"
sign.

Finally, the red hand
turned into the figure
of a white man walking.

Not wanting to offend
anyone, I did my best
imitation of a white
man walking, and
crossed the street.

Journal Entry
Evolved into "fly don't walk" art piece.

The above was about what happens when an Indigenous person is set loose in the big city. The intellectuals like to talk about semiotics, or the study of signs or symbols. As a Tlingit and Nisga'a kid growing up in Juneau, our tribe of kids had our own semiotics that included teasing and making fun of anything and everything; nothing was sacred. Everything and everyone was fair game. Our creation story has Yéil, *or* Raven *the trickster, doing what kids do naturally; i.e., exploring shiny things, figuring out how things work, teasing people that really need it, overcoming difficult odds, and generally loving life as it presents itself each day, no matter how challenging. Laughing at the ironies that present themselves is a critical part of our identity, and in my opinion, a key reason why we are still here. Whenever I see a red don't walk traffic sign, I think of my own brown hand, yet when I see a walk sign, I think of White Man and how I actually did get in trouble as a kid for imitating a classmate's walk. I have come to believe that this holdover from being a tribal kid is still pretty lively in me and is really what my art and writing is all about. I tell my son T'naa that I'm the oldest kid in Idaho and he easily believes me, even at almost eleven.*

The following is a true story. The last time I saw my daughter she was somewhere in her 70s and so happy to see me that she gave me a shopping bag full of my favorite foods. Half dried sockeye, jars and jars of her homemade blueberry jam, smoked salmon strips, black seaweed, and so on. I knew it was getting more difficult for her to make all this, so I refused and told her that I have plenty of my own, and thank you my daughter for being so thoughtful. Her eyes were twinkling bright and I saw a momentary flash of the little girl in her surfacing only long enough for a father to see. I was glad to see that she

fly
don't
walk
...after watching a bird and shadow dance on a very white wall, I was going to cross the street, but came to a "don't walk" sign.
Finally, the red hand turned into the figure of a white man walking.
Not wanting to offend anyone, I did my best imitation of a white man walking, and crossed the street.

2. *Fly don't walk*, 1998. Digital print.

still had her wits about her and was still working as hard as when she was a young girl. She forcefully shoved the bag back into my arms and said gently, "Take it, dad." Her strength was a bit startling; I didn't expect her to be so strong. She easily looked 20 years younger than her years, had a rich tan from working outside, artfully butchering fish by the Chilkat River and picking berries from the side of the mountain. She was a true child of Klukwan, our ancestral home of the Northern Tlingit.

We were at an impasse. Dang. She always was more stubborn than me and even in her 70s a force to be reckoned with. I looked to my own mom for guidance. She shrugged and smiled, letting me figure this one out for myself. In the end her obstinacy or just plain old willpower won out again. We eventually hugged and said our goodbyes, with her beaming and me carrying a bag of pure Tlingit love.

Long before I was born, a Tlingit Elder wanted to give her long-deceased husband's name to her good friend, my grandmother, Mary Brown Betts' next grandson. This is the way it was done in the old days. The women in the clans would have a definite say with who got which names. After all, we are powerfully matriarchal, and perhaps even more significantly, our Tlingit women are a natural force of nature not to be trifled with, *as the English would say. Believe me, I know because I grew up with four older sisters and enough strong willed aunties to make your head spin. You always hear about Tlingit warriors and how fiercely they defend their homeland. Guess what? Their mothers, sisters, daughters, aunties and grandmothers are where that fierceness and intelligence originates. They are the true ones that make us Tlingit who we are.*

At any rate, my mother Anita McNeil had four girls in a row and no namesake in sight. Our oldest brother Chris already had a name. It didn't look good for passing on the name *Xhe-Dhé*, and having it fade into time was simply not acceptable, it *had* to live on. Eventually I showed up and unlike the more traditional naming ceremonies, I received my name as an infant from the Elder Killer Whale ladies in the clan, or as we say back home, Keet Hít. It was a brokered deal, Tlingit style.

Xhe-Dhé was born in the 1840s or so and was living at the time when the American White Man was trying to establish themselves in our homeland. The first wave of White Man (Russians) was already driven off. It was kind of a stalemate, with both sides winning hard fought battles, but they finally gave up, and went searching for easier lands to colonize. As we all know, the Americans later won a foothold, even as we held our own. Other authors in this text write very eloquently about this history. *Xhe-Dhé* lived near what is now the Juneau waterfront where the large oil tanks and the Alaska State Museum reside. He was hounded out of town by the newly arrived White Christians and they never compensated him for his land and he lived out his years at Tee Harbor north of town with his wives and family. In the traditional Tlingit custom, one is obliged to ridicule a debtor until the debt is repaid. Needless to say, ridiculing has been literally raised to a high art in Tlingit country, with many raised totem poles owing their existence to the act of ridiculing. Ridiculation should be a new word coined to *really* talk about Northwest Coast art. It is no accident that a bird that mocks and mimics plays such a key role in our creation story. I never really thought about how the words ridicule and ridiculous have such a close kinship until now . . .

What this is all leading to is that my name comes with the obligation to tease Christians until the land is either paid for or returned. In the finest Tlingit tradition, I continue the act of ridiculing—in this instance, our good friends the Christians. In 2002 I made a piece titled *Tee Harbor Jackson* that told the above story. It features an image of *Xhe-Dhé* (aka Tee Harbor Jackson) as an Elder in the early 1920s. He has part of his nose cut off from various Tlingit wars and is standing in front of an early automobile that looks like a beat up Model A or T (I can't tell them apart) Ford. I notice that my landscapes are not really landscapes in the tradition of Western art, but rather a landscape that has people and stories as a key part of what it is about. I thought it was ironic that the administrators at the Alaska State Museum in Juneau refused to let me exhibit my work there because I am no longer an Alaskan resident (I am an art professor in Idaho). I told them that they are literally right on top of *my* land and that they should be the ones asking *me* for an exhibition of my work. Life is strange and one would think that the White Alaska State Museum administrators would be more enlightened about culture and identity, especially right beneath their (ahem—here goes) big feet. A few years ago I was interviewed by a graduate student about the politics of representation with museums and it essentially turned out to be a Master's Thesis where I talked about Western museum practices and how they often do not serve the needs of the Indigenous people that are represented in peculiar ways within their institutions. My line of reasoning, based on decades of academic and professional art experience, was that in order for Indigenous people to be represented accurately they simply need a museum director that is Indigenous too. It is amazing how many silly issues, challenges, and practices get cleared up in very short order when an Indigenous person is in charge. It is clear to me that there needs to be more Indigenous art administrators in our public museums and until that happens, those institutions will continue to miss the mark and generally be compromised with issues relating to Indigenous people.

Kincolith
Kincolith, the name of our village
translates to
place on the beach
where our enemy
skulls are planted.

It helped us live in peace
and an added bonus
was that we didn't have
many Jehovas witness types
ringing our doorbells.
It was a dark time in our history.

Anyone got any spare skulls
hanging around?

Kincolith killer whales love '59 Cadillacs for some reason

(see plate 2)

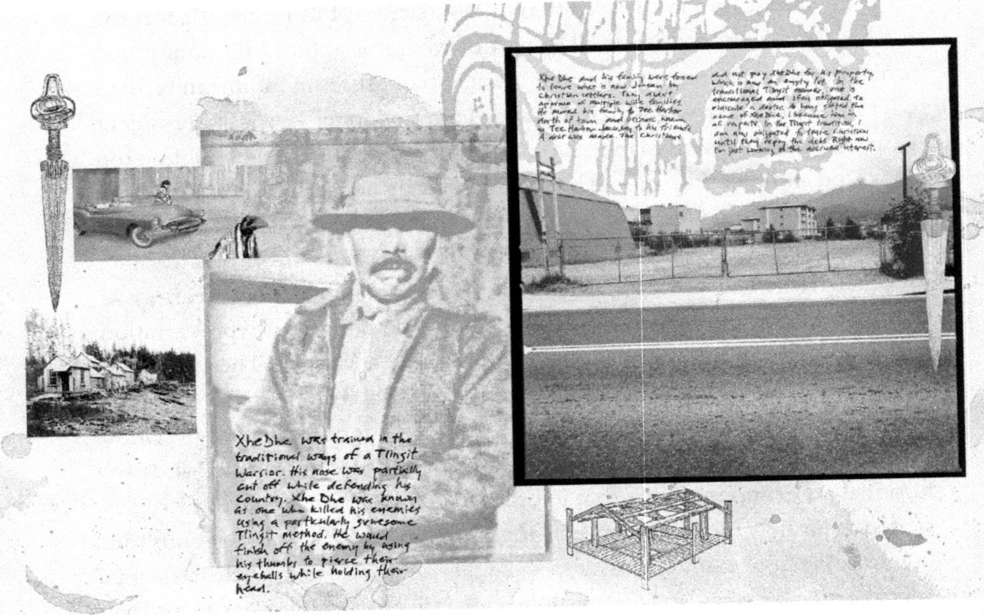

3. *Tee Harbor Jackson*, 2002. Digital print.

One of my Nisga'a aunties told me the story of planting skulls on the beach to deter attacks from neighboring tribes (as she was fitting my father with a traditional robe for his potlatch ceremony initiating him as a Nisga'a chief). An uncle disputed the story, clearly a bit put off, but what the heck. I thought it was a great story and I'm sure there is a juicy marbling of truth running throughout the legend. When I first showed the piece to my father, I wasn't sure if he'd be offended and be disappointed in me, or find it a bit amusing. I hardly ever have any apprehension with the creative process, but this piece was the singular exception; although I must say that it just *felt right* while photographing the various parts and pulling it all together. I brought the piece to his house full of apprehension, not sure if I'd have to censor myself for the first time; not a healthy thought for an artist. He put on his reading glasses and quietly studied it for a couple of minutes and looked at me critically. Then he laughed out loud and pointed at one of the skulls and said that it looked like one of the people from the neighboring tribes and howled with laughter again. When he asked for a larger print to put in the center of his wall, I knew things were all right.

It seems to me that the theory of the origin of our universe, and or life on Earth is rife with controversy, depending on whether you are talking to a physicist, theologian, evolutionary scientist, anthropologist or just your plain everyday person on the street. This question arose because the nature of the *fly by night mythology* work includes a mythological creation story, and inspired the piece titled *Cosmological Status*. I really love this piece because it is about our creation story with Raven playing a central role. I found an image of two skeletons, one a human and the other a bird in a Smithsonian text. In 1902 a Smithsonian scientist was putting forth the admittedly peculiar theory that humans were descended from birds; there was all the proof I needed for legitimizing our story. According to the Smithsonian scientist, humans were in fact descended from birds, which validated our creation story. This piece shows Billy Graham cruising around the Northwest coast in a Cadillac with Raven. After all, if scientists support our theory, it is only natural that Christians do too, right? The piece was made for a public art project in New Mexico and was on a billboard for a month.

One of the most challenging pieces for me to make was the one simply titled *Dad*. It was challenging because our father was my first real mentor, having taught me how to make a living on the ocean and be a fisherman like the thousands of generations of our ancestors. It was also challenging because his life was anything but simple and layered with events that essentially formed a large portion of our family identity. Part of his story is poignant, like just about all of the Indigenous people from his generation; part of it is plain silly, yet full of honor; and yet other parts are serious and note landmark events in our family. Even though it is about our father, it is really about our family because we are literally intermeshed and always will be whether we like it or not. I am not ashamed to say that this piece struck an emotional chord, because I wanted to try and figure out what it means to have not only our family persevere and prosper, but our entire Native Nations. Like so many other thousands (or was it millions?) of Indigenous children in both America and Canada for almost one hundred years, our father was put in a boarding school institution as a very young child. It was the old White Man tactic first put forth in 1875 by an evil man that would be jailed for child abuse today by the name of Richard H. Pratt. He founded the Carlisle Indian School and his driving philosophy was, "There is no good Indian but a dead Indian. Let us by education and patient effort kill the Indian in him and save the man." It is clear to anyone who studies the Indian Boarding Schools that they were a key component of an entire spectrum of genocidal practices against Indigenous people that included simply murdering them on a massive scale. I am very proud to say that when they did in fact try to kill the Indian in my father, that part of him survived, which is one of the reasons why our family was able to hold on to our traditional identity when it was almost wiped out in my

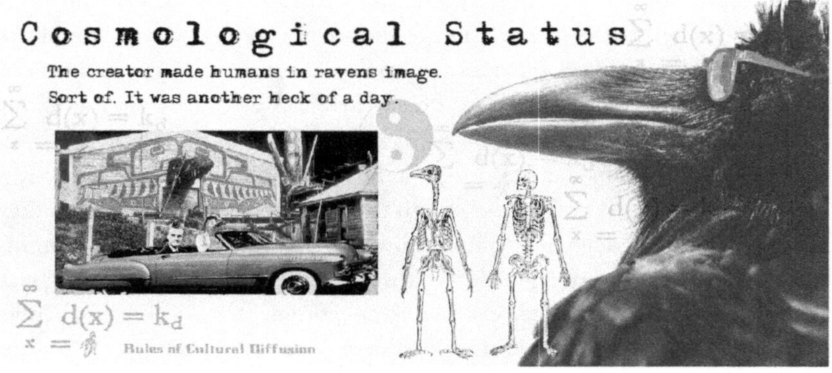

4. *Cosmological Status*, 1998. Digital print. Copyright 2008, Larry McNeil. All rights reserved.

parents' generation. I think of the untold numbers of young Native children that did not survive that portion of the North American Holocaust that was without a doubt all about genocide[1] (see plate 3).

After the 2001 World Trade Center bombing, I got to thinking about terrorism and what a horrific act it was. I thought of what a beautiful morning September 11, 2001, started out as, and how everyone was going about their business as usual, whatever it might have been. Of course, the morning of September 11 is etched in everyone's psyche by now, having watched the unbelievable horror unfold live on television right in the front room of our homes. The cold, calculating act of murdering innocent people by the thousands should surprise even the most jaded human, regardless of their ethnicity or cultural background. Like just about everyone else, the shock took a while to wear off, and really hasn't yet totally dissipated.

One irony in all of the above has to do with the American's role in the genocide of the Indigenous Peoples of this land. It got me to thinking about the United States and how they themselves played a role in what could be interpreted as terrorist acts throughout their history. What most Americans refuse to acknowledge is that what happened to them on September 11 is precisely what they did to the Indigenous Americans for so long. Their military campaigns were mostly directed at innocent and unarmed children and women who were often caught unaware and going about their usual lives, just like the victims of September 11. An objective person would not call this a military campaign or doctrine, but rather continuous acts of terrorism on a massive scale that hasn't been matched since, even counting what the Nazis did in the twentieth century. America has yet to really acknowledge this part of their history and it is common knowledge that what they call their Indian Wars was nothing more than terrorism that resulted in the murder of millions of innocent people; people who were mostly unarmed and certainly not at war, at least in the traditional sense of how one would define a war.

Just this week (June 2006), Ward Churchill (a professor of ethnic studies at the University of Colorado at Boulder) was put on notice that he is to be fired by their interim chancellor. Churchill wrote an essay comparing the victims of September 11 to *little Eichmanns*, a reference to Adolf Eichmann, one of the German Holocaust strategizers. I wrote an essay for our local newspaper in early 2002 that generally contains what I said in the previous paragraph, but my job wasn't threatened. I think that the distinction between our essays was that I did not call the victims Nazis, because I do not think that they were. They were innocent victims. I believe that what Churchill was trying to say was that we as members of a culture need to be held accountable for what our leaders and businesses are doing, plus our ancestors' acts. I could be wrong, but if his argument were true, I would be responsible for any atrocities that my ancestors perpetrated on their own people or neighboring tribes. I am sure that there were many, as we come from a warrior tribe, and we owned slaves, just like the southern plantations of old. I am not proud of that fact, but have come to terms with it and do not ignore this part of our identity; I explained to my son that we were not all good either, and it was wrong for our people to own slaves. This does not mean that I should be persecuted as a slave owner myself, because I am against slavery, and fiercely oppose it. However, it does mean that I should acknowledge this negative part of our history and tell our children all of the truths, not just what makes us look heroic.

This all led to my making this last piece titled *In the True Spirit of White Man*, which is about hypocritical patriotism. It is about White Man needing to come to terms with their own terrorist past and to stop waving their flags as if they're the only good guys left in the world. Like much of my other work there is text imbedded in the work and it talks about Edward Curtis and how he played a role in perpetuating the idea of *The Vanishing Race*, which is the entire premise for his large body of work about photographing Indians. His *Vanishing Race Series* is just a pretty way of saying genocide, and he makes it palpable, and even heroic, which is not good. It inspires White Man to view the *true* Indigenous people of America as being vanished, because after all, he offers photographic proof with his large body of work. The surviving Indigenous people of the Americas are relegated to pitiful wannabe Indians, not real, because according to Edward Curtis, we all vanished. This in itself unleashes an entire spectrum of negative activities from all across the mainstream culture, including termination policies by the federal government that continue to this day, and the simple attitude by White Man, or the mainstream culture, that we Indigenous people simply do not exist anymore.

My new work is about putting forth my own interpretation of our shared histories, including making art that has the silly Tonto character as a leading man, and the Lone Ranger as his somewhat illiterate sidekick. I would like to think that if my ancestors were alive that they would find it amusing; Raven the ultimate transformer would certainly approve (see plate 4).

Note

1. Editor's note: The history of Indian boarding schools in the United States and Canada is a painful one which has left a deep scar on the Native communities.

Kodiak Masks: A Personal Odyssey

Perry Eaton *(Alutiiq/Sugpiaq)*

Perry Eaton (Alutiiq/Sugpiaq) was born on Kodiak Island and grew up on his father's fishing boat. Although his college major was in art, he has largely pursued a career in rural economic development that has aided many rural Alaska Native communities. He was the founding president and chief executive officer of the Alaska Native Heritage Center. He also served seventeen years as chief executive officer of Alaska Village Initiatives. Always drawn to the arts (especially photography and mask carving), Eaton has conducted extensive research, traveling to museums in Russia, Europe, Canada, and the United States to photograph and study the cultural patrimony of Kodiak Island, from which artifacts were removed in the nineteenth century and the early twentieth by collectors, museums, archaeologists, and anthropologists. In this selection, Eaton discusses his work as an artist, his response to Kodiak masks, and his desire to contribute to a renaissance in Alutiiq cultural expression.

The masks of the Island have always been a part of the people and the people's story; in fact the modern story of the masks in many ways parallels that of the people. I first became aware of the existence of mask use on the Island in 1958. It's one of those moments in your formative years when something just sticks with you for the rest of your life.

We were living in Seattle at that time and I was coming home to Kodiak to fish salmon with my father each summer. 1958 was a terrible year. There were no fish and everybody was scrambling to see if they could figure out a different angle to come up with a few fish. We were rehanging our seine to fish deeper in the hopes of keeping the dogs (chums) from sounding (going under the net) on us. During a cannery coffee break, Charlie Christofferson and my father were talking about the fact that Charlie had heard that "them guys in Karluk had done a devil dance that week." With eyebrows lifted my father's interest perked up and of course I became very attentive as Charlie was one of my heroes. The conversation went something like, "Wow. I didn't think they did that anymore." Charlie said, "Yes, they paint their face with soot and jump around and do drumming. You know in the old days they used to wear mask and everything." At this moment an elderly woman who was visiting her daughter on her cannery break, Mrs. Heitman, joined the conversation and said, "That mask stuff all ended and they took all the masks away. They are all gone, there are none left on Kodiak. They took them all away." The cannery whistle blew ending the break, sending everyone back to work. And leaving a thirteen-year-old boy with a deeply implanted life quest to find and see these masks.

Little did I know that this saga of our masks would weave in and out of my life and ultimately lead to me becoming a mask maker.

In 1971 the United States of America settled the Alaska Native land claims and I have been involved in that great adventure ever since. One of the features of the Act is to exclude any ethnic perpetuation as a direct piece of the settlement. It is designed along the lines of a straightforward capitalist economics model. Tribal members convert to shareholders of a corporation entitled to all the traditional rights of shareholders of corporate America. The only thing Native in the Act was that an individual had to have a minimum of one-fourth blood quantum in order to enroll and participate, and had to be born before December 18, 1971. For years this has caused serious identity issues with the people. But on the up side it forced the question "What does it mean to be Native?" and for many, me included, a close examination of our roots and the evolving culture of the Island.

Over the years my involvement with the Native corporations and a career in economic development has required a significant amount of travel over a large portion of the globe. Washington, D.C., has been a frequent destination over the many years and gave me access to the Smithsonian's collection of Kodiak material. In the early 70s I made a bee line there to see the masks collected by William Dall on his trip to Kodiak in 1872. What I found was less than exciting visually: two small 8" × 5" bird-like carvings that had had their feathers and appendages broken off. In my heart I had wanted to find "OUR ART"! Something significant. Something spectacular. Something to rival coastal Indian art. Something that defined me and the Island. I left slightly disappointed but a little excited because I had come in contact with the past and with something that the "Smithsonian" thought was valuable. I felt validated.

After that one visit followed a long period of casual research, a few drawings, lots of conversation and most importantly, being a witness to the re-emergence of a visible cultural identity on the Island. It started with a few of our women (doesn't it always) bringing the dance back.[1] In the beginning it made me feel a little awkward and maybe a little embarrassed. But as I saw the process around the activity I began to realize the significance of what was happening. I became very proud and, at times, quietly emotional.

As a result of my work in rural economic development I had the opportunity to become involved in activities resulting from the opening of the borders with Russia. Being from the Island, I have always felt a strong pull to things Russian and jumped at the chance to visit the country. On a trip in 1989, I had the opportunity to be in St. Petersburg and found myself at the Kunstkamera museum (which is none other than Peter the Great's ethnology museum) standing in front of an exhibit of Alutiiq masks from Kodiak Island. There were seven of them and they *were* spectacular! They were different and distinctive. They were large, beautifully painted and adorned with feathers and fur and bangles that wanted to dance! They were the Island, they were us, they were me!

I returned home with some marginal photographs, many, many questions and a desire to make one . . . someday (see plates 7a and 7b).

I think the story might have ended here had it not been for the research of Professor Lydia Black. She had rediscovered facts around a certain French linguist named Alfonse Pinart who visited the Island in 1872 and collection of a large number of our stories and a significant number of masks. She encouraged one of her doctoral candidates, Dominique Desson, to do her thesis on the collection, resulting in Desson's "Mask Rituals of the Kodiak Archipelago." Submitted in May 1995, it has proven to be pivotal to the emergence of the mask in today's Alutiiq identity. It presents the collection and other collections in their entirety and develops a rich and learned dialogue. The work is a wonderful jumping off place to begin the exploration of masks and their meaning for today's Alutiiq people.

Supporting and backing up works such as these, the creation of the Alutiiq Museum and Archeological Repository proved to be a major boon to the people of the Island. Under the leadership of Dr. Sven Haakensen Jr. it has been a never-ending support unit for cultural enrichment.[2]

I have always been an artist. I took private art lessons when I was young and followed by majoring in art in college. Up until my mask making, my self-expression has taken many forms over the years, settling in black and white photography in the 80s. The discovery of the masks and the linkage they potentially had to our culture and identity began to capture my imagination and interest. There had been some artists from the Island, most notably Jacob Simeonoff, Doug Inga, and Jerry Laktonen, who had begun to pave the way in defining Alutiiq art with well-crafted and defining work.

Supported by their influence and based on some old photos and some illustrations from books, I decided to carve a mask of my own. I had learned from one of the books "the Kodiak people carve a unique type of mask called a plank mask." Good enough for me; I set out to make a plank mask. Of utmost importance for me was how to construct it in a manner that it could be danced. It was not obvious how this "plank" could be tied to the face and allow movement for a dance. This naturally led to the philosophical question "Why are you making this mask, to hang on the wall or to dance?" It was at that point that I decided to be a mask maker and not an "artist" in the western sense. I think if you use the mask format as a base for artistic creations that are to be hung on the wall in a western mentality they are "art." If you make masks to be worn and danced they are artifacts. The primary difference being, you can display artifacts but you can't dance "art." That takes nothing away from an artist and in fact I have done several pieces of art using the masks as a base but I don't consider them masks in the true sense. For me an Alutiiq mask must have the capability to be danced.

I had stumbled through about three-fourths of the work when a mutual friend suggested I meet Helen Simeonoff because she had been to France and had some pictures of the masks in the Pinart collection.

My meeting Helen and talking with her probably did more for my mask making than any other relationship. Her pictures were incredible. She was so encouraging and so open in sharing her knowledge and materials. It was just what I needed to really motivate me to move forward. As a result of her encouragement I went to France to see the masks first hand. Being in the presence of the collection was breathtaking to say the least. I was totally absorbed with and by them and what they mean and meant to the people of the Island (see figure 1).

The collection has proven to be an emotional experience that continuously inspires and fascinates me. The first time I saw it I was just speechless. The size and shapes were so different from what I had expected, having studied the available photographs. It's unfortunate that almost all photographs of masks are direct face-on shots. There are very few profiles or images that show the relief of the carving. Some of the masks were six and seven inches deep and it is impossible to appreciate this quality from photographs because they flatten the 3-D object to a 2-D image (see figures 2, 3, and 4).

After I recovered from the initial impact I began to have many questions: Why Pinart? Why France? Why did some of the masks look the same but different size and shape? And most importantly: What were the uses of these masks?

One thing was obvious. Here was the answer to the riddle of the chance conversation on the Kodiak dock in 1958. Alfonse Pinart was the son of a French industrialist and a linguist studying American indigenous language looking for

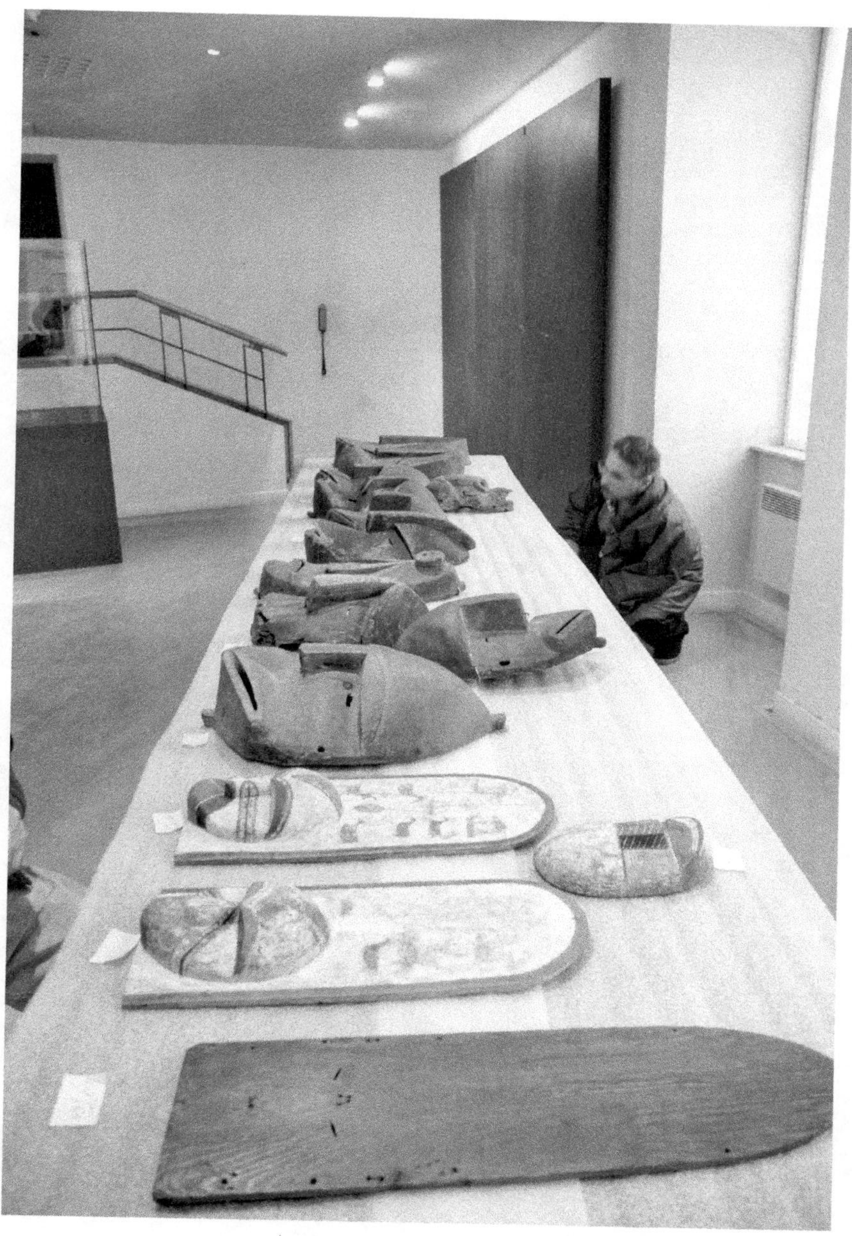

1. Photograph taken at the Chateau-Musée de Boulogne-sur-Mer in France, when a group of Sugpiaq people visited the Pinart collection. The masks were spread on a large table so they could be examined in detail. Photo by Perry Eaton.

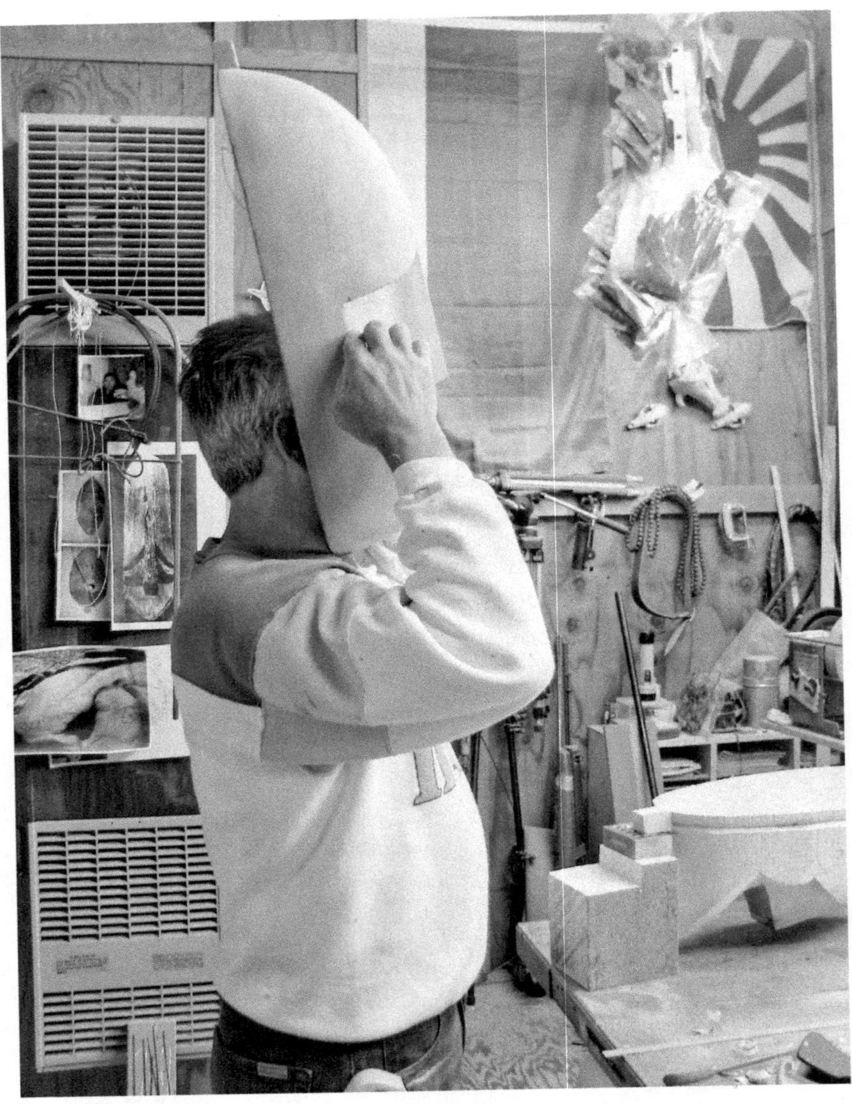

2. A central "rib" carved into the mask helps to support it on the dancer's head. Photo by Perry Eaton.

3. One of the largest masks in the Pinart collection. Photo by Perry Eaton.

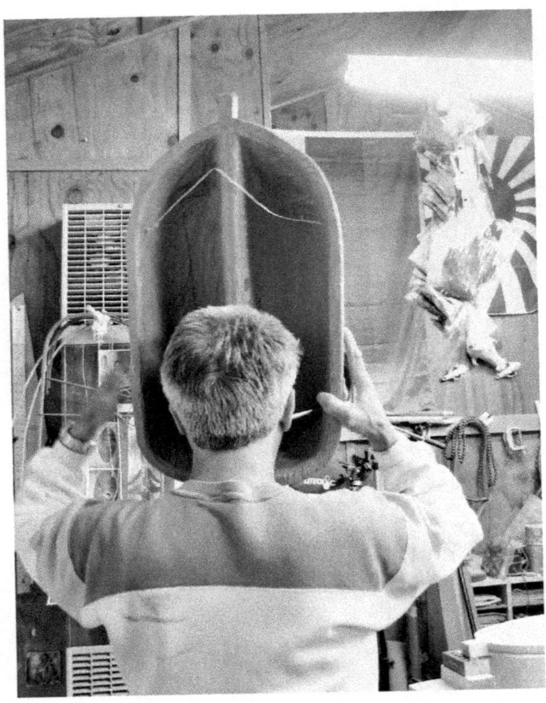

4. Rear view of a mask showing the center "rib." A covering of woven grass or a hide was tied on the back. Photo by Perry Eaton.

links between Native inhabitants and Asian origins. He arrived in Kodiak on November 8, 1871, after a two-month trip by kayak from Unalaska. He stayed until the spring of 1872, spending time in Afognak. Old Mrs. Heitman was right when she said "they took them all away." She was born Juliana N. Kasharavov in 1885 in Afognak. Her father Nikolai, who would become a powerful member of the Russian Orthodox clergy, would have been fourteen when Pinart visited and it would be highly unlikely he would forget such an important visitor. The young Juliana would have heard the stories of his visit first hand, and because Alfonse spoke perfect Russian it's easy to see why people thought it was the Russians that "took" the masks.

In my continuing search for answers I turned to the experts; those that had knowledge. I read primary sources such as the Russian accounts; published works by Hrdlicka, Heizer, Dall, Black, Desson, Richard Pierce's collection of translations, and a variety of miscellaneous articles and reports. Actually, I read anything that I could get my hands on, but I began to see some limitations.

There is a significant absence of firsthand discussion with the makers, users, and participants around the masks, and no known record of the technology of construction methods. Pinart's work, much of it yet to be published, may be the exception as his mission was to study the language and not just the objects as physical things.

It has become apparent to me that many "experts" base their opinions on their worldview and personal life experience, which, I suppose, is as it should be or maybe as it can only be. Religions and most notably Christianity have played a significant role in shaping our current view of the masks. We were taught that the "graven image" is all about devil worship and is evil in all cases and should be cast out and avoided in any and all forms. Naturally with this assimilated value there can be no open discussion or dialogue among the Island people. Consequently we end up with conversations like the one I heard as a boy that are skewed and incomplete in the extreme and often much abbreviated.

While tremendously important and ethically responsible, educational institutions, and intelligentsia, with their published and unpublished documents also have limitations. While far less restricting and crippling to diverse cultures, the application of accepted methodologies has sometimes led to conclusions that are questionable and occasionally completely incorrect.

As I studied the Pinart collection several things kept coming forward. The sheer size of some of the masks was awesome. Several of the larger ones were over twenty-three inches tall and as much as seventeen inches wide and eight inches in depth. It has been said that these masks were too large and heavy to be worn and were used as back-drops for plays, by being attached to ropes and swung behind the dancers. As a carver of masks and a craftsman I don't believe this. They were worn and they may well have also been attached to ropes and swung but from my examination of the backs they definitely were made to be worn. The mask is carved in such a way that a portion of the back is not hollowed out and left as a "spine" that comes approximately one third of the way down the center of the back and curves gently into the hollowed-out area at the nose, forming in some cases a perfect headrest. There is a hole cut in this spine to attach the harness to hold the mask in place over the face. The idea that this was done to suspend the mask is just not logical from a construction standpoint. First, recognize it's a tremendous amount of work to hollow out the areas adjacent to the spine. Even with my modern tools, I often groan at the prospect of this work. In addition, any attachment to this area would make the mask dance in an imbalanced manner. If you were to make the mask to be suspended it would be constructed in a manner that at least had the mask balanced and I believe my ancestor would do it in the most expedient manner possible. It is illogical to think a craftsman would sit with a beaver-tooth tool and needlessly do useless work.

The idea that they were too heavy also warrants comment. These masks were worn by men who lived in a kayak. They grew up with a paddle in their hand. Long hours of propelling their boats with paddles developed very strong upper bodies. I don't think balancing a ten-pound head piece was that much of a challenge.

There were collections within the collection of masks made by the same artist. There are at least eleven masks made by the same artist in one series. They are easily recognizable by their similar "paint box," size, carving technique, lack of attachment holes, and not being hollowed out on the back side. In my readings, the scholars dance around these masks and have a hard time dealing with them. I believe we are looking at the very first masks made for a consumer market. I believe these were made for Pinart to be used in his lectures. They are probably his "trunk show" illustrations. Several things lead me to believe this. First, they are not alive. They cannot see, breathe, or speak. In other words, they have no spirit and cannot be worn. They are somewhat worse for wear than other similarly painted pieces, suggesting considerable handling (or travel). They are the only artifacts in the collection like this. Secondly, they *all* are copies of the other older masks in the collection. What are the odds of a collector finding a complete body of work from one artist that *exactly* replicates the work of numerous older artists in the same collection? The question for me is: Where and when and by whom were these masks made? (see plates 5 and 6).

There are multiple works of at least three other artists in the collection. Most notably are ten small well-executed pieces that are designed to be held with the aid of a big stick. There are no teeth marks visible on any of the pieces, suggesting they were never danced. These masks are (were, as many have lost all adornment over time) fitted out with considerable feather, fur, and wood adornments and show real artistic talent. However, they, like the previous group mentioned, can have their shape and origin traced to the older masks in the collection. Were these made for Pinart? Were they the "original trunk show" and proved to be too frail so the other more robust versions were made? Did Pinart commission them to have locals reenact the plays the old one were originally intended? After all, he was a linguist collecting the stories and mythology of the people.

One of the most fascinating and telling things about our masks is what isn't there. After studying the collected pieces I began to compare form and subject with other masks from around the world in an effort to better understand the context of the society in which they were produced. African masks that deal with the diverse animals of the continent and Pacific coast Indian art that deals with the clan crests and mythical creatures all were testimony to the cohabitation of the living word. Our masks seemed to be missing some basic elements when the Island environment is considered.

There are no teeth, no fangs, no claws, and no ears. What an enigma. Our home is shared with the largest land carnivore in the world; the Kodiak bear.

I feel a great debt of gratitude to Mr. Pinart for having taken the opportunity, 134 years ago, to preserve a small piece of my material culture. It has proven to be and is destined to become one of the great sources for discussion and focus in the never-ending quest for Island identity. And in spite of all the questions and rabbit trails of intrigue and speculation the collection invokes, it is and will remain the fundamental baseline for the exploration of the Alutiiq mask as a cultural icon.

Taken as a whole, on the most elementary level, what the masks represent is sculpture of a very distinctive and highly stylized nature, representing the unique art form of the Kodiak People.

Notes

1. Editor's Note: In the 1980s a renaissance in traditional dance practices occurred throughout Alaska, resulting in new dance groups and festivals.

2. Dr. Haakensen received his Ph.D. in anthropology from Harvard University and is the son of recognized Alutiiq culture bearers Sven Haakensen Sr. and Mary Christenson Haakensen. He is currently the director of the Alutiiq Museum and Archaeological Repository.

Artifacts in Sound: A Century of Field Recordings of Alaska Natives

Craig Coray

Craig Coray was born and raised in Alaska. He currently resides in Anchorage with his wife and is a music instructor and composer at the University of Alaska, Anchorage, where he has been on the faculty since 1974. A recurrent theme in his compositions has been Alaska Native songs, stemming from his early childhood in Alaskan villages where his father collected songs of the Native people. He currently serves on the advisory group for Arctic Smithsonian's exhibit which includes recorded songs and stories. His essay here is about his research, acquisition, and repatriation of recorded song material of Alaska Native groups dating from 1899 to 1978. Most of these field recordings had been inaccessible to Alaskans because they were housed in out-of-state archives or were poorly or not at all catalogued. The recordings and field notes that Coray acquired are now being indexed and catalogued in the University of Alaska, Anchorage library, soon to be archived in the Alaska Collection. In 2007 Coray collaborated with the National Park Service and the Nandalton Tribal Council in publishing Dnaghelt'ana Qut'ana K'eli Ahdelyax *(They Sing the Songs of Many Peoples), a book and audio disc of rare Dena'ina Athabascan songs recorded by his father in Nondalton, Alaska, in 1954.*[1]

In the distant past, Sugpiaq hunters were said to have improved their hunting prowess by learning the songs of animals. It was believed that singing the song of the sea otter could lure it within striking distance. What songs might have emanated from a Sugpiaq kayaker in the Gulf of Alaska four hundred years ago as he serenaded the sea otter he hoped to spear? With no notated music and only a fragmentary oral history to draw from, we can do little more than speculate, and in addition, rely on audio recordings made in the twentieth century.

The musical tradition of Western culture is preserved due to a written system of musical notation with fixed values for pitch and duration; written records of music exist that were created over a thousand years ago. In contrast, the music of northern indigenous peoples has been preserved exclusively by oral transmission until very recently. Oral song tradition relies on the memory and interpretation of individual singers. Many traditional singers know hundreds and hundreds of songs, all from memory, which is a remarkable quality that is not found in Western tradition.

Musical change over time is to be anticipated: a song created centuries ago might be sung differently today. Consciously or unconsciously, Native singers will be influenced by other musical styles, whether from neighboring cultures or from the broader impact of Euro-American music after first contact. Proprietary songs belonging to individuals or family groups and clans may be neglected and forgotten. Songs associated with rituals no longer practiced (such as shamanism), or those using archaic words or special dialects, will lose their meaning. Given that change will occur, a distinction must be made between change that comes about gradually, allowing a culture to evolve, and change that comes about catastrophically, leading to erosion and possible extinction. In the case of Alaska Natives (as with many indigenous cultures), foreign imperialistic dominion has played a significant role in the demise of music and dance, whether through genocide, disease, relocation, or governmental/religious suppression of language and cultural practices. It is a testament to the resilience of Alaska Natives that in recent decades there has been an unprecedented revival, statewide, of neglected song/dance traditions.

One can argue, rightly, that change is part of any culture: witness the evolution of European art music from Gregorian chant to serialism or the more rapid evolution of jazz in the United States. Significantly though, Western culture has the means not only to revisit older musical traditions but to cultivate them in musical performances tailored to the stylistic nuances of the age in which they flourished. For cultures dependent on oral transmission by generations of singers, there will be less meaningful delineations between old and new styles.

The best documented links we have to an older "Alaskan" music are the written records of explorers, followed somewhat later by the writings and field recordings of ethnologists, anthropologists, folklorists, and linguists, as well as missionaries and educators. Written documents date from the late 1700s (Coxe, in the Aleutian Islands, observed Unangan singers in 1765), but early descriptions are often compromised by insufficient musical expertise on the part of the observers. Exceptions are the reports of Beresford at Sitka in 1787, and Haenke, a musician, at Yakutat during the Malaspina expedition of 1791. Unfortunately, Haenke's transcriptions have apparently been lost. The most reliable records we have are actual songs and narratives, recorded on various media over roughly a century beginning in 1899 (with the Harriman expedition) and now preserved in a handful of institutions across the nation, notably the American Folklife Center in the Library of Congress, the Archives of Traditional Music in Bloomington, Indiana, and the Alaska Native Language Center in Fairbanks, Alaska. The earliest of these recordings were made on wax cylinders by intrepid researchers and offer a fascinating, albeit frustrating glimpse of an earlier Alaskan musical culture; this is frustrating because the audio quality of wax field recordings varies from rough to unintelligible. Later recordings made on disc and magnetic tape are far superior in quality. The hiatus of field recording in Alaska is a period of roughly thirty years spanning the middle of the twentieth century and coinciding with the advent of the reel-to-reel tape recorder. The recorded material from this brief era represents the culmination of a long tradition of fine solo *a capella* singing by informed elders still connected to ancestral ways, gradually to be supplanted by group singing combined with drumming and dancing, geared toward entertainment at cultural festivals.

Early in my career as a composer, I became acquainted with some published recordings of Iñupiaq and Yup'ik music, notably the Smithsonian Folkways series and another collection by Lorraine Koranda titled *Alaskan Eskimo Songs and Stories*. Some of the songs on these recordings inspired my work as a composer. My own research of extant Alaska Native recorded music began in earnest when I was asked to develop a curriculum for a course on northern indigenous music for the University of Alaska, Anchorage (UAA) in 2002. I found that most of what was written on the subject resided in journal articles and that sound recordings were either scarce, severely restricted, or both. The Alaska Native Language Center and the University of Alaska, Fairbanks have large inventories of recordings but due to insufficient staffing virtually nothing was in place to provide access for research. I also found that the Library of Congress American Folklife Center has a large Alaska collection that includes some very important material, and that permission could be obtained for duplication for the University of Alaska, Anchorage, library. This collection amounts to some forty-four hours' worth of recorded sound and includes the field recordings and notes of such luminaries as Frederica de Laguna, Laura Boulton, and John Swanton. I felt it was important that the UAA library acquire these materials and successfully applied for grants from the Rasmuson Foundation and the Alaska Humanities Forum to fund both the purchase of copies and time to research the material and provide written annotations. From its inception this project took over three years to complete. The annotating alone took 482 hours and filled 91 pages.

The recordings with written documentation in the form of field notes or published texts were most informative and the best of these included text translations as well. Such is the case for the 1904 Sitka Recordings made by John Reed Swanton on wax cylinders. Though only 87 of the recorded songs have survived, lyrics for 107 of them were published in *Tlingit Myths and Texts, Bureau of American Ethnology Bulletin* (BAE) 39. In addition, the *Federal Cylinder Project*, edited by Judith Gray from the American Folklife Center, includes a sixteen-page section on the Swanton recordings, summarizing the audio on the thirty-two surviving cylinders and coordinating the songs with the listings in the BAE bulletin. This large collection has two shortcomings: the sound quality leaves much to be desired, and the songs are nearly all performed by one singer, a man by the name of Jacob Morris whose Tlingit name was Dekinaku. So while the songs in no way can be said to be representative of Tlingit musical style in 1904, the best of them are coherent enough to be transcribed and offer a basis for comparison against later fieldwork. Most intriguing perhaps are the lyrics, all of which have been paraphrased (presumably by Swanton) and which take us deep into Tlingit mythology, customs, and conflicts.

A significant wax collection not in the American Folklife group, but held at the Archives of Traditional Music in Indiana, is that recorded by Waldemar Jochelson in the Aleutian Islands in 1910–11 during the Aleut-Kamchatka Expedition. Consisting of seventeen songs and a number of narratives, this collection has figured prominently in the recent revival of Aleutian singing and dancing pioneered by the Unangan historian and dance leader Ethan Petticrew.

A collection of great interest to the Deg Hit'an Athabascan people and my research project are the recordings made by John Wight Chapman, educator and Episcopal clergyman at Anvik in southwest Alaska in 1925. Chapman recorded eight songs and also wrote a small book titled *Tena Tales and Myths*. As part of my research a copy of these songs has now been repatriated to the Deg Hit'an people.

In 1920 a musician named Carol Beery Davis moved to Juneau and began recording Tlingit material. Her accounts, along with song descriptions and photos, are documented in the publications *Songs of the Totem* and *Totem Echoes*. Unfortunately Davis brought a very ethnocentric view to her analysis of Tlingit music, providing "corrected" transcriptions of indigenous songs, which included Western-style keyboard accompaniments. Nevertheless the recordings, made on early disc technology and having survived three transfers to other media, feature genuine Tlingit songs and narratives by Native singers using traditional drums and rattles and are a valuable addition to the musical legacy of Southeast Alaska.

Laura Boulton's work in the Arctic has been best known through the Smithsonian Folkways collection titled *The Eskimos of Hudson Bay and Alaska*. Included in the American Folklife purchase and now held at the UAA library is the unpublished work of her extensive 1946 field sessions in Barrow, Alaska. Although accompanied by scant field notes, the 112 songs are mostly of high quality and are a valuable supplement to the published material. One published song tells of a hunter who was killed by another hunter and robbed of a seal. An unpublished song recorded immediately afterward tells how the murder was avenged after being revealed to the village by the murdered man's brother, who had transformed himself into a fox. The collection must be examined in its entirety, both published and nonpublished, to get a more dimensional perspective of Boulton's recordings and understanding of what songs the Barrow people recorded for her.

By far the most comprehensive collections I researched are those made between 1950 and 1958 by the acclaimed anthropologist Frederica de Laguna, working with fellow anthropologist Catherine McClellan. De Laguna made her first Alaskan field recording in Angoon in 1950 on a wire-spool machine. The centerpiece of this recording is the tragic recounting by Billy Jones of the destruction of Angoon in 1882. The narrative is in Tlingit but an English translation is provided in the field notes. In addition there are five songs, notably the slow, stately "Song of the Beaver Hat" which tells of the origin of Angoon, where the *Deisheetaan* clan were led by their founding ancestor-spirit to what became their village site.

Subsequent fieldwork took place in Yakutat, where de Laguna spent parts of two years becoming intimately acquainted with Tlingit culture. This work is detailed in her monumental three-volume series *Under Mt. St. Elias*. She also studied Ahtna culture in the Copper River Valley and Tutchone culture in the Yukon Territory. Altogether she recorded close to forty hours of songs, narratives, folklore, and linguistics. The sound quality varies considerably, mostly quite good but occasionally overmodulated to the point of distortion. Throughout one hears de Laguna's trademark system of monitoring speed fluctuations by blowing an "A" on her pitch pipe prior to recording.[2]

Space limitations make it impossible to list the most significant of the 306 songs in the 1952, 1954, and 1958 de Laguna collections. The Tlingit material from 1952 and 1954 is thoroughly documented in *Under Mt. St. Elias*, with complete musical texts, analyses, translations, and transcriptions (by the noted ethnomusicologist David McAllester) provided in the appendix (vol. 3). Two songs were published in the Smithsonian Folkways album *The Southeast Alaska Folk Tradition, Vols. I–III*: the "Song of the Golden Eagle" and the "Song for

Kagwantan Children" (incorrectly titled "Lament of the Lonesome Wolf"), both sung by Olaf Abraham. The only documentation for the Ahtna and Tutchone Athabascan recordings from both 1954 and 1958 is a brief description of the recorded contents on each reel, with timings.

Thorough and meticulous, de Laguna cross-referenced all the song material in the appendix of *Under Mt. St. Elias* with stories and anecdotal information in the text proper. She also researched the song lyrics published by Swanton in *Tlingit Myths and Texts*, providing a comparative analysis of songs that appear to be of the same origin, but which of course were recorded fifty years apart. One such song is "Funny Peace Dance Song: Raven Loses His Nose," appearing in Swanton as "A Song About Raven's Travels Through the World." The song lyrics describe how Raven lost his bill on a hook while stealing bait from a fisherman, and then had to fly down the smoke hole of a house to retrieve it. The Swanton lyrics parallel the de Laguna lyrics quite closely, being almost identical in places. A musical analysis of the recorded songs reveals a less convincing parallel, though certain similarities in contour could be construed to suggest a common musical origin.

It was my great pleasure to correspond with de Laguna shortly before her death, seeking permission for the use of her recorded materials in my research. While supportive of my research, she felt, and I concurred, that ownership of these many songs and narratives ultimately should reside with the communities where they originated. Through negotiations between myself, Judith Gray from the American Folklife Center, and Ralph Courtney from the UAA Consortium Library, procedures are now being implemented for duplicating these and other recordings for Native groups or individuals who have a vested interest in them. The essence of our plan is that American Folklife will provide primary permission and UAA will then act as an authorized agent for duplicating the materials, at a cost considerably lower than that charged by the American Folklife recording lab.

Occasionally, significant fieldwork will be discovered belatedly or posthumously, especially work carried out by amateurs unconnected to a scientific or educational knowledge base. Such is the case with a recording made by John Coray (my father) of Dena'ina singers and speakers in Nondalton, Alaska, in 1954. John Coray was a schoolteacher with an abiding interest in indigenous culture. The hour-long tape was intended as an audio dispatch to his parents in southern California, affording them a glimpse of life in a remote Alaskan village. It contains twenty-eight songs in five languages (Dena'ina, Yup'ik, Deg Hit'an, Iñupiaq, and church Slavonic), some of which are quite old. Recently the Lake Clark/Katmai National Park Cultural Resources Office took

Song About Raven's Travels

1. "A Song about Raven's Travels." Transcription by Craig Coray.

Funny Peace Dance Song: Raven Loses His Nose

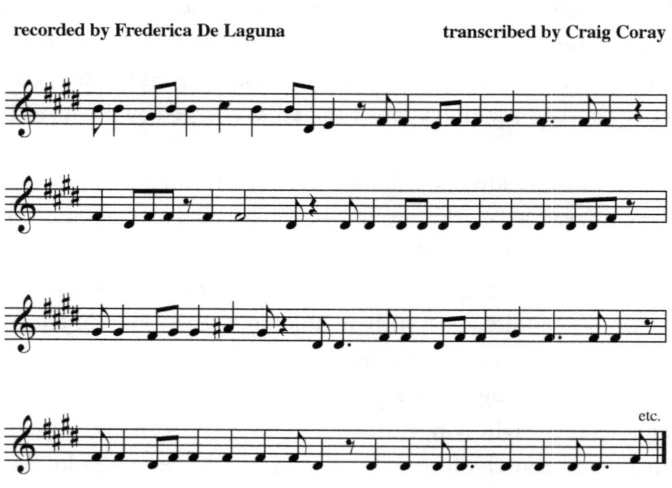

2. "Funny Peace Dance Song: Raven Loses His Nose." Transcription by Craig Coray.

an interest in the recording and brought it to the attention of the Dena'ina linguist Dr. James Kari, who has pronounced it the earliest known recording of Dena'ina song and speech. Dr. Kari in turn has been working with elders to translate the Dena'ina and Deg Hit'an portions, and has discovered some very rare material which articulates old belief systems. At the time of this writing the National Park Service is joining with Kijik Corporation and the Nondalton Tribal Council to publish the recorded songs on a compact disc along with a booklet containing song descriptions, translations, and transcriptions authored by myself, elders from the community of Nondalton, and Dr. James Kari.

A genre that features prominently in the 1954 Coray collection and appears to be unique to the Inland Dena'ina is the "solo" song. In conventional Western analysis it is characterized by the use of ungapped scales, free improvisatory melody with melisma and ornamentation, and complex syncopated rhythm making abundant use of triplets, dotted-note groups, and "swing" figures. The expressive element lies more in the flowing impassioned delivery than in the song lyrics, which like those of most other Alaska Native songs tend to be cryptic. A fine example of this genre is the Dena'ina Love Song quoted below, sung by Wassillie Trefon of Nondalton.

DENA'INA LOVE SONG (TRANSLATED BY JAMES KARI)

1.

Ts'iq'u yu niqu hnel'an yeha.
still for you I look there.
Nch'a eshchegh.
I cry to you.
Nda ya t'ghesht'ih ni yahi yuk'hdi yihe?
What can I do about it, in the sky there?
Nda ya t'ghesht'ih ni yahi yuk'hdi yi?
What can I do about it in the sky there?

2.

Yuyeh gu yu nuqu hne l'an yeha.
I look for you inside there.
Nch'a eshchegh.
I cry to you.
Nda ya t'ghesht'ih ni yahi yuk'hdi heya?
What can I do about it, in the sky there?
Nda ya t'ghesht'ih ni yahi yuk'hdi?
What can I do about it in the sky there?

Dena'ina Love Song

3. "Dena'ina Love Song." Transcription by Craig Coray.

3.
Nunudeɫi yi nuqu hneɫ'an yeha.
In an airplane I look for you there.
Nch'a eshchegh.
I cry to you.

Another significant collection was recorded by the Swedish folklorist Anna Birgitta Rooth in 1966 and 1978. Rooth's main informants were Dena'ina, Tanana, Gwich'in, Tanacross, and Ahtna Athabascan people from southwestern and interior Alaska. The collection consists of myths, stories, songs, and interviews, many of which were published in *The Alaska Expedition 1966*. This publication is essentially a literal transcription of the words as dictated by the informants, but also includes song transcriptions by Hakan Lundstrom, who was doing postgraduate work under Dr. Rooth at the time. A later publication titled *The Alaska Seminar* contains more song transcriptions and a musical analysis by Lundstrom. In my research I found several references to the recorded song material, but no copies were known to exist in the United States. Correspondence with the Anthropology Department at Uppsala University connected me with Dr. Gosta Rooth, husband of the late Anna Birgitta, who had accompanied his wife on her Alaska expeditions. Dr. Rooth was able to put me in touch with Hakan Lundstrom, currently Dean of Arts at Lund University, who owned a copy of the original tapes. Dr. Lundstrom enthusiastically agreed to provide me with a copy of the collection but explained that there had been speed fluctuations on the original tape which he had attempted to correct with varying success, and that his copy was incomplete. He speculated that some of the recordings had been made with a dictaphone, which uses a constant reel speed rather than a constant tape speed. He had intended to find a repository for the tapes in Alaska and took the opportunity to discuss the matter. I concluded that the logical place for this would be the Alaska Native Language Center in Fairbanks and put him in touch with Dr. James Kari. It was agreed that Dr. Lundstrom would secure the original tapes and remaster them using state-of-the-art software to make the necessary speed corrections. At the time of this writing Dr. Lundstrom is in the process of remastering and digitizing the tapes for archiving at the Alaska Native Language Center.

Rooth's is an extremely important collection, if somewhat flawed due to poor recording technique and/or equipment. She recorded several important creation myths and the songs associated with them. One example is "Animals Locked Up in Mountain," an Inland Dena'ina origin myth from Nondalton. It tells of a shaman who created a rift in Telaquana Mountain (an 8,070 foot peak in the Chigmit range in Southwest Alaska) allowing the animals of the Dena'ina world to emerge one by one. Of particular interest in this myth is the role of singing. In an earlier version told by Andrew Balluta in *Nuvendaltin Quht'ana*, the shaman opened the mountain with his staff and the rock rabbit sang a song for each animal prior to its liberation. In the version told by Alexie Evan in Rooth's transcript, the shaman required the people's help in opening the mountain. He instructed them to sing a series of songs, and it wasn't until the fourth song that the mountain opened and released the animals. Now, with the acquisition of the recordings from Sweden, one can hear the four songs sung by Alexie Evan as he related the myth. There are many other songs on the Rooth recordings which are attached to stories or myths, several of them featuring animals or animal-human interaction. The collection deserves much study, which hopefully will be facilitated by the reengineering of the tapes and access to the Alaska Native Language Center at the University of Alaska, Fairbanks. My most recent research of recorded song history has taken me back to the nineteenth century, before the advent of audio recording technology. In 1872 a Frenchman named Alphonse Pinart spent considerable time on Kodiak and Afognak Islands among the Sugpiaq people, collecting masks and other artifacts which later became a permanent collection in the Boulogne-sur-Mer Museum in France. Pinart also witnessed and made written records of eighteen masked dances. The song descriptions and lyrics were translated from Sugpiaq into Russian and then into French, eventually to be published along with photographs of the masks in *Kodiak Alaska: Les Masques De La Collection Alphonse Pinart*.[3] When the Sugpiaq historian Helen Simeonoff visited my northern indigenous music class in 2005, she shared the Pinart material with the class. Only one of the dances had been translated, and she hoped to find a translator for the remaining seventeen. It is fortuitous that my mother, Claudine Wright, is a native of Switzerland and is fluent in both French and English. She agreed to do the translating, with myself and Helen Simeonoff serving as consultants. At the time of this writing she is doing the final editorial work. Copies of the finished translations will be forwarded to Helen Simeonoff for her personal collection and to Dr. Sven Haakensen, director of the Alutiiq Museum in Kodiak.

The dance descriptions and song lyrics captured by Pinart provide a compelling vision of a world inhabited by powerful spirits journeying through multiple planes. Viewing the masks and reading the descriptions of the dance movements, one lacks only the sound to assemble a fairly complete picture of what Pinart witnessed. Claudine Wright's translation of one of the dances is quoted below.

> CHUMUGIIAK S'UMASHEDSHII
> (The one who went out of his mind, who is mad, insane)
>
> Song: My house / up there / in the universe / up there / my house/ you do not know it exists / the sun / the one that is up there/ behind the sun / up there / Spirit / I [?] tried on many occasions to approach you/from up there / I tried [?] to come to you / the earth / the one that is up there / of the entertainers [?] Legend: The legend says that one day, a man, wishing to become a shaman, withdrew to the woods. Once there he became inspired, saw the evil spirits and turned into this mask.
>
> Dance: Two persons arrive, one following the other. The second person, who wears the mask, takes his place in the left corner, hidden by a *kamleika* (waterproof garment made from animal intestines). He (unintelligible word) and dances on his knees during the first part of the song. Then he

gets up and, holding rattles, dances by bounds around the place, sometimes falling and, picking himself up, resumes dancing.

Sugpiaq dancers have expressed an interest in reviving the Pinart dances, which would entail restoring the Sugpiaq song lyrics and reinventing the choreography. If they do, the English translations will be the penultimate step in a convoluted linguistic metamorphosis through four languages, beginning and ending with the original Sugpiaq. Some of the original meaning will be lost, either in translation or through the loss of old belief systems. But much as a vessel can be reassembled from broken shards, these songs and dances, and the aura of power and mystery they engender, can be made to endure.

Notes

1. James Kari and Andrew Balluta, *Draft of Lyrics and Translations for 1954 Coray Recording*, 2004 (revised 2006).

2. If the "A" plays back as a "B-flat" then the tape recorder was operating too slowly, resulting in an increase in pitch when played back at normal speed.

3. See Perry Eaton's essay in this volume.

Digital Media as a Means of Self-Discovery—Identity Affirmations in Modern Technology

Frank Francis-Chythlook (*Yup'ik*)

Frank Francis-Chythlook was born in Dillingham, Alaska, and is Yup'ik. He is a media specialist and lives in Anchorage. In this essay he examines how digital media such as video and sound recording are being used by indigenous communities in Alaska to document oral histories, cultural activities, and history.

When the term "Native Video" is uttered in Alaska, it's likely images of feathers, fish, and traditional dance come to mind first. Farther down the list may be political activism—the annual live broadcast of the Alaska Federation of Natives Convention, or perhaps a persuasive televised announcement either for or against the opening of ANWR. A Caucasian journalism student fishing for video gigs recently approached me, asking if I film "all that Native stuff." He had been eavesdropping as I told a friend about some work I was doing, and couldn't help but interrupt to ask whether he could help me do it, since he's always looking for work. Pressed for time, I didn't explore what he meant by his reference to Native culture. I didn't feel I needed to—I could see potlatches dancing in his blue eyes and almost picture salmon swimming upriver in his golden locks.

It reminded me of a past discovery of my own pompous arrogance. I myself held an illusion of what material produced by Native videographers would and should be as I was teaching a course to Native teenagers in Anchorage. Yes, I was looking for heartfelt discussions about beading, Elders, hunting, gathering, and the difference between Yup'ik and Iñupiaq drum styles. Yes, I can admit I had the notion of taking old tales and having my students act them out. True, true it is that I wanted them to make a video about bows and arrows as part of a series demonstrating ancient hunting technologies.

The teenagers, in their own way, corrected my vision by knocking off the cultural blinders I was wearing. I was force feeding these notions of proper topics for Native videographers, stuffing them down their throats like a mother seagull regurgitating a salmon smolt to her chicks. But these young Athabascan, Iñupiaq, Aleut, Yup'ik, and Tlingit men and women are not seagull chicks, nor are they necessarily hungry for fish. By insisting that they choose only within these topics and be completely politically correct, and by allowing them only limited freedom all the while trying to teach them complex nonlinear editing software, I found that out of a pool of around fifty to seventy kids expressing an interest in making a video, only one or two students would be dedicated enough to put up with me for more than a few days a month. The program was available daily, and entirely voluntary. Something had to give, and rather than forcing what few teenagers I had to do my bidding, I admitted that my approach was perhaps off-key and needed to change. I adapted a more heuristic approach, teaching technique and placing fewer limits on the topics. I rewarded those who did well on the precursory projects with more freedom on the successive videos. I taught when they needed it. I listened to my students. I offered what I knew, rather than injecting it. My small lab's capacity was about eight to twelve students, with eight being one person to a computer and twelve taxing the oxygen potential of the room. Every day there were eight or more self-motivated individuals competing for my time and attention. Kung Fu, skateboarding, football, and family discord turned out to be the topics that they brought back with them.

I found that I could not stop the students from working on their projects. There were days when a barbeque or birthday cake could not pull any of the growing teenagers away from the editing stations. Indeed, the learning was raised on several levels—the students learned the editing software in-depth and I learned not to pigeonhole my own producers. The works that came out of the lab were truly artful. For example, the first skateboard video featuring Native skateboarders and Native Youth Olympics athletes. Short films that ask the question—"What is family?" A martial arts style film using football as a motivator for elevating the tension to violence. Some of these things have never been done before, and all have never been created in exactly this way before. The common thread in all cases—the students say, "Don't you tell me who I am, let me do that for myself!" What merit do these themes have in (Alaska Native) cultural preservation? The teenager who learns the skills of video editing and storytelling will revisit the cultural preservation idea later—gathering interviews with elders and editing them or creating DVDs. Spreading the vision of brown people doing their own thing on a skateboard or in a martial arts setting also has its positive effect. Now, others will see, yes, Natives can be on television. Integration of urbanism in Native culture is not only possible but happening all around. Skateboarding is now an Athabascan trait. Native Youth adapt to the circumstances they are in. Urban or rural, these youngsters are looking for ways to fit in. From seal hunting at fish camp to perfecting the "bluntslide,"[1] the need for reality and confirmation of existence is solid.

* * *

Claims of potential cultural revolution not substantiated by empirical data. Personal accounts of Frank Francis-Chythlook's adventures subject to copyright. Statement of video as a Native pride.

Notes

Video works referenced in this essay include *Big UnHappy Family*, *Toit like a Toiga*, *Shiver Me Timbers*, and *Animosity*. All were produced by students during the school year 2004–5 at the Alaska Native Heritage Center, High School Program Communication through Technology component. Portions of each are included on the DVD *Year End Wrap 04–05*. Availability is limited to personnel, students, and their families affiliated with the Anchorage School District. It is not approved for public showing.

1. See article describing this skateboard maneuver at http://www.skateboard.com/frontside/101/tricktips.

America's Wretched

Erica Lord (Iñupiaq and Athabascan)

Erica Lord (Athabascan/Iñupiaq) was born in Alaska and lived between her home village in Alaska and Upper Michigan. An interdisciplinary artist, Lord explores race, ethnicity, gender, and memory—universal aspects that in her experience seem to surface and diminish within her constantly changing persona, most times depending on the context or present environment. Lord has exhibited in the Smithsonian's National Museum of the American Indian, the Carl N. Gorman Museum, and the Schopf Gallery on Lake in Chicago. She received a B.A. in liberal arts and studio arts from Carleton College in 2001 and an M.F.A. in sculpture and photography at the School of the Art Institute of Chicago. "America's Wretched" is a critical examination of the portrayal of Native Americans and Alaska Natives in the media, incorporating the theories of Frantz Fanon and Paolo Freire to establish a theoretical platform for commenting on how photography and media represent Native peoples. See plate 8 in this volume for images of her own work that explore issues of identity.

> The proud spirit of the original owners of these vast prairies, inherited through centuries of fierce and bloody wars for their possession, lingered last in the bosom of Sitting Bull. With this fall the nobility of the redskin is extinguished, and what few are left are a pack of whining curs. The whites, by law of conquest, by justice of civilization, are masters of the American continent, and the best safety of the frontier settlements will be secured by the total annihilation of the few remaining Indians. Their glory has fled, their spirit broken, their manhood effaced; better that they die than live the miserable wretches that they are.
> —L. Frank Baum, *Abeerdeen Saturday Pioneer*

Indigenous peoples from around the world seem to share a common past, a parallel history of oppression. Summed up simply as the process of colonization, the steps include disease, conversion, and assimilation. Later, preconceptions or residual prejudice form between cultures. While nations have experienced the process differently, parallels exist both within their historical development and within the contemporary experiences and politics of what may at first seem dramatically different cultures. This may in part stem not from the Native peoples themselves, but more with the relationship to the colonizer; which follows a similar pattern on disparate continents. Following the western European colonial expansion, European ideals, perceptions, and concepts of racial and cultural superiority have affected Native peoples from Africa to the Americas, Asia, and Australia. Now, as educated and worldly people, we understand and accept that history; however, we forget to analyze the ways in which those antiquated ideas still exist. When reading and studying American visual culture, it becomes apparent that there still exists a sort of distancing of "western," or Euro-American people from the Native; an attempt (even if it is unconscious), to keep the Native in the past, easily recognizable, simple, and, essentially, separate and different from "us." The racial and cultural stereotypes of what an Indian looks like was constructed by whites, eventually accepted and digested by Natives, and have now been perpetuated for so long that we do not even question if this is who Indians really are. Contemporary images do not show the ethnocentric views as clearly as the old images, but they do continue to separate, exoticize, and mark as strange or bizarre, differentiating the Native from the Euro-American. This treatment has the dual effect of dividing the two as people of different levels of civilization or advancement, and denying the identities of contemporary Natives who do not fulfill the traditional stereotypes. Using the postcolonial theories of Frantz Fanon as a conceptual base, I want look critically at contemporary images of Native people and question if these new images are challenging the romantic ideals that exist in our post-colonial visual culture.

In *Wretched of the Earth* (1963), Frantz Fanon discusses how the master or oppressor seeks to dehumanize the Native, reducing him to animal, and thus metaphorically separating him from a human level, and defining him as a different species.[1] Later, when the anger of the oppressed turns to violence and that violence turns inward against other Natives, the oppressor reacts with surprise, as if his oppression of the Native had nothing to do with the Natives' violent demise. This moral distancing allows the colonizer to further separate himself from the Native, despite the relationship between the action and reaction, the learned violence and eventual counter-violence. "In order to free themselves they even massacre each other. The different tribes fight between themselves since they cannot face the real enemy—and you can count on colonial policy to keep up their rivalries."[2]

Obviously, these tactics were not unique to African colonizers. In modern times, these tactics have led to current ideas and perceptions of the Native and Native-like. In contemporary American life, though they are not "Native," the oppressed share a position in society; the American "Native" lives in the ghettos of America: from inner-city Black and Hispanic ghettos to the third world reality of Native American reservations and villages. The Natives' faces have changed along with their environment, but the story remains the same. Unfortunately, the perceptions and violence have remained the same as well.

On numerous occasions I have heard people comment on how they just don't understand why *they* (very pointedly marking them the "other") live in such poor conditions, why *they* have such a problem with violence, alcohol, or drugs. In the visual documentation of the ghetto or the reservation, it is no coincidence that the decay of the community is enlarged, that the subject continues to be the depressed, broken, and hopeless faces, that the images elicit overwhelming fear or pity. The continued focus on the violence and corrosion helps the oppressor to continue to separate himself from the other, as well as dividing the oppressed community itself. These images aid in identifying these people, the *they*, as a different variety of people, one that does not share any humanistic qualities, one that is not equal. "One step more, and the leader of the nationalist party keeps his distance with regard to that violence. He loudly proclaims that he has nothing to do with those Mau-Mau, those terrorists, those throat-slitters."[3] And similar to the African oppressor, you can count on colonial policy, or rather, economic and capitalist policy, to keep up the rivalries.

Fanon states that colonization and decolonization are both violent processes. In the American West, there were numerous accounts of violence—books, reports, and word of mouth—all described the ruthless savagery of the Indian. Settlers feared Indians, and what you fear you begin to hate. So began the process of colonization—all-out war against the Native, killing, and claiming the land. Did the fear of the savage, the Indian, begin here? When describing the Indian, there are accounts of noble chiefs, but more describe the faces with reference to primitive features, fearsome faces. Did this fear of the Indian, in particular, of that of the male, carry through to modern times? Does this also parallel the fear of the black man that Fanon describes; a fear of both physical power as well as untamed sexuality? To control this fear, we emasculate the men, rendering them harmless, and no longer a threat to the society. Bluntly speaking, is this fear of the sexuality, or the power of the Native, part of the reason that images of mixed-blood Natives are rare—visual proof of miscegenation is dangerous because it accepts the idea that the Native and the settler are one in the same, the same people, and the same species. Once the Native has been converted to believing in white society, there is no longer a threat: "[The Native] is told frequently that decolonization need not mean regression, and that he must put his trust in qualities which are well-tried, solid, and highly esteemed . . . In the colonial context the settler only ends his work of breaking in the Native when the latter admits loudly and intelligibly the supremacy of the white man's values" (Fanon, 43).

As long as there is a fear of the Native, there simultaneously exists a fascination with their primitivism. In America, it was accepted that the Native was to eventually die out by law of the conqueror (Fanon, 84), so in order to preserve the dying past, photography was introduced as an indispensable tool; Wild West shows and circus sideshows became popular. The Natives were tamed and put on display before they met their just and ultimate destiny of vanishing. "A Vanishing Race" was a "picture opera" by Edward Curtis depicting the old-time Indian. Curtis almost single-handedly created the image of the noble savage, documenting both the curiosities of the culture and people before they both disappeared. Curtis's photos did not alter the general attitude toward Native people. Natives continued to be feared and seen as savage. Misused or misunderstood, Curtis's photos could be used to support these ideas—these Natives wore animal skins, the women walked around indecently, their faces were brutal and fierce—maybe some were the noble savage, but the images supported the idea that they all possessed an animalistic fever deep within.

Curtis's photographs were taken between the time of contact and what is known as the "reservation period." Photography was introduced as a vital tool to document the rapidly changing culture; however, there are flaws in that these documents, which are supposed to be an objective view into another world, were often biased and constructed; secondly, the implied objective is that film is capturing something that will no longer exist after that moment; in the case of the Indian, to capture them before they changed or disappeared forever. As Indians became more remote and separate on their reservations, photography of the Native also transformed.

One of the first Native photographers, Lee Marmon, showed that the Native was still alive and presented the culture from a sensitive perspective that comes from his essential internal point of view. Though I am a fan of Marmon, his photographs are part of the continuum of photography that continues to show Natives as single-faced, an old culture, as part of the past. Photography is still often accepted as truth, and because it is coming from Natives themselves it is accepted as authority. The problem is the image is supposed to reflect reality, and in relation to the face of the Native, reality no longer reflects the image. To this day, the majority of photographs of Native people are historic, or historically referencing, images. For the viewer, it is easy to conclude that Natives are of the past, a primitive culture, and very clearly not part of modern life. Those that are left are documented in a different manner. The epigraph to this essay reveals a belief that once there was a noble time in the history of the Native, but now the few that are left are "whining curs" and "miserable wretches." It seems that the majority of Native photographs show one of two extremes: either the continuance of the noble savage or the depression and desperation of the reservation. Narrow opinions of the Native are kept alive; the subtle attempt to place them apart from the settler, or rather, contemporary American, still exist visually through the shooting and editing of Native photographs. Antiquated anthropology of racial science bleeds into our perceptions of the Native, both in our private thoughts and the public portrayal in visual media.

For the Native, the photographs set up a visual precedent that contemporary individuals cannot live up to. Contemporary Natives cannot honestly believe that we are the representations we see: the noble savage, the wise medicine man, the Indian maiden. In addition to these archetypes, we cannot fit the image visually because the photographs continue to portray faces that have not changed in the past two hundred years. In reality, most Natives are mixed blood of some sort. A visual representation of a mixed-blood individual could mean several things: that the threatening idea of miscegenation exists, that the culture is diluting and dying through the "breeding out" of the Native, or simply that these mixed-blood images do not exist because they are not as visually interesting—they do not create a story to believe in.

"People have come to expect Indians to look a certain way, and many Natives willingly delivered that stereotype as long as they made money at it. This is why stereotypes are so deeply ingrained into both American and Indian popular culture" (Hill 1998, 153). These poses were accepted by Americans as "Indian," but just as quickly accepted by Natives, even if it was an act, in an effort to make money and survive as a people. "Through the influence of the popular Wild West shows, Indians began to strike the stereotypical poses as they associated with those performances. It is an aboriginal form of 'mugging' for the camera" (148). However, with any act, if you perform it long enough, the line between reality and fiction blur; if the only remaining evidence of Indians were these constructed images, then we, Americans and Indians, begin to believe in the myth of the warrior.

In addition to acting Indian, the other essential factor in constructing the image of the warrior is his racial and physical "Indian-ness." Despite the reality that racial mixing had occurred since contact, there is little evidence of any Indian racial "impurity." Natives have been intermarrying throughout time; whether it was inter-tribal or with African Americans, Mexicans, or Europeans, there has never been a "pure" Indian race. However, Natives and non-Natives accepted the myth of racial purity; the effects of this type of racism are present in photographic evidence as well as oral and written history. In scientific methods, photographs were used as records for racial identification and taxonomy. "Many photos of Indians were used to document genetic features and to illustrate how bloodlines were either maintained or 'contaminated' due to interracial breeding" (Hill 1998, 158). There is little portraiture existing that shows "mixed-blood" Natives; though at first this may have been due to small numbers, it is more likely that there was an intentional editing of what was to be shown as Indian, as well as a denial of the existence of miscegenation. In modern times there is even more interracial mixing, as the majority of Natives admit to having non-Native blood of some sort. Despite this admittance of racial mixing, the visual evidence, through contemporary film and photographs, does not reflect the reality. There still continues the practice of editing to perpetuate this rather solid idea of "Indian"; it complies and continues a tradition begun over a hundred years ago. The Indian is still dark-skinned; always has angular features, commonly has long hair; and often still wears traditional clothing (e.g., the popularity of powwow photos). The stereotype of Indian is the same as it was generations ago despite the changing reality of Native America.

The government-regulated definition of "Indian,"[4] combined with visual reinforcement of what Indian is supposed to look like, creates a nearly unachievable level of Indian-ness and very small room for mixed-race acceptance. The blood-quantum regulations create a questioning of cultural authenticity that is always underlying. The visual example parallels the quantum issue in that it is easier to subscribe to a simple idea of Indian rather than work through the complex reality that exists (Hill 1998, 142). The difference exists in the levels of Indian-ness: The United States government initiated a minimum blood quantum of one-quarter to be nationally recognized as Native. Beginning in the 1990s many tribes began to shed the U.S. government's initial blood quantum approach, so tribal recognition may have a lower quantum requirement or use other methods such as lineal descent. Unfortunately, to be nationally recognized, one must comply with tribal, state, and national standards, despite their tribal criteria. In regard to image, there is no one model to show an "Indian enough" or one-quarter-Indian-blood-person visually; as a result, the visual culture subscribes to an easily defined "full-blood" appearance. This is easy because full-blood appearance has been defined by culturally stereotypical images that originated over a hundred years ago. Does this perpetuated image continue to exist because of a desire within the Native community to isolate themselves from other races and cultures; or does it exist because Americans

(Native and other) have created a nearly impossible definition of Indian-ness, reinforced by the image, and perpetuated by the Native community, visual artists, and scholars?

Is the time of the Native a time of the past? If you went by the names of the monuments and memorials around us, you would believe this to be true. If we go by Fanon, Whites, by law of conquest, have right to the American land, and thusly name monuments to the successors. "Every statue . . . all these conquistadors perched on colonial soil do not cease from proclaiming one and the same thing: 'We are here by the force of bayonets'" (Fanon, 84). Throughout America, there are constant reminders as to who the conqueror is. Universities, government buildings, and statues: all these become monuments to the conquest and defeat of the land and the people. Photographs became a different type of monument to the success of civilization; Indians were seen as dangerous, but simultaneously exciting and fascinating. By shooting the Indian in the studio, it tamed the savages and brought them into the home. Continuing to resurrect the last of the real Indians allows us to glamorize our past, selectively remembering and believing in romantic stories of chiefs and warriors, in turn, allowing us to avoid confronting a complex and difficult reality.

It appears that the majority of images of the American Native still exist as a distorted view of the people. This continuance of subliminal visual messaging does nothing to end the tension between Natives and non-Natives (or between Natives themselves); instead, it reinforces stereotypes, creating feelings of inequity for the Native, and ultimately further divides the people. "Whether or not Native practitioners will alter photographic conventions or have a radical effect on the kinds of imagery we generally revere, only time can tell" (Mitchell 1994, xvii). To create a simple, palatable, and safe version of Indian is what the directors of the Indian image have been doing for generations. Whether change comes from Natives who hold leadership roles or from our friends and family, it will take an intelligent and conscious analysis of our own colonized minds, understanding and critiquing our own preconceived notions, characters, and stereotypes.

In present times, it is true that we have all accepted some form of the values and ideas of the majority, of the "settler"; in fact, it could be said we are all settlers and we are all colonizers. Now begins the formidable task of understanding and living peacefully with each other and the complexity of our reality: "It is understandable that in this atmosphere, daily life becomes quite simply impossible. You can no longer be a fellah, a pimp, or an alcoholic homogeneity" (Fanon, 88). Politically, the Native still has a long way to come; whether it is through education, art, or one-on-one contact, success of my fellow Natives and overall equality is the goal. As I have mentioned, the visual and culturally "pure" warriors of the past are unattainable for the modern Native, but as Fanon stated, maybe the warriors still need to be called upon, but we must update the idea of who they are and what they do. "During the colonial period the people are called upon to fight against oppression; after national liberation, they are called upon to fight against poverty, illiteracy, and underdevelopment. The struggle, they say, goes on" (88). Indeed it does.

Imagery and History

In cultures throughout the world, there is a very human need to mark one's existence in history, to leave traces of one's life and work; clues that may unravel the story of that person, their culture, or situation. The earliest ochre markings of Aboriginal hands on rock, pilings of stones along trails, or even tagging or graffiti are all means of verification, a mark to evoke the simple message of "I was here."

I am an artist, and therefore visual iconography is something I examine. I am from Alaska, a place that throughout history has been a crossroads of cultures, a unique intersection of populations—human, animal, and spiritual. I think these origins—a lineage that I was born into, and a land I removed from, my cultural limbo and precarious balances—have molded my identity and fueled my artistic expression. As I continue to move in this space of translation, I maintain a constant balancing act between what seem to be opposing aspects of my life. I become an emigrant to my home, or more accurately, homes. Through art or ritual, I discover ways to find a root and affirm my position as a shifting self, understanding that in order to survive, identity and culture cannot be static. In order for cultural survival, we must review our visual philosophy, deconstructing the imposed images as well as our own colonized mind. Through this, the multiplicity of self will evolve along with our expanded notions of what is authentic, traditional, or real.

I want to explore the world in which translation is suspended, the space beyond singular identities where worlds collide, merge, or resist. In the context of my individual and cultural framework, I move through different identities, languages, and experiences. Art has become my tool of translation, addressing the merging of blood, culture, gender, memory, and the idea of home. The qualities that define my identity become an overlapping and blurring of lines creating an amalgamation in which the multiplicity becomes indivisible. However, since archetypes are easier to understand, a multifaceted identity is often rejected or narrowed into effortless characterizations. Therefore, it is most often the context of my environment or the company I choose that determine which of my qualities emerge. To sustain a genuine self, art becomes my means, creating a world in which I can shift and become one or all of my multiple visions of self.

Considering the history of "identity art," I want to explore the next wave of cultural examination, an evolution of new ways to demonstrate cultural identity beyond the polar ideas that exist in a solely black/white diaspora. I want to challenge ideas of cultural purity or authenticity as well as discuss ideas of attraction, repulsion, exoticism, and gender or feminist notions. Besides a few individuals, there has been a lack of the indigenous voice in the art world. Taking into consideration this challenge, I want to raise questions as well as declare convictions; challenge, deconstruct, and influence a new way of thinking about contemporary Native people, our life, and our art. It is time to redefine our representation as Native people. Until recently, it has been mostly cultural outsiders who have dictated images of Native people; when Natives have spoken, it is most often directed toward the cultural tourist. Through art and media, the cultural shapers of this generation, it is time for us to self-determine, to control our representation and image, to address modernity, development, and to discuss the myth of an authentic culture.

Though I mostly live in urban spaces and cities, I always return home; the movement between the two becomes a vital part of my life. Each time, I try rooting myself, attempting to leave my mark in a rapidly changing environment. Each of us has our small ceremonies or tiny rituals, everyday habits that become events of special circumstance. Through my work, I want to discover how ideas and concepts about identity, culture, and image come together with material experiments to compose my stories. The worlds that exist within me—such as Native, Woman, Artist, Other—continue to separate and merge again, coming together in a voice that seems to be growing louder every day. I want to merge the knowledge of my communities with the individual experience to create stories that grow and shift along with the worlds within and around. Through my art, I will become part of the growing wave of voices, redefining our selves, our communities, and our beliefs.

Notes

Epigraph quote: L. Frank Baum (author of *The Wizard of Oz*), in *Aberdeen Saturday Pioneer* (South Dakota), December 20, 1890, 10.

1. Jean-Paul Sartre in his preface to Fanon's *Wretched of the Earth*, 17.

2. Ibid., 18.

3. Fanon, *Wretched of the Earth*, 62. Subsequent page references are in parentheses.

4. To be considered "Indian" by the Bureau of Indian Affairs, one must be one-quarter Native blood quantum from a federally "recognized" tribe.

The Alaska Native Arts Festival

Tim Murphrey

Tim Murphrey is one of the former student coordinators for the Festival of Alaska Native Arts. He was the main coordinator for more than three years and then a volunteer for two years. The Festival of Alaska Native Arts started in 1973 and was one of the first statewide dance festivals. It was and still is primarily organized by the Alaska Native students in addition to local volunteers. Murphrey's essay addresses the history of the Festival. Murphrey works for the University of Alaska, Fairbanks and continues to be involved with the Festival as a volunteer.

The University of Alaska, Fairbanks (UAF) is situated atop a hill traditionally called *Troth Yeddah,'* or wild potato hill, by the Tanana Athabascan people. According to the late Traditional Chief Peter John, Athabascan Indians from this and surrounding areas would gather annually on the hill to pick the *troth*, wild potatoes that grew there. The purpose of the gathering was two-fold: it provided much-needed subsistence, but also allowed elders and leaders from all over to communicate with each other on important upcoming decisions and other news.

Not long after the turn of the twentieth century, the Dena or Athabascan people learned that *Troth Yeddah'* would be used as the place of learning of a different sort, with the founding of the University of Alaska. The elders saw this as an opportunity for their young people to learn, and gave their approval of the coming change. The University of Alaska, Fairbanks now accommodates a strong Alaska Native student body. It is their traditions and culture that are celebrated each year through the Festival of Native Arts.

In 1974, a group of Alaska Native students at the University of Alaska, Fairbanks began to feel the pressure of being away from home through the long cold winter. They felt that the best way to remind them of home would be to do as their ancestors had always done—sing. The spark turned into an idea, which grew into a plan, and eventually drew the interest of more and more students. The result was the first Festival of Native Arts. The Festival represents the growing renaissance or return of traditional dance that began occurring throughout Alaska in the 1970s. The Festival was one of the first statewide dance festivals that made efforts to represent all of Alaska's indigenous peoples.

The Festival of Native Arts has seen many changes over the years. Starting as a loosely organized group of students performing traditional songs, it has evolved into an annual three-day event, usually occurring on the first weekend in March. In years past, dance groups have performed in the Patty Center Gym, the Wood Center commons, and, most recently, the Charles Davis Concert Hall at the University. The Festival of Native Arts has been documented via video recordings beginning in the 1980s, when funding was available. These videos included interviews of dance leaders and elders by Rose Atuk Fosdick (Iñupiaq) of the Institute of Alaska Native Arts, or IANA. These are housed at the Polar Archives at the University of Alaska, Fairbanks.

The event is organized by the administrative assistant of the Alaska Native Studies Department and a part-time position filled by a student of UAF. The event, however, would not happen without countless hours of sacrifice by volunteers, both students and community members. There are many things to do in preparation for the Festival, starting with deciding which groups would be featured. Performance slots are usually first come, first served. As funding is tight, dance groups must raise the funds to fly to and from Fairbanks from their home villages. The University provides housing and meals for upwards of twenty-five dance groups, once they arrive. Each dance group can have membership ranging from twelve to over twenty. Hotel arrangements, in-town transportation, scheduling, and stage management are only a few of the major logistics to be taken care of by volunteers.

The Festival is vital to the preservation of Alaska Native culture and certainly validates the cultural heritage of Alaska. In preparation for the annual event, dancers spend the year performing and practicing their traditional songs and dances. Elders are able to teach younger generations the language and stories needed to carry on these important parts of their history and culture. In many rural areas, it is common to find young people too busy with school and sports that they have little time for cultural education such as traditional dance, language, art, and regalia making. For those students who take the extra time and hours of practice, and whose families often make their dance regalia, the reward is attending the Festival of Native Arts in Fairbanks. It provides that extra incentive to teach and learn.

The Festival of Native Arts provides a much-needed venue for Native people to share their culture with the world. Dancers from as far north as Barrow and as far south as the Aleutian Islands attend the event every year. Cultural groups include Iñupiaq, Yup'ik, Athabascan, Tsimshian, Tlingit, Haida, and Aleut or Unangan. There are several local powwow groups who perform in a style that is originally from the Plains area of North America. Other international guest performers in the past have been from Norway, Japan, Russia, Brazil, and various tribes from around the continental United States. These performers all have the opportunity to share their culture with an audience who may know nothing at all about Native people or dance. The current location of the event allows for an audience of over a thousand people at any given time, and every year patrons will find standing room only. All three nights of the Festival are free and open to the public. That, in conjunction with one of the largest Native arts and crafts sales in the state, is a major draw for newcomers to the Alaska Native culture. The celebration brings in not only locals but also transient visitors from two nearby military bases, as well as travelers from around the country.

The Festival of Native Arts sustains Alaska Native culture through education, sharing, and celebration. Whether it is sharing the beauty of your culture as a performer, or taking a piece of that experience with you as a spectator, the Festival of Native Arts is an exciting and special event.

Conflict and Counter-Myth in the Film *Smoke Signals*

Anna Smith-Chiburis (Tlingit)

Anna Smith-Chiburis is Tlingit, of the Deisheetaan clan of the Raven moiety. She received an M.F.A in creative writing from the University of Alaska, Anchorage and an M.A. in English from the University of Alaska in 2006. This selection addresses the film Smoke Signals, *based on the book by the Coeur d'Alene writer Sherman Alexie. As Chiburis reveals, Alaska Native scholarship does not invariably focus on Alaska Native culture, literature, or language but also explores other indigenous perspectives and ideas. Chiburis is currently at work on her first novel.*

He dazzles you right out of the water/right out of the moon, the sun and fire./Cocksure smooth talker, good looker,/Raven makes a name for himself/ up and down the coast from Nass River./stirs things up.

—Robert H. Davis, *Saginaw Bay: I Keep Going Back*

History. History is never the truth.

—Sherman Alexie, *Crazy Horse Speaks*

O, the glorious things / we do to survive.

—Sherman Alexie, *Toward Conception*

All films contain conflict. This is the central driving force behind plot. The creative process of weaving conflict into character is a complex one. In their informative text on playwriting, William Missouri Downs and Lou Ann Wright relate conflict to the crisis of human struggle: "plays [or films] are about conflict occurring in crisis" (Downs and Wright 1998, 60). Likewise, Downs and Wright identify obstacles and complications as important components of conflict. In relation to this, the central plot of the film *Smoke Signals* focuses on two American Indian men who live on the C'oeur d'Alene reservation. One of them, Victor, must travel south to Phoenix, Arizona, in order to pick up his deceased father's remains. His friend Thomas goes with him on the road, but from the start of their journey, both men are at odds with each other. Thomas tells stories about past events that Victor would just as soon forget. Also, Thomas embellishes the stories he often relates, which annoys Victor.

Also and with regard to character conflict, there is a certain duality of self in relation to the more concrete aspects of Victor's personality, which threatens to overshadow his, as well as more abstract and metaphoric qualities that are related to Thomas.

This struggle is mirrored by Victor's volatile relationship with Thomas, whose stories embody those very abstract and metaphoric qualities that Victor throughout the film strives to suppress. From another perspective, the stories Thomas tells are in conflict not only with Victor but also with a colonial perspective that threatens to overshadow that of his traditional culture, just as they play with concepts related to consciousness such as the concrete over the abstract, the verifiable over the imaginary, the known over the unknown, and the perceptible over the imperceptible. Also, his stories, due to their more abstract, metaphoric nature and their connection to indigenous traditional oral narrative, mirror a struggle over words and consciousness that is played out via his central conflicts with Victor.

With regard to the origins of this sense of duality, Euro-American colonization suppressed many aspects of traditional indigenous culture. As a result, a fair amount of dehumanization was an unfortunate part of the colonial process. As Paulo Freire relates in his text *Pedagogy of the Oppressed* (1994), "Dehumanization, which marks not only those whose humanity has been stolen, but also (though in a different way) those who have stolen it, is a distortion of the vocation of becoming more fully human" (30). Freire believes that colonized people experience certain aspects of dehumanization that can traumatize and linger for generations. He postulates that this gives rise to a dual sense of self in which one side is dominated by and lessened by the colonial aspect:

> A particular problem is the duality of the oppressed: they are contradictory, divided beings, shaped by and existing in a concrete situation of oppression and violence. (37)

Freire suggests there is a way to overcome or resolve this: "The correct method lies in dialog" (49). While he focuses more on aspects of teaching or pedagogy, the kind of dialogue he refers to can occur in any work of literature and art. The basis for this dialogue is counter-myth, which works to recreate the reality that myth always contrives to present. Likewise, Freire has explored the importance of language with regard to people finding a coherent outlet for their feelings and thoughts: "To exist, humanly, is to name the world, to change it" (69). When the colonized achieve a better sense of awareness about the origins of their duality, this can strengthen their sense of balance regarding this: "As they attain this knowledge of reality through common reflection and action, they discover themselves as its permanent re-creators" (51).

With this in mind, the stories Thomas relates could be viewed as sources of conflict and counter-myth. As they question and challenge certain myths regarding indigenous people, especially those related to cinema. Yet his stories are not only a kind of counter-myth, they are also entertaining, just as they present a sophisticated play of words utilized to add depth to both meaning and reality. For example, toward the beginning of the film, there is a scene where Thomas tells a story about how Victor's father, Arnold Joseph, was a hippie during the sixties:

> Thomas (Voiceover): During the sixties, Arnold Joseph was the perfect hippie, since all the hippies were trying to be Indians anyway. Both because of that, he was always wondering how anybody would recognize when an Indian was trying to make a social statement. But there's proof, you know? Back during the Vietnam War, he was demonstrating against it, and there was this photographer there. He took a picture of Arnold that day it made it onto the wire services and was reprinted in newspapers throughout the country. It even made the cover of *Time* magazine . . . [Later] Arnold got arrested . . . He got two years in Walla Walla. (Alexie 1998, 39)

Upon hearing this story, Victor becomes angry because he feels the story Thomas has told is not completely accurate. When asked if the story is true, Victor responds, "Thomas is full of shit" (39). One of Victor's central issues with Thomas's stories is that he doesn't feel they are truthful or factual accounts of the past. However, Victor doesn't relate what he believes might be a more accurate rendition. At other times, Victor complains that he doesn't understand Thomas's stories.

It could be argued that Thomas's stories tell another kind of truth, just as they strive for a greater sense of meaning beyond the concrete. For example, his story about Arnold Joseph plays with the issue of image directly related to how people dress and wear their hair, which he connects to how American Indian people are often stereotyped by the media, especially by cinema, with regard to their appearance and demeanor. Later, Arnold Joseph has his picture taken at a Vietnam War protest, which makes the cover of *Time* and he is eventually arrested and sent off to the Walla Walla penitentiary for two years.

From yet another perspective, the Arnold Joseph story plays with the concept of indigenous appearance as related to photography and publicity. That is, like a film, a photographic image and its surrounding headlines can convey a powerful message or myth to its viewers. Also, the idea that Arnold Joseph gets incarcerated carries the potential implication that he is, in some way, already imprisoned or confined by his own image, which has been created by his colonizers and is epitomized in American cinema.

Nowhere is this image of the American Indian more prevalent than in western films where the focus is, generally, on the distant past and before the closing of the American frontier. In many respects, *Smoke Signals* and its central characters and the stories Thomas relates could be viewed as a response to those American Indian mythic stereotypes that tend to dominate films of the western genre. Basically, those films have created a certain kind of myth with regard to American Indian people, which over time has come to be viewed as truth, when it is really a form of illusion.

Essentially, this film's unique response via the stories Thomas relates works to recreate and challenge those myths. At the same time, a dialogue is opened where there was none. As a result, *Smoke Signals* via its counter-myth plays off this mythic sense of cinematic illusion with regard to truth. Likewise, it could be said that the truth Victor seeks in others is, in itself, a form of illusion. That is, truth is related and meant to reflect reality: yet isn't there more than one way to interpret this and aren't there greater as well as lesser truths? Also, a thoroughly accurate account of an event, while informative, is made more meaningful when taken to the level of metaphor. It could be argued that only through metaphor can a greater sense of truth be realized. At the same time, there is the discrepancy of the colonial mythic truth that distorts and limits other relevant aspects of historical truth, therefore controlling this sense of truth. Thomas's metaphoric stories contrast with Victor's more concrete sense of reality. Also, his stories reflect differing aspects of his own indigenous duality. In relation to this sense of indigenous duality, American history, especially that of the West, has tended to reflect the colonial side. Simon Ortiz (2000) discusses aspects of his Acoma Pueblo culture's traditional storytelling, which he views as a way to create a deeper sense of meaning with regard to the indigenous historical past:

> Throughout the difficult experience of colonization to the present, Indian women and men have struggled to create meaning of their lives in very definite systematic ways. The ways or methods have been important, but they are important only because of the reason for the struggle. (122)

Also, Ortiz acknowledges this struggle with regard to the indigenous educational experience, which was a central creator of that part of the duality that diminished and oppressed their traditional culture:

> Some would argue that this means that Indian people have succumbed or become educated into a different linguistic system and have forgotten or have been forced to forsake their native selves. This is simply not true. (122)

In relation to this, while the English language is the dominant language of the North American continent, and it has become the language through which its contemporary indigenous people often express their voice, elements of their traditional culture still exert a fairly powerful influence. For example, though Thomas is a fictional character in a film, his stories represent the contemporary indigenous writer's hybrid fusion and the balance of at least two languages and cultures. At the same time, his stories reflect a certain resistance to allowing the colonizing culture to take over or dictate aspects of self that are related to traditional culture.

The supplanting of traditional indigenous language and culture with English was not and is not a completed process. More than likely, it never will be, as this would mean indigenous people would have to relinquish all ties to their traditional culture. However, when a balance can be found where the best of both cultures can be utilized to achieve a certain verbal fluency, this can translate into new innovations regarding narrative. Likewise, Thomas's stories, due to their metaphoric as well as dialogic nature and connection to indigenous traditional oral narrative, strive to recreate the world.

At the same time, it is important to add relevant context to his stories by acknowledging that the early process of eradicating traditional indigenous languages and replacing them with English was an educational strategy. It was also a dehumanizing process, because shame was often used to oppress innocent children. During the boarding school era, indigenous students were often punished for speaking their traditional language. Likewise, education had questionable quality as it was designed not to raise the consciousness and intellect of its students, but to limit them. It was important that they not be educated to the point where they might question the exploitation of their labor, land, rights, or selves. Freire (1994) refers to this kind of oppressive educational indoctrination and one-sided dialogue as a key characteristic of the legacy of cultural invasion:

> The theory of antidialogical action has one last fundamental characteristic: cultural invasion, which like divisive tactics and manipulation also serves the ends of conquest. In this phenomenon, the invaders penetrate the cultural context of another group, in disrespect of the latter's potentialities; they impose their own view of the world upon those they invade and inhibit the creativity of the invaded by curbing their expression. (133)

This antidialogical action represents only the voice of the colonizer and dominates only so long as it diminishes the voice and sense of self-expression of the colonized. For the colonized, the route to fluency in the dominant colonizing language, and culture is not only lined with obstacles, but comes at great sacrifice, which is, generally, the diminishment of traditional language and culture. As a result, a duality is created where the traditional indigenous culture is viewed as less than that of the colonizer's.

At the same time, Freire's ant-idialogical action conforms to Mikhail Bakhtin's concept of the monologic, which he defines in his text *Problems of Dostoevsky's Poetics* as something that strives to dominate verbal interaction and which therefore places limits on avenues of self-expression:

> Monologism, at its extreme, denies the existence outside itself of another consciousness with equal rights and equal responsibilities, another *I* with equal rights (*thou*). With a monologic approach (in its extreme or pure form) *another person* remains wholly and merely an *object* of consciousness, and not another consciousness. Monologue is finalized and deaf to the other's response, does not expect it and does not acknowledge in it any decisive force . . . and therefore to some degree materializes reality . . . [and] pretends to be the *ultimate word*. (Bakhtin 1984, 293)

Monologism epitomizes the manner in which the history of the American West has often been related, just as its antidialogic action strove to create a colonized that didn't answer back or challenge that monologue. In contrast to this and opposed to a single voice of authority, Bakhtin and Freire refer to dialogic or "the very fact of a plurality (in this case a duality) of unmerged consciousnesses" (Bakhtin 1984, 17). In part, Bakhtin is referring to a dialogue that is directed at others and where no voice has authority over others and meaning emerges as more multi-faceted and open. At the same time, with regard to dialogic, Bakhtin defines double-voiced discourse as that which is "directed toward another's discourse, toward someone else's speech" (185).

For example, much of the dialogue in *Smoke Signals*, especially Thomas's stories, could be viewed as a response and therefore a resistance to past American films that have tended to stereotype and to appropriate indigenous people and their culture. When this cinematic monologue and its authority and privilege to stereotype and to appropriate is questioned by the dialogic of a film like *Smoke Signals*, its illusionary power to coerce is diminished and a dialogic discourse is achieved, which also increases meaning and understanding. Most importantly, this dialogic aspires to transcend the monolog of western films, which tend to portray indigenous people in a certain stereotypical and therefore limited fashion.

It is important to note that Freire (1994) does not believe that dialogical action intends to end the dominant culture's dialectic:

> Dialogical cultural action does not have as its aim the disappearance of the permanence-change dialectic . . . it aims, rather, at surmounting the antagonistic contradictions of the social structure, thereby achieving the liberation of human beings. (160)

Otherwise, the dialogic would become the monologic and fall into that same oppressive role as those of their colonizers.

It could be argued that Thomas's stories personify Freire's dialogic as they are an attempt to overcome the colonizer's "antagonistic contradictions" by not allowing it to dominate or to silence important aspects of his traditional culture. Moreover, his essentially dialogic, heteroglossic, double-voiced stories represent the contemporary indigenous writer's fusion of at least two languages and cultures; his opposite counterpart can be found in the character of Victor. As his uncompromising tendency to want only the truth and nothing less places him in a rather oppressive role.

For example, there is a scene from Smoke Signals where Victor and Thomas ride a bus to Phoenix, Arizona. Whereupon they encounter a fellow passenger, a woman who tells Thomas her story about being an alternate on the United States Olympic gymnastic team. Due to a U.S. boycott, she says that she was unable to compete and missed her chance at Olympic gold. Thomas is sympathetic to her story while Victor, in his quest for absolute truth, accuses the woman of lying because as an alternate, she most likely would not have been able to attend the Olympics unless someone else on the team was unable to do so.

Yet Victor's high standard of the truth leaves little room for creative self-expression or any other kind of digression. While the woman exaggerates her gymnastic skills and Olympic moment, it doesn't really matter to Thomas, who was simply making casual conversation with her. Instead, Thomas simply accepts the woman's story for what it is. He empathizes with the woman. Whereas Victor, due to his strong sense of adherence to fact and truth as well as his sense of mistrust, does not. Freire might go so far as to describe Victor's actions toward Thomas and the woman on the bus as oppressive. Ultimately, Victor's excessive reliance on concrete truth, which he applies to everyone he meets, causes him to oppress those that don't fall into line. Yet, for Freire, Victor's need to oppress is understandable:

> The very structure of their thought has been conditioned by the contradictions of the concrete, existential situation by which they were shaped.

> Their ideal is to be men; but for them, to be men is to be oppressors. This is their model of humanity. (27)

Also, Freire might view Victor's zeal for truth as an illusion that he only utilizes to oppress others as he has been. That is, Victor's struggle is evidence of his own internal one-sided duality of self in relation to who he is as an indigenous man. He identifies with aspects of his colonial oppressors and then manifests this behavior by displacing it, rather ironically, onto his concept of truth, in which he gains power via oppressing those who don't conform to his high expectations. Likewise, his high expectations cause most to fall short, which leaves Victor always in the strong role of oppressor and all others as oppressed. Since Victor appears to view the oppressor as strong and the oppressed as weak, his innate survival skills have inspired him to forge a connection to the oppressor.

For example, there is a scene in the film where Victor and Thomas walk across the Arizona desert and Thomas relates his comments on their journey so far:

> I mean, I just want to know if you have any idea how long it's going to take. We've been traveling a long time, enit? I mean, Columbus shows up and we start walking away from that beach, trying to get away, and then Custer moves into the neighborhood, driving down all the property values, and we have to walk some more, then old Harry Truman drops the bomb and we have to keep on walking somewhere, except it's all bright now so we can see exactly where we're going, and then you and I get a beach house on the moon, but old Neil Armstrong shows up and kicks us off into space. And then your mom gets that phone call about your dad being dead, and jeez, he had to be living in Mars, Arizona, and we ain't got no money, no car, no horse, so we have to take the bus, all the way down here. I mean, we ain't got nobody can help us at all. No Superman, no Batman, no Wonder Woman, not even Charles Bronson, man. (beat) Hey, did you ever notice how much your dad looks like Charles Bronson? (Alexie 1998, 68)

Victor ignores most of Thomas's interesting outlook on their situation, and his brief response is directed only at Thomas's very last statement about how Arnold Joseph looks like Charles Bronson. Victor doesn't think that his father looked anything like Bronson. Once again, Victor only focuses on the smallest, most concrete aspect of Thomas's dialogue, just as he almost compulsively negates and strives to oppress his friend's discourse.

However, the rest of Thomas's humorous and metaphoric take on their road trip is actually quite interesting and revealing. He compares his and Victor's journey to that of the larger indigenous colonization experience, which is characterized by displacement of self, language, culture, and land. Thomas links Columbus arriving on the shores of the New World and Custer's fateful stand at the Little Big Horn and to the legacy of indigenous displacement. From there, he links it to the post-war nuclear era, which shaped the American political landscape with far-reaching effect. Then Thomas relates how he and Victor get kicked off the moon, whereupon they find themselves walking across the arid, desolate terrain of the Arizona desert with no money and with no way to save themselves. Yet Thomas believes Arnold Joseph, the man that inspired their journey, is capable of saving them. Thomas subtly implies that Arnold Joseph is a hero waiting to be recognized. However, Victor is not ready to acknowledge the more positive traits of his father.

Another interesting aspect related to character conflict is the distinct difference in personality and temperament between Victor and Thomas. Victor is an angry young man while Thomas is less so, just as his stories annoy Victor to no end. This sense of opposition adds depth to the key conflicts of this film. Karen Jorgensen (1997) discusses Alexie's use of doppelgangers or doubles or twins with regard to how his central characters tend to conflict in his novel *Reservation Blues*:

> In *Reservation Blues*, Alexie makes . . . use of Doppelgangers; they serve as foils to each other, reflecting and elucidating the personality differences of the characters in the novel. (20)

This is quite apparent in *Smoke Signals*, where some of the other personality issues also include the fact that Victor is more concrete but Thomas is not. Victor desires an absolute truth, whereas Thomas is more open to the idea that truth is relative. Like the characters in *Reservation Blues*, Thomas and Victor serve as foils to one another, which works to make the unique proclivities of each man stand out more. This intensifies and adds complexity to the element of conflict that exists between these two characters. For Jorgensen, the conflict and contrast of Alexie's two opposing characters strengthens their individual characteristics:

> Analogous to the implementation of intense chiaroscuro in a work of art, this side-by-side placement of character pairs by virtue of their differences accentuates the unique meanings of either one alone. (1997, 20)

Also, the duality of the two central yet dissimilar characters in *Smoke Signals* presents an elemental aspect of their conflicted relationship, in which it could be argued that one character is more akin to light while the other is to shadow:

> Alexie's use of Doppelgangers, then, provides character doubles with greater texture and definition, much like light and shadow sharpens the dimension in a work of art. (1997, 24)

While Jorgensen is referring to the conflicting complements of Alexie's characters, there is a certain shadowlike quality related to Victor's more oppressive nature, just as light and renewal are more related to Thomas and his stories. Moreover, Victor's concrete outlook on life and his tendency to oppress others if they digress from this shows this shadowy aspect of his personality.

However, Thomas's stories resist being overshadowed by Victor, as they continue to reveal different levels of meaning from seemingly ordinary events. For example, his story about Arlene's magic fry bread is life affirming. According to Thomas, there once was a feast on the rez, but there wasn't enough fry bread to go around:

> Thomas: You see, there was a hundred Indians at that feast and there were only fifty pieces of fry bread. Arlene kept trying to figure out what to do. I mean, it was her magical fry bread that everybody wanted. I mean, you know what happens when there are too many Indians and not enough fry bread. (beat) A fry bread riot. (beat) But Arlene knew what to do . . . You see, Arlene's fry bread was magic. Arlene was magic. (Alexie 1998, 74–75)

Arlene's answer is to split the fry bread in two; that way there would be enough to go around the feast. That way everyone there got to have some of Arlene's magic fry bread. Perhaps her fry bread is magic because it nourishes and heals those that partake of it, just as it symbolizes the importance of traditional indigenous feasts, an important link to traditional culture.

At the conclusion of the film, Victor tosses his father's ashes into the Spokane Falls River and he sends his father's spirit into the water to join the ghosts of salmon. For Victor, this is an act of redemption not only for his father, but also for him. When he pours his father's ashes into this river, he acknowledges the importance of that place and its stories and Victor appears to realize that with regard to his father, truth can be relative and complicated and open to meaning, as is demonstrated by the metaphor inherent in the stories Thomas relates; and as he esoterically foretold, they are saved by Victor's father.

Just as his stories metaphorically play with the concept of truth, just as his stories shed new light on the past, this film is a counter-myth that plays with western cinematic illusions or sets of codes that create the myth that is American Indian. Also, this film is not set in the past, but in the present where its two main indigenous characters must find a way to deal with the legacy of their own colonization. In relation to this, Thomas's stories reflect a contemporary as well as a uniquely indigenous duality of self that shows he has achieved a certain balance, which he tries to communicate to Victor, who instead wants a truth he thinks is based on fact, but is actually only an illusion and a defensive tool that allows him to coerce others so that he doesn't have to deal with or confront his own issues. Yet, eventually, Victor does face his own issues when he honors his father by throwing his ashes into the river.

Ultimately, as Freire (1994) notes and as the stories that Thomas relates reveal, words have two components, "reflection and action" (68). For Freire, when a language is utilized oppressively and restricts access to its center of meaning, the people negatively affected exist powerlessly on the periphery of the language of their colonizers:

> But while to say the true word—which is work, which is praxis—is to transform the world, saying that word is not the privilege of some few persons, but the right of everyone. Consequently, no one can say a true word alone—nor can she say it for another, in a prescriptive act which robs others of their words. (69)

The stories Thomas relates don't gain strength or meaning from oppression. Instead, they create a dialogue that challenges the monologue of his colonizers, but does not aspire to silence it. Likewise, Freire (1994) believes that, ultimately, dialogue must answer oppression with love and hope, which must be reclaimed by the colonized, or for that matter anyone disenfranchised from the power of the dominant language:

> Nor yet can dialogue exist without hope. Hope is rooted in men's incompletion, from which they move out in constant search—a search which can be carried out only in communion with others. (72)

In relation to this, Thomas's stories reclaim just as they impart love, hope, humor, and survival. Though his stories drift from concrete fact, they find a greater sense of metaphoric truth that reflects his people's experience on the American West, a place composed of many stories, some true, some not. In a way, Thomas is also a messenger whose stories mirror a struggle over words and consciousness. At the same time, his stories strive to recreate and reconfirm a reality not diminished by or beholden to the myth of his colonizers, which for Ortiz is of great import:

> This perception and meaningfulness has to happen; otherwise, the hard experience of the Euroamerican colonization of the lands and people of the Western Hemisphere would be driven into the dark recesses of the indige-

> nous mind and psyche. And this kind of repression is always a poison and detriment to creative growth and expression. (2000, 121–22)

In the end, the stories Thomas relates reflect conflicts that are unique to contemporary American Indians, but his stories also include universal themes such as desire, crisis, and complication, and yet, they are also in every sense of the word, a counter-myth. They are also stories that are open to meaning, which means they have the potential to liberate and in doing so, they recreate myth and reaffirm life. As Thomas's grandmother Builds-the-Fire says to him, "Tell me what happened Thomas. Tell me what's going to happen" (146).

Alaska Native Literature: An Updated Introduction

James Ruppert

In this essay, James Ruppert reviews the publication of Alaska Native literature, exploring common themes and structures as they reveal a changing response to colonialism and concern with identity and continuance. Alaska Native literature and authors are not commonly known outside of Alaska; Ruppert's essay provides a concise overview for potential new audiences. An advocate of Alaska Native literature throughout his career, Ruppert is a professor of English and Alaska Native studies at the University of Alaska, Fairbanks. He is the author of Mediation in Contemporary Native American Fiction *and editor of* Nothing but the Truth: An Anthology of Native American Literature *and* Our Voices: Native Stories of Alaska and the Yukon. *He is a past president of the Society for the Study of American Indian literatures and a frequent contributor to national journals on the subject of Native oral and written literature.*

When I wrote the introduction to Joe Bruchac's *Raven Tells Stories: An Anthology of Alaskan Native Writing* years ago, I kept wishing that there was an outline or survey of Alaska Native literature to help orient me. However, I found none and even today I am unaware of any such review. This is terribly unfortunate because I am sure there are plenty of people who know more than I do about the subject. But if I were to write that introduction today, I would include something of the history of Alaska Native literature to complement my generalizations about the literature and the writers in that anthology. I offer the following outline with the hopes that others will chink the gaps and finish the logs of this rough edifice. I do not claim to be definitive; rather, I see my comments as a starting point for those interested in an account of Native literature in Alaska. I intend to limit my remarks to Native writers who have authored books in the *belles lettres* tradition. Though I have the greatest respect for Native elders who have told their stories and life histories to non-Native editors and compilers, their works are the subject of another piece.

Certainly there are many Native writers I will not be able to mention who have published works of literature, but not yet in book form.

As we start this history of the publication of Alaska Native literature, it is clear that oral tradition was the source of much inspiration. As early as the 1950s, Emily Ivanoff Brown (Ticasuk) had collected legends and family histories from northwest Alaska and published them locally. In 1981, larger publishers brought out *The Roots of Ticasuk: An Eskimo Woman's Family Story* and *The Longest Story Ever Told: Qayaq, the Magical Man*. Later she published *Tales of Ticasuk: Eskimo Legends and Stories* (1987). Ticasuk was a much beloved writer and educator whose work inspired other Native writers.

Also in the 1950s Lela Oman was also collecting oral narratives, and in 1956, the Nome Publishing Company printed her collection *Eskimo Legends: Authentic Tales of Suspense and Excitement*. She continued to work with oral narratives, and in 1975, it was republished by Alaska Methodist University Press. In 1967 she published *The Ghost of Kingikty and other Eskimo Legends* and in 1995, *The Epic of Qayaq: The Longest Story Ever Told by My People* was issued. Both women helped demonstrate that there was an interest in Alaska Native voices and that there was a place for successful authors.

Alaska Native writing and publication grew as the Native American Renaissance began to influence writers here. Public visits and workshops by Native American writers such as Joy Harjo, Geary Hobson, Wendy Rose, Joe Bruchac, and others encouraged Alaska Native writers. Leslie Silko even briefly lived in Ketchikan. In the 1970s, as the nation's interest grew in all things Indian, publishers, editors, and writers sensed a rising interest in the voices of Alaska Natives. In 1971, the Indian Historian Press published Joseph Senungetuk's *Give or Take a Century: An Eskimo Chronicle*. Senungetuk's personal memoir of life in the Nome area resonates with larger questions of historical witness and cross-cultural contemplations.

In 1974 Fred Bigjim collected a series of letters he wrote for the *Tundra Times* on the ANCSA, and published them in a book, *Letters to Howard: An Interpretation of the Alaska Native Land Claims*. Bigjim's fusion of humor and political commentary placed him squarely in the tradition of American dialectical humor. Later in 1983 Fred Bigjim began a long and fruitful publishing career with the publication of a book of poems titled *Sinrock*. Much of his poetry contrasts traditional life with contemporary experience. He broadened his range with *We Talk You Yawn: A Discourse on Education in Alaska* (1985), and returned to more literary forms with *Walk the Wind* (1988), *Plants: A Novel* (2000), and *Echoes from the Tundra* (2000).

The 1980s saw much interest in writing coming from southeast Alaska. Andrew Hope began editing and publishing, and his volume *Raven's Bones* came out in 1982. Later, his Raven's Bones Press published a powerful book of poems by Robert Davis titled *Soulcatcher* (1986). Davis merged Tlingit life and myth with poems about change and growth. Moreover in 1982, the field of Alaska Native writing grew when Sister Goodwin published a book of poems with I. Reed Press in California.

Nora Marks Dauenhauer has worked for years with her husband Richard to collect, document, and archive Tlingit narratives and language. Her publications are many, but she has authored two literary books. A book of poetry, *The Droning Shaman*, came out in 1988 and in 2000 she published *Life Woven with Song*, a collection of poetry, fiction, and plays that present her cultural heritage and unique vision.

Also from the Southeast came one of the few novels published by a Native writer. *When Raven Cries: A Novel* (1994) was written by Kadashan, later republished in 1997.

Mary Tallmountain was one of the best-known Alaska Native writers. She lived in Nulato as a child before she was adopted and spent most of her life outside Alaska. In 1981, she published *There Is No Word for Goodbye*. This began the publication of a series of chapbooks that centered on her connections to Alaska: *Green March Moons* (1987), *Continuum: Poems* (1988), *Matrilineal Cycle* (1990), *The Light on the Tent Wall: A Bridging* (1990), *A Quick Brush of Wings* (1991), and *Listen to the Night: Poems for the Animal Spirits of Mother Earth* (1995). Her papers are archived at UAF. That same area of Alaska is given narrative treatment in a book that Poldine Carlo wrote about her experience in interior Alaska. *Nulato: An Indian Life on the Yukon* was published in 1978.

Interestingly, in one of the few works of fiction written in an Alaska Native language, Anna Jacobson published a novel in Yup'ik, *Elnqug* (1990).

Perhaps the best-known contemporary Alaska Native writer is Velma Wallis. Her first two books were oral narratives that she heard from her mother in which she fleshed out the characters to create a form of fiction somewhere between documenting oral narratives and Western notions of fiction. *Two Old Women: An Alaska Legend of Betrayal, Courage and Survival* (1993) was an international hit. She followed with *Bird Girl and the Man Who Followed the Sun: An Athabascan Legend from Alaska* (1996) and *Raising Ourselves: A Gwich'in Coming of Age Story from the Yukon River* (2002).

The new century promises a growth in Native writing. In 2000 Jan Harper-Haines brought out *Cold River Spirits: The Legacy of an Athabaskan-Irish Family from Alaska's Yukon River*. The well-known writer, actor, and activist Diane Benson published a book of poetry, *Witness to the Stolen* (2002). And recently, Loretta Outwater Cox reworked stories she heard into a fictional format and published two books, *A Winter Walk: A Century-Old Survival Story from the Arctic*

(2003) and *The Storytellers' Club: The Picture Writing Women of the Arctic* (2005). While it is clear that oral tradition will continue to inspire Native writers, some are striking out into new genres. Mary Tony, under the pen name Aurora Hardy, published a thriller titled *Terror at Black Rapids* (2004).

There have been a few anthologies that surveyed the field. In 1986, the *Alaska Quarterly Review* published a special issue titled *Alaska Native Writers, Storytellers and Orators*. It was later expanded and reprinted in 1999. Joe Bruchac from Greenfield Review Press collected material from Alaska Native writers for his 1991 anthology, *Raven Tells Stories: A Collection of Alaska Native Writing*. Later that decade Susan Andrews and John Creed from Kotzebue published a collection of student writing called *Authentic Alaska: Voices of Its Native Writers* (1998).

There are many Alaska Native writers I have not mentioned here. Many have written autobiographical, historical, or scholarly works. Many writers have published literature in periodicals and newspapers. I wish I could list them all. The literary arts are thriving in Alaska and I am sure that in the future you will see many more books on the shelves. Alaska Native writers are vital contributors to Alaska's literary future.

V

Ravenstales

This final section of the volume is titled "Ravenstales," which is a play on words. *Ravenstail* is a style of weaving found in southeastern Alaska and parts of northern British Columbia. It is well known for its distinctive black-and-white geometric design. Of course, Raven, the hero and trickster of virtually all indigenous groups in Alaska, is notorious for both his remarkable feats, including his insatiable curiosity (which always seems to get him in some kind of trouble), and his longtime association with people.

Throughout *The Alaska Native Reader*, categorizing the selections has not always been easy, though most of them, in subject and style, accord largely with the themes by which this book is organized. Here in part V we encounter works that are disparate—from each other, and often from other selections in this reader: an interview, selections of poetry, a recipe, a description of life in the Arctic, and a personal narrative that provides insight into life in Alaska.

The poem by C. G. Williams reflects on the all-important four-wheeler because of its importance in rural Alaskan villages, where cars are not practical, given the absence of roads. Four-wheelers or all-terrain vehicles are the norm for the more than two hundred villages in Alaska.

I thought it important to include recipes for delicious Alaskan Native foods. In the villages in Alaska, hunting and gathering from the land still supply the greater part of the diet. There are so many different kinds of foods—meats, birds, eggs, greens, berries, fish, and small game—that it would take far more space than we have to offer a truly representative range of recipes. I have chosen to include one recipe from Daisy Demientieff, a wonderful cook, which describes how she prepares moose meat.

Personal narratives provide a unique voice and perspective for this volume. Eleanor Hadden writes about her dedication to education and being a "non-traditional" student, that is, one older than twenty-five, with a husband, children, and extended family as well as community responsibilities. Denise Wartes's essay on how she learned to live in a remote Arctic village and adapt to a lifestyle in which she was not raised provides a compelling view for people who live in the "lower 48" (states), which do not present the same challenges as Alaska in terms of extreme climate, distance, and lack of roads.

Richard and Nora Marks Dauenhauer are well known in Alaska for their work in education and language revitalization and their publications on history and oral narrative. They are also poets. Included here are several previously unpublished poems by both Nora and Richard, illustrating their creativity, humor, and skill.

All in all, part V of *The Alaska Native Reader* has everything that Raven would approve of—humor, food, poetry, and real-life stories.

Poems

Nora Marks Dauenhauer (Tlingit) and Richard Dauenhauer

Nora and Richard Dauenhauer are well-known linguists, writers, and poets who have devoted much of their life's work to researching and publishing books on Tlingit language and oral literature. Nora Marks Dauenhauer is Tlingit and her husband Richard was ceremonially adopted into a Tlingit clan. Their joint publications include Haa Shuka, Our Ancestors: Tlingit Oral Narratives (1987); Haa Tuwunaagu Yis, for Healing our Spirit: Tlingit Oratory (1990); Haa Kusteeyi, Our Culture: Tlingit Life Stories (1994); *and two forthcoming volumes: one on the Russian-Tlingit battles of Sitka of 1802 and 1804, and one of Tlingit Raven stories. They have also coauthored many essays and books for Tlingit language instruction. Richard is a former poet laureate of Alaska (1981–88), and Nora is a widely anthologized poet, traditional singer, and dancer. Nora's books include* The Droning Shaman (1988) *and* Life Woven with Song (2000). *Richard's poetry publications include* Glacier Bay Concerto (1980), Frames of Reference (1987), Phenologies (1988), *and numerous journal publications and translations of German, Russian, Finnish, and classical Greek poetry.*[1]

Poems by Nora Marks Dauenhauer

GATHERING AT WILLIAM TYSON ELEMENTARY SCHOOL, ANCHORAGE, ALASKA

At the entrance: three figures dancing,
happy,
hands raised, as if laughing—
drumming,
        singing,
                dancing.

Inside, on the wall, in Northern Lights:
dancing cranes, killer whales, caribou, deer, beaver—
happy hands
stream across a wall.

Below, a chair of owl,
of bear and wolf,
feasting on vertebrae.

Above a hallway entrance, branching off:
a head protruding—Raven
dances with the sun in his beak.

Above the books,
a super-imposing Eagle
dances with salmon in its clutches,
getting away, too.

Children laughing,
          streaming voices,
                    dancing into classrooms.

FOR MY GRANDDAUGHTER AMELIA CHEERLEADING AT HOMECOMING '98, JUNEAU-DOUGLAS HIGH SCHOOL

Tears of pride fill
my eyes to the brim
shaping you into
a painting by Picasso,
gem-like, diamond-cut,
into one of his
sultry beauties.

COLE SEWING

My great-grandson Cole, age 6,
wants to make a robe.
I prepare
a sewing kit for him,
telling him, "You treat your needle

like it's the only needle in the world."
He's so excited,
I wonder if he heard me.
I put a spool of thread
in the kit,
a piece of felt
to practice sewing on.
Some safety pins,
some common pins,
a piece of chalk,
a thimble,
a measuring tape,
some beeswax:
all of my hopes went into the kit
with the sewing equipment.

GABE'S BIRTHDAY

Gabe, three today,
runs around
lowest to the floor.
It seems as if
he's carried above the guests,
his great-grandma Nora,
Grandma Le.
His gifts are piled
three times as high
as he is.

REPATRIATION

—for John Feller

A Killer Whale, you bend,
entering the Chilkat robe.
The hands of holders tremble.
The robe ripples
with its multiplying pods
of killer whales.
You dance

to an ancestor's song.
The sea of killer whales
splashes on your back.
We can smell the sea
laced with iodine on beaches
at low tide.

Poems by Richard Dauenhauer

Group One: Some Family Poems

MOTHER'S DAY 1988

—*for Andrea, at Twelve*

Rise and shake your skirts
to the buttercups, yellow as polished gold.
—William Carlos Williams ("The Words, the words, the words," *Collected Later Poems*)

In sunlight, twirling, Andrea
observes her hemline
flowing in the gentle breeze
and from the motion of her own
body. Her skirt becomes
a field of summer flowers
responding to command.

JAMIE, RACING OFF

Granddaughter Jamie, now
fourteen, downhill racer
in braces, embracing

speed, off to Statewide
and next the Western
Regionals, all aglow.

Yesterday in France
in the Winter Olympics
her older teammate

Hilary Lindh took home
a silver medal
in the women's downhill

and Juneau goes crazy
with welcome home posters.
I super-impose

our flashbacks of Jamie—
color slides and prints: first
downhill on the bunny

slope in gold and silver
winter sunlight; first
ski-steps, cross-country

with Gramma; very first
steps across our living-
room, the rug once stained

with brown-spot, diaper leak.
But now, with Jamie three
weeks shy of fifteen, now

in love with speeds that none
of us have ever reached—
it's me scared crapless.

SOCCER SQUAD

—for our Granddaughters:
Andi, Rissa, Jamie, Teresa

Like storm winds
off the glacier
that looms above the soccer field:

the Ransom and Florendo girls
charging downfield,
eyes and cleats
gleaming in the sun.

Reflection of this image:
how wonderful for them
to be a teenage girl;

how wonderful for me
not to be
a teenage boy or goalie.

BREAKFAST AT GRANDMA NORA'S

—for Cole, Gabe, Mikaela, Grandma Nora, & Grandma Le

Cole (age 6) is into
rocks and drawing Zuni
symbols. He demonstrates
on paper, shows his crystal,
and tells about his rock
collection. Grandma Nora
shows her rocks to Cole.
Every fossil, every
pebble has a story:
Alsek River rafting,
Copper River fishing,
jars of Anchorage
volcanic ash. They trade.

Gabe (age 4) is con-
trary today. He spec-
ulates on pancakes:
"I'm gonna feed my butt
and poop out my mouth!"

Grandma Nora expounds
on coprolites, the poop
that turns to stone. What a
concept! Fossil doo-doo!
The final word on turds.

BASED, OF COURSE, ON HEARSAY

(Based, of course, on hearsay—
the folk tradition now
illegal—), "This is how
we ate them, once a year."

Take only from a nest
with one or two eggs.
If there are three eggs, there's
an embryo inside.

Appreciate the weathered,
speckled-granite look
of the rock-like egg.

Hard boil gently,
eat when warm.

Crack, peel, cut.
Lightly salt and pepper,
drizzle seal oil
on the orange yolk to taste.

Savor the faintly fishy taste
from seagulls feasting
on the herring run.

Group Two. Congestive Heart Failure: Letting Go

—in memory of Leonard Dauenhauer (April 2, 1914–February 7, 2000)

DREAM POEM: TWO BY TWO

In my father's campground there are many tentsites;
I go to prepare a place for you.
—John 14:2 (Camper's Translation)

I often dream
of Follensby,
family camping
from childhood on.

I saw you there
again with Mom,
together now
by fireside.

From dreams so warm,
we often wake
to emptiness.
But this was warm

and comforting.
I woke and knew:
you wake to grief
with every day,

a widower
for eighteen years.
It's time to go,
ok to go.

The camp is made,
the fire set,
awaiting spark;
at fireside

your waiting chair.
The tent is up.
The sleeping bag
is warm.

SPRING SKIING

In Memory of Leonard Dauenhauer (April 2, 1914–February 7, 2000)
—for Tom

Two weeks beyond your death, we ski
cross-country, as you ran in youth
to victory. In brilliant mid-
day February sun, I pause
to meditate on snow as shroud
of winter death in spring. The sun-
down crust incises boots and traps
the ski tips, and induces
fall—a season of entrapment and
release; of death, yet lingering
in life and memory, the time
for balancing of joy and grief
about to slip to timelessness
through lenten disciplines of dark
to disorienting paschal
brilliance, with no night. But now
the tease of gliding for the last

time in sunlight, survivors
traversing turns of memory
and faith, knowing home is downslope,
through shade, still navigating far
upslope from Pentecostal green.

Group Three: Harvesting

SEPTEMBER MORNING FOG

September morning fog, the foraging
cheeps of chickadees, the splash and clatter
of anchor chains of unseen fishing boats.
Closer in the garden: clearing now.
Gray currants, each berry like a gem
strung on a naked vine. The other
berries memories of summer: raspberries,
strawberries, blueberries, salmon berries;
cherry shrubs too immature to bear.
Birds foraging. The rhubarb going dormant.
But in the garden heart, potato plants
still grow, each yellow, shriveled stalk leading
to hopes of gold below the fog and earth.

THE TIDES FORECASTING WINTER

The world becomes a harp
that gives forth no sound
but in response to the finger of God.
—St. Nicholas of Zicha

The tides forecasting winter touch
far in- and up-land now, almost
reaching fallow autumn gardens,
the intertidal shallows masked
with the face of the deep: the last
October weekend, when we play
with time in northern latitudes,
adjusting human measurement
to realities of nature.

Fall migration. Rainy, late
October afternoon. I do
my yard work to a varied thrush
and Oregon junco, working
through the yard and garden, blending
with decay in camouflage of
orange, brown, and black, sorting
through what's left beyond the brilliant
bloom of summer, ostentatious
fruits of warmth and sunlight gone
to seed again, as kernels
of the heat and light, preparing,
adjusting to the growing dark.

DIGGING SPUDS

> *May you live to see your children's children*
> *like olive shoots around your table.*
> —Orthodox Wedding Prayer

> *Nothing gold can stay.*
> —Robert Frost

This year, I hoard it for myself,
avoiding all the family kids.
In seasons past I always
coached the growing generations
on harvesting potatoes. Now
greedy for the solitude
to meditate on memories
of those who gave us seed,
too feeble for the energy
of any kids, I dig alone
in guilt, and meditate on life,
somewhere in the moment now
between inheritors and donors,
the time we need to be alone
with our dead, the treasure trove
of life. Below the peaks of mountains
honey-combed with gold mines, I turn
the earth, and gold unfolds by fork-

fulls, nuggets shining in dark soil,
indigenous potatoes, gift
of gardeners now gone, nothing
standard here in shape or size
or uniformity of store-
bought seeds like Yukon Gold or Yellow
Finn; another crop gone feral,
returning to Alaskan earth,
responding in the humid dark
to midnight sun on leaves. If nothing
gold can stay, it can at least
return, returning gold each fall.

HARVESTING POTATOES

Nondescript: the autumn
of our lives. A kinglet?
Basking in the spruce top
in fading sun? Juncos
flashier, more ener-
getic. In my rusty
garden chair I rest from
harvesting potatoes
this crisp September day,
savoring the sunlight
after weeks of steady,
unrelenting rain—com-
munion of sorts, in turned
potato beds, all those
upright stems of summer
fallen of their age
and weight. Our faith is gold,
of bounty more obscure
beneath the waiting earth.

POTATOES, 2003

On one of few non-rainy afternoons
in waning, low-angle October sun
I dig more equisetum roots than root
crops, potato yield this year the smallest
ever. Always harvesting the season
of atonement, meditating each
pitch-fork turn, with less and less to show:
is this the autumn of my life, body
weakening, most hopes of vernal seed
now manifest, for better or for worse?
I pace myself, the autumn garden still
full of life designed for emptying.
I work along each row, curious, plant
after plant. What will the earth disclose?

Note

1. Editor's note: In a communication about contributing to this volume, Richard and Nora wrote: "When we were invited to contribute to the present collection, we found ourselves 'written out' on essays. This is still the case. Having published a number of essays in recent years, we have nothing new to say or add at the moment. We offer here, instead, some poetry, a genre we have both sadly neglected in our recent years of writing essays on Tlingit culture and language revitalization, and working to publish Tlingit folklore texts and a range of instructional and reference materials for Tlingit language. For the last twenty years, 1986 through 2006, we have published something every year, either singly or collaboratively: poetry, articles, and books."

Poem

C. G. Williams (Tlingit)

C. G. Williams (Tlingit) lives in Anchorage, Alaska, and is a creative writer and arts administrator.

4 WHEELERS

Women and girls Ride 4 wheelers
With the cocky confidence of a cowboy
Leaping off their mounts
Drawing them to an abrupt halt
Sometimes there is a baby at the back of their coat
Sometimes a brother and sister
And there are the days of freedom where they ride
With nothing to impinge
Nothing to shake that deft governance at the helm of a 4 wheeler

Living in the Arctic

Denise Cross Wartes

Denise Wartes is currently the program coordinator of the Rural Alaska Honors Institute or RAHI at the University of Alaska, Fairbanks. Denise is originally from the Upper Peninsula of Michigan. As a newlywed, she moved with her husband, Mark, to the edge of the Arctic Ocean, where they lived and raised a family. Her essay describes her life in the remote Arctic village where there were no grocery stores—food came once a year via plane. Eventually Denise, Mark, and family moved south to Fairbanks where Denise has worked with RAHI since 1989.

The oldest of nine children, I grew up in the Upper Peninsula of Michigan in a small town called DeTour Village, sixty miles from the Bay Mills Indian Reservation. The day after I married Mark, we moved to the edge of the Arctic Ocean where we lived for the next several years on a homestead in the Colville River Delta. Mark had grown up in Barrow and along the Arctic coast, the son of a missionary pastor pilot, and considers the Arctic to be home. I joined him there and together we've had many adventures since. While we were living in the Arctic, our two children were born. We were very fortunate to live on Alaska's North Slope prior to the development of the oil fields, as the lifestyle we experienced really doesn't, and can't, exist anymore. We lived on a remote homestead, forty miles west of Prudhoe Bay or 180 miles east of Barrow.

Our groceries arrived on a C-46 plane once a year in the fall. Imagine the grocery list I had! What a learning experience. Mark shared with me the grocery list he had developed over the years, but I learned to do my own food ordering, expanding it considerably, as a bachelor's idea of meal planning left room for improvement. If we started to run out of something, we slowed down on that particular item or switched to a similar one that could be substituted, or just went without. Then next year we looked at what we'd run out of and decided what changes needed to be made. We mailed our grocery list to a grocery store in Fairbanks that dealt with supplying people in bush areas. They, in turn, would take our list, knowing that if they didn't have a particular item, they should substitute something close to it, as there wasn't any way to contact us and ask what we'd prefer. Several grocery carts and many, many cases of food and hundreds of pounds of flour and sugar later, they boxed up all of our food, put it on pallets, and transported it to the Fairbanks charter airline company that was going to transport our food north to us.

Now you may wonder how we found out when our food and supplies were to be shipped to us, so that we would have the runway all ready, smoothed out, and packed down, with lighted flare pots along its length. In Alaska, commercial radio stations send out twice daily messages to people living in the bush, messages from families stating that they'd arrived safely in town, that Grandma Susie says hello, that new baby Jonathan was born, that the tundra tires we'd ordered would be shipped by mail next week. We eagerly sat by our radio awaiting word of the long anticipated flight, sometimes to be disappointed when the weather was poor and they had to turn back because of fog or wind over the Brooks Range. Then came the day that we heard the drone of the C-46 in the distance. Everyone grabbed their parka and mukluks, jumped on their snow machines, and quickly drove to the runway so that the flare pots could be lit alerting the pilot of the runway.

Then what does one do with all these supplies? This day was better than Christmas and birthday wrapped together. Imagine, several trips with the snow machine sledding supplies up to the house, where I would unload the sled, separating out the perishable supplies and bringing them into the house, along with checking the unmarked boxes that may contain catsup or mayonnaise or some other item that couldn't be frozen. Then there was the mail, such a welcome event. Over the next several weeks we would open more mail each day, read magazines or newspapers with what might seem to be "stale" news, but to us was news that had happened the day before. In addition, the Alaska public library had a system where they send out ten books each month to us, keeping track of the books they'd sent, so there would be no duplication. When we finished reading the books, we would close up the mailbag and send it back to them on the next mail flight, usually every three to four months.

Each spring we went out onto the ice pack, living there for a couple weeks at a time, hunting seals for our dog team and using the skins for spring clothing. Each summer we traveled the Colville delta hunting and fishing. We stacked and gathered driftwood for winter, which we would later retrieve with snow machines, as we heated our home by driftwood. The Arctic Slope has no trees, so we gathered the driftwood that collected along the shores in the Harrison Bay area, wood that had drifted down the Mackenzie River in Canada and floated over into Harrison Bay, where our island juts out.

Come fall we would travel inland hunting ducks and geese, moose, caribou, and Dall sheep, preparing ourselves for the winter. From late September to mid-November we fished for Kaktak (Arctic Cisco) with nets under the river ice, fishing for our personal use and food for our dog team. We also sold these fish to the stores in Barrow and Fairbanks. The sale of these fish helped offset the cost of the C-46 flight that was chartered each fall, bringing in our year's supply of food, and things such as building materials, propane, and mail. Electricity was a luxury we used on an occasional basis from a small generator. Water came from a lake, snow, or ice (depending on the season).

Imagine my washday! Mark would spend the day before washday by chopping a hole in the lake ice, a task of several hours, dipping five gallon cans into the water, and transporting these cans of water to the house by snow machine and sled, where I would transfer the water to large clean garbage cans to bring the icy water up to room temperature. The next day we would put as much water as we could into large cooking pots or containers and heating them on our barrel stove and wood burning kitchen range. Then we added this hot water to the cold water placed in our washer, so as to have a warm water wash. Next came the drying of all these wet clothes, wet laundry hung everywhere, especially with two babies in diapers. In between major washdays I washed clothes by hand in a big washtub.

The Iñupiaq people of the Colville River are close friends and family. We traveled with them, helped them, and they helped us. We shared their lives. From them, we learned many lessons, such as how to sew skin clothing. Mark was fortunate to be tutored by two respected Iñupiaq elders, George Woods and Samuel Simmonds. The lessons he learned continue to shape his life today. This is also true of me.

The rapid expanse of oil development was fast changing our subsistence lifestyle. We moved to Fairbanks and entered our children in public school. While raising our family and working, I continued to take the occasional course, eventually attaining my certified professional secretarial rating. This certification transferred into university credits on my transcript, and I continued, frequently one course a semester, occasionally three courses, to work for a college degree. In 1996 I earned an associate's degree and in 2001 an interdisciplinary bachelor's degree in Alaska Native studies and business at UAF; in 2007 I earned a master's degree in cross-cultural studies at UAF.

I have a lifelong interest in working with Native peoples, personally and professionally. Presently I work at UAF with the Rural Alaska Honors Institute (RAHI), a college prep bridge program for rural and Alaska Native high school students. In the past I have worked with UAF Alaska Native studies, the Festival of Native Arts, and the Elder-in-Residence class. In addition, I taught a course in federal Indian law at UAF and have served as an unofficial teaching assistant for a number of courses in Alaska Native education, comparative

Aboriginal rights and policy, Native self-government, and Alaska Native Elder-in-Residence.

When growing up in northern Michigan, living on the Arctic Coast, and now in Fairbanks, I have always interacted well with people of differing ages, races, cultures, and philosophies. I have been and continue to be active within the Native community of Alaska, especially through my work with the university. I am fortunate enough to travel occasionally to Native villages, many Alaska Federation of Natives conventions, and Bilingual Multi-Cultural Conferences, to have participated in, assisted with, and attended the Festival of Native Arts for the last eighteen-plus years. I have assisted with the World Eskimo Indian Olympics, along with numerous other events such as potlucks at UAF and throughout the community, such as the Presbyterian Church Eskimo Thanksgiving feasts, Christmas feasts, the Christmas Nativity program, and many funeral potlatches. I continue to work with the Native people, especially the Iñupiaq people of the Arctic, because of my family's long history of friendship with them. They frequently call on me or Mark to assist them with filling out governmental forms, picking up freight at an airline and transporting it to a family member who doesn't have transportation, or telling a family member that someone is ill or in the hospital. In return, they share Native food such as muktuk, caribou, moose, berries—as an expression of thanks and with the knowledge that we appreciate so much what they share with us.

Tunnel? . . . What Tunnel?

Eleanor Hadden *(Tlingit, Haida, Tsimshian)*

Eleanor Hadden currently lives in Anchorage, Alaska. She is a graduate student at the University of Alaska, Anchorage. She has worked with Professor Jeane Breinig on Haida language projects and is currently doing her own research on language. Her essay addresses her thoughts on being an Alaska Native graduate student.

University students have various categories of challenges while attending college. There are the normal challenges of being far from home and family, budgeting time for studying and classes, and financial obligations. Then, there is another category of challenges: the non-traditional student vs. the traditional student. University students vary in age; some are a "traditional" student, the eighteen- to twenty-five-year-old; others are the non-traditional student, an individual who has had life experience before graduating from college.

I am currently a non-traditional Tlingit, Haida, Tsimshian student. I began my academic career as a traditional student and eventually graduated with a B.A. in anthropology as a non-traditional student. As a traditional student, I attended a university for two years and then married, had children, and traveled with my air force husband for an around-the-world life experience. We returned to Alaska, where I had planned on either returning to the work force or returning to college, as I had been a stay-at-home mom. We decided I was to return to college and finish my degree that had been started years before, thus fulfilling a promise given to my parents many years earlier. I had promised my parents if they gave approval for my marriage that I would finish my college education. So, to fulfill a promise given, I returned to college.

Family responsibilities are strong in our family. My grandmother guided my mother through words to "take care of each other." This meant to take care of her brothers, her mother, and children as well as "take care of each other." This concept of caring for our parents, children, and grandchildren means to support, take care of, nurse, watch over, protect, and nurture them when needed. This family responsibility challenges my time needed for graduate work. A mother's primary responsibility is family; however, in graduate school, a student's first responsibility is research and writing. In a family emergency, the first response is to take care of the family member who needs care without regard to graduate work.

Another of my challenges was balancing my life as a student, wife, mother, and daughter. Little was I to know fourteen years ago, when I told my family about returning to school, what challenges would occur in our household. The first household challenge was chores: who would do the chores, and when the chores would be done, etc. These changes would only be a source of concern to the family when I was studying for finals, or researching for or writing my papers. These household challenges were some of the compromises I made while attending college. This challenge was easier than the ones that would follow.

My university challenges were what class should I take as well as figuring out how to apply and register for the classes, finding a parking space, finding buildings where classes are held, figuring out how the library works, taking notes and studying, similar to and the same as challenges for traditional students. Since it had been about fourteen years since I had taken a class, I thought I should take something "easy." The anthropology department has a class, "Alaska Natives," that sounded "easy." Since I am Tlingit, Haida, and Tsimshian, I figured I should know something about Alaska Natives. The class was informative and I thought I was doing well as a returning non-traditional student, until the professor gave us our first test. One question asked, "What is it called when the uncle raises the nephew?" When professors give you a test, they usually do not give you the answer in the question, so I knew the answer to the question was not "the uncle raises the nephew." The answer was revealed when the professor returned the test. This question and answer was my first realization that there are anthropological terms for what I do in my life and a discipline that encourages me to ask questions I have always contemplated. This was a source of intrigue and I wanted to know more about anthropology, so I pursued a degree in anthropology.

My challenge of being a mother was continuing to support my children in their education and after-school activities so I decided to return to college as a part-time student. As a part-time student, I graduated after six years of attending the university. In those six years, my oldest child graduated from high school and left for his post–high school education. The month I graduated from college, my youngest child graduated from high school, and my husband and I celebrated our twenty-fifth wedding anniversary and I fulfilled a promise given to my parents twenty-five years earlier. I just was not specific as to the exact year of when I would fulfill the promise.

When I graduated with a B.A. in anthropology, there was no graduate program in Anchorage and I did not want to relocate to another city or state. Two years later, the university began a new master's in anthropology program so I applied. I did not realize the two-year hiatus was my "calm before the storm" period.

Students in a graduate program of anthropology have to analyze how people live their lives and then interpret that analysis in writing. I made that adjustment to analytic thought, and just when I was entrenched in my graduate work, more challenges surfaced in the manner of family medical emergencies.

Family emergencies create additional challenges to graduate studies. The first emergency was a minor car accident during my final and pro-seminar presentation. I had to present my semester's project and final paper with whiplash, pain medication, and muscle relaxants. It was not my best but that's the way of graduate school. My next challenge was a year's leave of absence to care for my mother, who was to have major surgery, and I needed to be with dad during this stressful time. Little did I know, not only would I help dad through mom's recovery from foot reconstruction and fusion of her ankle, but I would also be with mom while dad was hospitalized in Ketchikan and Seattle. I was then with my mom when my dad had his surgery and while he was in an intensive care unit (ICU) in Ketchikan and then meeting her in Seattle after dad was medevaced there. After his weeklong stay in ICU in Seattle, he had an additional two weeks in a rehabilitation facility in Seattle. My thoughts were not in my graduate studies.

I was able to return to Anchorage and do some preliminary work on gathering information for my bibliography so I could study for my graduate program comprehensive exams. I had the next step completed, the date set to take my exams, so I took a day off to relax. My husband and I decided to go berry picking as a relaxing method to prepare me for my examination. So much for relaxing. I fell and dislocated my right elbow. This next "adventure" in my life took over two months to recover, and after two long months recovering, I took my comprehensive exams, and passed. Life was returning to normal and I was beginning to prepare for my thesis and then the next challenge occurred.

During the Christmas holidays, my dad had to make another emergency trip to Seattle. This time the trip was shorter, but it still took time and effort away from my graduate work. I had already realized the importance of family over anything else in life but came to fully understand the importance of parents. The stress of worrying about them had made it difficult to study and to research my thesis topic, much less to think about writing my thesis. I have had to learn how to give time to my husband, my children, and to my parents, while balancing that time with work on my graduate studies.

Some Native students have to learn how to live in a "city" rather than in a village; or some students have to learn how to study college material. These have not been my challenges in college or graduate work. My challenges have been how to divide time between responsibilities as a student, wife, mother, daughter, and graduate work.

At some point in my pursuit of a college degree, when I felt as though I were drowning in family emergencies, studying, research, and writing papers, someone asked me if I saw the light at the end of the tunnel. My response was, "Oh, *that's* where I am!! Now that I know I'm in a tunnel, as it has been dark and I wasn't sure where I was, and now, that I know I'm in a tunnel, I know there will be a light at the end."

My light at the end of this academic tunnel is my granddaughter and future grandchildren. My grandmother, parents, and family are advocates of a college education and they wanted me to obtain this education to be a role model for our grandchildren and for other Native students. By meeting the responsibilities of family and their needs, and graduate work, I am fulfilling a family goal of acquiring an advanced college education.

Daisy's Best-Ever Moose Stew

Daisy Stri da zatse *Demientieff* *(Athabascan)*

Daisy Stri da zatse *Demientieff is Deg Xitan Athabascan. She was born in the 1930s in a small traditional fish camp above Anvik, Alaska, near the Yukon River. Daisy's mother, Belle Deacon, was a well-known basket maker and traditional artist. These are skills that she passed on to Daisy. Daisy was married to Mike Demientieff (Koyukon Athabascan) for nearly fifty years before he passed away. They enjoyed a traditional Athabascan lifestyle, spending each summer at their fish camp. Daisy often played music with her husband at the Traditional Athabascan Fiddle Festival, held each November in Fairbanks. A DVD titled* Beautiful Journey *(Anaguina Productions 2008) is a documentary of Daisy's journey down the Yukon River to gather material to make her traditional baskets. Daisy has many talents, including her basket making, music making, and cooking. This is one of her special recipes.*

1 pound of moose ribs — nice fat ones
4 cloves of garlic
1 cup of celery cut into pieces
2 carrots diced
2 beef bullion cubes
1 tablespoon dried onion flakes
1 small rutabaga chopped
Salt and pepper to taste

Simmer the above 2½ hours

Then add:
3 medium potatoes cut into 1-inch pieces
1 small onion chopped
½ cup rice
½ cup noodles
1 can diced tomatoes

Let simmer 20 minutes—So Good!!!

Put moose ribs in cold water to soak—wash and place in stew pot with enough water to cover. When this comes to boil, skim all the foam off the top. Only then start putting in the veggies and simmer.

Suggestions for Further Reading

Print Sources

Adams, David Wallace. 1995. *Education for Extinction: American Indians and the Boarding School Experience, 1875–1928*. Lawrence: University of Kansas Press.

Alaska Blue Book, 1993–1994. 1994. 11th ed. Juneau: Department of Education, Division of State Libraries, Archives and Museums.

Alaska Native Policy Center (Greta L. Goto, George Irvin, Sarah Sherry, Katie Eberhart). 2004. *Our Choices, Our Future: Analysis of the Status of Alaska Natives Report 2004 Prepared for the Alaska Federation of Natives*. Anchorage: Alaska Native Policy Center, First Alaskans Institute.

Andreev, A. I., ed. 1948. *Russkie otkyrtiia na Tikhom okeane I v Severnoi Amerike v. XVIII veke* [Russian Discoveries in the Pacific Ocean and North America in the Eighteenth century]. Moscow: OGIZ.

Andrews, Susan, and John Creed, eds. 1998. *Authentic Alaska: Voices of Its Native Writers*. Lincoln: University of Nebraska Press.

Anzaldúa, Gloria. 1987. *Borderlands: La Frontera*. San Francisco: Aunt Lute Books.

Arctic Village Council. 1991. *Nakai ti'in'in "Do It Yourself!": A Plan for Preserving the Cultural Identity of the Neets'aii Gwich'in Indians of Arctic Village*. Arctic Village, Alaska: Arctic Village Council.

Arndt, Katherine. 1996. "Dynamics of the Fur Trade on the Middle Yukon River, Alaska, 1839–1868." Ph.D. dissertation, University of Alaska, Fairbanks.

Arnold, Robert, et al. 1976. *Alaska Native Land Claims*. Anchorage: Alaska Native Foundation.

Attla, Catherine. 1983. *Sitsiy Yugh Noholnik Ts'in': As My Grandfather Told It*. Fairbanks: Alaska Native Language Center.

Bakar, O. B. 1991. "The Unity of Science and Spiritual Knowledge." In *Science and Spirit*, edited by R. Ravindra. New York: Paragon House.

Bakhtin, M. M. (Mikhail Mikhailovich). 1973. *Problems of Dostoevsky's Poetics*. Translated by R. W. Rotsel. Ann Arbor, Mich.: Ardis.

Balcom, Mary G. 1970. *The Catholic Church in Alaska*. Chicago: Adams Press.

Balluta, Andrew, and Linda Ellanna. 1992. *Nuvendaltin Quht'ana: The People of Nondalton*. Washington: Smithsonian Institution.

Bancroft, Hubert Howe. 1959. *History of Alaska: 1730–1885*. New York: Antiquarian Press. Originally published: San Francisco: A. L. Bancroft, 1886.

Banerjee, Subhankar. 2003. *Arctic National Wildlife Refuge: Seasons of Life and Land.* Seattle: Mountaineers Books.

Baudet, Henri. 1988. *Paradise on Earth: Some Thoughts on European Images on Non-European Man.* Middleton, Conn.: Wesleyan University Press.

Benson, Diane. 2002. *Witness to the Stolen.* Escondido, Calif.: Raven's Word Press.

Berger, P. L. 1976. *Pyramids of Sacrifice.* New York: Anchor Doubleday.

Berger, Peter, Brigitte Berger, and Hansfried Kellner. 1974. *The Homeless Mind: Modernization and Consciousness.* New York: Vintage Books.

Bergland, Knut, and Moses Dirks. 1990. *Unangam Ungiikangin kayux Tunusangin/ Unangam Uniikangis ama Tunuzangis/Aleut Tales and Narratives Collected 1909–1910 by Waldemar Jochelson.* Fairbanks: Alaska Native Language Center, University of Alaska, Fairbanks.

Berman, Matthew. 1991. *Violent Deaths in Rural Alaska.* Institute of Social and Economic Research, no. 804. Anchorage: University of Alaska, Institute of Social and Economic Research.

Bielawski, E. 1990. "Cross-Cultural Epistemology: Cultural Readaptation through the Pursuit of Knowledge." Paper presented at the 7th Inuit Studies Conference. Fairbanks: University of Alaska, Fairbanks.

Bigjim, Frederick (Seaguyuk). 1974. *Letters to Howard: An Interpretation of the Alaska Native Land Claims.* Anchorage: Alaska Methodist University Press.

———. 1983. *Sinrock.* Portland: Press-22.

———. 1985. *We Talk You Yawn: A Discourse on Education in Alaska.* Portland: Press-22.

———. 1988. *Walk the Wind.* Portland: Press-22.

Birket-Smith, Kaj. 1953. *The Chugach Eskimo.* Copenhagen: Nationalmuseets Skrifter, Etnografisk Roekke VI.

———. 2000a. *Echoes from the Tundra.* Kearney, Neb.: Morris Publishing.

———. 2000b. *Plants: A Novel.* Kearney, Neb.: Morris Publishing.

Bodley, J. H. 1982. *Victims of Progress.* Menlo Park, Calif.: Benjamin/Cummins.

Bolkhovitinov, N. N., ed. 1997–99. *Istoriia Russkoi Ameriki* [The History of Russian America]. 3 vols. Moscow: Mezhdunarodnye otosheniia.

Boulton, Laura. *The Eskimos of Hudson Bay and Alaska.* Washington: Smithsonian Folkways Records, 1954.

Boyd, Robert T. "Demographic History: 1774–1874." 1990. In *Handbook of North American Indians*, vol. 7, ed. Wayne Suttles. Washington: Smithsonian Institution.

Bradley, C. 1987. "Responses of American Indian Students in a LOGO Environment." Ph.D. dissertation, Harvard Graduate School of Education.

———. 2002. "Traveling with Fred George." In *The Earth Is Faster Now: Indigenous Observations of Arctic Environmental Change*, edited by Igor Krupik and Dyanna Jolly, 240–65. Fairbanks: Arctic Research Consortium of the United States.

Brown, Caroline, et al. 2005. *Contemporary Subsistence Uses and Population Distribution of Non-Salmon Fish in Grayling, Anvik, Shageluk, and Holy Cross.* Technical Paper no. 289. Fairbanks: Alaska Department of Fish and Game, Tanana Chiefs Conference.

Brown, Stephen, ed. 2006. *Arctic Wings: Birds of the Arctic National Wildlife Refuge.* Seattle: Mountaineers Books.

Bruchac, Joseph, ed. 1991. *Raven Tells Stories: A Collection of Alaska Native Writing.* Greenfield Center, N.Y.: Greenfield Review Press.

Burch, Ernest S. Jr. 1975. *Eskimo Kinsmen—Changing Family Relationships in Northwest Alaska.* New York: West Publishing Company.

Burger, J. 1990. *First Peoples.* New York: Anchor Doubleday.

Burroway, Janet. 1992. *Writing Fiction: A Guide to Narrative Craft.* 3rd ed. New York: Harper Collins.

Caduto, M. J., and J. Bruchac. 1989. *Keepers of the Earth.* Saskatoon: Fifth House Publishers.

Cajete, Gregory A. 1988. "Motivating American Indian Students in Science and Math." ERIC *Digest,* ED296812. http://www.ericdigests.org/pre-929/indian.htm (accessed July 7, 2006).

———. 1999. *Igniting the Sparkle: An Indigenous Science Education Model.* Sky Land, N.C.: Kivaki Press.

———. 2000. *Native Science: Natural Laws of Interdependence.* With introduction by Leroy Little Bear. Santa Fe: Clear Light Publishers.

Carlo, Poldine. 1978. *Nulato: An Indian Life on the Yukon.* Fairbanks: Carlo.

Carrol, J. B., ed. 1956. *Language, Thought, and Reality: Selected Writings of Benjamin Lee Whorf.* Cambridge, Mass.: MIT Press.

Chafe, Wallace L. 1981. "Differences between Colloquial and Ritual Seneca, or How Oral Literature Is Literary?" (Department of Linguistics, University of California, Berkeley) *Reports from the Survey of California and Other Indian Languages,* no. 1: 131–45.

Chaussonnet, Valérie. 1995. *Crossroads Alaska: Native Cultures of Alaska and Siberia.* Washington: Arctic Studies Center, National Museum of Natural History, Smithsonian Institution.

Cogo, Robert. 1979a. *Haida Months of the Year.* Ketchikan: Ketchikan Indian Corporation.

———. 1979b. *Haida Storytelling Time.* Ketchikan: Ketchikan Indian Corporation.

Cogo, Robert, and Nora Cogo. Ca. 1980. *Haida Food from the Land and Sea.* Anchorage: University of Alaska Materials Development Center.

———. Ca. 1983. *Haida Stories.* Anchorage: University of Alaska Materials Development Center.

———. 1983. *Remembering the Past: Haida History and Culture.* Anchorage: University of Alaska Materials Development Center.

"Comity between Denominations in the Home Field." 1874. *The Home Missionary* 47, no. 8. New York: Home Missionary Society, December.

Cone, Marla. 2005. *Silent Snow: The Slow Poisoning of the Arctic.* New York: Grove Press.

Coray, Craig. 2007. *Dnaghelt'ena Qut'ara K'eli Ahdelyqx* [They Sing the Songs of Many Peoples]. Anchorage: Kijik Corporation.

Crowell, A. 1992. "Postcontact Koniag Ceremonialism on Kodiak Island and the Alaska Peninsula: Evidence from the Fisher Collection." *Arctic Anthropology* 29, no. 1: 18–37.

Cruikshank, Julie. 1991. *Reading Voices: Oral and Written Interpretations of the Yukon's Past*. Vancouver: Douglas and McIntyre, 1991.

Dall, William Healey. 1884. "On Masks, Labrets, and Certain Aboriginal Customs, with an Inquiry into the Bearing of their Geographical Distribution." *Third Annual Report of the Bureau of American Ethnology*. Washington: Smithsonian Institution.

Dauenhauer, Nora. 1988. *The Droning Shaman: Poems*. Haines, Alaska: Black Current Press.

———. 2000. *Life Woven with Song*. Tucson: University of Arizona Press.

Dauenhauer, Nora, and Richard Dauenhauer, eds. 1987. *Haa Shuká, Our Ancestors: Tlingit Oral Narratives*. Seattle: University of Washington Press.

———. 1990. *Haa Tuwunáagu Yís, for Healing Our Spirit: Tlingit Oratory*. Seattle: University of Washington Press.

———. 1994. *Haa Kusteeyi Our Culture: Tlingit Life Stories*. Seattle: University of Washington Press.

Dauenhauer, Nora, Richard Dauenhauer, and Gary Holthaus, eds. 1986. "Alaska Native Writers, Storytellers and Orators." Special issue of *Alaska Quarterly Review* 4, nos. 3–4.

Dauenhauer, Richard L. 1999. *Conflicting Visions in Alaskan Education*. Fairbanks: University of Alaska Fairbanks.

Davis, Carol Beery. 1939. *Songs of the Totem*. Juneau: Empire Printing.

———. 1984. *Totem Echoes*. Juneau: Miner Publishing.

Davis, Robert. 1986. *SoulCatcher*. Sitka, Alaska: Raven's Bones Press.

Davydov, G. I. 1810, 1812. *Dvukraitnoe puteshestvie v Ameriku morskikh ofitserov Khvotsova I Davydova, napiannoe sim poslednim* [The Twofold Journey to America of Marine Officers Khvostov and Davydov Written by the Latter]. 2 parts. St. Petersburg.

———. 1977. *Two Voyages to Russian America, 1802–1807 (Materials for the Study of Alaskan History, No. 10)*. Edited and translated by Colin Bearne and Richard A. Pierce. Kingston: Limestone Press.

Deacon, Belle. 1976. "The First Man and Woman." In *Athabascans: Strangers of the North*. Anchorage Historical and Fine Arts Museum Exhibit and Lecture Series. Anchorage: University of Alaska Media Services, Alaska Native Cultural Heritage and Information Bank.

———. 1987a. *Engithidong Xugixudhoy: Their Stories of Long Ago*. Fairbanks: Alaska Native Language Center.

———. 1987b. *"Nił'oqay Ni'idaxin: The Man and Wife."* In *Engithidong Xugixudhoy*, 5–40.

de Laguna, Frederica. 1972. *Under Mount Saint Elias: The History and Culture of the Yakutat Tlingit*. 3 vols. Washington: Smithsonian Institution Press.

Deloria, V. Jr. 1991. "Higher Education and Self-Determination." *Winds of Change* 6: 18–25.

———. 1994. *God Is Red: A Native View of Religion*. Golden, Colorado: Fulcrum Publishing.

———. 2006. *The World We Used to Live In*. Golden, Colo.: Fulcrum Publishing.

DeNevi, Don. 1969. "Hudson Bay." *Music Educators Journal* 56: 66–68.

Desson, Dominique. 1995. "Mask Rituals of the Kodiak Archipelago." Master's thesis, University of Alaska Fairbanks.

Desveaux, Emmanuelle, ed. 2002. *Kodiak Alaska: Les Masques de la Collection Alphonse Pinart*. Paris: Adam Birot.

Dixon, M., and S. Kirchner. 1982. "'Poking,' an Eskimo Medical Practice in Northwest, Alaska." *Études/Inuit/Studies* 6, no. 2.

Doroshin, Peter P. 1866. *Doroshin, Russian Engineer, Prospected for Gold in Russian America, 1848–1858*. Translated by unknown editor from "Diaries Kept in Russian America." *Gornyi Zhurnal* 2, no. 3: 365–400.

Downs, William M., and Lou Ann Wright. 1998. *Playwriting from Formula to Form*. Fort Worth, Tex.: Harcourt Brace, 1998.

DuBois, J. 1986. "Self-Evidence and Ritual Speech." In *Evidentiality: The Linguistic Coding of Epistemology*, edited by Wallace Chafe and Johanna Nichols. Norwood, N.J.: Ablex.

Duckworth, Eleanor. 1996. *"The Having of Wonderful Ideas" and Other Essays on Teaching and Learning*. New York: Teachers College Press.

Dunaway, Finis. 2006. "Reframing the Last Frontier: Subhankar Banerjee and the Visual Politics of the Arctic National Wildlife Refuge." *American Quarterly* 58, no. 1 (March): 159–80.

Edenso, Christine. Ca. 1983. *The Transcribed Tapes of Christine Edenso*. Translated by Robert and Nora Cogo. Anchorage: University of Alaska Materials Development Center.

Eglash, Ron. 2003. *Alaskan Basket Weaver: Cartesian Coordinates*. Troy, N.Y.: Ron Eglash and Rensselaer Polytechnic Institute. http://www.ccd.rpi.edu/eglash/csdt/na/weavework/ (accessed July 8, 2006).

Engblom-Bradley, Claudette. 2005. "Math in Tlingit Art: A Culture-Based Technology and Mathematics Project for K-12 Classrooms in Southeast Alaska." *2004 National Council of Supervisors of Mathematics*. http://www.ccd.rpi.edu/Eglash/nasgem/ncsm04/ (accessed July 7, 2006).

———. 2006. "Learning the Yup'ik Way of Navigation: Studying Time, Position, and Direction." *Journal in Mathematics and Culture* 1, no. 1 (May). http://www.ccd.rpi.edu/Eglash/nasgem/jmc/ (accessed July 8, 2006).

Engblom-Bradley, C., and M. Reyes. 2004. "Exploring Native Science: An Innovative Summer Camp Involves Alaska Native Elders to Excite Students about Science and Culture." *Science and Children* 41, no. 7 (April): 25–29.

Enrico, John R. 2003. *Haida Syntax*. Lincoln: University of Nebraska Press.

Ewing, Susan. 1996. *The Great Alaska Nature Factbook: A Guide to the State's Remarkable Animals, Plants and Natural Features*. Anchorage: Alaska Northwest Books, 1996.

Fall, James A. 1987. "The Upper Inlet Tanaina: Patterns of Leadership among an Alaskan Athabaskan People, 1741–1918." *Anthropological Papers of the University of Alaska* 21, nos. 1–2: 1–80.

______. 2004. "Dena'ina Elena, Dena'ina Lands." Lecture delivered at the Anchorage Museum of History and Art, October 3, Anchorage, Alaska.

Fanon, Frantz. 1963. *Wretched of the Earth*. Preface by Jean Paul Sartre. New York: Grove Press.

Fast, Phyllis Ann. 2002. *Northern Athabascan Survival: Women, Community and the Future*. Lincoln: University of Nebraska Press.

Feld, Steven, and Keith H. Basso. 1996. *Senses of Place*. Santa Fe: School of American Research Press.

Fienup-Riordan, Ann. 1986. "Nick Charles, Sr.: Worker in Wood." In *The Artists behind the Work*. Fairbanks: University of Alaska Museum.

———. 1990. *Eskimo Essays: Yup'ik Lives and How We See Them*. New Brunswick, N.J.: Rutgers University Press.

———. 1991. *The Real People and the Children of Thunder: The Yup'ik Eskimo Encounter with Moravian Missionaries John and Edith Kilbuck*. Norman: University of Oklahoma Press.

———. 1996. *Agayuliyararput: Kegginaqut, Kangiit-Llu: Our Way of Making Prayer, Yup'ik Masks and the Stories They Tell*. Seattle: University of Washington Press.

Fison, Susan. 2006. *Anchorage Indicators: Neighborhood Sourcebook*. Anchorage: Municipality of Anchorage.

Fortuine, Robert. 1989. *Chills and Fever: Health and Disease in the Early History of Alaska*. Fairbanks: University of Alaska Press.

Freeman, M., M. R. Milton, and Ludwig N. Carbyn. 1988. *Traditional Knowledge and Renewable Resource Management in Northern Regions*. Edmonton: IUCN Commission on Ecology and the Boreal Institute for Northern Studies.

Freese, Barbara. 2004. *Coal: A Human History*. New York: Penguin.

Freire, Paulo. 1994. *Pedagogy of the Oppressed*. New York: Continuum, 1994.

Gibson, J. R. 1980. *Russian Dependence upon the Natives of Russian America*. Washington.: Kennan Institute for Advanced Russian Studies.

Gladwin, Thomas. 1975. *East Is a Big Bird: Navigation and Logic on Puluwat Atoll*. Cambridge: Harvard University Press.

Goodwin, Sister. 1984. *A Lagoon Is in My Backyard*. New York: I. Reed Books.

Gray, Judith. 1984. *The Federal Cylinder Project: A Guide to Field Cylinder Collections in Federal Agencies*, vol. 3. Washington: American Folklife Center, Library of Congress.

Gruening, Ernest. 1968. *The State of Alaska: A Definitive History of America's Northernmost Frontier*. New York: Random House.

Hadleigh-West, F. 1963. "The Netsi Kutchin: An Essay in Human Ecology." Ph.D. dissertation, Louisiana State University.

Hanable, William S. 1982. *Alaska's Copper River, The 18th and 19th Centuries*. Anchorage: Alaska Historical Society.

Hardwick, S. 1991. "I Serve Them . . . I Am Their Leader." *Winds of Change* 6: 32–27.

Hargus, Sharon, and Alice Taff. 1994. *Deg Xinag axa Nixodhil Ts'in': Deg Xinag Verb Lessons*. Anvik: Anvik Historical Society.

Harper-Haines, Jan. 2000. *Cold River Sprits: The Legacy of an Athabaskan-Irish Family from Alaska's Yukon River*. Kenmore, Wash.: Epicenter Press.

Harrison, B. G. 1981. "Informal Learning among Yup'ik Eskimos: An Ethnographic Study of One Alaskan Village." Ph.D. dissertation, University of Oregon.

Henkelman, James W., and Kurt H. Vitt. 1985. *The History of the Alaska Moravian Church 1885–1985: Harmonious to Dwell*. Bethel, Alaska: Moravian Seminary and Archives.

Hill, Richard W. 1998. "Developed Identities: Seeing the Stereotypes and Beyond." In *Spirit Capture*, edited by Tim Johnson. Washington: Smithsonian Institution Press.

Himmelheber, Hans. 1987. *Eskimo Artists*. Introduction by Ann Fienup-Riordan. English translation of 1938 German original. Fairbanks: University of Alaska Press.

———. 1984. *Yup'ik Eskimo Dictionary*. Fairbanks: Alaska Native Language Center, University of Alaska.

Hinckley, Ted C. 1972. *The Americanization of Alaska, 1867–1897*. Palo Alto: Pacific Books.

Hinton, Leanne. 1998. "Language Loss and Revitalization in California: Overview." *International Journal of the Sociology of Language* 132: 83–95.

———. 1999. "The Master-Apprentice Language Learning Program." In *The Green Book of Language Revitalization in Practice*, edited by Leanne Hinton and Ken Hale, 217–26. San Diego: Academic Press.

Hope, Andrew III, ed. 1982. *Raven's Bones*. Sitka, Alaska: Sitka Community Association.

———, ed. 2000. *Will the Time Ever Come: A Tlingit Source Book*. Alaska Native Knowledge Network. Fairbanks: University of Alaska.

Institute of Social and Economic Research. 2004. *Status of Alaska Natives Report*. Anchorage: University of Alaska.

Jacobson, Steven A. 1984. *Yup'ik Eskimo Dictionary*. Fairbanks: Alaska Native Language Center, University of Alaska Press.

———. 1995. *A Practical Grammar of the Central Alaskan Yup'ik Eskimo Language*. Fairbanks: Alaska Native Language Center, University of Alaska Press.

Jette, Jules, and Eliza Jones. 2000. *Koyukon Athabaskan Dictionary*. Fairbanks: Alaska Native Language Center.

John, Fred, Sr., and Katie John. 1973. "The Killing of the Russians at Batzulnetas Village." *Alaska Journal* 3, no. 3: 147–48.

Jojola, T. 1998. "Indigenous Planning: Clans, Intertribal Confederations, and the History of the All Indian Pueblo Council." In *Making the Invisible Visible: A Multicultural Planning History*, edited by Leonie Sandercock. Berkeley: University of California Press, 1998.

Jorgensen, Karen. 1997. "White Shadows: The Use of Doppelgangers in Sherman Alexie's *Reservation Blues*." *Studies in American Indian Literature* 9.

Kadashan (Bertrand J. Adams). 1994. *When Raven Cries: Novel*. Yakutat, Alaska: Kadashan Enterprises; reprint, Anchorage: Earthpulse Press, 1997.

Kaplan, Lawrence J., ed. 1988. *King Island Tales*. Fairbanks: Alaska Native Language Center, University of Alaska Press.

Kari, James. 1978. *Deg Xinag: Ingalik Noun Dictionary* (preliminary). Fairbanks: Alaska Native Language Center.

———. 1990. *Ahtna Athabaskan Dictionary*. Fairbanks: Alaska Native Language Center.

———. 1994. "Dictionary of the Dena'ina Athabaskan Language" (manuscript). Fairbanks: Alaska Native Language Center.

Kari, James, and James A. Fall. 2003. *Shem Pete's Alaska: The Territory of the Upper Cook Inlet Dena'ina*. 2nd ed. Fairbanks: University of Alaska Press.

Kawagley, Oscar Angayuqaq. 1995. *A Yupiaq Worldview: A Pathway to Ecology and Spirit*. Prospect Heights, Ill.: Waveland Press.

Kessing, R. M. 1979. "Linguistic Knowledge and Cultural Knowledge." *American Anthropologist* 81, no. 1.

Ketz, James A. 1983. *Paxon Lake: Two Nineteenth Century Ahtna Sites in the Copper River Basin, Alaska*. Fairbanks: University of Alaska Anthropological and Historic Preservation, Cooperative Park Studies Unit.

Khlebnikov, K. T. 1835. *Zhizneopisanie Aleksandra Andreevich Baranova, glavnogo pravitelia rossiiskikh kolonii v Amerike* [The Biography of Alexander A. Baranov, the Chief Governor of Russian Colonies in America]. St. Petersburg.

Kilbuck, John. 1894. "Report of the Mission Stations on the Kuskoquim River, Alaska, for the Year 1893–94." *Proceedings of the Society for Propagating the Gospel among the Heathen for the Year 1893–94*. Bethlehem, Pa.

Kingston, Deanna M. 1996. "Illuweet or Teasing Cousin Songs as an Expression of King Island Iñupiaq Identity." *Northwest Anthropology Series No. 9*. Corvallis: Department of Anthropology, Oregon State University.

———. 1999. "Returning: Twentieth Century Performances of the King Island Wolf Dance." Ph.D. dissertation., University of Alaska, Fairbanks.

———. 2005. "Song Duel." In *The Encyclopedia of the Arctic*, edited by Mark Nutall. New York: Routledge.

Kistorii Rossiisko-Amerikanskoi kompanii [Related to the History of the Russian-American Company]. 1957. Collection of Documents. Krasnoiarsk.

Koranda, Lorraine. 1972. *Alaskan Eskimo Songs and Stories*. Seattle: University of Washington Press.

Krause, Michael. 1975. *Native People and Languages of Alaska*. Fairbanks: Alaska Native Language Center, University of Alaska.

———. 1980. "Alaska Native Languages: Past, Present and Future." *Alaska Native Language Center Research Papers*, no. 4. Fairbanks: Alaska Native Language Center.

———. 1996. *Lecture on Alaska Native Languages*. Anchorage: Museum of History and Art, October 1996.

Krupa, David J., ed. 1996. *The Gospel according to Peter John*. Fairbanks: Alaska Native Knowledge Network.

Langdon, Steven J. 2002. *The Native People of Alaska: Traditional Living in a Northern Land*. 4th ed. Anchorage: Greatland Graphics, 2002.

Lawrence, Erma, and Robert Cogo. 1975. *Xaadas Gutiláa Gyaahlangáay: Haida Stories and History*. 2nd ed. Ketchikan: Society for the Preservation of Haida Language and Literature.

Lawrence, Erma, ed. 1977. *Haida Dictionary*. Fairbanks: Alaska Native Language Center, University of Alaska.

———, ed and trans. 1978. *Ki'ilang Sk'at'áa: Haida Reading Book*. Ketchikan: Ketchikan Indian Corporation.

———. 1982a. *Sáa Nang I'itl'aakdáasgyaa Sgalanggáay: Haida Gospel Songs*. Ketchikan: Society for the Preservation of Haida Language and Literature.

———. 1982b. *Xaadas Gyaahláang K'wándaa Short: Haida Stories*. Ketchikan: Ketchikan Indian Corporation.

Leer, Jeff. 1977. Preface. *Haida Dictionary*. Edited and compiled by Erma Lawrence. Fairbanks: Alaska Native Language Center.

Leggett, Aaron. 2006. "Dena'ina Heritage in Anchorage—Unveiling What Has Previously Been Unrecognized." *Raven's Circle Newsletter* 31, no. 4 (May): 5.

Lipka, Jerry, Gerald Mohatt, and the Ciulistet Group. 1998. *Transforming the Culture of Schools: Yup'ik Eskimo Examples*. Mahwah, N.J.: Lawrence Erlbaum.

Locust, C. 1988. "Wounding the Spirit: Discrimination and Traditional American Indian Belief Systems." *Harvard Educational Review* 58: 315–31.

Lomawaima, K. Tsianina. 1994. *They Called It Prairie Light: The Story of Chilocco Indian School*. Lincoln: University of Nebraska Press.

Lopez, Barry. 1986. *Arctic Dreams: Imagination and Desire in a Northern Landscape*. New York: Bantam Books.

Lord, A. B. 1960. *The Singer of Tales*. Cambridge: Harvard University Press, 1960.

Lower Kuskokwim School District. 1979. *Yut Qanemciit-Yup'ik Lore*. Bethel, Alaska.

Lundstrom, Hakan. 1980. "North Athabascan Story Songs and Dance Songs." In *The Alaska Seminar*, edited by Anna Birgitta Rooth. Stockholm: Acta Universitatis Upsaliensis, Studia Ethnologica Upsaliensis.

Lyons, W. 1969. "Society of Jesus." Ph.D. dissertation, University of Alaska.

Manuelito, Kathryn. 2005. "The Role of Education in American Indian Self-Determination: Lessons from the Ramah Navajo Community School." *Anthropology and Education Quarterly* 36: 73–87.

Mather, E. 1995. "With a Vision beyond Our Immediate Needs: Oral Traditions in an Age of Literacy." In *When Our Words Return: Writing, Hearing and Remembering Oral Traditions of Alaska and the Yukon*, edited by P. Morrow and W. Schneider. Logan: Utah State University Press.

———. 1984. *Cauyarnariuq (A Time for Drumming)*. Bethel, Alaska: Lower Kuskokwim School District.

McCarty, Teresa L. 1993. "Federal Language Policy and American Indian Education." *Bilingual Research Journal* 17, nos. 1–2: 13–34.

McGrane, Bernard. 1989. *Beyond Anthropology: Society and the Other*. New York: Columbia University Press.

McKennan, R. A. 1965. *The Chandalar Kutchin*. Montreal: Arctic Institute of North America.

Mead, Marie. 1996. *Agayuliyararput: Kegginaqut, Kangiit-Llu, Our Way of Making Prayer*. Transcribed and translated by Marie Meade; edited by Ann Fienup-Riordan. Seattle: University of Washington Press.

Meade, M. 1988. "Sewing to Maintain the Past, Present and Future." *Études/Inuit/Studies* 14, nos. 1–2: 229–39.

Milan, Frederick A. 1964. "The Acculturation of the Contemporary Eskimo of Wainwright, Alaska." *Anthropological Papers of the University of Alaska* 11, no. 2: 40–65.

Mitchell, Lee Clark, and Alfred L. Bush. 1994. *The Photograph and the American Indian*. Princeton, N.J.: Princeton University Press.

Mithun, M., and E. Ali. 1995. "The Elaboration of Aspectual Categories: Central Alaskan Yup'ik." *Folia Linguistica Europaea* 30, nos. 1–2: 111–27.

———. 1996. Introduction. *Prosody, Grammar, Discourse in Central Alaskan Yup'ik*. Santa Barbara Papers in Linguistics 7: 4–16.

Monument Valley High School (MVHS). 1995–2000. *Overview of 'Ndahoo'haa*. Monument Valley High School, Monument Valley, Utah. http://www.math.utah.edu/~clemens/ (accessed July 7, 2006).

Moore, John H. 1998. "Truth and Tolerance in Native American Epistemology." In *Studying Native America: Problems and Prospects*, edited by R. Thornton, 271–305. Madison: University of Wisconsin Press.

Moore, Kathleen Dess, Kurt Peters, Ted Jojola, et al. 2007. *How It Is: The Native American Philosophy of V. F. Cordova*. Phoenix: University of Arizona Press.

Morrow, P. 1981. "It Is Time for Drumming: A Summary of Recent Research on Yup'ik Ceremonialism." *The Central Yupik Eskimos, Etudes/Inuit Studies* 8: 113–40, supplementary issue, edited by E. S. Burch Jr.

———. 1995. "On Shaky Ground: Folklore, Collaboration, and Problematic Outcomes." In *When Our Words Return: Writing, Hearing, and Remembering Oral Traditions of Alaska and the Yukon*, edited by P. Morrow and W. Schneider. Logan: Utah State University Press.

Muktoyuk, Mary. 1988. *Iñupiaq Rules for Living*. Anchorage: Alaska Methodist University Press.

Nakai Ti'in'in [Do It Yourself]: *A Plan for Preserving the Cultural Identity of the Neets'aii Gwich'in Indians of Arctic Village*. 1991. Arctic Village, Alaska: Arctic Village Council.

Napoleon, Harold. 1990. *Yuuraraaq: The Way of the Human Being*. Anchorage: University of Alaska.

National Council of Teachers of Mathematics. 2000. *Principles and Standards for School Mathematics*. Reston, Va.: National Council of Teachers of Mathematics. http://standards.nctm.org.

Natkong, Jesse, Christine Edenso, and Robert Cogo. 1973. *Xaadas Kil Agyaan Gin-gaay: Haida Language Workshop Reader*. Transcribed by Charles Natkong Sr. and Erma Lawrence. Ketchikan: Society for the Preservation of Haida Language and Literature.

Nelson, Richard K. 1983. *Make Prayers to the Raven*. Chicago: University of Chicago Press.

Netting, Robert M. 1986. *Cultural Ecology*. Prospect Heights, Ill.: Waveland Press.

Nieto, Sonia. 1998. *The Light in Their Eyes: Creating Multicultural Learning Communities*. New York: Teachers College Press.

Oman, Lela. 1956. *Eskimo Legends: Authentic Tales of Suspense and Excitement*. Nome: Nome Publishing Company; reprint, Anchorage: Alaska Methodist University Press, 1975.

———. 1967. *The Ghost of Kingikty and other Eskimo Legends*. Anchorage: K. Wray's Print Shop.

———. 1995. *The Epic of Qayaq: The Longest Story Ever Told by My People*. Ottawa: Carleton University Press.

O'Neill, Dan. 1994. *The Firecracker Boys*. New York: St. Martins Press.

Oosten, J. G. 1984. "Male and Female in Inuit Shamanism." *Études/Inuit/Studies* 10, nos. 1–2: 115–31.

Orth, Donald J. 1971. *Dictionary of Alaska Place Names*. Washington: U.S. Government Printing Office.

Ortiz, Simon. 2000. "Towards a National Indian Literature: Cultural Authenticity Nationalism." In *Nothing but the Truth: An Anthology of Native American Literature*, edited by John L. Purdy and James Ruppert. Upper Saddle River, N.J.: Prentice-Hall.

Osgood, Cornelius. 1940. *Ingalik Material Culture*. Vol. 22. New Haven, Conn.: Human Relations Area Files Press.

———. 1958. *Ingalik Social Culture*. Vol. 53. New Haven, Conn.: Yale University Press.

———. 1959. *Ingalik Mental Culture*. Vol. 56. New Haven, Conn.: Department of Anthropology, Yale University.

Oswalt, Wendell H. 1967. *Alaskan Eskimos*. San Francisco: Chandler Publishing Company.

Papert, Seymour. 1993. *Mindstorms: Children, Computers, and Powerful Ideas*. 2nd ed. New York: Basic Books.

———. 2000. "What's the Big Idea? Toward a Pedagogy of Idea Power." IBM *Systems Journal* 39, nos. 3–4. http://www.research.ibm.com/journal.

Philips, Susan Urmston. 1983. *The Invisible Culture: Communication and Community on the Warm-Springs Indian Reservation*. New York: Longman Press.

Posey, Darrell Addison. 2001. "Intellectual Property Rights and the Sacred Balance: Some Spiritual Consequences from the Commercialization of Traditional Resources." In *Indigenous Traditions and Ecology: The Interbeing of Cosmology and Community*, edited by J. A. Grim, 3–23. Cambridge: Harvard University Press.

Pulu, Topou L. ca. 1983. Introduction. *Haida Stories*, edited by Robert and Nora Cogo. Anchorage: University of Alaska Anchorage, Materials Development Center.

Ransom, Jay Ellis. 1978. "Alaxsxaq: Where the Sea Breaks It Back." *Alaska Journal* (summer).

Ray, Dorothy Jean. 1975. *The Eskimo of the Bering Strait: 1650–1898*. Seattle: University of Washington Press.

Reed, Irene, Osahito Miyako, Steven Jacobson, Paschal Afcan, and Michael Krauss. 1977. *Yup'ik Eskimo Grammar*. Fairbanks: Alaska Native Language Center, Yup'ik Language Workshop.

Renner, Louis L., S.J. 1979. *Pioneer Missionary to the Bering Strait Eskimos: Bellarmine Lafortune, S.J.* Portland: Binford and Mort.

Richtmyer, Richard. 2006. "City Center Could Honor Athabascans." *Anchorage Daily News*, June 27, A1, A8.

Rooth, Anna Birgitta. 1971. *The Alaska Expedition 1966: Myths, Customs, and Beliefs among the Athabascan and the Eskimos of Northern Alaska*. Lund: Acta Universitatis Lundensis, Sectio I, Theologica Juridica Humanoria 13.

Rosaldo, Renato. 1993. *Culture and Truth: The Remaking of Social Analysis*. Boston: Beacon Press.

Rossiiskii gosudarstvennyi arkhiv drevnikh aktov [Russia's State Archive of Ancient Acts]. Moscow: RGADA.

Rossiiskii gosudarstvennyi arkhiv Voenno-morskogo flota [Russia's State Archive of Navy]. St. Petersburg: RGA VMF.

Rude, Robert. 1996. *ANCSA: An Act of Deception*. Anchorage: Salmon Run Publishing.

Ruppert, J. 1995. "A Bright Light ahead of Us: Belle Deacon's Stories in English and Deg Hit'an." In *When Our Words Return*, edited by P. Morrow and W. Schneider. Logan: Utah State University Press.

Ruppert, James, and John W. Bernet. 2001. *Our Voices: Native Stories of Alaska and the Yukon*. Lincoln: University of Alaska Press.

Russkaia Amerika po lichnym vpechatleniian missionerov, zenilprokhodtsev, moriakov, issledovatelei I drugikh ochevidtsev [Russian America in Personal Impressions of Missionaries, Pioneers, Mariners, Explorers, and Other Eyewitnesses]. 1994. Collection of documents. Moscow.

Sarris, Greg. 1993. *Keeping Slug Woman Alive: A Holistic Approach to American Indian Texts*. Berkeley: University of California Press.

Scollon, Ronald, and Suzanne Scollon. 1979. "Bush Consciousness and Modernization." In *Linguistic Convergence: An Ethnography of Speaking at Fort Chipewyan, Alberta*. New York: Academic Press.

Senungetuk, Joseph. 1971. *Give or Take a Century: An Eskimo Chronicle*. San Francisco: Indian Historian Press.

Shelikhov, G. I. 1971. *Rossiiskogo kuptsa Grigoriia Shelekhova stranstvovanie iz Okotska po Vostochnomu okeanu k Amerikanskim beregam* [The Travel of Russian Merchant Shelikov from Okhotsk in the East (Pacific) Ocean to American Shores]. Edited with an introduction by B. P. Polevoi. Khabarovsk.

Sherzer, J. 1981. *Kuna Ways of Speaking: An Ethnographic Perspective*. Austin: University of Texas Press.

Simeone, William. 1995. *Rifles, Blankets and Beads: Identity, History and the Northern Athapaskan Potlatch*. Norman: University of Oklahoma Press.

Skinner, Ramona. 1997. *Alaska Native Policy in the Twentieth Century*. New York: Garland Publishing.

Smith, Graham Hingangaroa. 2000. "Protecting and Respecting Indigenous Knowledge." In *Reclaiming Indigenous Voice and Vision*. Vancouver: University of British Columbia Press.

Smith, Linda Tuhiwai. 1999. *Decolonizing Methodologies: Research and Indigenous Peoples*. London: Zed Books.

Spatz, Ronald, ed. 1999. "Alaska Native Writers, Storytellers and Orators: The Expanded Edition." *Alaska Quarterly Review* 17, nos. 3–4.

Stephan, Alberta. 1996. *The First Athabascans of Alaska: Strawberries*. Pittsburgh: Dorrance Publishing; reprint, Anchorage: Todd Communications, 2002.

———. 1998. *Report on the Dena'ina Team's Second Trip on Elmendorf Air Force Base Lands*, August 19. Files, Alaska Department of Fish and Game, Anchorage.

———. 2001. *Cheda (Athabascan for Grandma)*. Anchorage: Todd Communications.

Stewart, R. L. 1908. *Sheldon Jackson: Pathfinder and Prospector of the Missionary Vanguard in the Rocky Mountains and Alaska*. New York: Fleming H. Revel.

Strong, Stephen B. 1972. "An Economic History of the Athabascan Indians of the Upper Copper River." M.A. thesis, McGill University.

Stuck, Hudson. 1989. *Ascent of Denali: A Narrative of the First Complete Ascent of the Highest Peak in North America*. 1914. Lincoln: University of Nebraska Press.

Sturtevant, William, ed. 1984a. *Handbook of North American Indians*, Vol. 5, *Arctic*, edited by David Damas. Washington: Smithsonian Institution.

———. 1984b. *Handbook of North American Indians*, Vol. 6, *Sub Arctic*, edited by David Damas. Washington: Smithsonian Institution.

Sullivan, Lawrence, ed. 2003. *Native Religions and Cultures of North America: Anthropology of the Sacred*. New York: Continuum.

Suzuki, David, and Peter Knudtson. 1992. *Wisdom of the Elders*. Toronto: Stoddart.

Swanton, John R. 1905a. *Contributions to the Ethnology of the Haida*, vol. 10, part 2. Publications of the Jesup North Pacific Expedition. New York: G. E. Strechart.

———. 1905b. *Haida Texts and Myths: Skidegate Dialect*, vol. 5. Publications of the Jesup North Pacific Expedition. New York: G. E. Strechart.

———. 1908. *Haida Texts: Masset Dialect*. Memoirs of the American Museum of Natural History 10. Washington: Smithsonian Institution.

———. 1909. *Tlingit Myths and Texts*. Bureau of American Ethnology Bulletin 39. Washington, D.C.: Bureau of American Ethnology.

———. 1912. *Haida Songs*. Publication of the American Ethnological Society, vol. 3 (with Franz Boas, *Tsinshin Texts*). Leiden: E. J. Brill.

———. 1971. *The Haida Indian Language*. Seattle: Shorey Book Store.

Talamantez, I. M. 1977. "Ethnopoetics Theory and Method: A Study of 'Isánáklésde Gotal with Analysis of Selected Songs, Prayers, Ritual Structure, and Contemporary Performance." Ph.D. dissertation, University of California, San Diego.

———. 1987. *Green March Moons*. Berkeley: New Seed Press.

———. 2005. *Seeing Red: American Indian Women Speaking about Their Religious and Political Perspectives*. Lanham, Md.: Altamira Press.

Tallmountain, Mary. 1987. *Green March Moons*. Berkeley: New Seed Press.

———. 1988. *Continuum: Poems*. Marvin, S.D.: Blue Cloud Quarterly.

———. 1990. *The Light on the Tent Wall: A Bridging*. Department of American Indian Studies, University of California, Los Angeles.

———. 1990. *Matrilineal Cycle*. Oakland: Red Star Black Rose.

———. 1991. *A Quick Brush of Wings*. San Francisco: Freedom Voices Publications.

———. 1995. *Listen to the Night: Poems for the Animal Spirits of Mother Earth*. San Francisco: Freedom Voices Publications.

———. 1999. *Keeping Alive the Visions of the Ancestors: The Integrated Approach to Native American Religious Studies*. Milan: Jaca Books. English translation, in *Native Religions and Cultures of North America*. New York: Continuum International Group, 2000.

Tedlock, D. 1981. *The Spoken Word and the Work of Interpretation*. Philadelphia: University of Pennsylvania Press.

Thompson, Chad. 1990. *K'etetaalkaanee: The One Who Paddled among the People and the Animals: An Analytical Companion Volume*. Fairbanks: Alaska Native Language Center.

Ticasuk (Emily Ivanoff Brown). 1981a. *The Longest Story Ever Told: Qayaq, the Magical Man*. Anchorage: Alaska Pacific University Press.

———. 1981b. *The Roots of Ticasuk*. Anchorage: Northwest Publishing Company.

———. 1987. *Tales of Ticasuk: Eskimo Legends and Stories*. Fairbanks: University of Alaska Press.

Tikhmenev, P. A. 1861, 1862. *Istoricheskoe obozrenie obrazovaniia Rossisk-Amerikanskoi kompanii I deistvie eio do nastoiashchego vremeni* [A Historical Review of the Establishment of the Russian-American Company and Its Activity Up to the Present Time]. 2 parts. St. Petersburg.

———. 1978. *A History of the Russian-American Company*. Edited and translated by

Richard A. Pierce and Alton S. Donnelley. Seattle: University of Washington Press.

Tinker, G. E. 1991. *Missionary Conquest: The Gospel and Native American Cultural Genocide*. Minneapolis: Fortress Press, 1991.

Tiulana, Paul. 1987. *A Place for Winter: Paul Tiulana's Story*. Alaska: CIRI Foundation.

Tony, Mary (as Aurora Hardy). 2004. *Terror at Black Rapids*. Baltimore: Publish America.

Van Stone, James. 1979. *Ingalik Contact Ecology: An Ethnohistory of the Lower-Middle Yukon, 1790–1935*. Chicago: Field Museum of Natural History.

Veniaminov, Ivan. 1840. *Zapiski ob ostorvakh Unalashkinskogo otdela* [Notes on the Islands of Unalaska District]. 3 vols. St. Petersburg: Academy of Sciences. English translation: *Notes on the Islands of the Unalaska District*, translated by Lydia T. Black and R. H. Geoghegan, edited by Richard A. Pierce. Kingston: Limestone Press, 1984.

Wallace, Kristi, Robert G. McGimsey, and Thomas P. Miller. 2000. "Historically Active Volcanoes in Alaska—A Quick Reference." *U.S. Geological Survey Fact Sheet 118-00*. Online version. http://geopubs.wr.usgs.gov/fact-sheet/fs118-00.

Wallis, Velma. 1993. *Two Old Women: An Alaskan Legend of Betrayal, Courage, and Survival*. Fairbanks: Epicenter Press.

———. 1996. *Bird Girl and the Man Who Followed the Sun*. Fairbanks: Epicenter Press.

———. 2002. *Raising Ourselves: A Gwich'in Coming of Age Story from the Yukon River*. Seattle: Epicenter Press.

Warbelow, C., D. Roseneau, and P. Stern. 1975. "The Kutchin Caribou Fences of Northeastern Alaska and the Northern Yukon." Studies of Large Mammals along the Proposed Mackenzie Valley Gas Pipeline Route from Alaska to British Columbia. Biological Report Series, vol. 32. Calgary.

Wheeler, Priscilla Carvill. 1997. "The Role of Cash in Northern Economies: A Case Study of Four Alaska Athabascan Villages." Ph.D. dissertation, University of Alberta.

Williams, Maria. 1992. "Alaska Native Music and Dance: The Spirit of Tradition." In *Native American Dance: Ceremonies and Social Traditions*, edited by Charlotte Heth, 149–67. Washington: Smithsonian Institution.

———. 1996. "The Rise of Native Solidarity." Three-part series. *Tundra Times*, October.

———. 2001. *Our Culture and Way of Life: Alaska Native Music and Dance*. Anchorage: Anchorage Museum of History and Art.

———. 2005. "To Dance Is to Be: Heritage Preservation in the Twenty-First Century." *Alaska Park Science* 4, no. 1: 33–37. http://www.nps.gov/akso/AKParkScience.

Witherspoon, Gary. 1977. *Language and Art in the Navajo Universe*. Ann Arbor: University of Michigan Press.

Woodbury, H. 1981. "Translation Glosses and Semantic Description." In *Extending the Rafters: Interdisciplinary Approaches to Iroquoian Studies*, edited by M. Foster, J. Campisi, and M. Mithun. Albany: State University of New York Press.

Wright, Miranda Hildebrand. 1995. "The Last Great Indian War (Nulato 1851)." M.A. thesis, University of Alaska, Fairbanks.

Zagoskin, Lavrenti A. 1967. *Lieutenant Zagoskin's Travels in Russian America, 1842–1844: The First Ethnographic and Geographic Investigations in the Yukon and Kuskokwim Valleys of Alaska*. Edited by Henry N. Michael. Translated by Penelope Rainey. Arctic Institute of North America, Anthropology of the North: Translations from Russian Sources, no. 7 (Russian edition, 1956). Toronto: University of Toronto Press.

Audio and Video Recordings and Films

Alexie, Sherman. 1998. *Smoke Signals*. New York: Hyperion Films.

Ali, E., and J. Active. 1982. *Masking Making Project*. Audiotape. Bethel, Alaska.

Ayaginar (Charles N.). 1975, 1980, 1994. Audio and video tapes.

Brink, I. 1974. *Alaska, Family Story*. Kasigluk, Alaska.

Brink, T. 1955. *Family Story*, Kasigluk, Alaska.

Brink, Frank, and Jo Brink. 1988. *Tubughna: The Beach People*. Filmed and narrated by Frank and Jo Brink. Tyonek Film project supervisor, Emil McCord Sr. Anchorage: CIRI Foundation.

Camai Festival 1996. 1996. Bethel: KYUK.

Camai Festival: First Dance 2000. 2000. Bethel: KYUK.

Deacon, Belle. 1973. Interview of Belle Deacon by Karen McPherson, April 17. In *Grayling, Alaska* (audiotape). Alaska Native Oral Literature Project. Anchorage: Alaska State Library Media Services.

Highlights of Celebration '90: Continuing Our Traditional Way of Life: In Our Ancestors' Trail. 1990. Juneau: Sealaska Heritage Foundation.

Kaligtuq (Marie Nichols). 1981. *Bethel and Kasigluk*. Audio and film clip from *Yup'ik Eskimos*. Anchorage: Chevron.

Kivgiq. 1992. Barrow: North Slope Borough.

Makalria (Nicoli Nichols). 1954. Kasigluk family story.

Nengqeralria (Charles and Elena Nichols). 1975, 1980, and 1994. Audio and video tapes.

———. 1998. *Heart Beat 2: More Voices of First Nations Women*. Washington: Smithsonian Folkways.

Nilgaq: Fifth Annual Kingikmiut Dance Festival. 2004. Native Village of Wales, Alaska.

Nome Elders Conference, 1984. Field recordings.

Quyana Alaska: A Celebration of Traditional Native Dance. 1991. Anchorage: Blueberry Productions.

The Wolf Dance. 1984. Fairbanks: Learn Alaska Network and University of Alaska.

This Land Is Ours. 1996. Video. Written by Laurence A. Goldin and Bradford C. Matsen. Produced by Laurence A. Goldin. Juneau: Aurora Films.

Websites

Ahtna: http://www.ahtna-inc.com.

Alaska Commission on the Status of Women: "Profiles in Change: Names, Notes and Quotes from Alaskan Women": http:// alaskool.org/projects/women.

Alaska Department of Education: http://www.eed.state.ak.us/stats/statewidebyethnicity.

Alaska Federation of Natives: http://www.nativefederation.org.

Alaska Native Arts Foundation: www.alaskanativearts.org.

Alaska Native Knowledge Network: www.ankn.uaf.edu.

Alaska Native Language Center, University of Alaska, Fairbanks: http://www.uaf.edu/anlc.

Alaskool: www.alaskool.org.

Aleut History, Aleut Corporation: http://www.aleutcorp.com/culture_history.html.

Alutiiq Museum: http://www.alutiiqmuseum.com

Anchorage Daily News index of articles: www.alaskool.org/projects/ancsa/articles/newspaperindx.html.

Arctic Slope Regional Corporation: http://www.asrc.com.

Bering Straits Native Corporation: http://www.beringstraits.com.

Bristol Bay Native Corporation: http://www.bbnc.net.

Calista Corporation: http://www.calistacorp.com/culturalinformation.asp.

Chugach Alaska Corporation: http://www.chugach-ak.com.

CIRI: http://www.ciri.com.

Doyon: http://www.doyon.com. Gwich'in Steering Committee: http://www.gwichinsteeringcommittee.org.

NANA Regional Corporation: http://www.nana.com/the_people.htm.

Neighborhood Sourcebook for the Municipality of Anchorage, Alaska: http://www.muni.org/oecd/neighborhoodsourcebook.cfm

Traditional Tlingit Map and Tribal List, Alaska Native Knowledge Network, University of Alaska, Fairbanks: http://www.ankn.uaf.edu/ANCR/Southeast/TlingitMap/index.html.

Acknowledgment of Copyrights

Permission is gratefully acknowledged to reproduce the following copyrighted material. Every reasonable effort has been made to obtain permission. We invite copyright holders to inform us of any oversights.

Part I. Portraits of Nations: Telling Our Own Story

"*Lazeni 'linn Nataełde Ghadghaande* / When Russians Were Killed at 'Roasted Salmon Place' (Batzulnetas)." As told by Katie and Fred John, transcribed and edited by James Kari, from *Tatl'ahwt'aenn Nenn' The Headwaters Peoples' Country* (Alaska Native Language Center, Fairbanks, Alaska, 1986).

"The Fur Rush: A Chronicle of Colonial Life." From *The Fur Rush: Essays and Documents on the History of Alaska at the end of the Eighteenth Century* by Katerina G. Solovjova and Aleksandra A. Vovnyanko, translated by Richard L. Bland and Katya S. Wessels (Anchorage: Phenix Press, 2002).

"Memories of My Trap Line" by Maria Bolanz. From her novella.

"Cultural Identity through Yupiaq Narrative" by George P. Charles (Kanaqlak). *Senri Ethnological Studies* 66 (2002): 41–62.

"*Dena'ina Ełnena*: Dena'ina Country: The Dena'ina in Anchorage, Alaska" by James A. Fall. Based on a presentation at the Cook Inlet Historical Society, Anchorage, October 2004.

"*Qaneryaramta Egmiucia*: Continuing Our Language" by Walkie *Kumaggaq* Charles. *Anthropology and Education Quarterly* 36 (2005).

"The Alaskan Haida Language Today: Reasons for Hope" by Jeane Breinig. Portions of this selection, significantly revised, appeared in "Alaskan Haida Stories of Language Growth and Regeneration," *American Indian Quarterly* 30, nos. 1–2 (spring 2006) and "Wahligidouk: Giver of Gifts," *Atlantis: A Women's Studies Journal* 29, no. 2 (spring-summer 2005).

Part II. Empire: Processing Colonization

"*Yuuyaraq*: The Way of the Human Being" from *Yuuyaraq: Way of the Human Being* by Harold Napoleon. Center for Cross-Cultural Studies, University of Alaska, Fairbanks, 1991.

"Why the Natives of Alaska Have a Land Claim" by William *Iggiagruk* Hensley. From a talk presented in France in November 1969. Copyright by William L. Hensley.

"A Brief History of Native Solidarity" by Maria Williams. *Tundra Times* 35, no. 26 (October 1996).

Part III. Worldviews: Alaska Native and Indigenous Epistemologies

"A Yupiaq Worldview: A Pathway to Ecology and Spirit," from *A Yupiaq Worldview: A Pathway to Ecology and Spirit* by Oscar *Angayuqaq* Kawagley. 2nd edition (Long Grove, Ill.: Waveland Press, Inc., 2006). Reprinted by permission of Waveland Press, Inc.

"The Cosmos: Indigenous Perspectives" by Gregory A. Cajete. Based on *Native Science: Natural Laws of Interdependence* by Gregory A. Cajete (Sante Fe, N.M.: Clear Light Books, 1999).

Part IV. Native Arts: A Weaving of Melody and Color

"*Ugiuvangmiut Illugiit Atuut*: Teasing Cousins Songs of the King Island Iñupiat" by Deanna *Paniataaq* Kingston. Based on her master's thesis.

"*fly by night mythology*: An Indigenous Guide to White Man, or How to Stay Sane When the World Makes No Sense" by Larry McNeil. Copyright 2006, all rights reserved.

"Conflict and Counter-Myth in the Film *Smoke Signals*" by Anna Smith Chiburis. Based on her master's thesis.

Part V. Ravenstales

"For My Granddaughter Amelia: Cheerleading at Homecoming '98, Juneau-Douglas High School" by Nora Marks Dauenhauer. Previously published in *Life Woven with Song* (Tucson: University of Arizona Press, 2000); copyright Nora Marks Dauenhauer.

"Repatriation" by Nora Marks Dauenhauer. Previously published in *Alaska Quarterly Review* (University of Alaska, Anchorage), edited by Ronald Spatz, 24, nos. 1–2 (2007).

"Based, of course, on hearsay" by Richard Dauenhauer. Previously published in *Tidal Echoes* (University of Alaska, 2008).

"Harvesting Potatoes" by Richard Dauenhauer. Previously published in *Alaska Quarterly Review* (University of Alaska, Anchorage), edited by Ronald Spatz, 24, nos. 1–2 (2007).

Index

Maria Williams is an assistant professor in the Departments of Music and Native American Studies at the University of New Mexico.

The Alaska native reader : history, culture, politics / edited by Maria Shaa Tláa Williams.
p. cm. — (The world readers)
Includes bibliographical references and index.
ISBN 978-0-8223-4465-0 (cloth : alk. paper)
ISBN 978-0-8223-4480-3 (pbk. : alk. paper)
1. Indigenous peoples—Alaska—Civilization. 2. Alaska—Civilization.
3. Alaska—History. 4. Indians of North America—Alaska. 5. Eskimos—Alaska.
I. Williams, Maria Shaa Tláa.
II. Series: World readers.
F904.A364 2009
305.897′0798—dc22 2009007570

CPSIA information can be obtained
at www.ICGtesting.com
Printed in the USA
BVHW040601230821
614886BV00004B/321

9 780822 344803